D1285660

CASSIRER: SYMBOLIC FORMS AND HISTORY

Cassirer

SYMBOLIC FORMS AND HISTORY

JOHN MICHAEL KROIS

Yale University Press
New Haven and London

Published with assistance from the foundation
established in memory of Philip Hamilton McMillan
of the Class of 1894, Yale College.

Designed by Sally Harris
and set in Melior type by
Keystone Typesetting, Orwigsburg, Pa.
Printed in the United States of America by
The Murray Printing Company, Westford, Massachusetts.

Library of Congress Cataloging-in-Publication Data

Krois, John Michael.
  Cassirer, symbolic forms and history.

  Bibliography: p.
  Includes index.
  1. Cassirer, Ernst, 1874–1945.   I. Title.
B3216.C34K76   1987   193   86–11185
ISBN 0-300-03746-5 (alk. paper)

The paper in this book meets the guidelines for
permanence and durability of the Committee on
Production Guidelines for Book Longevity
of the Council on Library Resources.

10   9   8   7   6   5   4   3   2   1

To Hannelore

CONTENTS

PREFACE

To enter into Ernst Cassirer's philosophy is to become immersed in the history of philosophy and the general historical development of culture. Probably no other twentieth-century philosopher has been as steeped in the history and theory of as many different fields of study as Cassirer. His writings have found a wide audience among readers of divergent interests and have influenced such figures as the art historian Erwin Panofsky, the theologian Paul Tillich, the aesthetician Susanne Langer, and the Renaissance scholar Paul Oskar Kristeller. Cassirer's philosophical concerns were so wide-ranging that he engaged in theoretical controversies with such different thinkers as Moritz Schlick and Martin Heidegger. The secondary literature on Cassirer reflects the encyclopedic character of his work; there are essays on many topics in numerous fields. But there is a dearth of critical analysis on Cassirer as a systematic philosopher. Although he is respected as a historian of philosophy, Cassirer's own thought has attracted little sustained philosophical criticism.

In this study I have sought to provide a systematic, structural analysis of Cassirer's thought that cuts across all his specific theoretical investigations as well as his historical works, from his earliest writings to his last. My aim has been to show the unity of Cassirer's thought. Although my approach has been systematic rather than developmental, it has nonetheless sometimes been necessary to shift perspectives to that of intellectual biography or cultural and political history. My interpretation depends upon an awareness of the way Cassirer's ideas emerged in the course of his life, but it is not simply a reiteration of their development. All this is, of course, in Cassirer's spirit. In writing a book about a thinker for whom the dialectic between philosophy and history was of philosophical importance, I have found it necessary to bring this dialectic to my own study as well.

The reader should not expect a complete reconstruction of every aspect of Cassirer's philosophy. For example, I say relatively little about his theory of art, his theory of mathematics, or his philosophy of religion, and I cannot claim to have given an exhaustive exposition of his philosophy of language, myth, or science. I have discussed Cassirer's many works with the objective of determining and clarifying his general philosophical position. This approach was motivated by the belief that no genuine understanding of particular problems in Cassirer is possible unless his general theoretical position is clearly defined.

Early in the preparation of this study it became apparent that the currently accepted understandings of Cassirer's thought were wholly insufficient to make sense of what Cassirer had actually written. Two interpretations had become established: a Continental and an Anglo-American one. The former sees Cassirer as a neo-Kantian epistemologist representing the Marburg school; the latter sees no theoretical position at all in Cassirer's writings, but only the attempt to clarify problems through historical scholarship. Neither of these interpretations does justice to Cassirer's thought as a whole. Again and again in the course of my investigations I have encountered these interpretations, and I have showed repeatedly that they are incapable of making sense of Cassirer's writings. These incursions, sometimes in the text and sometimes in the notes, have been necessary in order to extricate Cassirer's actual position from claims about what it "must" be.

The intellectual climate in a country can affect the reception of a thinker's ideas just as profoundly as the hasty categorizations of historians of philosophy. Even though Cassirer has been widely read in the English-speaking world and, judging by the quantity of secondary literature, most studied there, the interpretation of his philosophy that prevails there is no more satisfactory than the one entrenched on the Continent. This is due in part to the philosophical climate of opinion that governed after World War II; the spirit of analytic philosophy was inhospitable to Cassirer's systematic philosophizing. In his preface to the English translation of the first volume of The Philosophy of Symbolic Forms Charles Hendel recalled that when Cassirer came to the United States in 1941 "he found himself welcomed everywhere in the guise of his earlier self, as it were, the philosopher of science. . . . Cassirer was hardly regarded as a philosopher who had developed an original philosophy" (PSF 1:viii). Even with the publication of the English translation of *The Philosophy of Symbolic Forms* in the 1950s the nature of Cassirer's original philosophy remained unclear, at least partly because philosophers in the English-speaking world preferred to approach the works of past thinkers only in the context of particular problems.

The philosophy of symbolic forms is neither simply a "theory of knowledge" nor unsystematic historicism. Myth, technology, language, ethics and law, the sciences and the humanities all have a place in its theory of cultural and historical life. Cassirer's systematic writings and his historical works are different aspects of one project of thought: to philosophically understand historical life.

Cassirer brings his theory of symbolic forms to bear on social reality, but he is not a social philosopher in the sense that his contemporaries at the Institute for Social Research in Frankfurt were—social critics for whom philosophy and politics were closely entwined. Nor was Cassirer's thought oriented to religion as was the late work of his teacher Hermann Cohen or followers of Cohen such as Franz Rosenzweig. Cassirer proposed to develop a systematic philosophy based on his interpretation of the history of philosophy from the Renaissance to Hegel.

If one were to describe Ernst Cassirer's character and philosophy in one word, it would be *conciliatory*. Unlike the philosophical revolutionaries Wittgenstein and Heidegger, Cassirer held to the tradition of systematic thought even though he predicated his whole philosophy on a criticism of idealism. Yet Cassirer's project of thought was hardly a moderate undertaking. He sought to accomplish no less than a reconstruction of twentieth-century philosophy, reintegrating the two hostile directions of science-oriented philosophy (best represented by the Vienna Circle of logical positivism) and (often antiscientific) *Lebensphilosophie*—which for Cassirer includes the whole lineage of postidealistic philosophy from Kierkegaard to Heidegger. Cassirer's means for this reintegration were later to be hailed as "new" under such names as "semiotics," "structuralism," and "hermeneutics." Much more could be said about Cassirer's relationship to these and other trends in philosophy, including contemporary metascience, but this is not the place for such comparisons. So, too, much more could be said about the influences on Cassirer's thought, for example, Vico, Kant, Hegel, Goethe, Cohen, Dilthey, Husserl. If we are to understand Cassirer's position as Cassirer's, however, the search for antecedents and influences can never provide what is sought. The present study claims to make a start in this direction, but more remains to be done. In particular, further exploration is needed of the philosophy of symbolic forms' metaphysical foundations. Cassirer's appropriation of Goethe's idea of the *Urphänomen*—the primary phenomenon—and, especially, Cassirer's metaphysical conception of *Leben* or "life" as an *Urphänomen* (along with the other "primary phenomena" he mentions) are topics that require further analysis and explication. This task must wait until Cassirer's own efforts in this direction become accessible. The unfinished fourth volume of *The Philosophy of Symbolic Forms* was devoted to these questions. Donald P. Verene and I are presently editing Cassirer's manuscript of this work for publication.

Throughout this study I have used the available translations of Cassirer's writings. Where none was available or when the existing translation was faulty, I provided a translation or rectified the existing one (with explicit acknowledgment that I have done so). References to *The Philosophy of Symbolic Forms* are given with the pagination of both the English translation and the German edition.

This study has been aided by many people in the United States and Germany. I am indebted to Gerard Radnitzky, University of Trier, West Germany, whose efforts made possible my stay from 1980 to 1983 at Trier, where the final research for this study was completed and the manuscript written. Norbert Hinske and Ernst Wolfgang Orth were also supportive of this work at Trier.

I wish particularly to thank the *Deutsche Forschunggemeinschaft* for its financial support of my work at Trier, which made possible the completion of this project.

Gunnar Andersson (University of Trier), Don Howard (University of Kentucky), and Rudolf Makkreel (Emory University) have read portions of the manuscript and made helpful suggestions. Peter Cassirer (University of Göteborg) and Irene Kajon (University of Rome) kindly provided me with documentation of Cassirer's teaching and with bibliographic material that would otherwise have been unobtainable. I have discussed my interpretation of Cassirer over the years with students and colleagues and have benefited from their comments. I wish to give special thanks to two persons whose critical comments on fundamental questions were particularly helpful: Karl-Otto Apel of the University of Frankfurt and Klaus Oehler of the University of Hamburg. My greatest intellectual debt is due to Donald P. Verene of Emory University, the director of my doctoral thesis on Cassirer at Pennsylvania State University during the early 1970s. Our discussions and his work on Cassirer have been of continuing help in the development of my ideas.

I also wish to thank the rights and permissions department of Yale University Press for permission to quote from Cassirer's unpublished papers, housed at Yale's Beinecke Rare Book and Manuscript Library. Thanks are also due to the members of the staff of the Beinecke Library, who on my numerous visits have always been helpful and forthcoming in the cumbersome process of consulting the Cassirer papers. Finally, I am grateful to Rita M. Furman for her patient attention to detail in typing the final version of the manuscript.

ABBREVIATIONS

Works by Cassirer

AH "Axel Hägerström: Eine Studie zur Swedischen Philosophie der Gegenwart." *Göteborgs Högskolas Årsskrift* 45 (1939): 1–119.

D *Descartes: Lehre–Persönlichkeit–Wirkung.* Stockholm: Bermann-Fischer Verlag, 1939.

DI *Determinism and Indeterminism in Modern Physics* [1936]. Translated by O. T. Benfey, with a preface by Henry Marganau. New Haven: Yale University Press, 1956.

EM *An Essay on Man.* New Haven: Yale University Press, 1944.

EP *Das Erkenntnisproblem in der Philosophie und Wissenschaft der neueren Zeit* [1906–57]. Reprint. 4 vols. Darmstadt: Wissenschaftliche Buchgesellschaft, 1971–74. Volume 4 appeared first in 1950 in an English translation; see PK.

FF *Freiheit und Form: Studien zur deutschen Geistesgeschichte* [1916]. Reprint. Darmstadt: Wissenschaftliche Buchgesellschaft, 1975.

GGW *Goethe und die geschichtliche Welt: Drei Aufsätze.* Berlin: Verlag Bruno Cassirer, 1932.

IC *The Individual and the Cosmos in Renaissance Philosophy* [IK, 1927]. Translated by Mario Domandi. New York: Harper & Row, Harper Torchbooks, 1964.

IG *Idee und Gestalt: Fünf Aufsätze* [1921; 2d ed. 1924]. Reprint. Darmstadt: Wissenschaftliche Buchgesellschaft, 1971.

IK *Individuum und Kosmos in der Philosophie der Renaissance*

[1927]. Reprint. Darmstadt: Wissenschaftliche Buchgesell-schaft, 1963.

KLL   *Kants Leben und Lehre* [1918]. Reprint. Darmstadt: Wissen-schaftliche Buchgesellschaft, 1972.

KLT   *Kant's Life and Thought* [KLL, 1918]. Translated by James Haden. New Haven: Yale University Press, 1981.

KW   *Zur Logik der Kulturwissenschaften* [1942]. Reprint. Darm-stadt: Wissenschaftliche Buchgesellschaft, 1961.

LH   *The Logic of the Humanities* [KW, 1942]. Translated by Clar-ence Howe. New Haven: Yale University Press, 1961.

LM   *Language and Myth* [1925]. Translated by Susanne K. Langer. New York: Harper and Bros., 1946. Reprint. New York: Dover Publications, 1953. Reprinted in *WW*.

LS   *Leibniz' System in seinen wissenschaftlichen Grundlagen* [1902]. Reprint. Darmstadt: Wissenschaftliche Buchgesell-schaft, 1961.

MS   *The Myth of the State*. New Haven: Yale University Press, 1946.

PE   *The Philosophy of the Enlightenment* [1932]. Translated by F. C. A. Koelln and James P. Pettegrove. Princeton: Princeton University Press, 1951.

PK   *The Problem of Knowledge: Philosophy, Science, and History since Hegel*. Translated by William H. Woglom and Charles W. Hendel. New Haven: Yale University Press, 1950. For German edition see *EP*.

PRE   *The Platonic Renaissance in England* [1932]. Translated by James P. Pettegrove. Austin: University of Texas Press, 1953.

PsF   *Philosophie der symbolischen Formen* [1923–29]. Reprint. 3 vols. Vol. 1, *Die Sprache;* vol. 2, *Das mythische Denken;* vol. 3, *Die Phänomenologie der Erkenntnis*. Darmstadt: Wissen-schaftliche Buchgesellschaft, 1964.

PSF   *The Philosophy of Symbolic Forms* [PsF, 1923–29]. Trans-lated by Ralph Manheim. 3 vols. Vol. 1, *Language;* vol. 2, *Mythic Thought;* vol. 3, *The Phenomenology of Knowledge*. New Haven: Yale University Press, 1953–57.

QR   *The Question of Jean Jacques Rousseau* [1932]. Translated and edited by Peter Gay. New York: Columbia University Press, 1954.

RKG   *Rousseau, Kant, Goethe: Two Essays*. Translated by James Gutmann, Paul Oskar Kristeller, and John Hermann Randall, Jr. Princeton: Princeton University Press, 1945. Reprinted with an introduction by Peter Gay. New York: Harper & Row, Harper Torchbooks, 1963.

SF/ET *Substance and Function* [1910] *and Einstein's Theory of Relativity* [1921]. (Both books bound as one.) Translated by William Curtis Swabey and Marie Collins Swabey. Chicago: Open Court Publishing, 1923. Reprint. New York: Dover Publications, 1953.

SMC *Symbol, Myth, and Culture: Essays and Lectures of Ernst Cassirer, 1935–1945*. Edited by Donald Phillip Verene. New Haven: Yale University Press, 1979.

STS *Symbol, Technik, Sprache: Aufsätze aus den Jahren 1927– 1933*. Edited by Ernst Wolfgang Orth and John Michael Krois. Hamburg: Felix Meiner Verlag, 1985.

WW *Wesen und Wirkung des Symbolbegriffs*. 1956. Reprint. Darmstadt: Wissenschaftliche Buchgesellschaft, 1969.

ZMP *Zur modernen Physik* [1921/1937]. Contains reprints of German *ET* (in *SF/ET*) and *DI*. Darmstadt: Wissenschaftliche Buchgesellschaft, 1964.

Works on Cassirer

PEC Paul Arthur Schilpp, ed., *The Philosophy of Ernst Cassirer*. Library of Living Philosophers, no. 6. 1949. Reprint. New York: Tudor Publishing, 1958.

INTRODUCTION

On Ernst Cassirer's sixtieth birthday in 1934 he was presented with a collection of essays written in his honor, a festschrift entitled *Philosophy and History*.[1] The title was significant for several reasons. Cassirer was known both as a philosopher and as a historian of philosophy. A dialectic between philosophical and historical perspectives pervades all his writing. His best-known theoretical work, *The Philosophy of Symbolic Forms*, interprets historical life philosophically, while his classic historical studies, *The Individual and the Cosmos in Renaissance Philosophy* and *The Philosophy of the Enlightenment*, portray philosophical ideas as living forces in historical epochs. But the title of the festschrift had a further significance: it was in English, as were all the contributions; the few that originated in Germany had been translated.[2] During the Weimar Republic Cassirer was one of Germany's most prominent philosophers, a professor in Hamburg and for a time the university's rector. In 1933, at the height of his career, he emigrated from Germany, almost immediately after Hitler became Reich's chancellor. As an active supporter of the Weimar Republic and a Jew, as well as a person in public office, Cassirer was directly confronted by the new regime. The rise of the Third Reich affected his life and, to an extent, his thought. In *The Myth of the State* (1946) and other later writings he sought to understand philosophically the catastrophe that in 1933 was only beginning. The new political situation forced Cassirer to change his sphere of activity; he left Germany for the English-speaking world. Cassirer's reception as a thinker has been in part determined by this fact.

The editors of *Philosophy and History* included in the book a bibliography of Cassirer's writings, grouping them under the headings of "systematic" and "historical" works. This division is acceptable for bibliographic purposes, but Cassirer's writings cannot be understood in this way. His systematic works abound with historical discussions while his historical works are interwoven with philosophical arguments and often develop systematic theses. Hans Morgenthau once described this feature of Cassirer's works thus: "There never was a less antiquarian historian than Cassirer. In truth, he was not a historian of philosophy, but a philosopher who used history as a vehicle for philosophic thought, as others have used the aphorism or the system for the same purpose."[3] Cassirer's writings are united by his concern to understand history, especially the history of philosophy and its relation to the development of culture. It is not a coincidence that Cassirer devoted most of his historical research to the Renaissance and the Enlightenment. For him these two periods illustrate best how a rejuvenation of intellectual activity can change human life. But thought is not unaffected by historical reality. Cassirer's own writings show this. His interest in ethics and political philosophy grew in response to the political events of the early 1930s and after. Reflecting the different intellectual climates in which he lived after emigrating from Germany, Cassirer had to make his thought understandable to readers with different philosophical presuppositions; he even changed from writing in German to English. Despite all this, Cassirer's philosophy reveals a remarkable continuity.

An attempt to understand Cassirer's philosophy in a comprehensive way must strive to see his systematic and historical works as aspects of one project of thought. It requires taking cognizance of the early writings and mature works from Cassirer's career in Germany as well as the later writings from his years in England, Sweden, and the United States. My aim is to provide such an interpretation.

Most of the secondary literature on Cassirer consists of essays and reviews, and although these investigations vary in the degree of their comprehensiveness, they do not, either individually or collectively, provide a complete, systematic interpretation. The largest, most complete volume on Cassirer, *The Philosophy of Ernst Cassirer*, in the Library of Living Philosophers series edited by Paul Arthur Schilpp, is typical in this regard. Its twenty-three essays by different authors serve more to show the need for a comprehensive interpretation of Cassirer than to provide one. In his review of the book Iredell Jenkins wrote that the reader's general impression is that the only thing uniting the contributors' works is their inability to define Cassirer's position:

What comes as a definite and cumulative shock is the uncertainty that these authors evidence concerning their interpretations and criticisms: their seeming inability to be satisfied as to what Cassirer's position actually is. . . . There is apparent throughout these essays the sense that their authors are groping for some concretions within the flux of Cassirer's dialectic: for some bed-rock on which issues can be debated and for some constant frame-of-reference in terms of which difficulties can at least be defined.[4]

These comments were published in 1950; since that time the need for comprehensive interpretation has remained basically the same.

There have been few efforts to provide an extended analysis of Cassirer's thought. In 1956 Carl Hamburg published *Symbol and Reality: Studies in the Philosophy of Ernst Cassirer*, which draws attention to what is clearly the core of Cassirer's thinking, his concept of symbolism.[5] I agree with Hamburg's emphasis on this matter, even though I cannot agree with his interpretation of Cassirer's theory of symbolism. Nor can I follow Hamburg in considering Cassirer's philosophy to represent essentially the Marburg school of neo-Kantianism or to chiefly stand for epistemology and the philosophy of science. This is a prevalent view of Cassirer. It also underlies Seymour Itzkoff's *Ernst Cassirer: Scientific Knowledge and The Concept of Man*.[6] Itzkoff contends that Cassirer's theory of science is based upon his philosophical anthropology. This leaves the origin of Cassirer's basic philosophical position, from which this philosophical anthropology itself derives, unaccounted for. Itzkoff's volume on Cassirer for Twayne's World Leaders Series exposits *The Philosophy of Symbolic Forms* in a manner consistent with his earlier book. He says that the third volume of the *Philosophy of Symbolic Forms* "is probably Cassirer's central work," but in this work, *The Phenomenology of Knowledge*, he finds "no transcendental position on knowledge."[7] His appreciative depiction highlights Cassirer's detailed investigations, but these appear to lack a basic unifying theory. In a different vein, David Lipton's *Ernst Cassirer: The Dilemma of a Liberal Intellectual in Germany, 1914–1933* approaches Cassirer via the sociology of knowledge. His use of this method, I have argued elsewhere, prevents him from considering the question of the unity or even the content of Cassirer's philosophy.[8] Lipton looks to outside, political forces to explain Cassirer's works and leaves untouched the problem of the foundations of his thought and the viability of his ideas. His book calls attention, however, to aspects of Cassirer's work that few philosophical interpreters have recognized: his awareness of and interest in social and political reality.[9]

These five works exhaust the English monographs on Cassirer. They contain helpful analyses of specific aspects of Cassirer's work, but they do not address the systematic nature of his thought as a whole or investigate the relationship between his "historical" and "systematic" works.

Cassirer's thought has been much neglected in the German-speaking world.[10] There has been no postwar reinstatement of Cassirer in German scholarship; he remains today a respected but unexamined figure.[11] Nonetheless, due to the many-faceted nature of Cassirer's publications, his work has influenced thinking in many fields, including linguistics, semiotics, anthropology, art history, education, psychology and psychoanalysis, and history.[12] My concern with Cassirer's reception is not how he may have affected other scholars or disciplines, but how his thought has been understood as an original philosophy.

In many ways Cassirer stands alone in contemporary philosophy. No other philosopher in this century has given such prominence to the study of myth.[13] No other philosopher has given as much emphasis to the plurality of the "worlds" we experience—the worlds perceived through language, art, science, myth, and other forms of interpretation—or used this idea as a way to answer traditional philosophical questions.[14] No other philosopher has based his work on the analysis of meaning in the way that Cassirer has done, focusing on expression, rather than reference, while at the same time including both, along with abstract symbolism, in a comprehensive theory of signs and meaning. Yet Cassirer's explication of symbolic forms also exemplifies the mainstream of twentieth-century philosophy because of the fundamental importance it grants to problems of meaning.[15] Why, then, has Cassirer been so neglected? Part of the answer to this question can be found in the two prevailing views of Cassirer's thought. One view, which I call the Continental interpretation, takes Cassirer's philosophy to represent neo-Kantian epistemology; the other, which I call the Anglo-American interpretation, takes Cassirer to be a scholarly investigator and historian of ideas, a representative of historicism without a philosophical position of his own. According to the former view, Cassirer's thought can be subsumed under the Marburg school of neo-Kantianism founded by Cassirer's teacher, Hermann Cohen. Interpreters of this persuasion give primary attention to Cassirer's intellectual beginnings and identify his intellectual deelopment with this milieu. On this view Cassirer's thought is a carry-over from a movement that began in the nineteenth century rather than a new philosophical outlook. This is a standard history-book view.[16]

On the Anglo-American interpretation, based primarily upon those works of Cassirer's that are available in English, his numerous historical writings and the continual historical references in his systematic works are taken to indicate that he is really a historian of ideas who does not articulate a philosophical position of his own. The Marburg school, and neo-Kantianism generally, are little known among philosophers in the English-speaking world, so that movement does not play a significant role there in the attempts to interpret Cassirer's thought. For many of his Anglo-American interpreters, Cassirer seems at best to represent a kind of late, idealistic historicism such as Croce's, an equation of philosophy with the study of history.

Cassirer's philosophy—taken as an epistemology or as historicism—could hardly be considered to have room for metaphysical or ethical questions. The prevailing preconceptions about Cassirer's philosophy discourage considering it in such terms. Confusion about Cassirer's theoretical position has often been accompanied by a failure to recognize the normative dimension in his thought. In fact, these are actually two aspects of the same problem. According to both prevailing views of Cassirer's thought, his ethical position must be complete relativism. This is obviously the case for those who take him to uphold a type of historicism, but even for those who take the philosophy of symbolic forms to be an epistemology, his thought must seem completely relativistic. According to this view, Cassirer's philosophy of "symbolic forms" expanded epistemology to include additional forms of cognition neglected in previous theories of knowledge. In addition to scientific knowledge, Cassirer investigated our knowledge of the world as it is found in language, art, religion and myth, and other forms of culture. On this view, Cassirer has *multiplied* the forms of knowing. It is typical to find critics attributing to Cassirer the position that there are many forms of knowledge, all of them equally valid, and then concluding that his philosophy leaves him with no standards—theoretical or practical.[17]

Yet Cassirer developed a normative theory of ethics as well as a theory of truth. For him these are aspects of a systematic philosophy in which the theory of knowledge is a part, not the whole. Systematic philosophy, Cassirer said, "extends far beyond the theory of knowledge" (SF, 447). In saying this he had in mind philosophy in general and his philosophy of symbolic forms in particular. To conceive the philosophy of symbolic forms as a "theory of knowledge" must lead to the kinds of misunderstandings and confusion that have prevailed in the literature on Cassirer's thought.

The Continental Interpretation Cassirer's thought has usually been approached through Kant and neo-Kantianism.[18] Hermann Cohen (1842–1918) and Paul Natorp (1854–1924), the main figures in the Marburg school of neo-Kantianism, were Cassirer's teachers. Cassirer often defended Cohen's thought against criticism. These are facts. But to hold that Cassirer's philosophy can be described adequately as a form of neo-Kantianism assumes much more. Helmut Kuhn wrote in his biographical article for the *Neue Deutsche Biographie* that "despite all the independence which he soon displayed to his teachers, he remained in method and basic philosophical conviction a representative of the Marburg form of Neo-Kantianism" (s.v. "Cassirer, Ernst Alfred"). To see what this means it is sufficient to look at the same author's review of Cassirer's *Essay on Man* (1944). Over a page of the review describes the Marburg school's doctrines, pointing out that "the Marburg Kantians are primarily concerned with the object as construed by science," and that Cassirer's thought "may be construed as the consummation of Marburg Kantianism."[19] Kuhn concludes that Cassirer's neo-Kantianism forces him to hold an abstract view of man that regards him as a knower and not an actor. This emphasis on cognition results in a "failure to come to grips with the problem of man as a unity of body and mind"; hence the ethical dimension—action by real individuals—is not taken into account (ibid., 502). Kuhn concludes: "The *Essay on Man* has no room for an ethics—no room for a man confronted with a choice of good and evil" (ibid., 504).

An *Essay on Man* was also characterized in Fritz Kaufmann's review as "one of the latest and, perhaps, the last documents of the Marburg Neo-Kantian school."[20] This "Continental" view of Cassirer is not confined to German scholars. Seymour Itzkoff's first monograph on Cassirer begins with a chapter on "Cassirer's Kantianism" and then presents his philosophy as a "theory of knowledge."[21] Iredell Jenkins claims that Cassirer's philosophy is a kind of Kantian idealism that conceives man abstractly—in purely intellectual terms— recognizing only his cognitive relationship to the world and overlooking all his vital (and moral) ties.[22]

This interpretation of Cassirer focuses on one of the most salient features of the Marburg school of neo-Kantianism: its emphasis on epistemology and the supreme status given by Cohen to cognition in the mathematical natural sciences. In a position paper in the Marburg school's own journal, Cohen and Natorp state: "Philosophy to us, is bound to the fact of science, as this elaborates itself. Philosophy, therefore, to us is the theory of the principles of science and therewith of all culture."[23] Scientific knowledge is the primary object of concern to the Marburg school, and scholars who assert that Cassirer is a Marburg neo-Kantian hold that his philosophy also is basically an epistemology, and, more specifically, that it is primarily an epistemology of scientific knowledge, or at least that scientific knowledge is its major paradigm for thought. Further, it is assumed that neo-Kantianism, and Cassirer's thought in particular, is a kind of subjective idealism. In a summary essay on Cassirer in a 1973 German volume on contemporary philosophy, the author states flatly that Cassirer's philosophy is a kind of *Bewusstseinsidealismus*, an idealism of consciousness.[24] Cassirer is presumed to hold that consciousness is the ultimate philosophical starting point, interpreting "consciousness" to mean the ego in a Cartesian sense. Yet even Cohen stressed that transcendental logic and his own chief work, the *Logik der reinen Erkenntnis* (1902), have nothing to do with such an "Idealismus des Bewusstseins."[25] Cassirer upheld no such primacy of consciousness, but rather the primacy of meaning and the fact that the person is bound to a body. This view of Cassirer as a philosopher of consciousness results from the fact that his readers have brought an interpretation to his works, rather than taking them in their own terms. The currency enjoyed by the view that Cassirer upholds a subjective idealism stems from a number of false conceptions about neo-Kantianism and Cassirer's relationship to this movement. The true test of the adequacy of this view is to consider how Cassirer actually develops his philosophy in his works over the years.

The view that Cassirer is a subjective idealist is nowhere as pronounced as it is among contemporary German philosophers. Since World War II Germans have shown great interest in American Pragmatism, particularly in the philosophy of Charles S. Peirce. His work— like Cassirer's—gives prominence to the theory of signs and symbols, to what Peirce called "semiotic." Cassirer's work on this subject has been ignored by German philosophers, but the prima facie similarity between this aspect of Peirce's thought and Cassirer's has elicited comments that reveal preconceptions of Cassirer's work. Jürgen Habermas, for example, notes a striking similarity between Cassirer's idea of a philosophy of symbolic forms and Peirce's theory of signs, but he then dismisses Cassirer's approach: "Unlike Cassirer, however, Peirce cannot base the process of semiotic mediation on the transcendental unity of consciousness."[26] Habermas does not demonstrate this point by reference to Cassirer's writings; he takes for granted that for Cassirer the unity of *consciousness* is logically prior to sign usage and that individual consciousness for Cassirer is, therefore, also prior to consciousness as constituted intersubjectively by means of sign interpretation.

Karl-Otto Apel, whose thought is even more strongly influenced by Peirce than is Habermas's, agrees with the latter's view of Cassirer. Apel, too, notes that Cassirer's philosophy appears at first to bear a striking resemblance to Peirce's theory of signs, but he finds fault in what he takes to be the foundation of Cassirer's theory:

This shortcoming of Kant's critique of reason [that the transcendental synthesis of apperception is insufficient to found knowledge], which had already been sensed by the fathers of German philosophy of language, Hamann, Herder and Wilhelm von Humboldt, could in fact be rectified in the development of neo-Kantianism by Ernst Cassirer who, in his *Philosophy of Symbolic Forms*, to some extent incorporated the sign function into the transcendental synthesis of apperception. Neo-Kantianism emerged at the same time as American pragmatism, but its *semiotic transformation of transcendental philosophy* differs from Peirce's conception in that—despite its semiotic embodiment of the mediating function of cognition—it leaves the Kantian presupposition of a transcendental idealism of consciousness [*Bewusstseinsidealismus*] unaltered as far as this mediated subject-object relationship is concerned. In this respect, Peirce's semiotic transformation of Kantianism is far more radical.[27]

Apel gives three reasons why Peirce's transformation of Kantian philosophy is more radical than Cassirer's: (1) "There can be no knowledge of something as something without a real sign mediation on the basis of material sign vehicles"; (2) "the sign can have no representational function for a consciousness without the presupposed existence of a real *world* which, in principle, must be thought of as being representable, and that means *knowable*, in various aspects"; and (3) "there can be no representation of something as something by a sign without *interpretation by a real interpreter*" (ibid., 100). These criticisms of Cassirer derive from the assumption that his position, as Apel says, is a form of *Bewusstseinsidealismus*, an idealism of consciousness. For such a philosophy, the ultimate presupposition and starting point is the mind, the "transcendental unity of apperception," rather than the phenomenon of meaning expressed through signs and symbols that interpret a real world for a community of real interpreters.

Klaus Oehler, the foremost German authority on Peirce's philosophy, makes the same criticism of Cassirer in still more explicit terms.

According to Oehler, Cassirer continued to uphold Kant's conception of *Bewusstsein überhaupt*, consciousness in general, while simply adding language as a medium. Oehler says that Cassirer's symbolic forms "have their place completely within the traditional modern framework of the transcendental theory of knowledge, and constitute means of mediation for consciousness, which continues to be conceived in solipsistic terms."[28]

These observations by Habermas, Apel, and Oehler show why contemporary German philosophers assume that Cassirer's philosophy offers little promise of a new direction in thought. These critics hold that Peirce and the recent Anglo-American philosophy of language take a significant step beyond the older idealistic form of philosophizing, with which they associate Cassirer. It is significant that none of these criticisms are presented as the result of a critical investigation of Cassirer's writings. They are remarks purporting simply to state the facts.

Cassirer has frequently been perceived as having no interest in problems of ethics or political philosophy. Helmut Kuhn asks: "Where is, we wonder, a place for ethics and political philosophy in the frame-work of the Symbolic Forms? For Cassirer, life comes into view only as *vita acta*, 'life that was lived,' never as *vita agenda*, 'life as it is to be lived.' "[29] In a more recent article Nathan Rotenstreich states bluntly: "Cassirer never developed an ethical theory of his own."[30] When *The Myth of the State* appeared, some reviewers found it to be lacking in this regard, showing the need for an ethics in Cassirer's philosophy. Leo Strauss contended that an adequate response to doctrines that favor political myth "would have been not an inconclusive discussion of the myth of the state, but a radical transformation of the philosophy of symbolic forms into a teaching whose center is moral philosophy."[31] Strauss did not realize that Cassirer had done precisely that; he transformed the philosophy of symbolic forms in the latter half of his career to create a teaching centered on the problem of the normative dimension of the idea of culture. The relative inaccessibility of some of Cassirer's work on these topics plays a role in these negative judgments, since a number of important papers in this area have only been available since 1979.[32] Yet the view that Cassirer has no ethical theory persists in even the most recent work on his thought. Heinz Paetzold, for example, asserts that "it is difficult to see how the basic problems of ethics can be solved through Cassirer's theory of the symbol," and hence, Paetzold charges, Cassirer "loses sight of the problems of ethics."[33] The inability to see how Cassirer could have an ethics reflects a particular philosophical interpretation of his thought that militates against understanding what he accomplished in this area. Whoever believes that Cassirer is a philosopher of "consciousness" cannot expect him to have developed an ethics based on a transcendental theory of the pragmatics of language. Whoever regards Cassirer's philosophy of language to treat only epistemological matters cannot expect this philosophy also to include a theory of the will and action. Clearly, Cassirer's contribution to ethics can only be understood if there is first an adequate understanding of his basic philosophical orientation.

The Anglo-American Interpretation In the English-speaking world relatively little attention has been given to the neo-Kantian movement, and this has resulted in a different view of Cassirer from the one normally found among his Continental interpreters. A few American interpreters have perceived a relationship between Cassirer's philosophy and American Pragmatism. John Hermann Randall has noted fundamental agreement between Cassirer and Dewey.[34] Felix Kaufmann discusses the agreement between Cassirer's views of science and Dewey's (PEC, 209–13). An examination of the pragmatic elements in Cassirer's thought or of his references to American Pragmatist writings, which are not infrequent, would be interesting but would lead beyond the present problem.[35] This is not a typical approach to Cassirer. Much more common in the Anglo-American world is to see his philosophy as a form of historicism. On this interpretation there are no fixed ends inherent in historical life and no objective norms or standards by which to regard it. The only constant is the development of the human spirit. John Passmore reports that in England the prevailing view of Cassirer is that he failed to distinguish between philosophy and history, that for him to philosophize is to study history. Passmore states: "In Cassirer's eyes, however, this is a distinction [that is, between history and philosophy] without a difference. Philosophy for him, as for Croce, is 'self-knowledge,' and self-knowledge is the knowledge of the human spirit at work in culture."[36]

This perspective is common in the English-speaking world. Adherents of this view overlook Cassirer's critical analysis of Croce's thesis of the identity of philosophy and history, a thesis Cassirer rejected categorically.[37] Cassirer charges Croce with upholding a skepticism in every field of knowledge except history, but even within that field, Cassirer concludes, Croce upholds a *schrankenlosen historischen Relativismus*, an unlimited historical relativism, so that "the whole doctrine, even though it proclaims logic as the basic science, in fact turns out to be an unlimited historical relativism in which change is studied so to speak for its own sake, in which no objective-logical enduring factors [*Bestand*] of any kind are discerned or set off" (ibid., 34).

For Cassirer, the Crocean position is ultimately self-contradictory: it is concerned with development, but nothing is recognized as developing; hence, this view deprives itself of any real content to reflect upon and to know. In addition to these logical considerations, the whole *retrospective* character of Croce's position puts philosophy in a fully passive position and condemns it to the role of a spectator with nothing to contribute to the positive shaping of culture. Cassirer argued against this view of philosophy again and again, especially in the latter part of his career and particularly in his frequent criticisms of Hegel.

The view that Cassirer upheld a vague, historist idealism is akin to saying that he had no position of his own. When Brand Blanshard reviewed Cassirer's *Essay on Man*, he saw the book in such terms. Unlike Helmut Kuhn or Fritz Kaufman, who found a "document of the Marburg Neo-Kantian Schooi," that is, an expression of a definite philosophical position, Blanshard found no position at all: "It is not hard to think as one reads a book so wealthy as this in historic and scientific erudition, but at the same time so oddly inconclusive, that Cassirer was rather a distinguished reflective scholar than a great speculative philosopher. The learning is not mobilized in the interest of any theory; the book is not so much an 'essay on man' as a series of essays, all suggestive and enlightening, which converge on—what? It is hard to say. Perhaps there *is* no end, or harmony of ends, towards which all these activities are moving."[38]

For Cassirer there was quite definitely an end upon which the activities discussed in the *Essay on Man* converged, and he stated it there succinctly: "Human culture taken as a whole may be described as the process of man's progressive self-liberation (EM, 228).[39] The *Essay on Man* is a work on philosophical anthropology, but the theory of man it presents is derived from a philosophical position that is developed elsewhere. In the preface to the *Essay on Man* Cassirer drew attention to this fact: "My critics should, however, be warned that what I could give here is more an explanation and illustration than a demonstration of my theory. For a closer discussion and analysis of the problems involved I must ask them to go back to the detailed description in my *Philosophy of Symbolic Forms*" (EM, viii). To look for Cassirer as a speculative philosopher in *An Essay on Man* is, therefore, to go against Cassirer's own instructions. Many of Cassirer's readers have tended to regard this late work as a summary or even a substitute for *The Philosophy of Symbolic Forms*, but this can only result in a distorted and incomplete view of his thought.[40] Since *An Essay on Man* is widely read in the English-speaking world but the *Symbolic Forms* is not, it is not surprising that Cassirer is widely thought of there to have no theoretical position.

The most recent attempt in the English-speaking world to come to grips with Cassirer's ideas is Nelson Goodman's *Ways of Worldmaking*. Goodman does not perceive himself as a Cassirer scholar or interpreter; on the contrary, he conceives his work to be purely philosophical and to treat objective problems. In order to resolve objective philosophical issues Goodman has been led to take up central theses of Cassirer's philosophy of symbolic forms and to introduce them into present-day philosophical discussion. The questions that this endeavor raises are, therefore, purely philosophical, not textual. Goodman sought to draw a line between his own work and Cassirer's by indicating a difference he perceived in their respective approaches. Goodman sees a basic agreement between his effort to distinguish different ways of "worldmaking" and Cassirer's effort to distinguish different "symbolic forms." The difference between his work and Cassirer's, Goodman says, is that "Cassirer undertakes the search through a cross-cultural study of the development of myth, religion, language, art, and science. My approach is rather through an analytic study of types and functions of symbols and symbol systems."[41]

Here Goodman gives expression to the widespread view that Cassirer is a scholar engaged in historical study rather than a philosopher engaged in a theoretical project. Even Susanne Langer, long regarded as the philosopher most influenced by Cassirer, stated that, although his concept of symbolism served her for years in her work on the theory of art, she understood it through Cassirer's usage of it, not from any explicit definition he may have given: "In many years of work on the fundamental problems of art I have found it [Cassirer's concept of the symbol] indispensable; it served as a key to the most involved question. But this symbol concept, as it emerges in use, in the course of work—which, after all, is the most authentic source of all concepts—cannot be defined in terms of denotation, signification, formal assignment, or reference. The proof of the pudding is in the eating, and I submit that Cassirer's pudding is good; but the recipe is not on the box."[42]

No matter how elusive Cassirer's conception of the symbol may seem to be, it is the key to his thinking on the issues that have concerned his critics—his theory of consciousness, his understanding of idealism, and his theory of ethics. The theory of symbolism is one of the main avenues of Cassirer's thought. Another is his thinking about history.

While the goal of my study is a systematic investigation of Cassirer's thought rather than an intellectual biography, it will nonetheless sometimes be necessary to adopt a biographical perspective. Hence it will be helpful to review how Cassirer's writings emerged throughout the course of his career.

Cassirer's Early Years

Ernst Cassirer was born on July 28, 1874, in the German city of Breslau (today: Wroclaw, Poland), a center of commerce in the province of Silesia. The Cassirer family operated the J & M Cassirer Breslau Sulfite-Cellulose Factory. Part of the family resided in Berlin, and as a youngster Cassirer often traveled there to visit his cousin Kurt Goldstein with whom, years later, he would collaborate.[43] Cassirer began his university studies in Berlin in 1892 in jurisprudence, changed to German literature, and then arrived at philosophy.[44] He changed universities often, going to Leipzig, then Heidelberg, and returning to Berlin before settling in 1894 upon Marburg, where Hermann Cohen held the chair of philosophy. Cohen was well known as the founder of the Marburg school of neo-Kantianism and as one of the greatest living authorities on Kant. Neo-Kantianism was a deeply divided movement, fraught with controversies, many of which were only slightly veiled personal animosities. Lewis White Beck writes that "men entered and left the [neo-Kantian] movement as if it were a church or a political party; members of one school blocked the appointments and promotions of members of the others; eminent Kant scholars and philosophers who did not found their own schools tended to be neglected as outsiders and condemned as amateurs" (Encyclopedia of Philosophy, s.v. "Neo-Kantianism"). Neo-Kantianism was in its heyday in Germany during Cassirer's student days, and its factionalism presented considerable difficulties to a beginner in philosophy. Each of the "schools" had a particular interest or doctrine that it took to constitute its inheritance from Kant, which it sought to develop as the "true Kantianism." Near the end of his life Cassirer wrote the following recollection about this confusing situation and the reasons that led him to study with Cohen:

It was then a generally admitted opinion that no one could enter the field of philosophy without a careful and thorough study of the work of Kant. . . . But this general agreement was only an apparent one. It contained the germs of a radical dissension. Nearly all the philosophical schools referred to Kant and appealed to his authority, but there was never a clear and unambiguous way of interpreting his fundamental doctrines. There was an empiristic view of the Kantian system side by side with a rationalistic view; there was a metaphysical conception side by side with a strict phenomenalism, nay a strict skepticism; there was a "realistic" explanation in contradiction to another that seemed to lead to mere "subjective idealism." It was extremely difficult to find one's bearings in this mass of opposite interpretations.[45]

Cassirer found his way out of the impasse posed by these conflicting interpretations during a lecture course on Kant given by Georg Simmel at the University of Berlin. After fifty years Cassirer recollected what occurred at that class:

In one of the first hours [Simmel] gave a short bibliography of the literature on Kant and it was on that occasion that I first heard the name of Hermann Cohen. Simmel emphasized how much he himself owed to the study of Cohen's books, but he immediately added that those books, in spite of their real sagacity and profundity, suffered from a very grave defect. They were written, he said, in such an obscure style that as yet there was probably no one who had succeeded in deciphering them. That was, of course, a great paradox that could not fail to make an impression on the mind of a young man. What a surprise to hear that, after all, there was a work on Kant which the best judges considered to be a true and thorough explanation of his fundamental thoughts but which at the same time was declared to be nearly inaccessible to the common reader!

Prompt in acting, as suits a boy of nineteen, I resolved to try the adventure myself. I bought Cohen's book, *Kants Theorie der Erfahrung*, and began to study it. And here I felt from the first pages, that I was on firm and secure ground. I could by no means overcome all the difficulties at once—the less so as I was still imperfectly acquainted with the technical language of philosophy. But I pursued the reading of Cohen's work, for I was convinced that here at last I had found the guide that I had so badly missed and so eagerly desired in my study of Kant's philosophy. After a short time I had gone through all the principal works of Cohen and it was only when I had come to this point that I felt prepared to make his personal acquaintance. I went to Marburg, where he held the chair of philosophy, and soon became a pupil of Cohen's and ultimately one of his most devoted and intimate friends. (Ibid., 222–23)

Cassirer was Cohen's student from 1896 to 1899 and completed his studies in Marburg with his inaugural dissertation "Descartes' Kritik der mathematischen und naturwissenschaftlichen Erkenntnis."[46] The thesis fell squarely within the field of study that most interested Cohen, the idealistic foundations of mathematics and natural science.

Following Cassirer's studies and his marriage to his cousin Toni Bondy, the Cassirers lived in Munich, but they were attracted to Berlin and moved there in 1903. Cassirer remained there for sixteen years, the longest he was ever to reside in one place during his career.

Berlin: 1903–1919

In Berlin Cassirer was exposed to the intellectual and cultural life of Germany's most important city. He was a part of a large, wealthy family that figured prominently in the arts and academic community in Berlin from the turn of the century until the end of the Weimar Republic.[47] During Cassirer's years in the city five cousins numbered among his closest friends. Fritz Cassirer (1871–1926) was a conductor, composer, and musicologist who had studied philosophy before taking up music. Bruno Cassirer (1872–1941) was a publisher, specializing in fine editions, particularly in books on art as well as literature and philosophy. Bruno Cassirer published the works of Hermann Cohen and, later, Ernst Cassirer's writings. In 1912 the Bruno Cassirer Verlag published Cassirer's most important work as an editor, his ten-volume edition of Kant's writings, the most complete collection of Kant's works to appear until then.[48] Richard Cassirer (1868–1925) was a noted physician and professor of neurology at the University of Berlin. The most well known member of the family was Paul Cassirer (1871–1926). His art gallery introduced French Impressionism into Germany, offering the first exhibitions in the country of the works of Cézanne, Monet, Renoir, Gauguin, Toulouse-Lautrec, and Rodin. Among the German artists he supported were Ernst Barlach, Max Slevogt, and Oskar Kokoschka. His exhibitions of van Gogh (1904), of Munch, Cézanne, and Matisse (1907), and of Kokoschka (1910) were internationally acclaimed. Among conservative circles he acquired the reputation of the man who, in the words of Kaiser Wilhelm II, brought "Pariser Dreckkunst" (Parisian Filthart) to Berlin.[49] Paul Cassirer was one of the leaders of the Berlin Secession, which provided artists with a forum outside the narrow stylistic limits of the Royal Academy's exhibitions. The Berlin Secession, says the historian Peter Paret, was "the aesthetic expression of doomed liberalism in Germany."[50] Paul Cassirer became the target of criticism for promoting an "un-German way of seeing nature" (ibid., 110). The art shown at the Berlin Secession, Paret says, emphasized the "symbolic function of art," and, because it deviated from tradition, seemed unsettling, so that many people "reacted with intense anxiety to an art that questioned familiar assumptions and showed them an unknown world" (p. 88). Paul Cassirer was also a publisher. Among his authors were Heinrich Mann, Else Lasker-Schuler, Ernst Toller, and Frank Wedekind. He also published the works of socialist theoreticians: Eduard Bernstein, Rosa Luxemburg, Erich Mühsam, and Ernst Bloch. Cassirer refereed philosophy manuscripts submitted to Paul Cassirer for publication.[51] Finally, Kurt Goldstein (1878–1965) was active as a physician in Berlin, where he laid the groundwork for his theories of the organism and aphasia. Goldstein's research on aphasia later played a significant role in Cassirer's philosophy of symbolic forms.[52]

In the midst of these people, in the cultural and political center of Germany, Cassirer developed the idea of his philosophy of symbolic forms.

Cassirer's earliest work centered on Leibniz, "the founder of German Idealism." His first book, Leibniz' System (1902) and the two-volume edition of Leibniz's writings that followed it, Leibniz, Philosophische Werke (1904–06), were eventually supplemented by an edition of the Nouveaux Essais in 1915.[53] From the standpoint of Cassirer's later development, it is interesting to note that he gave particular attention, even in these early works, to ethics and the theory of law. For example, Cassirer emphasized that Leibniz's introduction of the theory of individual, historical being into idealistic metaphysics enabled him to found a theory of "inalienable, individual human rights."[54]

Cassirer believed that philosophy can only progress by means of a critical reception of its own history. He believed that attempts at radical criticisms of previous solutions to problems actually prove philosophy's continuity: "Whoever follows the overall development of thought must come to realize that in it we find a slow, continuing progression of the same great problems. The solutions change, but the basic problems remain. Everything directed against them only serves to more sharply and clearly formulate them and in this way to prove that their vitality is constantly renewed."[55] Among the questions that are renewed again and again in the history of philosophy, and the one that most interested Cassirer at this time, is "What is knowledge?"

Cassirer's next project after his work on Leibniz was to begin what eventually became a four-volume work on the history of the problem of knowledge, the first two volumes of which appeared in 1906 and 1907. This work, Das Erkenntnisproblem in der Philosophie und

Wissenschaft der neueren Zeit (The problem of knowledge in philosophy and science in the modern age), covers in its first two volumes the period from Nicolas of Cusa through Kant. In the introductory discussion of his method in *Das Erkenntnisproblem* Cassirer sheds light on many of the themes that became the focal point of the development of his own theoretical philosophy, in particular his criticism of the concept of substance. The study of the history of philosophy, Cassirer says, must primarily be a method by which we learn to understand this history. This is what makes it a science or *Wissenschaft*, rather than just an enumeration of various collected facts (*EP*, 1:viii). The object of Cassirer's work is to understand the changing conception of knowledge in modern thought. He distinguishes this task from the "history of theories of knowledge" (*Geschichte der Erkenntnistheorien*), which "cannot give us a full or sufficient image of the inner, continual development of the concept of knowledge" (*EP*, 1:8).

Key turns in this development sometimes originate outside of philosophical systems, such as in Pico's criticisms of astrology, Leonardo's conception of imagination, or Galileo's science. Many forces affect the development in question: "Such an affective role is not the privilege of a single field, but rather holds in the same manner for all the contents and directions of culture" (*EP*, 1:10). Cassirer's objective in *Das Erkenntnisproblem* is to understand conceptions of knowledge as part of history: "We must make the attempt to reconstruct the governing, driving ideal of knowledge in an age as a comprehensive intellectual movement" (*EP*, 1:10).

Cassirer conceived the history of ideas as treating of living processes rather than finished, fixed facts. Ideas continue to live, are carried to new conclusions, and give birth to new thoughts. He attempts to show how the history of philosophy consists of different "directions" (*Richtungen*) of thought uniting diverse thinkers in— often unintended—joint efforts toward common goals. Unlike Hegel, who conceives the history of philosophy in terms of the development of the Idea, that is, his own metaphysical system, thereby relegating those thinkers that do not contribute directly to this end to a kind of antechamber of thought, Cassirer treats little-known figures in detail along with the great systematic philosophers because they contribute to the continuity of thought. Cassirer did not discuss his approach to writing history as such until much later,[56] but the theoretical foundations for his approach became apparent in his early systematic work *Substance and Function*. There the concept of function takes the place of the concept of substance as the basis of continuity. This conceptual shift is already evident in the *Erkenntnisproblem*'s introductory remarks on the continuity of the history of thought:

Every historical, serial development requires a "subject" [*Sub-jekt*] that lies at its base and is expressed outwardly in it. The mistake made by the metaphysical history of philosophy does not lie in the fact that it calls for such a subject, but rather in reifying [*verdinglicht*] it by speaking of the self-development of the "Idea," progress made by the "World Spirit" and so forth. We have to dispense with every such thing-like carrier that stands behind the historical movement; the metaphysical movement must be transformed into a methodological one. Instead of seeking and calling for a common substratum, we only require the continuity of thought in the individual phases of what occurs; it alone is what we require in order to speak of the unity of the process. (EP, 1:16–17)

Cassirer calls this unity a "hypothesis" and a "postulate," but he does not look upon it as something arbitrary. Despite his critical references to Hegel's way of characterizing the history of philosophy, Cassirer nonetheless ends the introduction to his method with a positive appraisal of what he calls the "deeper idealistic theme that is fundamental for Hegel, despite all of his metaphysical confusions" (EP, 1:17). By "idealism" Cassirer means here the methodological doctrine developed by Cohen, to whom Cassirer directs the reader in a footnote, that the logical unity which Kant had limited to certain categories of the understanding is necessary as an original "logical function" to the foundation of any science, including the historical study of philosophy (EP, 1:18n).

On July 26, 1906, Cassirer completed the formalities of his *Habilitation* at the University of Berlin and for the next thirteen years he lectured there as a *Privatdozent*. His *Erkenntnisproblem* was readily accepted as a *Habilitationsschrift*, but at the colloquium following the trial lecture, the neo-Kantian realist Alois Riehl charged that Cassirer denied the existence of physical objects, whereas Cassirer had only claimed that cognition determined the way we know. Riehl, since the previous year *Ordinarius* at Berlin as the successor to Dilthey's chair, would have prevented Cassirer from receiving the *venia legendi* had not Dilthey himself, who attended the lecture, spoken in Cassirer's favor.[57]

In 1910 Cassirer's first systematic theoretical work appeared: *Substanzbegriff und Funktionsbegriff* (*Substance and Function*). The problems discussed in this work were first examined in an article in the *Kantstudien* in 1907.[58] There Cassirer outlined his view of the philosophical significance of new developments in modern logic stemming from the creation of the formal logic of relations by Schroeder, Peirce, Couturat, and, especially, Russell. He pointed out that the objects of knowledge in modern science were laws whose mathematical expression could not be adequately grasped by the Aristotelian concept of substance (*ousia*) or understood by the classical logic of the syllogism, which was felt to be a "reaktionäre und hemmende Moment," a reactionary and restrictive element (ibid., 7). The new logic was based on the concept of relation, not substance, and dealt with functions, not classes. Cassirer argued that this new logic offered a more reliable guideline for a transcendental analysis than traditional class logic had provided to Kant. This idea, developed in the article "Kant und die moderne Mathematik," provided the seminal idea for *Substance and Function*.

Substanzbegriff und Funktionsbegriff (The concept of substance and the concept of function) develops a theory of the a priori "invariants" of experience. Cassirer argues that the method of science proves the felicity of such invariants: "Since we can never compare the system of hypotheses itself with the naked facts in themselves, but always can only oppose one hypothetical system of principles to another more inclusive, more radical system, we need for this progressive comparison an ultimate constant standard of measurement in supreme principles that hold for all experience in general."[59]

In *Substance and Function* Cassirer uses the term *experience* to refer primarily to scientific inquiry, and when he uses the term *reality* (*Wirklichkeit*) it designates the world as an object of scientific knowledge. He says: "The one reality can only be indicated and defined as the ideal limit of the many changing theories; yet the assumption of this limit is not arbitrary, but inevitable, since only by it is the continuity of experience established" (SF/ET, 321–22). It is interesting to note that Cassirer upholds this absolute standard of truth as well as an instrumental theory of hypothesis evaluation, for which he refers concurringly to the works of John Dewey and William James: "We call a proposition 'true,' not because it agrees with a fixed reality beyond all thought and all possibility of thought, but because it is verified in the process of thought and leads to new and fruitful consequences."[60] Cassirer's contention in *Substance and Function* that *both* absolute and instrumental criteria of truth are necessary to science reflects his interpretation in *Das Erkenntnisproblem* of the concept of *Erfahrung*, "experience," in Kant. There he points out that, in order to prevent confusion, it is necessary to specify whether we are speaking about the object of knowledge in terms of the results of inquiry present at hand or in terms of the unlimited continuity of the knowing process (EP, 2:752–53). Cassirer employs this distinction in *Substance and Function* in order to distinguish the philosophy of science as a theory of inquiry and theory formation from the general theory of knowledge.

In 1912 Hermann Cohen retired from the chair of philosophy at Marburg and moved to Berlin, where he lived until his death in 1918. During these years he taught in Berlin at the Hochschule für die Wissenschaft des Judentums, the "College for the Study of Judaism." Despite efforts by Cohen and Natorp to have Cassirer appointed as Cohen's successor in Marburg, this position was offered to someone else—an experimental psychologist. This appointment ended the identification of Cohen's chair with Marburg neo-Kantianism. "Marburg" had become synonymous not only with an approach to transcendental philosophy, but with the school's leader as well, who was disliked by many for his outspoken stand on the Jewish contribution to German culture and his socialist political views. Cassirer did not give traditional Jewish thought a central position in his philosophy (the feature of Cohen's late work that so appealed to Franz Rosenzweig), nor does socialist theory play an important role in his work.[61] That he was Cohen's choice was political reason enough for not appointing him, and as Natorp declared in the *Frankfurter Zeitung*, the appointment of Cohen's replacement was made on purely political grounds.[62]

Cassirer's lack of success in finding a professorship stood in marked contrast to his growing reputation as the author of *Das Erkenntnisproblem* and *Substanzbegriff und Funktionsbegriff*. In the spring of 1913 he received an invitation from Harvard University to spend the coming academic year there as a guest professor in the philosophy department, but he declined to accept the offer in deference to his family. In the same year *Das Erkenntnisproblem* earned Cassirer the Kuno Fischer Gold Medal, awarded by the University of Heidelberg for work on the history of philosophy.[63] Cassirer's next major work, *Freiheit und Form*, appeared two years after the outbreak of World War I. Unlike his previous publications, this work was dedicated exclusively to the *geisteswissenschaftliche* or humanistic side of philosophy: to the problem of human freedom, the relationship of the individual to society, and the general development of culture. *Freiheit und Form* is subtitled *Studien zur Deutschen Geistesgeschichte*, "studies of German cultural history," but Cassirer's interpretation deliberately seeks to avoid what he calls "narrow intellectual chauvinism" (FF, xvi). In Imperial Germany, in the midst of World War I, his approach to German culture contrasted sharply with the prevailing view, which, by emphasizing the medieval, mystical sources of German culture and ignoring its modernist elements, sought to divorce it from the general development of European culture.[64]

Cassirer begins by placing German culture in the context of a general European movement: the Renaissance. The Renaissance concern with individuality, he argues, is taken up in the metaphysics of Leibniz. Cassirer then shows how the growing emphasis on the individual developed in German culture up to the humanism of Humboldt, Goethe, and Schiller. He claims that their humanism avoids treating individual freedom egoistically because they relate it to the "general" task of giving human life a *cultural* form in which individual freedom can unfold.

German literature had a deep influence on Cassirer's philosophy. In an essay published a year after *Freiheit und Form* Cassirer gave an interpretation of poetry that marks a turning point in his philosophical development. In this essay, entitled "Hölderlin und der Deutsche Idealismus" (Hölderlin and German idealism), Cassirer for the first time presents myth and poetic vision as original, independent forms of understanding. They are neither early stages of thought on the way to science nor external ornament. Through myth and poetry the world and life are "erst wahrhaft erschlossen und gedeutet," first truly disclosed and interpreted (*IG*, 121). In the Hölderlin essay Cassirer concentrates again on individuality, but on its negative aspect, the tragedy of individual finitude (*IG*, 136–55). The concluding section contrasts Hölderlin's poetic vision of individual mortality with Hegel's attempt to see it in the larger context of his metaphysical system. The Hölderlin essay gives the first indication of a new direction in Cassirer's philosophy, away from the Marburg view that the principles of science are the principles of all culture.

It was about this time (1917) that Cassirer developed the theory of symbol forms. He told his friend Gawronsky that the idea first occurred to him as he stepped aboard a Berlin streetcar (*PEC*, 25).

The last major work to appear during Cassirer's years in Berlin was *Kants Leben und Lehre* (*Kant's Life and Thought*). This work, which examines Kant's entire corpus, attributes unusually great importance to the *Critique of Judgment* and to Kant's historical writings. Cassirer says that although the latter seem to be brief, quickly written, occasional pieces, their contribution to the conception of the state and history in German idealism is in fact hardly less important than that made by the *Critique of Pure Reason* itself in the sphere of its problems (*KLT*, 223). The historical writings, Kant's ethical works, and the *Critique of Judgment* together form a general teleological system of philosophy (*KLT*, 226). On this view, Kant's system coheres as a philosophy of historical life; it is not essentially a theory of knowledge.

Kants Leben und Lehre was published in 1918. In April of the same year Hermann Cohen died. In November, World War I ended, Kaiser Wilhelm abdicated, and Germany was declared a republic. The advent of the Weimar Republic brought a change in Cassirer's personal fortunes. In the spring of 1919 Cassirer was offered two chairs of philosophy at two newly founded universities, the University of Frankfurt and the University of Hamburg. Cassirer accepted Hamburg's offer, and that October he began what were to be the fourteen most productive years of his life.

Hamburg: 1919–1933

The University of Hamburg was officially founded on May 10, 1919, and Cassirer was named professor in the *geisteswissenschaftliche* faculty on June 18. In addition to the university, Hamburg offered another important intellectual resource that was to influence greatly the development of Cassirer's thought, the Kulturwissenschaftliche Bibliothek Warburg, the Warburg Library for Cultural Studies. Aby Warburg (1866–1929), the library's founder, was one of the major theoreticians of art history in this century.[65] His view of ancient Greek culture and the influence of the ancients on the modern world was radically different from the prevailing Winckelmannian conception of the ancient world as a culture of stillness and repose. For Warburg, classical art was the source of the archetypal forms of emotional expression found in Renaissance art—what Warburg called *Pathosformel*, formulas of pathos.[66] His interest in cult and ritual, astrology, magic, and primitive medicine gave another view, long overlooked, of ancient Greece and Rome. All this was documented in the Warburg Library.[67] Fritz Saxl, the library's director, showed Cassirer around the library shortly after Cassirer had settled in Hamburg and reports that when they were finished Cassirer said that the overwhelming collection of books was so close to his own area of interest that he would have to avoid the library for a while. It was not long, Saxl adds, until "Cassirer became our most assiduous reader" (*PEC*, 49; cf. *PSF*, 2:xviii; *PsF*, 2:xiii). In 1896 Warburg had made a trip to New Mexico to observe the ceremonies of the Indians in the Mesa Verde region, and in this way to observe firsthand the archetypal forms of expression that he believed were the roots of ancient art. Here Warburg led the way for Cassirer. In his account of Warburg's trip and the lasting influence it had on him, Saxl points out that, just as Warburg had sought to understand European Renaissance art directly through his experience in the Mesa Verde, Cassirer tried to understand preempirical thinking philosophically through his study of the anthropological material collected at the Warburg Library.[68]

During his first two years in Hamburg, Cassirer published two major works, the third volume of *Das Erkenntnisproblem* and his book on the epistemological problems posed by the theory of relativity, *Zur Einsteinschen Relativitätstheorie* (*Einstein's Theory of Relativity*). The new volume of *Das Erkenntnisproblem* (devoted to the post-Kantian systems of philosophy) contains a lengthy discussion of Hegel that sheds light on the fundamentals of Cassirer's own philosophical position as it emerges in *The Philosophy of Symbolic Forms*. Cassirer does not attempt to examine Hegel, Fichte, or Schelling in terms of epistemology. To try to see the Hegelian system or the other metaphysical philosophies as theories of knowledge would result, Cassirer says, in a negation of the principle upon which they are based (*EP*, 3:vi). As in the earlier two volumes, Cassirer regards the "problem of knowledge" as the problem of the methodology of thought in the broadest sense (*EP*, 3:v). In his next work, *Einstein's Theory of Relativity* (*SF/ET*), he concludes by arguing that even the whole of scientific knowledge cannot exhaustively represent reality without engaging in an unwarranted reduction (*SF/ET*, 446). Cassirer rejects the attempt to compress the totality of the forms in which we understand reality into a single, "*ultimate* metaphysical unity" (*eine letzte metaphysische Einheit*) (*SF/ET*, 446; *ZMP*, 109). In this discussion Cassirer uses the term *symbolic form* for the first time in print: "It is the task of systematic philosophy, which extends far beyond that of the theory of knowledge, to free the idea of the world from this onesidedness. It has to grasp the *whole system* of symbolic forms" (*SF/ET*, 447). It is noteworthy that Cassirer introduces the chief idea of his philosophy by contrasting the task of *systematic* philosophy with the task of the theory of knowledge and declaring the former to be his problem.

Cassirer does not explain or define the idea of symbolic form in the Einstein book; he does this in his essay "Der Begriff der symbolischen Form im Aufbau der Geisteswissenschaften" (The concept of symbolic form in the construction of the human sciences), which was included the next year in the first group of lectures published as *Vorträge der Bibliothek Warburg*.[69] His theory of myth was first presented in a Warburg Library monograph entitled *Der Begriffsform im mythischen Denken* (The form of the concept in mythic thought.)[70] These works were immediately followed by the first volume of the *Philosophy of Symbolic Forms: Language* in 1923. Volume two, *Mythic Thought*, appeared in 1925. Among the other smaller works written during this period, many of which were first published in the *Vorträge der Bibliothek Warburg* or as *Studien der Bibliothek Warburg*, is the study *Sprache und Mythos*.[71] Susanne Langer's translation of this work as *Language and Myth* has been perhaps the most widely read of Cassirer's works in English translation.

In 1927 Cassirer published two essays that are of particular importance for the understanding they provide of his general philosophical position. One of these ("The Problem of the Symbol and Its Place in the System of Philosophy") offers Cassirer's briefest statement of the organization of his philosophy of symbolic forms.[72] The other, "Erkenntnistheorie nebst den Grenzfragan der Logik und Denkpsychologie" (Theory of knowledge and borderline questions of logic and the psychology of thought), like a similarly titled paper published fourteen years earlier, gives Cassirer's reflections and critical comments on recent philosophical movements.[73] This essay is of particular interest because it includes a discussion of how he regarded his own, new conception of philosophy:

> More and more we have been forced to recognize that the sphere of theoretical meaning [*Sinn*] that we designate with the names "knowledge" [*Erkenntnis*] and "truth" [*Wahrheit*] represent only *one* (however significant and fundamental), layer of meaning [*Sinnschicht*]. In order to understand it, in order to see through its structure, we must compare and contrast this layer with other dimensions of meaning [*Sinndimensionen*]. We must, in other words, grasp the problem of knowledge and the problem of truth as particular cases of the more general problem of meaning [als Sonderfälle des allgemeinen Bedeutungsproblems]. (Ibid., 34)

Here Cassirer explicitly states that, with his *Philosophie der symbolischen Formen*, he has not expanded the theory of knowledge but rather has shifted the whole task of his philosophical investigations to new, more fundamental ground.

In 1928 Cassirer published yet another retrospective reflection on his earlier philosophical work, this time on his theory of the concept presented in 1910 in *Substance and Function*. This paper, "Zur Theorie des Begriffs" (On the theory of the concept), describes how Cassirer revised his earlier interpretation of the concept.

> For now it seems to me that the logical problem of the concept is far more closely connected to the general problem of meaning [*Bedeutungsproblem*] than was the case in my earlier presentation. It seems to me that the theory of the concept can only be sufficiently founded and completely developed in the context of a systematic "theory of meaning" [*Bedeutungslehre*]. What I now believe to see more clearly and sharply

than in the discussion in my earlier work is this: that for such a "theory of meaning" mathematics and the mathematical sciences . . . do not constitute the whole sphere of meaning itself, but rather, in order to be correctly understood, grasped, and assessed as particular kinds of meaning, they must be contrasted with other forms of giving meaning [*Sinngebung*]. . . . For we can no longer attempt to infer the general form of the concept itself from the particular form of mathematical and mathematical-physical concepts.[74]

With these words Cassirer disavows a position central to the Marburg school, that scientific knowledge—and mathematics in particular—has a privileged position for philosophical thought.

The systematic shift in Cassirer's philosophical point of view away from the epistemological also led him away from the view that mathematics or science can provide an adequate understanding of the function of concepts. After *Substance and Function* Cassirer began developing the theory of meaning through which he would approach the theory of the concept and a host of other philosophical questions. Cassirer's theory of meaning is developed in the third volume of the *Philosophy of Symbolic Forms: The Phenomenology of Knowledge*. This work, which Charles W. Hendel in his introduction to the English translation calls "truly the central work of Cassirer's genius" (*PSF*, 3:ix), offers Cassirer's statement of the general principles of his philosophy. Whereas the first two volumes had only illustrated aspects of the philosophy of symbolic forms, the third develops its general theoretical position. The third volume is not about a particular symbolic form, such as language or myth, although these are both discussed extensively in the first and second parts of *The Phenomenology of Knowledge*, just as scientific and conceptual knowledge is discussed in the third part of the volume. To a large measure, the interpretation given to this work determines the way Cassirer's philosophy is understood as a whole.

The Phenomenology of Knowledge appeared in 1929, but it was finished in manuscript in 1927, the same year that Cassirer published one of his most acclaimed works in the history of philosophy: *Individuum und Kosmos in der Philosophie der Renaissance* (*The Individual and the Cosmos in Renaissance Philosophy*). In the Renaissance book he embarked on a kind of historical project different from the one he developed in the four-volume *Erkenntnisproblem*. More than before Cassirer seeks to show how philosophy is part of history, one of the forces in an age. Philosophy does not follow the general movement of the time "as some abstract shadow," but actively affects and determines it (*IC*, 6). The forces of the Renaissance bring about the rise of modern individualism: "There can be no doubt that the Renaissance directed all its intellectually productive forces towards a profound examination of the problem of the *individual*" (*IC*, 35). Cassirer focuses on the Renaissance notion of the individual as a kind of Prometheus, the creator of culture. He thinks that this Promethean conception of humanity underlies the whole modern age and continues to develop in philosophy up to the Enlightenment, in which he believed it reached its fullest expression. In two other works, both published in 1932, Cassirer describes how this philosophical outlook was handed down to the eighteenth century: *Die Platonische Renaissance in England* (*The Platonic Renaissance in England*) and *Die Philosophie der Aufklärung* (*The Philosophy of the Enlightenment*).

In the latter work Cassirer regards the Enlightenment as a European movement. He defies the attempt to divide it according to different countries' varied outlooks and contributions. Cassirer's treatment is deeply sympathetic; he sees his work as a first step "toward a revision of the verdict of the Romantic Movement on the Enlightenment" (*PE*, xi). In the preface, Cassirer indicates that what he has described should not be regarded with purely historical interest: "The consideration of the philosophic past must always be accompanied by philosophical reorientation and self-criticism. More than ever before, it seems to me, the time is again ripe for applying such self-criticism to the present age, for holding up to it that bright clear mirror fashioned by the Enlightenment" (*PE*, xi). Cassirer's view of the Enlightenment sheds much light on the spirit of his own philosophy and on a number of his views on specific questions, some of which are clearly attempts to revive positions developed during the Enlightenment. Foremost among these is Cassirer's conception of "inalienable human rights."

The first steps in Cassirer's thinking on the subject can be found in two papers published while he was in Hamburg. The first, "Die Idee der Republikanischen Verfassung" (The idea of a republican constitution) was delivered in 1928 at the university's celebration of the tenth anniversary of the founding of the Weimar Republic.[75] Arguing against the widespread hatred of the Weimar Republic as a supposedly "un-German" form of government, Cassirer showed how republican government and even the French revolution in fact derived from the ideas of German philosophers. Cassirer's defense of the foundations of the Weimar Republic is closely related to his argument in a lecture published in 1932, "Vom Wesen und Werden des Naturrechts" (On the essence and development of natural law), in which he argues that the idea of inalienable human rights is indispensable to jurisprudence.[76] Cassirer's study of Rousseau, *Das Problem Jean*

Jacques Rousseau (*The Question of Jean Jacques Rousseau*), which also appeared in 1932, is a further example of his growing interest in this area of philosophy.

By the late 1920s Cassirer was at the height of his career in Germany. In 1928 he was again offered the chair of philosophy at the University of Frankfurt. To Cassirer's dismay the offer resulted in a kind of contest between Frankfurt and Hamburg to get or keep Cassirer. During the late 1920s Cassirer also traveled widely to various European countries to give lectures. The most discussed of these occasions was his participation in March and April of 1929 in Davos (Switzerland) in the "Davoser Hochschulkurse" where, in addition to lecturing, he met and debated publicly with Martin Heidegger (see chap. 1).

In the spring of 1929 Cassirer was elected rector of the University of Hamburg for the term November 1929 to November 1930. On the occasion of his acceptance of this post, Cassirer gave a lecture on "Formen und Verwandlungen des philosophischen Wahrheitsbegriffs" (Forms and transformations of the philosophical concept of truth).[78] With his assumption of this office, Cassirer held the highest position in the German university system, the first person of Jewish descent to do so. During 1930 a remarkable but little-known essay of Cassirer's appeared, "Form und Technik" (Form and technology). In this study he developed his conception of the crisis in contemporary social life caused by the spread of modern technology and also made important clarifications about his own general philosophical position. After his term as rector Cassirer returned to his academic work and received the summer semester of 1931 as a research term, much of which was spent in Paris in the Bibliothèque nationale working on *The Philosophy of the Enlightenment*.

The political events of 1933 brought an end to Cassirer's career in Hamburg and his life in Germany. On January 30 Hitler was named chancellor by Reich's President Hindenburg, and although the next election in March could have stopped the National Socialists' assumption of power, Cassirer was convinced that the democratic era of the Weimar Republic was over. When he heard for the first time the slogan "Recht ist, was dem Führer dient" (Law and justice is whatever serves the Führer), Cassirer said: "Either tomorrow all of Germany's legal scholars unanimously protest against this paragraph or Germany is lost."[79] Even in the first days of the Reich Cassirer saw no alternative to emigration. He had already requested an official leave of absence from the university before the first laws to bar Jews from state offices were enacted in April. When Cassirer received notification in July that he had been relieved of all his duties at the University of

Hamburg, it was not unexpected.[80] At the beginning of May the Cassirers had already left Hamburg for Vienna, convinced that they would never be able to return to Germany to live.

The Émigré Years

England. Cassirer received three teaching offers during the summer of 1933 for the coming academic year 1933–34, one from All Souls College at Oxford, one from the University of Uppsala in Sweden, and one from the newly founded University in Exile in New York. Cassirer decided to go to Oxford, where he spent two years teaching the history of philosophy. While at Oxford he made Albert Schweitzer's acquaintance, an event that made an indelible impression on Cassirer. Schweitzer's personality and his conception of the ethical duty of philosophy to further and guard the cultural values that protect human life struck a responsive chord in Cassirer.[81] These ideas become recurrent themes from this time on in Cassirer's works. In the only publication that Cassirer completed during his stay at Oxford, a paper on "Schiller und Shaftesbury," he argues that Schiller more correctly understood the central doctrine of Shaftesbury's ethics than did Kant and that Shaftesbury does not uphold hedonism or any other "material" principle of ethics, as Kant thought. For Shaftesbury, the summum bonum is above all else an *objective standard* or measure (Maß).[82] This defense of normative ethics is an indication of the way in which Cassirer attempts later to develop an ethical theory.

In September 1935 Cassirer left England for Sweden to assume the chair of philosophy at the University of Göteborg.

Sweden. Cassirer spent nearly six years in Sweden. He felt personally at home there, but, as in England, he was confronted with a different, and for him in many ways antagonistic, intellectual climate. Swedish philosophy was positivistic in spirit and its representatives were unsympathetic to transcendental philosophy. Cassirer's confrontation with this attitude led him to clarify his own position in papers published in the Swedish journal *Theoria*, generally in reply to published criticisms of his views. The most important of these papers are "Inhalt und Umfang des Begriffs" (Intension and extension in the concept), "Zur Logik des Symbolbegriffs" (On the logic of the symbol concept), and "Was ist Subjektivismus?" (What is subjectivism?).[83] At this time Cassirer also developed his philosophy of science to a fuller extent and in more detail than before. His book *Determinismus und Indeterminismus in der modernen Physik* (*Determinism and Indeterminism in Modern Physics*), published in 1936, provides the most explicit statement of his view of the method and foundations of science. The concluding chapter centers on ethics; in it Cassirer distinguishes physical and ethical points of view. When the English translation appeared years later, part of his discussion of ethics was published in *Saturday Review*.[84]

In Sweden Cassirer begins to develop an ethical theory from his philosophy of symbolic forms. In his inaugural lecture at the University of Göteborg in 1935, "The Concept of Philosophy as a Problem of Philosophy" he asks, "Are there general binding supra-individual, supra-state, supra-national ethical claims?" (SMC, 61), and he sets himself the task of answering this question. Three years after his inaugural lecture he gave his answer in his interpretation of the foundations of ethics and law in the study "Axel Hägerström." Hägerström was the originator of the emotive theory of ethics and the founder of the influential Uppsala school of legal thought. Hägerström's ideas served as a foil for Cassirer to present his own theory of the objective validity of ethical norms.

In a lecture given the year after his Göteborg inaugural address, he explains how history and the ethical point of view are combined in the concept of culture (SMC, 81). Cassirer had been attracted to the normative theory of history from the beginning of his work as a thinker. He praised Kant's normative concept of history, which relates events to "the ideal unity of an immanent end" (KLT, 227), emphasizing that this view of history transports us from the realm of "being" to the realm of "obligation" [Sollen] (KLT, 277: KLL, 241). This conception of immanent norms in history goes back to his first published work, *Leibniz' System*. In the section on the subject of ethics and the concept of history (LS, 425–49) he develops a view of history embracing the "Zweckeinheit des Ganzen," the unity of purpose in the whole (p. 449), a notion he traces to Vico.

Cassirer returns now to this notion, developing it in terms of his philosophy of symbolic forms in the Axel Hägerström study, but also fleshing it out in what is probably his most creative work on the history of philosophy, *Descartes: Lehre—Persönlichkeit—Wirkung* (Descartes: thought—personality—influence). In this work he examines the personality and works of Descartes the thinker, Queen Christina of Sweden, and characters from Corneille's dramas to construct a conception of the seventeenth-century "heroic" ethical personality. This idea has for him more than historical significance. Cassirer's 1941 essay "Logos, Dike, Kosmos in der Entwicklung der griechischen Philosophie" (Logos, dike, cosmos in the development of greek philosophy) also investigates the ethical import of culture.[85]

Among Cassirer's major publications from his years in Sweden is also Zur Logik der Kulturwissenschaften (*The Logic of the Human-*

ities), which offers his theory of the distinction between the natural sciences and the sciences of culture.

Prior to leaving Sweden, Cassirer completed the final volume of *Das Erkenntnisproblem* (volume 4, translated as *The Problem of Knowledge*). It examines the problem of knowledge in different fields, the growing fragmentation of the concept of knowledge, and the problematic state of philosophy among the sciences "after Hegel's death."

On June 2, 1939, Cassirer became a Swedish citizen. Along with the benefits that this brought him, it also meant that he had to retire from teaching at age sixty-five in accordance with Swedish law. Beginning with winter semester 1940–41 Cassirer was professor emeritus, but he took the opportunity to offer a "public lecture" course open to all students and the general public. His course on "Der junge Goethe" (the young Goethe) lasted two semesters (see chap. 5). He had always wanted to teach such a course, but now, in the midst of World War II, Goethe also epitomized for Cassirer the cultural tradition that had been betrayed by Nazi Germany. Cassirer was convinced that it was necessary for him to continue teaching and have an effect on the next generation of students, so he again began to consider emigration. He received an invitation to teach at Yale as a guest professor, and on May 20, 1941, the Cassirers left Sweden on board the Swedish freighter *Remmaren*. Among the other passengers was the linguist Roman Jakobson, with whom Cassirer daily had long conversations during the voyage.[86] These talks no doubt influenced his interest and work on structuralism, most evident in Cassirer's paper "Structuralism in Modern Linguistics."[87] He was so attracted to Jakobson's work that he suggested to Paul Arthur Schilpp in 1943 that Jakobson be invited to contribute the paper on Cassirer's philosophy of language to the Library of Living Philosophers volume, which was already in the planning stage.[88] After a hazardous crossing, the *Remmaren* arrived in New York on June 4, 1941.

The United States. At Yale Cassirer taught undergraduate and graduate courses, including an annual joint seminar with his colleagues. Cassirer readily adapted to the differences between European and American universities. He was familiar with American philosophy; there was no language barrier for him; and he found attractive the more open form of classroom work and freer discussion between colleagues.[89]

Cassirer taught at Yale from 1941 to 1944 and at Columbia beginning in the fall of 1944. He died suddenly of a heart attack on April 13, 1945.

In less than four years Cassirer wrote two books and fourteen articles and reviews, as well as an array of other lectures and essays that were not published. (Some have subsequently appeared in *Symbol, Myth, and Culture*.) "Albert Schweitzer as Critic of Nineteenth-Century Ethics," published in 1946, continues the explication of culture as an ethical concept, which Cassirer had begun to develop in Sweden.[90] But even the writings on the history of philosophy, mostly on Renaissance thought or on the philosophy of language, reflect an underlying concern for the normative sense of the idea of "culture." Cassirer came to see every problem in relationship to that of ethics in a broad sense, that is, the nature of man and the ends and limits for human action. *An Essay on Man* (1944) can and should be regarded in this context. The historical studies of Pico della Mirandola and Galileo are further instances of a desire to show how the modern age led to a "new spirit" of individual responsibility and reason. He planned to contribute the introduction to the *Renaissance Philosophy of Man*, which he was editing with Paul Oskar Kristeller and John Herman Randall, Jr., but he did not live long enough to write it.[91]

Language, as Cassirer first pointed out in 1933 in the expanded version of his paper on "Die Sprache und die Aufbau der Gegenstandswelt" (Language and the construction of the world of objects), is essential to the formation of the ethical world (STS, 140–43). Language seemed for him to be the key to a comprehensive theory of ethics, man, and history. All this enters into the new definition of man as "animal symbolicum" (*EM*, 26). When he writes in the preface of the *Essay on Man* that the "old problems" of the *Philosophy of Symbolic Forms* now appear to him "from a different angle and appear in a new light" (p. vii) he means this *normative* perspective. The symbol is "the way to civilization" (p. vii).

The prevailing irrationalism and savagery of World War II did not affect Cassirer's normative conception of "humanity," but he felt compelled to understand the reasons for this return to barbarism. His last book, *The Myth of the State* (1946) offers his explanation (see chap. 5). A collection of previously unpublished papers from the last decade of Cassirer's life (*Symbol, Myth, and Culture*, 1979) now makes available other writings that develop further the ideas in the *Myth of the State* and contains papers that document Cassirer's gradual turn to the problems of ethics.

Among the projects Cassirer left unfinished at his death, the most important and substantial is his fourth volume of the *Philosophy of Symbolic Forms*. Unlike his plan to write a volume on art as a symbolic form, the manuscript of volume four is the basis for a work of a general nature, on the "metaphysics of the symbolic forms." The volume on art was never written. Cassirer wrote to Schilpp that he had postponed writing it again and again because of the "unfavorableness of the times" (*Ungunst der Zeiten*).[92] But he did work on the fourth volume and a continuous manuscript of some 284 pages on "Zur Metaphysik der symbolischen Formen; Philosophie der symbolischen Formen, Bd. IV" (On the metaphysics of the symbolic forms; Philosophy of symbolic forms, vol.4) exists among his papers.[93]

According to James Pettegrove, who translated Cassirer's *Platonic Renaissance in England* and aided him with the stylistic revisions of *An Essay on Man* (EM, viii), Cassirer was planning at the time of his death to write next a book on Shakespeare (PE, 116–17n). Cassirer saw Shakespeare as the perfecter of Renaissance humor, stressing that for Shakespeare there is "no separation between comedy and tragedy" (PRE, 177). One of Cassirer's last publications, "Thomas Manns Goethe-Bild," concludes with a discussion of the correlation of the comic and tragic;[94] the Shakespeare book was most likely going to expand upon this topic. Cassirer was working toward a completion of his theory of culture, moving to the level of the emotions and the sense of life itself. These themes also figure in his late essays in *Rousseau, Kant, and Goethe*.[95]

Even an overview of Cassirer's work shows that his thought cannot be understood as a whole if it is interpreted as an epistemology, a theory of "mind," or even as a philosophy of "life" that simply portrays history as a factual, ever-changing flux of events. Cassirer's philosophy is a theory of historical life, but it is not a form of historicism; it conceives history in a normative sense. This conception of history depends upon a fundamental transformation of transcendental philosophy.

I

CASSIRER'S TRANSFORMATION OF PHILOSOPHY

In the latter half of the nineteenth century in Germany, philosophy was overshadowed by the developing natural sciences. Science's ability to offer testable explanations and its mathematical precision stood in sharp contrast to the speculative systems of German idealism. Scientific materialism spread.[1] Two influential figures in this movement were the physiologists Jacob Moleschott (1822–93), from whom derived the slogan "No thought without phosphorus," and Ludwig Büchner (1824–99). The latter's *Kraft und Stoff* (Frankfurt, 1855; translated as *Force and Matter*, 1884) was the chief compendium of scientific materialism, epitomizing its antimetaphysical and antiphilosophical attitude. Scientific materialism was symptomatic of far-reaching changes in German culture. These changes can also be seen, for example, in the writings of Büchner's eldest brother, Georg, whose dramas, in particular *Woyzeck*, mark the beginning of naturalist and even expressionist feeling in Germany. In the latter part of the nineteenth century the spirit of romanticism was on the wane. Neo-Kantianism arose in this climate.

In the fourth volume of *Das Erkenntnisproblem*, which deals with philosophy, science, and history after Hegel, Cassirer portrays German philosophy's quandary during the late nineteenth century. Caught in a dilemma between dissatisfaction with the older metaphysical systems of idealism and unphilosophical scientific materialism, philosophy provided what Eduard Zeller (1814–1908) described as a "spectacle of unmistakable bewilderment and uncertainty" (PK, 5) as thinkers gave up the attempt to develop a metaphysical system. In the midst of this situation some scientists, Hermann von Helmholtz in particular, became aware that the concepts and methods used in the study of nature are not part of the subject of this study itself. The need was felt for a "theory of knowledge" and a "philosophy of science." This need combined with the opinion that philosophy had taken a wrong turn after Kant. In his book *Kant und die Epigonen* (Stuttgart, 1865) Otto Liebmann criticized all the thinkers after Kant for their reception of Kantian philosophy, especially for their interpretations of the thing-in-itself. He concluded each chapter with a call to go "Back to Kant!" that gave the neo-Kantian movement its slogan.[2]

The most important criticism of scientific materialism to result from the return to Kant was Friedrich Albert Lange's *Geschichte des Materialismus* (1865). In this classic study Lange criticized materialism on epistemological grounds, thereby placing himself within the movement represented by Liebmann and his own younger colleague at Marburg, Hermann Cohen.[3] With Lange's support, Cohen completed the academic requirements for a German professorship. In 1876 he became a professor at Marburg as Lange's successor.[4]

The back-to-Kant movement itself bore the naturalistic, materialistic mark of the times. Lange, Helmholtz, and Zeller all saw the key to a revival of Kantianism in physiology. Helmholtz thought that study of the nervous system could reveal the "transcendental" forms of intuition.[5] Zeller and Liebmann also sought the conditions of knowledge in the physiology of sensation. Cassirer points out that this naturalistic view enjoyed "unquestioned predominance" among the early neo-Kantians in the 1860s (PK, 4).

Yet neo-Kantianism brought a reorientation in philosophy. Instead of pursuing a system of metaphysics, philosophers found their task in the "theory of knowledge." Cassirer was wrong to claim that Zeller, in his inaugural lecture in 1862, introduced the term *Erkenntnistheorie* (theory of knowledge) into German philosophical parlance, but he was right in regarding this lecture as a milestone in the development of neo-Kantianism.[6] German neo-Kantianism developed as a philosophy whose centerpiece from the beginning was the theory of knowledge.[7]

Cassirer describes the neo-Kantian movement and its sentiment this way: "In place of the metaphysical orgy inspired by post-Kantian philosophy, a complete sobriety appears. Logic has abandoned every pretension of reaching to the heart of absolute being and no longer purports to be the 'representation of God' in his eternal essence. But neither is it content with developing formal laws of thought and deduction. What logic seeks to clarify is the problem of knowledge of reality" (PK, 4–5). Cassirer finds this same "scientific" sobriety of thought in the French- and English-speaking worlds at the time, even though Comte and Mill and their followers differ methodologically from the neo-Kantians (PK, 8). This change in the spirit of late nineteenth-century philosophy threatened to restrict it to the position of handmaiden to science. Philosophy became a specialized discipline among many; as epistemology it no longer dared to proclaim a truth of its own. Cassirer describes the intellectual milieu of his student years this way: "The mood for an a priori metaphysics is gone, and with it, too, that for any thoroughgoing systematic thinking" (PK, 15).

Parallel to the development of science-oriented philosophy, which culminated in the logical positivism of the Vienna Circle, another, quite different variety of philosophy made itself felt. Thinkers such as Kierkegaard, Nietzsche, Bergson, Scheler, and Heidegger also rejected idealism and the attempt to conceive reality as a "system," but they treated epistemology and problems in the exact sciences as secondary concerns. To Cassirer these thinkers represent Lebensphilosophie, the "philosophy of life." Cassirer uses the term in a systematic, rather than a strictly historical, sense. He broadens its standard meaning (to refer to Dilthey, Simmel, Bergson, and their followers) so as to signify postidealistic thought in general. Hence, in Cassirer's vocabulary "life philosophy" does not refer just to a school of thought but to a broad fundamental shift in philosophical thinking.

One indication of Lebensphilosophie's significance for Cassirer is that he delayed publishing the third volume of the Philosophy of Symbolic Forms (PSF) for two years because he anticipated adding a final chapter defining the relationship between the PSF and contemporary philosophy as a whole. He says in the preface that he finally decided to publish this essay separately under the title " 'Leben' und 'Geist' zur Kritik der Philosophie der Gegenwart" ("Life" and "spirit"— toward a critique of contemporary philosophy) (PSF 3:vi; PsF 3:IX). For Cassirer, "contemporary philosophy" meant Lebensphilosophie. Cassirer did publish this essay (1930; an English translation appears in the Schilpp PEC as " 'Spirit' and 'Life' in Contemporary Philosophy"), but this was only the beginning. The manuscript of the fourth volume of the PSF shows that the work was conceived as a coming to terms with Lebensphilosophie, from which Cassirer intended to develop the relationship of the symbolic forms to the problem of metaphysics. The first chapter is a critique of Lebensphilosophie; the second focuses on "philosophical anthropology"; the concluding portion was to treat the problem of the Urphänomen, the primary phenomenon.[8]

Until the extensive material relating to the fourth volume of the PSF is available for study, all discussions of Cassirer's views of metaphysics can only be tentative in their claims. I will limit my references to this unpublished work to a minimum, but the question of Cassirer's attitude toward metaphysics is crucial to my attempt to show the direction of his thought and to indicate the way it constitutes a transformation of philosophy.

To speak of a transformation requires that some form of philosophy serve as the starting point. Cassirer indicates his starting point in the foreword to the first volume of the *PSF* when he expresses his belief that language "can be elucidated only within a general system of philosophical idealism" (*PSF*, 1:72; *PsF*, 1:IX). How does Cassirer transform idealism, in particular the transcendental idealism of Marburg neo-Kantianism? Cassirer introduced his idea of a philosophy of symbolic forms with a global criticism of modern idealist metaphysics from Descartes to Hegel: "They hold that philosophy can permeate the universitas, the concrete totality of the spirit (*Geist*), only if it can be deduced from a logical principle" (*PSF*, 1:72; *PsF*, 1:IX). For Cassirer this is an unacceptable reduction of the concreteness and variety characteristic of the human world to the rational order of a conceptual system. Different ways of having a world are all reduced to one—rational, conceptual order: "Of all cultural forms, only that of logic, the concept, cognition, seems to enjoy a true and authentic *autonomy*" (*PSF*, 1:83; *PsF*, 1:15). This reductionism is not an incidental problem but an inherent characteristic of idealistic philosophy: "Indeed, this ultimate reduction of all cultural forms to the one form of logic seems to be implied by the concept of philosophy itself and particularly by the fundamental principle of philosophical idealism" (*PSF*, 1:84; *PsF*, 1:16). Cassirer proposes therefore a different fundamental principle, that is, to begin with meaning and the symbol instead of logic and the concept. Symbolism is a phenomenon that "recurs in each basic cultural form but in no two of them takes exactly the same shape" (*PSF*, 1:84; *PsF*, 1:16). Cassirer hopes to preserve recognition of the autonomy of myth, religion, art, technology, science, and so forth to avoid the illusion that these ways of having a world all can be forced into a single rational, conceptual system.

Cassirer's objection that idealist metaphysics reduces all reality "to the one form of logic," that is, a panlogism, applies generally to Marburg neo-Kantianism and particularly to Cohen's "System der Philosophie."[9] In addition to this critical point concerning philosophical idealism generally, Cassirer has a specific criticism of neo-Kantian idealism.

The neo-Kantian schools focused upon scientific knowledge, on knowledge in mathematical physics or knowledge in historical study. But each school, Cassirer points out, spoke as though its orientation permitted it to speak for the whole of science, indeed for all of philosophy, whereas in reality there was "no tribunal" to resolve the conflicts of the schools (PK, 11). The notion of systematic thought was no longer recognized. Cassirer was unsympathetic with neo-Kantianism's renouncement of the autonomy of systematic philosophical thought: "Instead of assuming the role of leader and representing a determinate ideal of truth in the pride of its own strength and on its own responsibility, it [philosophy] allows itself to be led by the sciences and forced in a prescribed direction by each of them in turn" (PK, 17). His criticism is the same in substance as Walter Benjamin's judgment that neo-Kantianism's weakness lay in its unacknowledged "complicity with positivism."[10]

No matter how Cassirer may have viewed the Marburg school's epistemological conception of philosophy before he developed his philosophy of symbolic forms, his later thought moves far beyond it. As he remarks in a lecture from 1942, "every philosophy contains an ontology—a general theory of being. In this regard we may perfectly agree with Aristotle if he defines metaphysics as the doctrine of being as such—as being qua being" (SMC, 166–67). But Cassirer denies that ontology can explain or even describe absolute being in the sense of a substantial reality. In the same lecture he indicates his own view this way: "Life, reality, being, existence are nothing but different terms referring to one and the same fundamental fact" (SMC, 194). This fundamental fact cannot be explained by science or philosophy: "We cannot explain it, if explanation means the reduction of an unknown fact to a better-known fact, for there is no better-known fact" (p. 194). As early as 1920 Cassirer made this point in his critical account of Hegelianism in Das Erkenntnisproblem. There he denies that the fact of experience (Erfahrung) can be explained or shown to be necessary; it cannot be "derived from something else, something higher, and then justified through it as a kind of higher form of reason" (EP, 3:371). The "fundamental fact" of life, reality, being, existence, or experience, unlike the Faktum der Wissenschaft (the fact of science), cannot be accounted for by a transcendental philosophy. We can give no "conditions of the possibility" of the fundamental fact of existence.

Cassirer's conception of the fundamental fact of existence and metaphysics brings him into contact with what he calls Lebensphilosophie. This contact grows from the general tendency of his thought in the Philosophy of Symbolic Forms.

In the preface to the third volume of the Philosophy of Symbolic Forms Cassirer says that he has found a new approach to philosophy, different from the criticism of knowledge (Erkenntniskritik), phenomenology, or metaphysics (PSF, 3:xv–xvi; PsF, 3, vii–viii). In saying that his approach is not Erkenntniskritik he distances himself from the neo-Kantians: "The Philosophy of Symbolic Forms is not concerned exclusively or even primarily with the purely scientific, exact conceiving of the world [Weltbegreifen]; it is concerned with all the forms assumed by man's understanding of the world [Weltverstehen]" (PSF, 3:13; PsF, 3:16).

In what way is the PSF concerned with the forms of understanding the world? Cassirer describes his new approach as the "attempt to state the transcendental question itself in a more comprehensive sense" (ibid.). Cassirer's philosophy of symbolic forms is a transformation of transcendental philosophy. To understand Cassirer's philosophy we begin by asking, What does Cassirer mean by the "transcendental question"?

The "Transcendental" Question

Hermann Cohen's interpretation of Kant made an early, deep, and lasting impression on Cassirer. As a student Cassirer bought Cohen's Kants Theorie der Erfahrung and felt "from the first pages" that he was on "firm and secure ground."[11] The beginning of the book focuses upon what Cohen calls "die transzendentale Methode."[12] It was the "transcendental method" that Cassirer recollected as "firm and secure ground." In an article for the Encyclopedia Britannica Cassirer writes: "Cohen gave for the first time a critical interpretation of the entire Kantian system which, with all of its penetration into the specific detail of Kant's fundamental doctrines, sets, nevertheless, one single systematic idea into the centre of the investigation. This is the idea of the 'transcendental method'" (s.v. "Neo-Kantianism"). Cohen's concept of the transcendental method provides the chronological and logical place to start in examining Cassirer's thought.

Kant never speaks of a transcendental method. This idea was developed by the neo-Kantians and is associated with Cohen and his school in particular. To understand the "transcendental method" it is necessary to begin with Kant's conception of the transcendental.[13]

Kant indicated what he meant by transcendental first in the Critique of Pure Reason and later in the Prolegomena to Any Future Metaphysics. Kant's statements in the latter work, intended to correct the misconceptions of readers of the Critique, dissociate the term transcendental from the notion of a transcendent or "higher" reality: "High towers and metaphysically great men resembling them, round both of which there is commonly much wind, are not for me. My place is the fruitful bathos of experience; and the word 'transcendental' . . . does not signify something passing beyond all experience but something that indeed precedes it a priori, but that is intended simply to make knowledge of experience possible. If these conceptions overstep experience, their employment is termed 'transcendent,' which must be distinguished from the immanent use, that is, use restricted to experience."[14] *Transcendental* was meant to refer to the "cognitive faculty," not something beyond experience (ibid., 41). Kant gives two definitions of *transcendental* in the *Critique of Pure Reason* that state how he conceived his transcendental philosophy to constitute a turn toward the "cognitive faculty" and away from the objects of knowledge.

Kant's first definition reads: "I entitle *transcendental* all knowledge which is occupied not so much with objects as with the mode of our knowledge of objects insofar as this mode of knowledge is to be possible *a priori*. A system of such concepts might be entitled transcendental philosophy."[15] Kant's second definition reads:

Not every kind of knowledge *a priori* should be called transcendental, but that only by which we know that—and how—certain representations (intuitions or concepts) can be employed or are possible purely *a priori*. The term 'transcendental,' that is to say, signifies such knowledge as concerns the *a priori* possibility of knowledge, or its *a priori* employment. Neither space nor any *a priori* geometrical determination of it is a transcendental representation; what can alone be entitled transcendental is the knowledge that these representations are not of empirical origin, and the possibility that they can yet relate *a priori* to objects of experience. . . . The distinction between the transcendental and the empirical belongs therefore only to the critique of knowledge; it does not concern the relation of that knowledge to its objects. (Ibid., 96)

The first definition appears to be much broader than the second one. The former refers to how our knowledge of objects is possible a priori; hence, transcendental knowledge is knowledge of the mode of knowledge (*Erkenntnisart*) *as* a priori. The transcendental seems to be the theory of the a priori. This view of the transcendental was promulgated, for example, by Hans Vaihinger.[16] The second definition restricts the transcendental to our knowledge "that and *how*" certain elements of the cognitive faculty are a priori. This view limits the transcendental to the theory of the *possibility* of the a priori; it does not aim at providing what Kant in the first definition calls "a system of such [a priori] concepts," or at least it does not treat this as the chief object of a transcendental philosophy. For Hermann Cohen, transcendental theory is concerned with the possibility of the a priori. Cohen's step beyond Kant consisted in his particular interpretation of this theory as a "method."

The transcendental method, Cohen says, has as its principle and norm the thought that "such elements of consciousness are elements of knowing consciousness, which are necessary and sufficient to found and establish the fact of science [Faktum der Wissenschaft]."[17] Consciousness (Bewußtsein) for Cohen means universal "pure" consciousness, not the subject of psychology, and by science he means the fact of scientific knowledge, not a given stage of science. Cohen claimed that the transcendental method arose historically through Kant's reflection on Newton's Philosophiae naturalis principia mathematica (ibid., 94). This method makes possible the development of what Cohen called the philosophy of Reinheit, that is, of the pure (nonempirical) conditions of experience. The transcendental "method" for Cohen is a way of asking questions, the way we proceed when we question how the fact of science is possible. The fact of science is crucial in Cohen's conception of the transcendental method: "All philosophy depends upon the fact of the sciences. This dependency . . . is for us the eternal in Kant's system."[18] The fact of science refers to the reality of science as a fact and as something "generated" or, in Cohen's language, as a matter of Erzeugung, "generation." Cohen emphasized that modern science depends on the generation of the mathematical idea of the infinitesimal, that is, not the existence of any infinitely tiny things, but an ideal of thought.[19] This notion must be the result of Erzeugung, for it cannot be found in experience.

Cohen eliminates all the static givens in Kant's philosophy—sensibility, the categories, the object of knowledge, the subject as the giver of the moral law; they are no longer taken as given (gegeben) but rather set as a task (aufgegeben). Philosophy starts by asking about a "given" like the fact of science only to discover that this fact is a construction. Philosophy discovers in every given a generation. This notion that thought ultimately proceeds from itself Cohen called Reinheit (purity). Cohen's operationalization of transcendental philosophy was developed in three massive tomes on purity in knowledge, will, and feeling.

On numerous occasions Cassirer affirmed the importance of Cohen's notion of the transcendental method. In a 1920 lecture on Cohen he says that Cohen's "decisive contribution" to Kant's teaching was to place the "transcendental method" at the center of critical philosophy.[20] This was so important, he emphasized repeatedly, because Cohen thereby countered the prevailing naturalistic and psychologistic conceptions of Kantianism expressed by Helmholtz, Lange, Liebmann, Zeller, and others so as to emphasize again the pure, strictly logical character of transcendental philosophy.[21] The logical principles of knowledge do not originate in some sensory or intellectual

Gegebenheit, the givenness of our psycho-physical organization. As Cohen stressed first and foremost, they result from a *geistige Erzeugung*, an intellectual generative process. As a result, Cassirer said, Cohen's emphasis on the pure—nonpsychologistic—basis of Kantianism, led to a type of philosophy conceived in the same spirit as Husserl's phenomenology.[22]

The dynamic character of Cohen's notion of purity, coupled with the view that the transcendental method was really a way to ask questions and not a dogmatic doctrine about things, led Cassirer to regard "Marburg" thinking as an ongoing process instead of a rigid "school" outlook. He even held that it was possible to be part of the school and yet reach conclusions completely different from Cohen's. But Cassirer's attitude toward the Marburg school was not uncritical. In later years he spoke of his relationship to Cohen, the Marburg school, and neo-Kantianism with a sense of growing divergence and dissatisfaction that his thought was taken as representative of this movement. In the preface to *Kant's Life and Thought* (1918) he repeated his indebtedness to the focus provided by Cohen's concentration on the transcendental method, yet he also stated that his own conception of the problems of Kant's philosophy had taken a shape that diverged in many ways from Cohen's (*KLT*, 3; *KLL*, viii). By 1936 his tone had become sharper: "When my essay 'Einstein's Theory of Relativity' appeared [1921], there were many critics who agreed with the conclusions I had drawn from the development of the new physics but who supplemented their agreement with the question whether as a 'Neo-Kantian' I was permitted to draw such conclusions. This volume will probably be exposed in still greater degree to such questions and doubts" (*DI*, xxiii; *ZMP*, 132). It was not long until the book reviews confirmed Cassirer's suspicion (see chap. 3).

One of the frequent criticisms of Cassirer's thought was that he upheld a neo-Kantian subjectivism; to meet this charge he wrote the essay "Was ist Subjektivismus?" While upholding the importance of the idea of the transcendental, Cassirer denies that this is a "subjectivistic" phenomenon and adds that "many of the doctrines that are attributed in today's philosophical literature to neo-Kantianism are not only foreign to me, but diametrically opposed to my own views."[23] According to John Hermann Randall, Jr., who knew Cassirer at Columbia, Cassirer at the end of his life was "provoked that the label ["Kantian"] was still attached to him" (*PEC*, 711). When Paul Arthur Schilpp approached Cassirer to write an autobiographical statement for the Library of Living Philosophers volume on his thought, the thing foremost in Cassirer's mind was that this would finally provide him with the chance to clarify his relationship to

Cohen. Cassirer said: "Now I will be able to finally make clear for others my relationship to Cohen, and I'm glad to get to do this. My ties to him and my later separation from him—both are important."[24]

Cassirer died before writing this clarification, and nowhere does he discuss the issue in detail. This was no doubt due in part to the loyalty with which the heads of philosophical "schools" were regarded in Germany, but especially due to the deep personal friendship between the two men, an attachment heightened by the fact that attacks on Cohen's thought were often allied with anti-Semitic animosities.[25] Under such circumstances it is unlikely that Cassirer would step forward as a critic of Cohen or even indicate points of disagreement with him. Nowhere does Cassirer criticize Cohen's philosophy, but this need not mean that his thought did not in fact depart radically from that of his teacher.

Perhaps Cassirer's most important statement of his indebtedness to Cohen are remarks he made in 1929 in his debate with Martin Heidegger at Davos, Switzerland.[26] There Cassirer stated that for him neo-Kantianism is not a philosophy in the sense of a dogmatic system of doctrines (dogmatisches Lehrsystem) but a way of asking questions (eine Richtung der Fragestellung). He even went so far as to state that he believed that there was "no essential antithesis" (kein wesentlicher Gegensatz) between neo-Kantian criticism and Heidegger's own phenomenological criticism.[27] Heidegger replied that neo-Kantianism is basically a "theory of knowledge" and ultimately a theory of scientific knowledge, whereas these were not his own questions. But in 1929 they were no longer Cassirer's either. There was surprise among phenomenologists when Cassirer's Philosophie der symbolischen Formen appeared because it was neither a theory of knowledge nor a theory of science. Max Scheler saw the first volume of Cassirer's main work as the "clearest witness" of a turnaround in philosophy, a breaking away from the epistemology of science.[28]

At Davos Heidegger also called attention to the neo-Kantians' concentration on "consciousness" (Bewußtsein) and contrasted this with the fact that man is fundamentally "bound to a body" (Gefesseltheit in den Leib).[29] But the enbodied subject was also fundamental for Cassirer. When Maurice Merleau-Ponty wrote his phenomenological tour de force on the body-subject, The Phenomenology of Perception, he emphasized particular indebtedness to Cassirer's discussion of expressive meaning and the body in the third volume of the Philosophy of Symbolic Forms. Merleau-Ponty saw that this work avoids Bewußtseinsphilosophie, a position that Heidegger identifies as typical of neo-Kantianism.[30] I do not think that Cassirer and Heidegger offer a comparable philosophical outlook, but I also do not think that their differences are to be found at the level of these problems or the supposed conflict between the former's "neo-Kantian" and the latter's "phenomenological" approach. [31] Cassirer's response in Davos to Heidegger's view of neo-Kantianism shows how he avoided that movement's limitations and how he could break away from Cohen and yet regard himself as following him.

I remain within Kant's basic methodological version of the transcendental as Cohen so often formulated it. He saw the essential feature of the transcendental method in that this method begins with a fact; but he [Cohen] narrowed his general definition: begin with a fact in order to ask about the possibility of this fact, by repeatedly putting forth mathematical natural science as that which is worth asking about. Kant did not limit the question this way. But I ask about the possibility of the fact of language. How does it come about, how is it thinkable that we are able to communicate [verständigen] from one being to another [von Dasein zu Dasein] in this medium? How is it possible that we can see a work of art as something objective and definite, as an objective being, as something meaningful in its wholeness?[32]

Cassirer extends the transcendental question to the "more comprehensive" question of meaning.

The fact of the intersubjective understanding of meaning is the starting point for Cassirer's philosophy. He even claims that "only then, when this question [of the possibility of Verständigung] has been raised will the way be made free to come to Heidegger's question [of the meaning of Being]" (ibid., 267). The decisive fact for Cassirer, he says himself, is that language and other symbolic forms provide "a bridge from individual to individual."

This stands out for me again and again in the fundamental phenomenon of language. Everyone speaks his own language, and it is unthinkable that we should carry one person's language over into that of another. And yet we understand one another through language. And there is something like a unity throughout the unending variety of different ways of speaking. In this lies for me the decisive point. And that is why I begin with the objectivity of symbolic form, because here the inconceivable is accomplished. Language is the clearest example. We claim that we stand here on common ground [einen gemeinsamen Boden]. (Ibid., 265)

This emphasis on language as the common ground of human beings is antithetical to the tendency in *Being and Time* to regard authentic *Dasein* as isolated and discourse in the light of the analytic of Dasein.[33]

For Cassirer the most basic question of philosophy becomes: How is it possible that there is meaning? How is it that we understand one another? He has not merely broadened the philosophical task that Cohen envisioned, making the theory of knowledge into a more general discipline that studies a variety of forms of "knowledge"; Cassirer saw that the problems of the theory of knowledge, such as certainty or the criterion of truth, require a philosophical inquiry on the fundamental phenomenon of meaning. In the same year that Cassirer finished the manuscript of the third volume of the *Philosophie der symbolischen Formen* (1927), he published an article in which he described his own development this way:

> More and more we have been forced to recognize that that area of theoretical meaning [*Sinn*] that we designate with the names "knowledge" [*Erkenntnis*] and "truth" [*Wahrheit*], no matter how significant and fundamental, represents only *one* layer of meaning [*Sinnschicht*]. In order to understand them, in order to recognize their structure, we must compare and contrast this layer with other meaning dimensions. We must, in other words, conceive the problem of knowledge and the problem of truth as particular cases of the more general problem of meaning [*als Sonderfälle des allegemeinen Bedeutungsproblems*].[34]

Cassirer states here explicitly that the philosophy of symbolic forms does not expand the "theory of knowledge," but rather shifts his philosophical investigations to new, more fundamental ground. He *subsumes* the theory of knowledge under the more basic theory of meaning. Cassirer transforms transcendental philosophy from a critique of knowledge into a critique of meaning.[35]

Meaning and the Theory of Signs

Cassirer uses the term *symbolic form* in a variety of ways: to refer to particular occurrences of meaning, to pervasive kinds of symbolic relations, and to cultural forms or ways of having a "world," such as myth, language, art, or science. Unifying all these applications is a basic transcendental theory, for which Cassirer coins the designation "symbolic pregnance."[36]

Cassirer was not the first to develop a philosophical theory of signs, symbols, and meaning, and he appears to have been aware of others' efforts, with the important exception of the work of Charles Sanders

Peirce (1839–1914).[37] The term that Peirce utilized for his theory was "semeiotic," or, as it is more often spelled today, semiotic. Cassirer discussed Lambert's "Semiotik" in 1907 (EP, 2:418) and in later years he even came to use the term *semiotic* for this study of symbolic forms. For example, in an essay published in 1945 he states: "Language is a 'symbolic form.' It consists of symbols, and symbols are no part of our physical world. They belong to an entirely different universe of discourse. Natural things and symbols cannot be brought to the same denominator. Linguistics is a part of semiotics, not of physics."[38] In the *Essay on Man* Cassirer referred to Charles Morris's work on the theory of signs (*EM*, 32) in order to make his own ideas clearer to American readers. These references indicate his readiness to regard the theory of symbolic forms in the context of what the American Pragmatists called semiotic, yet the term itself is not important in Cassirer's vocabulary. He was put off, for example, by Moritz Schlick's use of the term to refer only to the "conventional" aspect of signs.[39] But this should not prevent us from seeing the inner connections that exist between Cassirer's philosophy of symbolic forms and what, for example, Peirce calls semiotic.

Cassirer's theory of signs stands in close proximity to Peirce's. In their attempts to come to grips with the tradition of philosophy, especially Kant and Hegel, both thought that the development of the logic of relations was particularly important in the endeavor to think beyond Kant or Hegel.[40] In fact, both were initially led to the theory of signs by reflection on the logic of relations.

The Logic of Relations

Cassirer believed that the logic of relations provided a more reliable guide for a "transcendental logic" than the logic that was available to Kant, that is, the traditional logic of classes and the syllogism. Cassirer stressed that class logic depends upon the logic of relations because every class can be defined as a series whose members are related to one another by a principle: "We must recognize first of all that the order in a certain 'bunch' [Schar] of elements never adheres to the individual elements themselves nor is given with them as a fixed, finished characteristic, but rather that it is first defined through the generating relation [erzeugende Relation] out of which the individual members proceed."[41] Kant's attempt to create a transcendental logic focused upon the deduction of the pure concepts of the understanding, which were categorical in nature. Cassirer regarded the logic of relations as a new and better way to approach transcendental logic because this perspective asked not about the "categories" that serve as a priori invariants of experience, but about the generating relations, *erzeugende Relationen*, that are the source of categories. This new approach to transcendental logic leads Cassirer to reconsider the nature and theory of what is usually considered to be the essence of thought itself: *der Begriff*, the concept.

At this early stage in Cassirer's thought he believed that the best approach to a reexamination of the concept was to consider its use in modern, mathematically oriented, natural science: "The fate and the future of critical philosophy is determined by its relationship to the exact sciences. If we attempt to cut through the bond between it and mathematics and mathematical physics, then it would be deprived of its value and content" (ibid., 1). Cassirer noted that traditional class logic is concerned with the subsumption of different contents under one another, a preoccupation determined by the centrality of the concept of substance or the "thing" in Aristotelian metaphysics: *ousia*. Modern science does not study "things." Its concern is with laws expressed as mathematical functions. The essence of the concept in modern science is found in the idea of function. Here Cassirer explicitly follows Russell and holds that "mathematics is in its whole development nothing other than a special application of the general logic of relations; the relational concept, however, can be traced back to the fundamental notion of 'functionality' " (ibid., 7). Using modern mathematical science as his guide, Cassirer's first systematic book reinterprets transcendental philosophy by reinterpreting the theory of the concept in terms of function.

The central theses of *Substanzbegriff und Funktionsbegriff (Substance and Function)* are based on Cassirer's reinterpretation of the theory of the concept. The weakness of the traditional theory becomes evident, Cassirer points out, when we consider the question of concept formation. Traditional theory began by proposing that concepts are formed by abstraction. On that view the task of thought is to consider a plurality of objects and sort out their unifying, common elements. This is a commonsense view: "Nothing is presupposed save the existence of things in their inexhaustible multiplicity, and the power of the mind to select from this wealth of particular existences those features that are *common* to several of them" (*SF/ET*, 4). The final goal of such a classification process, the most comprehensive concept, is a conception of all-inclusive "being" totally devoid of every characteristic. But the fatal flaw of this theory is that it makes a tacit and crucial assumption. The common features that are isolated by abstraction are assumed to be discovered by means of comparison, an activity guided by the similarity between things. But nowhere among the characteristics of a thing do we find its "similarity." This theory of concept formation surreptitiously introduces this *relation between* things into the sensuous qualities of a thing and then proceeds as though the real task were to ferret out these similarities. Once this assumption has been tacitly made, Cassirer explains, then "it can indeed appear as if the work of thought were limited to selecting from a series of perceptions $a\alpha$, $a\beta$, $a\gamma$ . . . the common element a. In truth, however, the connection of the members of a series by the possession of a common 'property' is only a special example of logically possible connections in general. The connection of the members is in every case produced by some general law of arrangement through which a thoroughgoing rule of succession is established" (*SF/ET*, 16–17). In other words, any reference to the "similarity" among things already assumes the function of the concept to relate them in a series or group of similar things.

According to Cassirer's view the concept can be formulated as a function of the general form: $F(a, b, c \ldots)$ (*SF/ET*, 26). A natural occurrence A is described by its inclusion in a network of various functional connections such as f(A, B, C . . .), (A, B', C' . . .), and (A, B", C" . . .) that stand for different spatial, temporal, causal, and other orders (*SF/ET*, 256). The point of conceiving concepts as functions is that concepts are rules or laws that generate series, not members of the series: "That which binds the elements of the series a, b, c, . . . together is not itself a new element, that is actually infused into them, but it is the rule of progression, which remains the same, no matter in which member it is represented. The function $F(a, b)$, $F(b, c)$, . . . , which determines the sort of dependence between the successive members, is obviously not to be pointed out as itself a member of the series, which exists and develops according to it" (*SF/ET*, 17).

Cassirer uses such formulas to call attention to the rule of progression (signified here by the F) that defines a particular series. He is not employing these formulas, as a formal logician would, in order to talk about sentences in a formal calculus,[42] that is, to refer to the logical form of a dyadic or triadic relational predicate.[42] Formal logic abstracts from all content in order to talk about the form of assertions and predicates per se. Cassirer focuses instead on the nature of the rule or law of progression (generating relation) by which members of a series are related to one another and so gain their cognitive identity. His concern is the conditions of the possibility that something is a *content* for thought, that is, transcendental, not formal, logic. When Cassirer uses formulas to describe the basic relationship between the concept as a rule of progression (F) and the members of the series which this rule relates to one another, his object is to explain the logical structure of experience.

We can elucidate Cassirer's theory of the concept in *Substance and Function* by contrasting it with Gottlob Frege's theory of function and concept, with which it bears similarities. Cassirer mentions approvingly, but does not examine, Frege's theory.[43] Cassirer explicitly agrees with Frege's assertion (contra Schröder) that "the concept [conceived intensionally] logically precedes its extension."[44] Yet he adds that "Frege himself did not adhere strictly and consistently to his own basic view [that the concept is essentially understood and defined as a function], but replaced it by a purely quantitative [that is, extensional] view of the concept." Cassirer gives no argument for his claim, stating simply that it "has been aptly shown by Wilhelm Burkamp in his *Begriff und Beziehung*" (PsF, 3:342n; PSF, 3:293n). Burkamp claims that Frege was forced to adopt such a "quantitative" view of the concept because it was needed for his project of deriving number from the logic of concepts. Burkamp argues that Frege's attempt to deduce the natural numbers as quantities from the essence of the concept required him to begin with an extensional notion of the concept, that is, with classes. The theory of concepts as functions is essentially intensional, however, because it takes concepts to be relational.[45] Frege, according to Burkamp, therefore upheld conflicting views about the essence of the concept. Cassirer agrees with Burkamp on the primacy of the intensional aspect of the concept (just as he agrees with mathematicians such as Weyl who regard the natural number series as primarily ordinal). We can account for Cassirer's strict adherence to the primacy or intension by recognizing the basic difference between Cassirer's theoretical project and Frege's.

Frege's application of the mathematical notion of function to language is concerned not so much with concepts per se as with propositions. This is why Frege devotes attention to the truth values "true" and "false" while Cassirer does not even mention them. Cassirer's application of the mathematical notion of function is concerned with concepts per se, that is, with entities that by themselves cannot be true or false. Frege himself pointed out that his starting point was propositions, not concepts, and that therefore he might not have chosen well when he named his 1879 work the *Begriffsschrift* (concept writing).[46] Frege had already distinguished in that work between a "function" and an "argument" in a proposition. A proposition, he says, "decomposes into a stable component, representing the totality of relations, and the sign, regarded as replaceable by others, that denotes the object standing in these relations. The former I call a function, the latter its argument."[47] For example, in the proposition "Hydrogen is a chemical element," "hydrogen" is the argument and "being a chemical element" is the function. On Frege's analysis, the argument of one proposition, if it is not an individual name, can be used as a function in another proposition. Hence, "hydrogen" (an argument in the above sentence) is a function in "The gas in the red container is hydrogen."

The functional nature of the terms in a proposition is seen in the fact that the truth value of a proposition is a function of the argument it contains. Frege calls particular attention to the fact that a function by itself is not a proposition. In this state a function is said to be "unsaturated."[48] For example, "——is a chemical element" is an unsaturated function. Frege's examination of the function stresses the incompleteness of such a formula because his chief concern is with propositions. From Cassirer's point of view "chemical element," as a concept, is not incomplete, or it would not be a concept.

The nature of concepts is to be general. Cassirer claims that this generality is best understood by means of the model of a mathematical function. As soon as we conceive of an order and connection among any elements of thought, "we have already presupposed the concept, if not its complete form, yet in its fundamental function" (SF/ET, 17). Our conceptions always involve a functional form that relates the members of a series to one another. A form of the series is involved, therefore, in the thought of any object. This form of the series is a function, "the rule of progression, which remains the same, no matter in which member it is represented" (SF/ET, 17). This "rule," the "form of the series," is never reducible to the members of the series, yet it does not have any reality apart from the series because its whole being is exhausted by determining a (at least ideal) series; otherwise it is not a concept. Cassirer explains this logical point this way: "The serial form F (a, b, c . . .) which connects the members of a manifold obviously cannot be thought after the fashion of an individual a or b or c, without thereby losing its particular character. Its 'being' consists exclusively in the logical determination by which it is clearly differentiated from other possible serial forms, $\phi, \psi, \ldots$" (SF/ET, 26). For Cassirer, all experience is determined by such serial forms. Transcendental philosophy becomes, at least in Substance and Function, the search for those serial forms that constitute the "invariants of experience" (SF/ET, 269).

This brings us to the basic difference between Cassirer's and Frege's applications of the mathematical notion of function to logic. Whereas Frege developed his ideas as part of his attempt to formalize language along mathematical lines, Cassirer was trying to reconstruct transcendental logic. His analysis of the concept as a function was directed toward a new theory of the a priori conditions of the possibility of any cognition. Therefore, Cassirer was inclined to reject any approach to the theory of the concept that did not clearly affirm the priority of intension over extension. Insofar as Frege did not do this, he did not share in Cassirer's project.

Cassirer did not adhere long to the conception of the transcendental that he began to elaborate in *Substance and Function*, for it soon appeared to him too mathematical to stand as the model of the conditions of experience in the most fundamental sense.[49] Even with *Substance and Function* he moves toward a more concrete principle. Cassirer begins by discussing the problem of the theory of the "concept," but by the time he nears the end of *Substance and Function* his viewpoint has shifted, and he refers to the logical theory of concepts as the problem of *Repräsentation*: "If we understand "representation" as the expression of an ideal rule, which connects the present, given particular with the whole, and combines the two in an intellectual synthesis, then we have in "representation" no mere subsequent determination, but a constitutive condition of all experience. Without this apparent representation, there would also be no presentation, no immediately present content" (SF/ET, 284; see also 282–85). With this, Cassirer has turned around the traditional conception of representation, according to which the sphere of signs and the sphere of the signified belong to completely different realms of being. On that view things are known immediately and subsequently represented by signs. As Cassirer understands it, representation is necessary even if we are to experience something as immediately present and "given." Representation becomes the "constitutive condition of all experience" and henceforth the focus of Cassirer's conception of the transcendental.

Symbolic Form There are many sources for this central concept—Wilhelm von Humboldt, Heinrich Hertz, Goethe—yet the term *symbolische Form* itself appears to be Cassirer's own creation.[50] Cassirer first gave a definition of symbolic form in 1921: "Under a 'symbolic form' should be understood every energy of mind [*Energie des Geistes*] through which a mental content of meaning [*geistiger Bedeutungsgehalt*] is connected to a concrete, sensory sign [*konkretes sinnliches Zeichen*] and made to adhere internally to it" (WW, 175). Two things about this definition should be noted—its breadth and its logical structure.

This definition is so broad that it admits much more to constitute a "symbolic form" than the cultural forms of language, art, or myth that Cassirer refers to in the essay in which he gives the definition. Cassirer speaks the language of German idealism when he refers to an *Energie des Geistes*. The word *Geist* (usually rendered in English as "mind" or "spirit") immediately calls to mind Hegelianism, whereas the term *Energie* reveals Cassirer's debt to the great German linguist Wilhelm von Humboldt, whose work he discusses at length in the first volume of the *PSF*. In a famous passage Humboldt distinguished between language as a formal system of rules and as a living, formative force, calling the former *ergon* and the latter *energia*.[51] This distinction is more familiar today in Saussure's expressions *langue* and *parole* or in Chomsky's terminology, competence and performance. When Cassirer calls a symbolic form an "energy" he has in mind Humboldt's conception of language as an ongoing process. Cassirer's idea of symbolic form is not limited to natural languages but refers to all types of signs. Thus "Energie des Geistes" means any act of interpretation, either finding or giving meaning.

What, then, constitutes a "concrete, sensory sign" for Cassirer? Anything can be a sign—and insofar as something is experienced, it is a sign. But this does not mean that there are an unlimited number of symbolic forms, ways in which concrete, sensory signs can receive a "content of meaning." Interpreters of Cassirer have questioned how many different symbolic forms there are.[52] If we use the term *symbolic form* in the broad sense of a sign situation, then the varieties of interpretation seem limitless, but if by a "symbolic form" we mean those specific cultural matrices by which we have a "world," then they are limited in number. The criterion of such cultural symbolic forms is universal applicability:

It is a common characteristic of all symbolic forms that they are applicable to any object whatsoever. There is nothing that is inaccessible or impermeable to them: the particular character of an object does not affect their activity. What would we think of a philosophy of language, a philosophy of art or science that began with enumerating all those things that are possible subjects of speech and of artistic representation and of scientific inquiry? Here we can never hope to find a definite limit; we cannot even seek it. (MS, 34)

A cultural symbolic form opens up an understanding of everything; it is a way of having a world. The number of such symbolic forms is limited by the criterion of universal applicability. An indirect shot in billiards—playing off the cushion or from one ball to another—is a symbolic act in that it is based upon regarding the immediate object of concern in relation to a further thing, and "such mediated operations are always symbolic" (*PSF*, 3:273; *PsF*, 3:320). While an indirect billiard shot may be a symbolic operation, it does not have universal applicability as a form of interpreting the world. Such universal symbolic forms are few.

It is also important to recognize, in addition to the breadth of

Cassirer's notion of a "symbolic form," its logical structure. Cassirer's conception of symbolic form has three elements. Mistaking the triadic character of Cassirer's theory of signs and symbolism for a dyadic one results in great confusion because such a perspective overlooks the pragmatic dimension of Cassirer's thought.[53] Recognizing the triadic structure of symbolic forms reveals several important points of agreement between Cassirer's theory and Pragmatist semiotic.

The three elements of Cassirer's definition of a symbolic form can be directly correlated with the function of the concept that Cassirer gave in *Substance and Function*, which he alternatively expressed as $F(a, b, c, \ldots)$ or $F(a, b), F(b, c). \ldots$ Cassirer refers to an "energy" of the mind because he envisions symbolism as a process. A dyadic relation, such as Saussure's sign standing in relationship to the signified, is static, leaving no room for the dimension of use.[54] *Energie des Geistes* expresses the original, formative power "through which the simple presence of the phenomenon assumes a definite 'meaning' [*Bedeutung*]" (*PSF*, 1:78; *PsF*, 1:9). In the tradition of American Pragmatist thinking on the theory of signs, this "energy" would be referred to as "interpretation." In the model developed by Peirce, which influenced Royce and Morris, we find the same basic *triadic* conception of the process that Cassirer had in mind.

The theory of symbolic forms does not stand on its own but depends upon Cassirer's transcendental theory of meaning, which he offers under the name *symbolische Prägnanz*. Symbolic pregnance is the key to understanding how Cassirer's thought constitutes a transformation of transcendental philosophy.

Symbolic Pregnance In his 1928 review of the second volume of the *Philosophy of Symbolic Forms* Heidegger said that a critical discussion of Cassirer's thought will only become possible "when the basic concepts of this system are worked out and brought to their ultimate foundations."[55] Cassirer does this in the third volume, the *Phenomenology of Knowledge*, which develops the dimensions of meaning and shows their "ultimate foundations" in symbolic pregnance. This doctrine provides the *PSF* with its "firm and solid ground." By considering this doctrine the way is open to understanding Cassirer's conception of metaphysics.

Cassirer conceives the symbolic forms of human culture—language, art, science, and the like—to be expressions of "artificial" symbolism since they all involve the "giving of signs" (*Zeichengebung*; *PSF*, 1:105–06; *PsF*, 1:43). Cassirer agrees with Saussure that the particular signs that constitute a natural language are cultural creations and, hence, conventional (*SMC*, 182–83). There is no reason to proclaim the designation *tree* to be any more "natural" than *arbor* or *Baum*. Unlike the later generation of French semiologists, however, Cassirer does not think that this conventional aspect of symbolism warrants an interpretation of signs that only affirms "freeplay" at the expense of recognizing anything in the origin of signs that is not conventional.[56] Such a conception reflects what has since been called the "prejudice of a contractual agreement," the outlook that the conventional character of the words and other aspects of particular languages can be transferred to language *as such* so that it too seems to be based upon a kind of contractual agreement or convention.[57] Cassirer called this extreme conventionalistic approach to language "naturalistic" and rejected it because it is based upon circular reasoning: "Language is said to be a convention, 'something agreed upon,' which the individuals simply encounter; political and social life is traced back to a 'social contract.' The circular nature of such arguments is obvious. For agreement is possible only in the medium of speech and, similarly, a contract has meaning and force only within a state and a medium of laws" (*LH*, 108). Language itself cannot be reduced to a convention. This is why Cassirer distinguishes between "artificial" and "natural" symbolism.

Human beings, individually and collectively, introduce specific, arbitrary signs to mean certain things; by virtue of this process of Zeichengebung (the giving of signs), the "artificial" symbolism of culture is produced (*PSF*, 1:105–07; *PsF*, 1:41–43). But the creation of culture does not create the phenomenon of meaning itself, for meaning is already found in the world as we perceive it through the senses: "We can understand how a sensuous particular, such as the spoken sound, can become the vehicle of a purely intellectual meaning, only if we assume that the basic function of signification [*des Bedeutens*] is already present and effective before the individual sign is produced, so that this productive act does not create signification itself, but merely fixes it, merely applies it to a particular case" (*PSF*, 1:106–07, translation altered; cf. *PsF*, 1:42). By "natural symbolism" Cassirer means the understanding of meaning that pervades all sense perception. His point is that the understanding of meaning, whether artificial signs of culture or the natural symbolism found in our perception of the world, cannot be explained as a matter of convention or agreement. Both kinds lead us to the *basic* phenomenon, "symbolische Prägnanz."

There is no English equivalent for *Prägnanz*, which derives from the German *prägen* (to mint or coin and give a sharp contour) and the Latin *praegnens* (laden or ready to give birth).[58] It embodies at once the ideas of giving form and fecundity. The term *Prägnanz* was crucial to Gestalt psychology, which flourished while Cassirer developed his notion of symbolic pregnance. Kurt Goldstein, Cassirer's cousin and close friend, was a leader of the Gestalt school represented by Max Wertheimer, Kurt Koffa, and Wolfgang Koehler, and he edited, along with them, the journal *Psychologische Forschung*. The fundamental principle of this school was the "law of pregnance" or "good gestalt," according to which "psychological organization will always be as 'good' as the prevailing conditions allow."[59] This principle, which was directed to the perceptual field as a whole, interpreted "good" to mean articulation in terms of unity, continuity, closure, simplicity, or other exemplifications of filling in or completing perception. Although Cassirer does not discuss this Gestalt principle, it surely inspired his conception of symbolic pregnance. As one author describes this principle, "Prägnanz affects shape, size, and surface attributes so that the most significant aspects of an object are preserved if the field conditions are not altered too severely; i.e. a 'thing' is invariant or transposable like a melody."[60] Gestalt psychologists studied this invariance or transposability as a perceptual phenomenon; Cassirer discerned in such phenomena a transcendental semiotic principle.

Cassirer gives this definition: "By symbolic pregnance we mean the way [*die Art*] in which a perception as a 'sensory' experience ['*sinnliches' Erlebnis*] contains at the same time a certain nonintuitive 'meaning' ['*Sinn*'] which it immediately and concretely represents" (*PSF*, 3:202; *PsF*, 3:235). Here again Cassirer speaks of three elements: a sense experience, a meaning, and the way the former contains the latter. Symbolic pregnance seems to be little more than a broadly formulated restatement of what Cassirer termed a symbolic form, but now he refers to the "sensory" in general instead of to a "sensory sign" and he speaks more broadly of the "way" this presents a meaning rather than of an "energy of mind" that connects it with a meaning. He speaks of meaning (*Sinn*) in general instead of an "intellectual content of meaning" (*geistiger Bedeutungsgehalt*) because symbolic pregnance pervades sensory awareness itself. Symbolic pregnance does not involve or depend upon the giving of signs (*Zeichengebung*) or a giving of meaning (*Sinngebung*). It is not a subjective activity, but the condition of the possibility of all Sinngebung and Zeichengebung.

Cassirer's chief discussion of symbolic pregnance occurs in a brief, crucial chapter in the third volume of the *Philosophy of Symbolic Forms*. He distinguishes there between symbolic pregnance and what Kant called "synthesis" and what Brentano and Husserl termed "intentionality."

Cassirer sees in Kant's *Critique of Pure Reason* a "difficulty and ambiguity," namely that Kant's discussion of synthesis suggests that there is a "self-subsistent transcendental subject" that is the "author" (*Urheber*) of the organization of the order we call perception. Yet there is no need for such an author to "give" meaning and order because these are *always already there* (*PSF*, 3:194–95; *PsF*, 3:226–27). There are no bare sensations that need a subject to give them meaning. The notion that there is a sensation distinct from meaning is a fiction.

Cassirer makes a similar objection to the phenomenological conception of the "intentionality" of consciousness. On that view, consciousness is always twofold: it is always consciousness *of* an object, a distinction that can be made within consciousness without assuming the externality of the object (*PSF*, 3:196–97; *PsF*, 3:228–29). Husserl distinguishes between two strata in the stream of phenomena, a material "hyletic" stratum and a "noetic" stratum. Cassirer finds fault with this distinction because it cannot be made without thereby introducing a difference that is not there *phenomenologically*. Phenomenology cannot remain within the descriptive sphere of meaning and speak of a stratum that is without meaning and must receive it. In this distinction Cassirer finds "a vestige of that dualism that sees a cleavage between the physical and the psychic, which instead of regarding body and soul as correlative sees them as different in respect to substance" (*PSF*, 3:198; *PsF*, 3:230). If we are to speak in strictly phenomenological terms, Cassirer continues, then we must recognize that "no content or consciousness is in itself merely present, or in itself merely representative; rather, every actual experience indissolubly embraces both factors. Every present content functions in the sense of representing, just as all representation demands a link with something present in consciousness" (*PSF*, 3:199; *PsF*, 3:231). Cassirer's response to the subjectivism he finds in Kant and Husserl is the doctrine of symbolic pregnance.

Cassirer devised a thought experiment to illustrate what he means by symbolic pregnance. He asks that we imagine a drawn line and consider its particular appearance, its shape, its spatial and other physical qualities.[61] It appears to us as an aesthetic phenomenon with a certain jagged or flowing form. A cultist might regard the line as a mark with magic significance; an art historian might think it illustrates a particular style or, perhaps, the kind of curved line that Hogarth called the "line of beauty."[62] It could even express graphically a certain functional development to a mathematician. In short, the line or design always appears in some framework of interpretation. Everything is always already in *some* context or field of meaning. This context is part of what Cassirer means when he says that symbolic pregnance is "*the way* in which a perception as a 'sensory' experience contains at the same time a certain nonintuitive 'meaning' which it immediately and concretely represents." Cassirer concludes that analysis can never lead us back to absolute elements; it is the relational element of *meaning* that stands out "as a genuine a priori, an essentially first factor [*Wesensmäßig-Erstes*]" (PSF, 3:203; PsF, 3:236). Symbolic pregnance is the transcendental element in Cassirer's philosophy of symbolic forms.

The shift from the theory of knowledge to the theory of meaning leads Cassirer away from subjectivism. Symbolic pregnance is not a new name for the Kantian "transcendental unity of consciousness." Its locus is not some "I think" that accompanies all our ideas.

We have designated as symbolic pregnance the relation in consequence of which the sensory [*ein Sinnliches*] embraces a meaning and represents it immediately [*unmittelbar darstellt*] for consciousness: this pregnance can be reduced neither to merely reproductive processes nor to mediated intellectual processes—it must ultimately be recognized as an independent and autonomous determination, without which neither an object nor a subject, neither a unity of the thing nor a unity of the self would be given to us. (PSF, 3:235; PsF, 3:275)

Symbolic pregnance is not an act of consciousness or "Energie des Geistes." It is the condition of the possibility of a consciousness and of the symbolic forms of culture. Unlike an idealism of consciousness, Cassirer's notion of symbolic pregnance required a conception of subjectivity that begins with the phenomenon of the body.

Cassirer traces the phenomenon of meaning and symbolism to the relationship between the body (*Leib*) and soul (*Seele*):

The relation between body and soul represents the prototype and model for a purely symbolic relation, which cannot be converted either into a relationship between things or into a causal relation. Here there is originally neither an inside and outside nor a before and after, neither an agent nor an effect; here we have a combination which does not have to be composed of separate elements but which is in a primary sense a meaningful whole which interprets itself, which separates [*auseinanderlegt*] into a duality of factors in order to interpret ['*auslegen*'] itself in them. A genuine access to the body-soul problem is possible only if we recognize as a general principle that all thing connections and causal connections are ultimately based upon such relations of meaning. The latter do not form a special class *within* the thing and causal relations:

rather they are the constitutive presupposition, the *conditio sine qua non*, on which the thing and causal relations themselves are based. (*PSF*, 3:100; *PsF*, 3:117)

Two questions arise here. How does the relationship between the body and the sensitive, "living" nature of the body, the soul, constitute the "prototype" of a *symbolic* relationship? How is this symbolic relation the conditio sine qua non of all other relations? The symbolic relationship of Leib and Seele is an instance of the type of meaning that Cassirer calls "expression" (*Ausdruck*).

Cassirer's point about the body-soul relationship becomes obscured if we insist on reserving the terms *symbol* and *symbolic* for phenomena in the sphere of culture.[63] Expressive meaning is not a product of culture; it characterizes the first stages of perception and bodily awareness. Cassirer argues at length that perception is originally expressive—expressiveness (for example, something as soothing to look at or "friendly") is more primitive than the epistemological notion of "sensation" (for example, the blue spot). Hence, the feeling of the body, our basic self-awareness, is an understanding of meaning. This is the prototype of all symbolic relations.

Expression

In a lecture presented in Berlin in 1931 Cassirer argues that if we conceive the body and soul in a Cartesian manner as different substances or things, then it remains inconceivable how they could ever be conjoined, yet we experience this conjunction whenever we speak to someone.[64] Language too is like an animated body. In a speech situation we understand the speaker through his gestures, tempo, and many other expressive qualities that underlie and support or distract from what he says. If communication is too greatly hindered, then instead of a "sinnbeseelten sinndurchdrungenen Sprachleib" (a speech body animated and saturated with meaning), we only hear sounds; understanding nothing, we are left with mere "isolated word objects" (*isolierter Wortkörper*; ibid., 24). He concludes that the same kind of expressive meaning necessary to even a rudimentary understanding of speech communication is required to understand the body-soul relationship. Body and soul "gehören zusammen wie ein geistiger 'Sinn' zu dem, worin dessen Sinn 'erscheint,' *sichtbar wird*, wie ein Zeichen zu dem, was es bezeichnet" (belong together like an intellectual "meaning" belongs to that in which it appears, becomes visible, like a sign [belongs] to that which it designates; ibid., 16). This kind of meaning is primordial; the problem is not how body and soul come together but how we learn to distinguish between them.

The interpretation that distinguishes the bodily and sensitive aspects of the person originates in physical action, the doing and feeling that accompanies one's physical confrontation with the world. Reflection enters as thinking about intelligent action in a bodily sense, not thinking about thought.

In his examination of the body-subject in *The Phenomenology of Perception*, Maurice Merleau-Ponty refers again and again to Cassirer's analysis of meaning in the *Phenomenology of Knowledge* and particularly to the key idea of symbolic pregnance.[65] Cassirer's thesis that the relationship between the body and sensitive nature (soul) constitutes the "prototype of all symbolic relations," that is, that the expressive meaning perceived in the world has its original seat in the body, is Merleau-Ponty's starting point in his phenomenology (ibid., 235). He explicitly follows Cassirer's doctrine that symbolic pregnance is anterior to any kind of "sense-giving acts," to the significance of signs, and even to expressive meaning (p. 291).

Cassirer could have agreed with Merleau-Ponty's description of perception: "Rationalism and skepticism draw their sustenance from an actual life of consciousness which they both hypocritically take for granted, without which they can be neither conceived nor even experienced, and in which it is impossible to say that *everything has a significance*, or that *everything is nonsense*, but only that *there is significance*" (p. 296). Philosophy can begin with the view that "there is significance." But Cassirer could not agree with Merleau-Ponty's terming this a "new *cogito*" (ibid.). Meaning in the sense of symbolic pregnance is the condition of the possibility of a cogito, not itself a cogito. Symbolic pregnance is neither something in the mind nor something in the world. The phenomenon of meaning itself is the necessary condition for the separation of the ego from the "other" and the world, a separation which, in turn, is "the necessary condition that the ego not only exists, but knows of itself."[66]

Cassirer completed the manuscript of the *Phenomenology of Knowledge* in 1927, the year Heidegger's *Being and Time* appeared. To his manuscript Cassirer added substantive footnotes agreeing with Heidegger's analysis of time, space, and the meaning of Being for *Dasein*. He indicates that these analyses fit into his conception of expressive meaning. About Heidegger's analysis of space Cassirer says: "What distinguishes our undertaking from that of Heidegger is above all that it does not stop at this stage of the at-hand and its mode of spatiality, but without challenging Heidegger's position goes beyond it; for we wish to follow the road leading from spatiality as a factor in the at-hand [that is, space with expressive meaning] to space as the form of existence, and furthermore to show how this road leads right through the domain of symbolic formation—in the twofold sense of 'representation' and 'significance'" (PSF, 3:149n; PsF, 3:173n). Cassirer's other comments offer the same assessment, the gist of which is that with his analysis of Dasein Heidegger has uncovered the world relation that Cassirer examines under the heading of expression.

When Heidegger recasts the epistemologist's notion of subjectivity as "consciousness" (Bewußt-sein) in terms of existence or Being-there (Da-sein), he regards language and all other types of meaning as derivative from Dasein's Being-in-the-world (in-der-Welt-sein).[67] His term for this ontological structure of meaning is Bedeutsamkeit (significance). Meaning (Sinn) is that through which Dasein understands something as something by virtue of the aim of some project (Entwurf).[68] He avoids in this way the subjective, mentalistic conception of the origin of meaning by Sinngebung through acts of mind. Meaning originates in the Sich-vorweg-sein (being ahead of itself) of Dasein in the sphere of action in the world of things. This primary Entwurf of Being Heidegger calls "care" or caring, Sorge. Cassirer agrees that meaning must be traced to the sphere of activity that Heidegger calls Sorge, but he does not share Heidegger's readiness to limit the phenomenon of meaning to the phenomenon of Dasein. Sorge is an example of expressive meaning (Ausdruck), but expressive meaning cannot itself be reduced to an ontological structure. Meaning is always symbolic pregnance and this, Cassirer claims, cannot be explained, reduced to, or even clarified by any ontology. His reasons for this view derive from the character of expressive meaning itself.

Cassirer's approach to the phenomenon of expressive meaning is threefold: phenomenological description; empirical research on perception, particularly by Gestalt psychologists; and myth interpretation.

Cassirer agrees with Scheler that phenomenological description must begin with whole experiences, the perception of someone smiling, asking a question, threatening us with a gesture, or turning red with shame (PSF, 3:87–88; PsF, 3:102). The unity of such experiences is more "primitive" than the epistemological notion of a sensation (Empfindung). Although Cassirer thinks that phenomenological description is indispensable for the study of expressive meaning, he also believes that it is subject to the pitfalls of introspection. In particular, Cassirer calls attention to the tendency to see expressive meaning originating in "acts" of "consciousness" (PSF, 3:88–89, 57; PsF, 3:104–05, 67). Expressive meanings—facial expressions, gestures, and the moods in an environment—do not as phenomena have such an interpretative character. This point is decisive for Cassirer. He contends that reliance on introspection has nourished numerous philosophical confusions, such as the pseudo-problem of "other minds." Subjective idealism presumes that we have a basic awareness of ourselves as consciousnesses and that we must infer the existence of "other persons" and the "external world." However, if we begin instead with the phenomenon of expression as it is found in myth and developmental psychology, that is, the actual beginning of thought, we must admit that the process of self-discovery proceeds in the opposite direction (PSF, 3:89; PsF, 3:105). Expressive perception of the world is characterized by awareness of living in a world of action (PSF, 3:83–84; PsF, 3:97–98). The genealogy of the ego in myth shows that individual consciousness develops from group consciousness.

The primacy of expression is corroborated by the work of Gestalt psychologists. Cassirer draws from the findings of this school and related empirical research, from Koffka, Bühler, Stern, Hering, Koehler, Werner, Katz, and others. Actual empirical research fails to discover "sensations" as conceived by empiricist epistemology. Cassirer cites Koffka: "We are left with the opinion that phenomena such as 'friendliness' or 'unfriendliness' are extremely primitive—even more primitive, for example, than that of a blue spot" (PSF, 3:65; PsF, 3:76). The world as it is first perceived is not an "assembly," but whole events emotionally saturated with feeling: "Where the 'meaning' of the world is still taken as that of pure expression, every phenomenon discloses a definite 'character,' which is not merely deduced or inferred but which belongs to it immediately. It is in itself gloomy or joyful, agitating or soothing, pacifying or terrifying" (PSF, 3:72; PsF, 3:84). Such perception is fundamental to the mythic world. In order to understand the original relationship to the world, Cassirer concluded, philosophy must begin with the study of myth.

Myth is an intersubjective phenomenon, a "symbolic form" that has "a grounding in an original mode of perception," that is, expressive meaning (PSF, 3:62; PsF, 3:73). Cassirer argues against the view that mythic or aesthetic awareness can be understood in terms of an "act of consciousness"; the whispering or rustling in the woods, a shadow darting along the ground, a light flickering on the water, all such phenomena, which seem animated in mythic awareness, are directly expressive. To see these expressive phenomena as the result of acts of interpretation, intentions, syntheses, or empathy introduces something into the phenomena that is not there and ignores what is unique about expression—its immediate, animated sensory wholeness.

Such views must, as Cassirer puts it, "kill perception by making it into a complex of mere sensory contents, before it can reanimate this dead matter of sensation by the act of empathy."

Actually, we arrive at the data of *mere* sensation—such as light or dark, warm or cold, rough or smooth—only by setting aside a fundamental and primary stratum of perception, by doing away with it, so to speak, for a definite theoretical purpose. . . . This expressive character is not intrinsically subjective, since it is what gives to perception its original color or reality and makes it a perception of reality. For the reality we apprehend is in its original form not a reality of a determinate world of things, originating apart from us [i.e., having no relationship to us]; rather it is the certainty of a living efficacy [*Wirksamkeit*] that we experience. (*PSF*, 3:73; *PsF*, 3:86)

We experience the expressive world through interaction with it as an embodied subject. The "subjective" and "objective" emerge through this interaction. Cassirer holds that "the horizon of the ego and of reality separate for him [man] within the totality of his bodily, emotional, and intellectual activities" (*STS*, 55). These activities are not the source or cause of the phenomenon of expressive meaning itself, however.

The examination of expressive meaning brings Cassirer to the limit of phenomenological investigation. In order to preserve the phenomenon of expression as it is lived, he rejects all subjective explanations of it—synthesis, intentionality, even the existential structure of "care." How, then, does he explain expressive meaning? Cassirer's answer is that it can have no explanation. Like symbolic pregnance, expressive meaning is an Urphänomen, a primary phenomenon.

Cassirer takes the idea of the Urphänomen from Goethe, for whom the Urphänomen is a perceptual phenomenon and also the limit of perception. Goethe points to the fact that it is not possible to translate differences of color into differences in number by using measurements without thereby losing the phenomenon to be explained.[69] The perception of a color—a hot red or a cool blue—is a "primary phenomenon," incapable of further explanation. For Cassirer, color perception is thus an instance of expressive meaning.

The thesis that meaning is an Urphänomen recurs in different shapes throughout Cassirer's *Phenomenology of Knowledge*. He refers to meaning as an Urphänomen to show that higher intellectual functions depend upon the original stratum of expressive meaning (*PSF*, 3:87; *PsF*, 3:102) and to show that the problem of body-soul dualism is caused by overlooking (and resolved by recalling) that the Urphänomen is an animated body (*PSF*, 3:99–103; *PsF*, 3:116–21). He points out that the phenomena of spatiality and temporality are fundamentally exemplifications of the Urphänomen of meaning: "What is given *here* points to a *not-here*, and what is given *now* points backwards to a *not-now*; without this, the phenomenon of an intuitive [*anschaulich*, that is, perceived by the senses] world could not be understood or even described" (*PSF*, 3:124; *PsF*, 3:144). Causal relations are secondary; symbolic relations, primary. Meaning, therefore, "cannot be explained by any causal derivation because it must be presupposed by every causal explanation" (*PSF*, 3:176, cf. 92; *PsF*, 3:205, cf. 68). This is true of meaning relations per se, true of representation as well as expression (*PSF*, 3:122–23; *PsF*, 3:141–42). Hence, symbolic relations are exempted from the "principle of sufficient reason" (*PSF*, 3:323, cf. 72–74; *PsF*, 3:377, cf. 84–87).

The recognition of meaning as an Urphänomen indicates that causal explanations do not exhaust the field of knowledge. Knowledge of form can only be exhibited (*aufweisen*) and its content grasped by a form of inventory (*als reiner Bestand*) (*LH*, 178ff; *KW*, 101). The assertion that meaning is an Urphänomen reformulates the contention that symbolic pregnance is an "essential first"; it is essential to understanding any proposition, no matter whether it is true or false, prior to knowing its truth or falsity. The epistemological problems of truth and certainty are secondary to the problem of meaning. The theory of symbolic pregnance does not permit inferring the truth of any empirical assertions. The theory of symbolic pregnance explains the possibility of forming any truth claim, any proposition, any image of a "world."

Symbolic Forms and the Metaphysics of Lebensphilosophie In his later work Cassirer surprises the reader by his readiness to speak a different kind of language, directed explicitly to metaphysical questions. His discussion of the "fundamental fact" of existence in his 1942 lecture on "Language and Art" is couched in the language of "life philosophy." He says "the ego, the individual mind, cannot create reality. Man is surrounded by a reality that he did not make, that he has to accept as ultimate fact" (*SMC*, 195); he refers to this ultimate fact simply as "life."

Cassirer's transformation of transcendental philosophy prepares the way for this new way of speaking. Symbolic pregnance stands as the condition of the possibility of *Weltverstehen* (understanding a world). But the fundamental fact of "having a world" falls outside transcendental philosophy. Cassirer sought to come to grips with this "fundamental fact" as he worked on the fourth volume of the *PSF*.[70] In this work he investigated Lebensphilosophie with the aim of showing the relation of the *PSF* to metaphysics.

Cassirer adopts the term *Leben* (life) from Goethe. His quotation from Goethe in "Language and Art" sets the stage for his remarks on the "fundamental reality" of "life": " 'Truth or, what means the same, the Divine is never to be grasped directly. We can see it only in a reflected light, in an example, a symbol, in single and related phenomena. We become aware of it as incomprehensible life and yet we cannot renounce the wish to comprehend it' " (SMC, 193; see also GGW, 75).

The framework for Cassirer's work on the metaphysics of the symbolic forms is Goethean: life as the conceptually incomprehensible Urphänomen, the symbol as its mode of expression. Cassirer does not comment on Goethe in the "Language and Art" essay; he uses Goethe's language and outlook as his own starting point. One of the three main parts of the fourth volume of the PSF is a critical discussion of the idea of the Urphänomen itself (Beinecke Ms 183c). For Cassirer, as for Dilthey, Lebensphilosophie originates with Goethe.[71] One reviewer of The Problem of Knowledge (written contemporaneously with part of PSF 4) was prompted to observe that, in that work, "Cassirer's references to Goethe suggest a certain completion to his thought which he himself could not, as a critical [i.e., epistemological] thinker, allow himself to formulate in a conclusive manner."[72] The reviewer, Isabel Stearns, holds that Cassirer was "prevented" from making an "adequate ontological use" of Goethe's thought (for example, its teleological component and Goethe's theory of the relationship of particular and universal) because of his own "epistemological assumptions."[73]

Yet Cassirer overcomes the hurdle of the epistemological strictures of neo-Kantianism—but not by developing an ontology. Just as he transformed transcendental philosophy as theory of knowledge into a theory of Weltverstehen and meaning, so, too, he reinterprets the problem of being and metaphysics in light of the problem of meaning.

For Cassirer, the history of metaphysical thought was determined largely by two concepts, that of the "thing" (ousia, substantia, Ding) and that of causality or, more generally, the principle of sufficient reason. These concepts take for granted the primary phenomenon of meaning. Truly "first" philosophy must begin with the phenomenon of meaning. Cassirer criticizes traditional ontology for passing over this primary phenomenon in order to speak directly of being: "It is everywhere the striving of ontology—a striving rooted in its original question—to transpose problems of meaning (Sinn-probleme) into pure problems of being (Seins-probleme). Being is the foundation on which all meaning must ultimately be in some way grounded. . . . And here it is above all two determinations which dominate the whole problem of metaphysics: the concept of the thing and the concept of causality. All other relations culminate in these two categories, which literally absorb them" (*PSF*, 3:94; *PsF*, 3:111). The source of this tendency to substantialization, Cassirer argues, is language itself, which spatializes and reifies even purely conceptual contents of thought (see below, chap. 2).

His criticism of the Kantian thing-in-itself illustrates how Cassirer coupled this criticism of language with a positive theory. In his chief analysis of the Kantian concept Cassirer says: "This concept [the thing-in-itself] can be no more than the border-limit [*Grenze*] of our empirical knowledge, the horizon that encircles our experience's field of vision. It will, therefore, have to give us a different sort of view, depending upon the field of vision itself and according to the contents that are given within it" (*EP*, 2:742). In other words, the "thing" in itself, as the "horizon" of experience, is not actually thinglike. It cannot be understood as a thing, Cassirer argues, because of the different forms in which it appears in the *Critique of Pure Reason*. In the transcendental aesthetic the thing-in-itself appears as the *Rezeptivität* (receptivity) of sensibility; in the analytic it represents the counterpart or object of the objectifying function of the pure concepts of the understanding; in the transcendental dialectic it is the schema of the regulative principle of reason that gives a systematic unity to all experience (see *EP*, 2:744–59). Cassirer does not think that the concept of the thing is the appropriate vehicle for Kant's meaning; the thing-in-itself for Cassirer becomes equivalent to the concept of the world (*der Weltbegriff*).

By conceiving the Ding an sich as a kind of thing, Cassirer says, a "grammatical" move is made by which Erfahrung (experience) is made into a "Substantivum," causing metaphysics to arrive at antinomies (*EP*, 2:751). By treating the thing-in-itself as a thing, the concept of the world is regarded in a single, fixed way, whereas in experience different ways of having a world cohere, just as different aspects of the thing-in-itself cohere in the *Critique of Pure Reason*. Cassirer's interpretation of the thing-in-itself is one reason for the centrality of the concept of the "world" in the *PSF*.

Traditional metaphysics treats the world primarily one way, as something created by God; the concept of being in traditional ontology amounts to a substantialization of the world as a thing.[74] Man, too, is considered part of this divine creation. History remains incidental to this conception of the world. When Cassirer speaks of understanding or having a world, for example, the world of myth, science, technology, or art, the "world" has an essential historicity. The symbolic forms are forms of life, not just forms of knowledge.[75] The world as historical reality is a living process, not a thing. The same is true of man. Man and world are aspects of life. For "life," Cassirer insists, there can be no metaphysical "ground."

Cassirer's objections to foundationalism figure prominently in his discussions of Hegelianism. At the point in Hegel's system where the theory of the idea is supposed to lead to the philosophy of nature (the resolve of the Idea to "go forth freely as nature,"), Cassirer says, "the language of Hegel's panlogism without transition turns into the language of myth."[76] The image of the created world emerging from the original being of God who gives up none of his essence here supplants Hegel's dialectic. The law of logical development cannot be consistently applied in metaphysics, Cassirer claims, without an unacceptable reductionism. Cassirer follows Goethe in rejecting Hegel's dialectical characterization of the growth of plants, which regards the bud as giving way to the flower and the fruit by "negation" so that the fruit becomes a "false existence of the plant" (EP, 3:375). This view undermines the continuity of nature, and—what is more important to Cassirer—it deprives nature of any Eigengesetzlichkeit, any lawfulness of its own (EP, 3:376). This point is echoed in Cassirer's frequent criticisms of Hegel's political theory as obscuring the "actual dynamics" of individual freedom due to its elevation of the state to a position of ethical supremacy (FF, 366; EP, 3:372, 369). Natural, organic growth and human activity both become subservient to the Hegelian Begriff. The price of coherence in Hegel's system is disregard for the significance of individual natural and historical reality.

Some of Cassirer's criticisms of Hegel have an existential character. In his essay "Hölderlin und der deutsche Idealismus" Cassirer examines Hegel's philosophical attempt to mitigate conceptually the suffering endured by individuals—accomplished by Hegel's shifting the perspective from that of the individual being to that of the Weltgeist (world spirit). Cassirer contrasts this to Hölderlin's tragic view of individuality: "When Hegel engages in tireless intellectual effort to resolve the dialectic of the general and the particular, the finite and the infinite, we marvel at this mighty effort that encompasses the entire breadth of the life of the mind and seems to let it all proceed from the pure movement of thought. Yet it is Hölderlin's basic sensibility that we feel more strongly and personally, a sensibility that does not feign to present a solution to this original conflict, but only wants to fathom it in its depth and to present it poetically" (IG, 155).

The general tendency of Cassirer's thought while he developed the PSF—away from epistemology and toward concrete historical life, as seen in his criticism of panlogism and his emphasis on the primacy of expressive meaning—inclines him toward sympathy with Lebensphilosophie. By contrast, Rickert's rationalistic prejudices prevented him from seeing the movement in such a positive regard.[77] Yet Cassirer is an Apollonian, antagonistic toward the irrationalistic elements in Lebensphilosophie, which, in vulgar form, eventually became a political force in the 1920s and 1930s.[78] The supposedly hostile relationship between the intellect and man's vital, feeling nature so passionately debated in the 1920s exemplified for Cassirer the same linguistic mistake typical of traditional metaphysics. Proponents on either side of the debate construed the intellect (Geist) and life (Leben) as thinglike entities, thereby turning a conceptual opposition into a real, spatialized one.[79] Cassirer emphasizes that the phenomenon of Geist is in reality a transformation of Leben: "a turning and about-face of Life itself—, insofar as it passes from the circle of merely *organic* creativity and formation into the circle of 'form,' the circle of *ideal* formative activity" (*PEC*, 875). Here (in his 1930 paper " 'Spirit' and 'Life' in Contemporary Philosophy") Cassirer speaks the language of Dilthey's Lebensphilosophie.[80]

The philosophy of Leben provides Cassirer with his access to the problem of metaphysics. A somewhat cryptic statement from the manuscript of the fourth *PSF* volume sketches his basic conception: "Unsere Metaphysik: Gewahrwerden des Lebens[.] Zurückgehen des Lebens in seinen 'Grund'—dadurch muss das Leben freilich zu Grunde gehen, aber es ist in der Sphaere des Geistes aufgehoben[.] [D]ie Subs [tanz] des Lebens ist zum *Subjekt* geworden seine Sinn-Sphaere über-dingliche u[nd] über-persönlich" (Our metaphysics: life's becoming self-aware. Life's return to its 'ground'—this of course must be life's destruction, but it is preserved in the sphere of mind. The substance of life becomes *subject*, its sphere of meaning, above things and transpersonal).[81]

This statement condenses themes found in the 1930 essay on "Spirit and Life" (that is, that Geist is the transformation of Leben) and other published writings (the irreducibility of the "primary phenomenon" of "life"—the inability to trace it to some further reality as its ground or cause). The fourth volume of the *PSF* was constructed as an explication of the notions of the Urphänomen of Leben and of Geist as the sphere of meaning. Given the present unedited state of the text it does not seem advisable to attempt here and now to investigate Cassirer's thinking on these questions in that work. But it is important to clarify at least one point, namely, how Cassirer understood his thought to differ from the general orientation of Lebensphilosophie.

The first principle of Lebensphilosophie, "life," is immanent, in contrast to the speculative grounds of traditional metaphysics. Nonetheless life cannot be fully articulated. As the primary phenomenon it can never be explained. Cassirer follows Goethe, holding that life is *unergründlich*, unfathomable, because it can have no ground, no explanation.[82] Life cannot be categorized for it is the source of all categories. To realize this is to be no longer limited to the immediacy of life. To what extent is it possible for Lebensphilosophie to recognize the phenomenon of transcendence? This is the main point of contention in Cassirer's critique of Lebensphilosophie.[83]

Cassirer cautions against understanding *Transzendenz* in its literal spatial sense of "übersteigen," of climbing or rising up. The notion of transcendence should not be confused with the concept of the transcendent in the sense of a *Jenseits*, a "beyond." Cassirer criticizes life philosophy, however, for truncating the meaning of *transcendence*. Simmel speaks of the "immanence" of life's transcendence.[84] Life is "more-life," that is, it always goes beyond itself in the sense that it is a self-perpetuating process. It is also "more than life" because it creates something which becomes autonomous and follows its own laws: culture. This is the source of what Simmel calls the "tragedy of culture," the fact that cultural works accumulate and finally overwhelm the creativity of life.[85] Simmel's concept of life as "more-life," like Nietzsche's emphasis on life as "overcoming" (*Überwindung*), emphasizes the here and now over the timeless and the particular over the general. This emphasis on the concrete is also illustrated by Bergson's appeal to the intuition of duration (*durée*) over the abstraction of clock time (*le temp*) or Heidegger's conception of "authenticity" in contrast to the lifeless formalism of "das man." Cassirer is critical of all these thinkers and of Lebensphilosophie in general for one fundamental reason: life philosophy's break with the idealist tradition limited the concept of transcendence in a way that made it impossible to conceive of generally valid ideals, be they ethical or theoretical. Instead of transforming the idealist tradition, Lebensphilosophie turned against it.

The autonomy of cultural creations arises, Simmel says, with the "Umschlag der Form aus ihrer vitalen in ihre ideale Geltung," the shift of form from its vital to its ideal validity.[86] For Simmel this is a tragic turn. Following Lotze's discussion of ideal validity, *Geltung* had been a prime topic of discussion among neo-Kantians. (Heidegger refers to the term as a *Wortgötzen*, an idolized word.)[87] Cassirer grants the social reality of the problem of alienation expressed in Simmel's conception of the tragedy of culture, but he rejects the tendency in Lebensphilosophie to limit transcendence to the sphere of "life" and so deny the transcendence of the ideal.

In a 1933 essay on Bergson's ethics and philosophy of religion Cassirer distinguished between a philosophy of life in which intuited time links us with the past so as to establish an ethics of repetition and a philosophy in which time is anticipatory in the sense of a vision of the future.[88] Time in the former sense limits us to an ethics of the family and the nation; time in the latter sense leads to the "Ethos der absoluten Gemeinschaft," the ethos of the absolute community, namely, the ideal of humanity (ibid., 28). The normative validity of the ideal is a problem for all Lebensphilosophie insofar as it remains bound to what occurs here and now. For such philosophy the ideal is a mere abstraction. The idea, as something "above time" and eternal (Unzeitliches, Ewiges) has no place in a "mere Lebensphilosophie."[89] As Cassirer formulates the key problem concerning life philosophy, "How can the transcendence of the Idea be reconciled with the immanence of Life?" (PEC, 866).

Despite Cassirer's criticism of idealism as panlogism, he upholds the idealists' claim that there is a reality above time (überzeitlich) and above the individual (überpersönlich).[90] This is the sphere of meaning, Sinn, which transcends existence. Cassirer insists upon distinguishing between meaning and existence. This was his main point of dispute with Heidegger's Being and Time. Cassirer differentiates his outlook from Heidegger's this way: "For us meaning is by no means exhausted by Dasein, rather 'there is' impersonal meaning ["es gibt" unpersönlichen Sinn] which, of course, is only experienceable for an existing subject. Cf. mathematical meaning, there is objective meaning in the sense of significance (= "mind" [Geist]). There is, finally, a breaking away from the merely ontological, without actually tearing the bond with it."[91] This "breaking away" of meaning from being is Cassirer's conception of transcendence. He rejects the existentialist view of meaning, which regards it solely as an epiphenomenon of "care" (Sorge), that is, attached to things in a way that is bound to the pragmatic dimension of life. Cassirer takes up Heidegger's play on the German es gibt, "there is" (literally, "it gives"). Heidegger challenges the idealist claim that "es gibt" eternal truth: "Because the kind of Being that is essential to truth is of the character of Dasein, all truth is relative to Dasein's Being."[92] Cassirer denies this. The fact that meaning is only experienceable for an existing subject does not limit its Geltung, its intersubjective validity, to finite experience.

Mathematical meaning is perhaps the clearest example of this transcendence of meaning. Cassirer stresses that the general phenomenological principle according to which being (Sein) is synonymous with "being constituted" does not permit introducing the temporality of the existing subject into this constitution process (PSF, 3:404; PsF, 3:472). In particular, he criticized Brouwer's version of intuitionism and Oskar Becker's phenomenological theory of mathematics for making such a mistake by misconceiving the role of time in mathematics. Brouwer and Becker (an associate and follower of Heidegger at Marburg) both conceive the time of mathematics as the time of the mathematician. But the psychological time in the act of counting, that is, the finite time of the mathematician's life, is not the time of number. The time of number is merely the relational element of "ordering or ordered sequence" (Reihung, geordnete Folge), not change. "This 'objective' time of mathematics must not be confused with 'historical' time, or with the 'experienced' time of the mathematician" (PSF, 3:404n; PsF, 3:472n). The "time" of mathematics is not that of things, events, or psychic acts but simply serial order. Mathematical truths can be considered eternal truths because mathematics is neither an empirical science of things nor a psychological activity creating imaginary objects. It is essentially a "new and powerful symbolism" (EM, 212).

In discussing the nature of mathematics (EM, 212–14; PK, 77–78; EP, 4:84–85; PSF, 3: part 3, chap. 4) Cassirer always makes the point that mathematics is not less ideally valid if conceived of as essentially a symbolic form than if conceived of as a Platonic form. Mathematics is essentially relational (PSF, 3:385, 395; PsF, 3:450,461). The system of numbers and natural number series is the simplest sort of mathematical relation, while higher mathematics consists of more complex systems of relations (EM, 213). Because of its relational character, mathematics can be conceived as an ordering, yet this is not to say that mathematical statements owe their validity to their actually being constructed. Cassirer disagrees with Brouwer's version of intuitionism because it follows such a line of thought, thereby "dissolving the objective idea of number in the subjective act of enumeration and hence submerging the principle of idealism in that of psychologism" (PSF, 3:373; PsF, 3:436). Similarly, Cassirer disagrees with the nominalistic tendency of Hilbert's "formalism," which reduces mathematics simply to signs conceived as marks on the page (PSF, 3:381; PsF, 3:445). Mathematical symbolism, like all symbolism, is for Cassirer rather "a mode of objectivization" (PSF, 3:383; PsF, 3:448).

Mathematics evolves through the production of ever more refined systems of signs. Cassirer indicates that his approach to mathematics shares Leibniz's conviction that it is the power of signs to concentrate thought and so liberate mathematical reasoning from the concrete (PSF, 3:389; PsF, 3:454). The spirit of Cassirer's "semiotic" approach to mathematics may be Leibnizian, but one can nonetheless discern that the basis of Cassirer's conception of mathematics is his own doctrine of symbolic pregnance. Although not mentioned by name, symbolic pregnance serves as the focal point of Cassirer's discussion of the power of mathematical symbols to formulate "transcendent" conceptions such as types of infinity: "We grasp 'meaning' [Bedeutung] only by referring it back to 'intuition' [Anschauung], just as intuition can never be given to us otherwise than in regard to meaning. If we hold fast to this insight, the symbolic factor in our knowledge will no longer be in danger of splitting into an immanent and a transcendent component. The symbolic is immanence and transcendence in one, for in it a fundamentally supra-intuitive meaning is expressed in intuitive form" (PSF, 3:385; PsF, 3:450). The signs used by mathematicians are always sensory objects, yet their significance transcends the intuitive world. Cassirer finds this systematic conception confirmed by Hilbert's famous formulation that in mathematics "the infinite is methodologically grounded and secured by means of the finite" (ibid.).

The validity of mathematics, its ideality, is based on the transcendence of meaning. In his theory of mathematics, as everywhere else in Cassirer's philosophy, the Urphänomen of symbolic pregnance is the final basis for the objectivity of understanding. In the case of mathematics, the world of "ordinative forms" (PSF, 3:383; PsF, 3:447), Cassirer finds the symbolic relationship in its purest sense. Yet mathematical relations are but an instance of the relationality of symbolic pregnance. This point provides Cassirer's solution to the problem of the objectivity of mathematics. By reference to the symbolic pregnance of signs themselves Cassirer does not need to postulate the existence of transcendent entities as the objects of mathematics or limit mathematics to the immanent psychological activity of the mathematician.

The philosophy of life would reduce all relations of meaning, including mathematical relations, to concrete existence. Taking mathematics as "the science which strives to master the infinite with finite means," Oskar Becker says that this definition points immediately and necessarily to the mathematician himself (PSF, 3:405n; PsF, 3:473n). Becker focuses on the mathematician's use of "finite means," Cassirer on the mastery of the infinite. Where Becker considers the mathematician, Cassirer considers the sign. Mathematical signs, while finite, transcend finitude. The time form of mathematics is eternity because it accrues not to the thought of the mathematician as a finite historical person but to a system of symbolism. The notion of mathematical "eternal truths" is justified because it refers not to the thoughts of persons or existing things but to meanings embodied by symbols.

Meaning itself is never merely a sensory psychological content. The

Urphänomen of symbolic pregnance cannot be explained by any psychological process because it is presupposed in every psychological phenomenon.

The symbol is Cassirer's master key to the problem posed by life philosophy: how to take full cognizance of historical life without sacrificing the transcendence of the ideal. As a philosopher of culture, Cassirer was concerned with this problem in other areas besides mathematics. The normative ideal of truth and, more important, ideals of morality were called into question by Lebensphilosophie. In these cases too, Cassirer's interpretation of normative ideals depends upon his theory of the symbol.

II

PHILOSOPHY AND CULTURE

The philosophy of culture originated in the eighteenth century with thinkers such as Vico, Herder, Voltaire, and Rousseau. In the late nineteenth and early twentieth centuries, the neo-Kantians developed their *Kulturphilosophie*. For Kant the concept of culture had its place in the philosophy of history. Kant contends that history has a purpose even though no plan can be attributed to the individuals who act out the course of history.[1] This purpose resides in the ideal of morality, which "belongs to culture" (ibid.). *Kultur* simply means the cultivation of man's capacities.[2] The concept of culture, like that of history, was important to Kant only insofar as it related to ethics. The neo-Kantians went much further, eventually taking Kulturphilosophie to encompass all of philosophy. In the Marburg school, culture was conceived as "the common effort of all mankind," yet this effort was taken to be essentially cognitive and focused upon the "work of science."[3] In the Baden school, the philosophy of culture was synonymous with the philosophy of history. Windelband asserts in his programmatic essay "Kulturphilosophie und transzendentaler Idealismus" (Philosophy of culture and transcendental idealism) that Kant's transcendental philosophy is itself essentially a philosophy of culture because culture is "the totality of that which human consciousness makes (*herausarbeitet*) of the given by virtue of its rational character."[4] In contrast to the Marburg view, Windelband maintains that Kant developed his philosophy through a critique of science merely because science was a way to limit the claims of metaphysics.

The main point of transcendental philosophy is Kant's insight that even in that which we are used to taking as something given, there is—as soon as something is present as a generally valid experience—actually a synthesis according to the laws of "consciousness in general" [Bewußtsein überhaupt], according to overreaching, objectively valid forms of reason . . . so it is by an inner necessity that critical philosophy, which was unfolded as a method in reference to the problem of science, has become, without intending to do so, in terms of what it achieves, a philosophy of culture—*the* philosophy of culture. With this consciousness of creative synthesis, culture has come to self-knowledge: for it is in its inner essence nothing else. (Ibid., 287, 289)

This line of thought permits Windelband to proclaim that "History is the true Organon of philosophy."[5]

Cassirer's conception of the philosophy of culture more closely resembles Windelband's view than it does the Marburg school's epistemological emphasis. Cassirer presents the philosophy of culture as the philosophy of history. In his 1936 essay "Critical Idealism as a Philosophy of Culture" (SMC, 64–91), he asserts that culture is not essentially something theoretical, a body of knowledge, but a "system of actions" (SMC, 65). In the *Essay on Man*, too, Cassirer speaks of culture as "the system of human activities" (EM, 68). Culture is the totality of activities that produce what we call human history. The paramount question raised by the philosophy of culture is, What is the goal of human activity? Cassirer's answer depends upon his conception of meaning and the symbol, which provides his first philosophy.

The first concept in Cassirer's philosophy of culture is meaning, not "consciousness in general." Cassirer seeks to understand the basis of culture by asking, What are culture's basic symbolic forms? His answer is myth, language, and technical activity (*Technik*). There are other important symbolic forms, such as art, science, or history, but these are not, in the literal sense of the word, "primitive" forms of culture since they can only develop from the fundamental forms. This also holds for philosophy itself.

Philosophy is a later development in the history of culture. Cassirer is acutely conscious of this and—like Hegel— he is especially aware of the place of his own thought in the history of philosophy. The philosophy of culture serves Cassirer as a medium for reflection on philosophy. In this regard it fulfills the function for Cassirer that the *Phenomenology of Mind* did for Hegel. The philosophy of culture enables Cassirer to give an account of the origin of philosophy and, ultimately, of the philosophy of symbolic forms. This origin is language.

Cassirer was a pioneer in the philosophy of language. He emphasizes that "philosophical awareness arises only in and through language" (PSF, 1:117; PsF, 1:55) and that without language there would be no culture. Hence, he considers it especially important for the philosophy of culture to begin with a philosophy of language. He notes that Cohen and Dilthey, among others, failed to see this.[6]

Cassirer's approach to language is historically reflective. Like Vico and Herder before him, Cassirer emphasizes the primacy of expressive, poetic speech over "ordinary," commonsense discourse about objects. Cassirer's attention to language's early fusion with mythic thought is diametrically opposed to the view expressed by Willard van Orman Quine that "our ordinary language of physical things is about as basic as language gets."[7] For Quine, Cassirer's claim that language originates with mythic thought is historical only, a description of the phylogenetic development of habits of symbolization (ibid., 122; cf. 80). But as Cassirer wrote in the Essay on Man, "In our study of language, art, and myth the problem of meaning takes precedence over the problem of historical development. . . . This structural view of culture must precede the merely historical view" (p. 60).

Cassirer uses the term structural here in its contemporary sense— for a methodology developed primarily in linguistics by Ferdinand de Saussure, N. S. Trubetzkoy, Roman Jakobson, and others, but with clear parallels in fields such as biology (in the evolutionary theory of Goethe, Cuvier, and Geoffry de Sainte-Hilaire) and in Gestalt psychology.[8] Cassirer's lecture "Structuralism in Modern Linguistics," read to the Linguistic Circle of New York on February 10, 1945, has been called the first pronouncement of structuralism as an interdisciplinary methodology.[9] Among the many points of agreement between Cassirer's own method of thought in the PSF and contemporary structuralism,[10] is his use of the concept of transformation rather than causality. "Transformations" in language, in perception, and in biological processes, Cassirer claims, are radically different from mechanical processes so that the concept of causality is inapplicable to them.[11] They can be described and systematized, but they are inaccessible to a causal explanation. Cassirer's developmental studies of symbolic forms are about structural transformations, which are not subject to causal explanation. I do not want to suggest that Cassirer's PSF should be understood primarily in terms of structuralism or to minimize the importance in Cassirer's philosophy of the "transcendental method" or dialectical thinking. Yet his claim to provide "structural" rather than "historical" explications of the symbolic forms should be taken seriously.

In the general introduction to the PSF, Cassirer proposes to pursue a method for understanding the development of culture that does not simply reiterate the history of the symbolic forms (PSF, 1:84; PsF, 1:16). The PSF approaches the history of culture as a study of the morphology of symbolic forms. The result is an *ideal* history. This ideal history includes a particular understanding of the history of philosophy based upon Cassirer's theory of language.

Cassirer's theory of language has been treated almost exclusively as epistemology while its ontological aspects have been largely ignored or misunderstood.[12] Thinking that Cassirer's theory of language commits a genetic fallacy, Quine feels justified in passing it by with the comment that it is "itself no argument against preserving and prizing the abstract ontology," that is, the ontology implicit in "our ordinary language about physical things."[13] Cassirer's philosophy does not permit such ontological favoritism. Being cannot be divorced from the ways of having a world; ontology cannot be separated from the philosophy of culture. Myth, language, and technology are ways in which the world has being: "The manifold character of the meanings of being do not stand in contradiction to the demand for the unity of being. It is this manifoldness that actually fulfills the demand for this unity."[14] Language is not only a way of having a world, it is the medium for discourse about the term *being*. Therefore Cassirer began the PSF with a discussion of language and being.

Cassirer begins the PSF with the statement: "Philosophical speculation began with the concept of *being*" (PSF, 1:73; PsF, 1:3). The question "What is being?" was at first taken concretely. "The early Pre-Socratic philosophers attempted to determine the beginning and origin, the ultimate 'foundation' of all being: the question was stated clearly, but the concrete, determinate answers given were not adequate to this supreme, universal formulation" (PSF, 1:73; PsF, 1:3). With Plato the question took a new turn; instead of directly inquiring about what is, Plato asked about the very concept of being (PSF, 1:74): "Plato claims that he is the first to attain the concept and problem of Being. Whereas all the earlier thinkers, as much as they sought to determine or define [*bestimmen*] being [*Sein*] as such, basically had only spoken about beings [*Seienden*]."[15] Plato reformulated the problem by showing the conflict between Parmenides' distinction of being and nonbeing and pointing out that in discourse these are interwoven. In the course of differentiating among things in language "what is not, in some respect has being, and conversely that what is, in a way is not."[16] For Cassirer, this paradox and the limits of Greek and medieval ontology derive from their interpretation of being as substance (*ousia, substantia*), unchanging thinglike reality. Even Aristotle's purely logical theories constantly refer to the basic conception of substance, which is the basis of the logic of generic classes. *Substance and Function* offers Cassirer's logical objections to the primacy of the concept of substance (*SF/ET*, 3–9); his ontological objections must be gleaned from his comments on the growing awareness of language among philosophers.

Scholasticism remained completely within the framework of the metaphysical conception of substance. The humanists of the Renaissance were the first to break sharply with this mode of thought. They focused upon the language of scholasticism and their criticisms, Cassirer points out, were not just stylistic. The humanists attacked the primacy scholasticism gave to abstract substantives, nouns like *entitas, quidditas, haecceitas*. In scholastic philosophy, Cassirer says, "all characteristics and activities were transformed into thing-like substances" (*EP*, 1:122). The humanists' view of man did not permit such an essentialistic, substantial, and nonhistorical metaphysics.

For Cassirer the Renaissance was not a mere rejuvenation of past philosophy, but a genuine new beginning. Ancient and medieval thought conceived being as the immutable and eternal. Renaissance thought reverses this evaluation of the timeless object of metaphysics and theology. The Humanist Giovanni Pico della Mirandola stands as the pivotal figure in this reevaluation.

It is an extraordinarily bold step of Pico's to reverse at this
point the conventional metaphysical and theological estimate.
The latter proceeds from the basic notion that the highest and
indeed in the end the only value belongs to what is immutable
and eternal. This notion pervades Plato's theory of knowledge
and Aristotle's metaphysics and cosmology. With them is
joined the medieval religious worldview, which sets the goal
of all human activity in eternity, and which sees in the multiplicity, in the mutability, in the inconstancy of human action
but a sign of its vanity. So long as man fails to master this inner unrest of his, and in so far as he fails to end and conquer
it, he cannot find the way to God. "Inquietum est cor nostrum,
donec requiescat in te."
But with Pico this inner unrest of man, impelling him from
one goal to another, and forcing him to pass from one form to
another, no longer appears as a mere stigma upon human nature, as a mere blot and weakness. . . . This is man's privileged
position: unlike any other creature, he owes his moral character to himself. He is what he *makes* of himself—and he derives from himself the pattern he shall follow. . . . The likeness
to God is not a gift bestowed on man to begin with, but an

achievement for him to work out: it is *to be brought about* by man himself.[17]

This turn toward the centrality of subjectivity in the modern epoch of philosophy has a characteristic expression in Kant's doctrine of the "primacy of practical reason." In Kant's philosophy, Cassirer says, "the world of being is transformed into a world of deed" (*KLT*, 420). To Cassirer Kant represents the peak of the Enlightenment, just as the Enlightenment represents the high point in the philosophical movement that began with the Renaissance. The pendulum swings back toward the philosophy of substance in Hegel's philosophy, which brought the modern epoch to a kind of end with the equation of "substance" and "subject." In Hegel's system the historical process "stands still."[18]

After Hegel's attempt to conjoin the metaphysics of substance with the centrality of the subjective, philosophy undergoes a reorientation. Now, action becomes the foremost concern of philosophy. "Its 'subjective' trend has led philosophy [in the early twentieth century] more and more to focus the totality of its problems in the concept of life rather than the concept of being" (*PSF*, 1:111; *PsF*, 1:48). Lebensphilosophie investigates the concrete world of human activity, that is, historical reality. This emphasis on action is the sense of Cassirer's oft-quoted remark in the *PSF* that "the critique of reason becomes the critique of culture" (*PSF*, 1:80; *PsF*, 1:11). The claim that philosophy after Hegel is concerned chiefly with action or praxis has been widely discussed;[19] Cassirer adopts the notion of "life" (Leben) as the name for this systematic focal point of thought.

Because of his emphasis on action, Cassirer uses traditional philosophical terminology in new ways, giving these terms a nonsubstantialistic meaning. A prime example of this is his use of the term *Geist* ("mind" or "spirit"). *Geist*, he says, is a transformation of *Leben*, not a substance or something static.

We must not understand the term "Geist" or spirit as designating a metaphysical entity opposed to another called "matter." If we accept the radical dualism between body and soul, matter and spirit, between "substantia extensa" and "substantia cognitians," language becomes, indeed, a continuous miracle. In this case, every act of speech would be a sort of trans-substantiation. Speech is meaning—an incorporeal thing—expressed in sounds, which are material things. The term "Geist" is correct; but we must not use it as a name of a substance—a thing "quod in se est et per se concipitur." We should use it in a functional sense as a comprehensive name for all those functions which constitute and build up the world of human culture.[20]

As proof of the indivisibility of language into material and meaningful aspects, Cassirer points to Trubetzkoy's founding of structuralist phonetics, in which the phoneme is a unit of meaning, a part of semantics, rather than something merely physical (ibid., 112–13; see also *EM*, 124–26).

Cassirer's analysis of symbolic pregnance provides his theory of the conditions of the possibility of *any* understanding of the world, but to understand the system of concrete cultural forms a shift in perspective is required akin to that between transcendental philosophy and what Hegel called "Phänomenologie."

For Hegel, phenomenology studies and recalls the way that mind "appears" (*als erscheinend*), that is, objectifies itself in things so as to appear for itself in these as something opposite to itself.[21] Cassirer follows Hegel here: the philosophy of symbolic forms studies the objectification of life in the works of culture and "recollects" it. This recollection is not merely historical. Hegel uses the word *erscheinend* (appearing) to call attention to the fact that the Phänomenologie is not history but the study of the essential. Cassirer stresses that the same dialectic between *Wesen* (essence) and *Erscheinung* (appearance) functions in the *Phenomenology of Mind* as in the *Logic* (*EP*, 3:347–59). When Hegel characterizes the study of the *Phänomenologie des Geistes* as the representation of "appearing knowledge" (*das erscheinende Wissen*) and as the way taken by natural consciousness to true knowledge, he means that it describes something that does not merely happen by chance but manifests itself by necessity.[22] Hegel's thesis that "Das Wesen muß erscheinen" (essence must appear) means in the context of the *Phänomenologie des Geistes* that true philosophical knowledge must appear at the end of a course of development. In every volume of the *PSF*, Cassirer explicitly states that he is following Hegel's conception of phenomenology; each volume shows how the essence of a symbolic form "appears," how each comes to fully present its unique view of the world (*PSF*, 1:83–84, 2:xv–xvi, 3:xiv–xv; *PsF*, 1:15–16, 2:ix–x, 3:vi–vii).

Cassirer wrote a plurality of studies on phenomenology and Hegel a single volume; this fact has architectonic significance. Hegel's *Phänomenologie* is hierarchical. In the *Phenomenology of Mind*, all the earlier stages of thought lead up to the final stage of philosophical knowledge; art and religion are *aufgehoben* in this final stage. Cassirer's conception of phenomenology does not take the different symbolic forms as stages in single, linear, overall development, but as forces effective in the development of culture at every point. For Cassirer, the different symbolic forms of culture enjoy an autonomy that Hegel's panlogism does not permit. The series of symbolic forms in Cassirer's *Essay on Man*, for example, does not constitute a hierarchy. The order in which he presents the symbolic forms does not entail seeing the last one—science—as replacing the earlier ones. Cassirer's architectonic is centrifugal. The symbolic forms separate and fan out from the first form of myth and henceforth remain opposed. Language, at first completely bound up with myth, becomes the vehicle for logical discourse and this in turn is the basis on which science evolves. Hand in hand with this, the technical manipulation of the world through tools (a feat which is also at first inseparable from mythic conceptions of the efficacy of things) leads to a view of the world composed of physical, "natural" things. But language leads not only to science; as poetry, language becomes art. The forms of social morality undergo similar development, from the stage of mythic taboo and custom to rule by law. Cassirer describes the process this way:

Here we encounter a law that holds equally for all symbolic forms, and bears essentially on their evolution. None of them arises initially as separate, independently recognizable forms, but every one of them must first be emancipated from the common matrix of myth. . . . Theoretical, practical, and aesthetic consciousness, the world of language and of morality, the basic forms of the community and the state—they are all originally tied up with mythico-religious conceptions. (*LM*, 44)

This "law that holds equally for all symbolic forms" is the principle underlying Cassirer's version of Hegelian phenomenology. In the third volume of the *PSF* Cassirer says that he follows Hegel's conception of phenomenology, but that he disagrees with its foundations and its development (*PSF*, 3:xv; *PsF*, 3:vii). Cassirer's objection to the reductionism of Hegel's panlogism was discussed above; in the *PSF* the theory of the symbol replaces "Logic." The "law" that underlies the development of the symbolic forms in culture derives from the nature of symbolism. Cassirer agrees with Hegel that "the whole cannot be presented all at once but must be unfolded progressively by thought in its own autonomous movement and rhythm" (*PSF*, 3:xiv; *PsF*, 3:vi), but for Cassirer this progressive unfolding ends with a series of autonomous symbolic forms.

Hegel compared his phenomenology to a ladder that had been extended to natural consciousness so as to permit it to attain the level of philosophy or "science." Cassirer says that to begin he "must first set this ladder lower" (*PSF*, 2:xvi; *PsF*, 2:xi). Hegel begins with the problem of certainty, which is already a matter of scientific concern. Cassirer begins with the mythic roots of scientific thought: "Our insight into the development of science—taken in the ideal, not temporal sense—is complete only if it shows how science arose in and worked itself out of the sphere of mythical immediacy and explains the law and direction of this movement" (*PSF*, 2:xvi; *PsF*, 2:xi).

The "law" and direction of the development of thought—from its origin in mythic thinking—derives from the nature of symbolism. For example, the development of language from its early fusion with myth stems from the direction of symbolism's "ideal, not temporal" development.

Cassirer identifies three stages in the development of symbolic forms, stages he terms "mimetic," "analogical," and "purely symbolic."[23] In the first, understanding adheres closely to the concrete sensory world of objects. In the second, understanding is oriented toward the activity of the subject. In the third, the symbolic character of interpretation comes to full realization and application. This is an ideal, not a historical, progression. Like the Hegelian dialectic's movement from *an-sich* to *für-sich* and, finally, to *an und für sich*, Cassirer's analysis of the mimetic, analogical, and purely symbolic meaning has methodological significance and application; it is not an empirical theory.

The development of the concept of number can serve as an example of Cassirer's dialectic. Ethnological research has shown that in primitive cultures numbers have names standing for things or parts of the body. The word for five can mean that "the hand is closed," the word for six that a jump has to be made to the other hand in counting (*PSF*, 3:342; *PsF*, 3:399). Clinical studies of patients suffering from aphasia show that they may be able to count concrete things or count on their fingers, but they find numerals meaningless (*PSF*, 3:253–54; *PsF*, 3:296–97). In both cases number only has a mimetic meaning, closely following objects in the world. In the analogical phase of meaning mental activity is the focal point. Number can be regarded in terms of mental activity, such as counting or computation, without regard to the particular counted objects; in this case, number is understood psychologically. A purely symbolic conception of number regards it neither in terms of psychological activity nor in reference to things, but as a specific form of symbolic interpretation with a validity of its own. In the philosophy of mathematics the series of natural numbers is regarded as a relational "order in progression" without reference to the counting subject (*PSF*, 3:404n; *PsF*, 3:472n). The validity of mathematics is thereby anchored in the medium of mathematics itself. The full development of mathematics disregards the question of how well it copies the world; rather, mathematics is perceived as a way of having or understanding a world. The same holds for all symbolic forms. The symbolic interpretation does not copy a given world; it makes a world accessible.

Cassirer makes use of the distinction between mimetic, analogical, and purely symbolic phases of understanding in his accounts of all the different symbolic forms.[24] One might ask whether this distinction can be applied to philosophy itself. This raises the question whether philosophy can be categorized as a symbolic form. Cassirer never discusses philosophy in such terms. To say that philosophy is a symbolic form would mean that it is a particular, unique way of having a world, but that it is not. Philosophy is for Cassirer the activity of reflecting on the unity and purport of the ways of understanding or having a world. Although philosophy does not provide a particular way of having a world, the history of philosophy as Cassirer understood it clearly reflects the process of interpretation defined by the three stages of mimetic, analogical, and purely symbolic meaning.

Philosophy began with reflection on being, discovered the activity of subjectivity, and, finally, arrived at reflection upon the phenomenon of meaning itself. This conception of philosophy's history puts Cassirer's own thinking on symbolic forms in the perspective in which he himself regarded it: as part of a new phase of philosophy in which language and meaning become its first concern. This development leads to a new formulation of philosophy's original questions. In order to develop the problem of meaning as first philosophy Cassirer had to broaden the ordinary conception of symbolism to give it a universal sense. To do so required distinguishing among three symbolic functions.

Expression, Representation, and Significance

Cassirer refers to the three symbolic "functions"—expression (*Ausdruck*), representation (*Darstellung*), and pure significance (*reine Bedeutung*)—as "dimensions" of meaning (*PSF*, 3:448; *PsF*, 3:525). These are not phases or stages, and they cannot be reduced to one another. None can assume the role of the other. Expression is the most elementary function of meaning because "it does not admit of a difference between image and thing, the sign and what it designates" (*PSF*, 3:93; *PsF*, 3:109). An image is expressive simply as a physiognomic configuration. As soon as an image is regarded as depicting something else, that is, as having a referential relationship to something else, its function is representative.

This difference can be illustrated with the one-word sentences "Yes" and "No." In the language of the child these initially have a purely expressive meaning; they are used to give vent to desire or dislike. They acquire a representative function when they are used logically to affirm or negate some propositional content (PSF, 3:109; PsF, 3:128). The prime example of the representative function of language is the copula is (see PSF, 3:450, PsF, 3:527; STS, 10). A sign has a representative function when "a relationship in being is asserted which is supposed to maintain 'in itself' and is conceived to be accessible and essentially understandable in the same way to every sensitive, perceiving, and thinking subject."[25] Language is essential to having such a "realistic" understanding of the world. Cassirer calls particular attention to the fact that the entire course of Hegel's *Phenomenology of Mind* depends upon the fact that thought is not just opinion, but something put forth in language and so capable of being contradicted (EP, 3:314–15). When "yes" and "no" are only used to express desire or repulsion they cannot be logically contradicted because they have no truth content. They express a wish, but they cannot be true or false.

This is the case with all expressive symbolism. It does not "represent." Cassirer says that the use of language in magic follows the principle that Freud calls the "omnipotence of thought," the belief that everything can be made to submit to desire (PSF, 2:157n; PsF, 2:188n). This occurs, for example, in the symbolism of dreams, which lacks the idea of contradiction.[26] Dreams, the magical worldview of myth, and the expressive awareness of the child all share the symbolism of the expressive image. Cassirer traces the function of expressive symbolism to sense perception itself. Insofar as perceived phenomena appear to us as agitating, soothing, gloomy, joyful, pacifying, or otherwise exhibiting a mood, they exemplify what Cassirer calls expressive symbolism.

Whereas the expressive and representative functions of symbolism are closely related to the world we live in and perceive with the senses, the significative function is purely conceptual. Cassirer's favorite example of purely significative meaning is an axiomatic system, whose sense does not rely upon or derive from sensory reality.

I should note that Cassirer's conception of symbolism has met with criticism. At a lecture given by Cassirer in 1927, one discussant claimed that Cassirer's theory regards meaning as fundamentally "not a phenomenon of culture, but a natural fact of animal life" (STS, 30). Cassirer could agree with the former statement but not the latter. The Urphänomen of meaning is not a product of culture, something made or invented. Yet it is not just a "fact of animal life" and can have no naturalistic explanation.

A more recent, but similar, criticism of Cassirer's conception of symbolism is found in Paul Ricoeur's *Freud and Philosophy*. Ricoeur claims that Cassirer's extension of the conception of symbolism to describe the whole field of awareness erases a true dividing line: the distinction between univocal and plurivocal expressions. The former do not demand interpretation, whereas the latter do. Hence, Ricoeur contends, the word *symbolism* is best reserved only for the latter. Plurivocal expressions constitute the field of hermeneutic research. Cassirer recognizes the distinction that Ricoeur wants to uphold; in *An Essay on Man* he adopts Morris's designations *signals* and *symbols* to mark this difference: "Signals and symbols belong to two different universes of discourse: a signal is a part of the physical world of being; a symbol is a part of the human world of meaning" (*EM*, 32). Signals, such as the Pavlovian dinner bell, are univocal; symbols are plurivocal. Hermeneutics is the process of interpretation (*Verfahren der Deutung*) of works of culture (*KW*, 97; *LH*, 173). It can attempt to determine the meaning (Sinn) these works had to those who produced them or show the different meanings they acquired historically. Cassirer's conception of hermeneutics does not differ essentially from Ricoeur's. But to define the symbolic function, as Ricoeur does, "to mean something other than what is said"[27] would destroy Cassirer's basic position that symbolism is the root of the perception of expression. Ricoeur points to the fact that dreams are the "royal road to psychoanalysis," in which the psychoanalyst interprets manifest meanings to find their hidden sense (ibid., 15). R. H. Hook, a psychoanalyst, says that Ricoeur's criticism of Cassirer begins with a view of symbolism that does justice to the psychoanalyst's effort of interpretation, which is a kind of logical reconstruction, but that Cassirer's conception of the expressive function of symbols provides a theory of meaning as it is immediately experienced, prior to such secondary interpretation. The psychoanalyst translates the expressive symbolism of the dream into the representational symbolism of discursive language. The formation of dream images occurs by different symbolic processes than those utilized for their interpretation. Hook says that "to follow Ricoeur would be to remain on the secondary process level and to fail to penetrate to the roots of symbolic formation."[28]

Cassirer himself gave little attention to the interpretation of dreams, but numerous authors have seen his theory of mythic symbolism in this light. Alfred Lorenzer calls attention to the fact that Freud's distinction between "primary process" (*Primärprozess*) and "secondary process" (*Sekundärprozess*) agrees in virtually every detail with Cassirer's distinction between mythic thought and the representational thinking inherent in discursive language (based on the *Darstellungsfunktion*). Lorenzer concludes: "It is remarkable that Cassirer arrives at a description of mythic thought that corresponds exactly to Freud's presentation of 'processes affected by a primary process.' "[29] The details of Freud's explication of a primary process, the condensation (*Verdichtung*) of content in a dream raising its intensity (*Intensität*), the free use of associations in forming images, the lack of contradiction, the predominance of an impossible wish or desire, the infantile disregard of practical feasibility—all these aspects are also found in Cassirer's theory of mythic thinking. Subsequent independent research on myth has substantiated many connections between mythic thought and what Freud called a primary process, as has the rise of the interdisciplinary field of ethnopsychoanalysis.[30]

One might ask, then, why Cassirer himself did not pay more attention to Freud's work. Susanne Langer explains Cassirer's neglect of Freud by pointing to Freud's strictly practical interest in adjustment and to his tendency to regard every aspect of culture—from religion, art, and learning to social reform—as so many avenues of personal gratification and sublimation of the passions. She rightly judges that this hedonistic view of culture had to seem devastating to Cassirer, since it obliterates the normative issue of the aim of culture.[31] I, too, think that this colored Cassirer's view of Freud and obscured for him their undeniable agreement on many questions, preventing Cassirer from considering the possible constructive results of comparing the theory of myth and the theory of the interpretation of dreams and psychoanalysis generally.[32]

In addition to these considerations, the attempt to limit the theory of symbolism in the way suggested by Ricoeur is also objectionable from Cassirer's point of view on purely philosophical grounds. It would deprive philosophy of a way to unite the different levels of meaning illustrated by the difference between a dreamed dream and a dream as the object of a psychoanalyst's interpretation. A dream subjected to conscious interpretation enters into the process of logical interpretation through verbal language. Manifest meanings experienced in the dream are then interpreted to stand for something else in the dreamer's waking life, a conflict or suppressed wish or fear of some sort. But the dream as dreamed does not "stand for" something else; its images affect the dreamer initially in a "naive" manner. The difference between the interpretation of a dream through language and the experience of a dream exemplifies the difference between what Cassirer termed the representational and the expressive function of symbolism.

Cassirer's hope of unifying the diverse forms of culture in a philosophy of symbolic forms requires a common denominator. Without it, he says, "we lose our eye for the whole" (PSF, 3:48; PsF, 3:57). The theory of expressive meaning is especially important because it provides access to the origins of culture.

Expression, the Image, and Myth

The perception of expressive meaning has a cognitive function: "it is the *image* which opens up the true essentially and makes it knowable" (PSF, 3:69; PsF, 3:81). Although the word *image* usually calls to mind something seen, the symbolism of the "image" does not just exist in the visual field; it is characteristic of sensory awareness as such. Cassirer says that "the reality we apprehend is in its original form not a reality of a determinate world of things, originating apart from us; rather it is the certainty of a living efficacy that we experience" (PSF, 3:72–73; PsF, 3:86). This "living efficacy" (*lebendige Wirksamkeit*) has the unity of a dramatic occurrence, not the static character of the "thing." In the perception of the world as expressive, "the being that is apprehended in perception confronts us not as a reality of things, of mere objects, but as a kind of presence of living subjects. . . . The farther we trace back perception, the greater becomes the preeminence of the 'thou' form over the 'it' form" (PSF, 3:62–63; PsF, 3:73–74). Cassirer's thesis is that perception "discloses certain original traits in which, one might say, it approaches the mode and direction of myth" (PSF, 3:61; PsF, 3:72). Cassirer's conception of the image should be understood in terms of the "living efficacy" of the mythic perception of expression.

For Cassirer, myth or mythic thought includes much more than narratives about heroes and gods. These occupy a later, less elementary place in the scheme of mythic thought. "Taken in themselves the mythical stories of gods or heroes cannot reveal to us the secret of religion, because they are nothing but the *interpretations* of rites. They try to give an account of what is present, what is seen and done in these rites" (MS, 28). Myths in this sense provide the epic element in mythic thought, but the rites are the drama itself. At a more basic level, mythic thought is a form of life that possesses a particular mode of perceiving, thinking, and acting. These aspects are seen in the phenomena of mana, taboo, totemism, magical practices, sacrifice, and other rites. From these develop alchemy, astrology, and religion.

Mythic "thought" is a midleading designation because it sounds like a form of ratiocinative activity. Cassirer denies that myth is essentially or primarily theoretical: "It is not mere observation [*Betrachtung*] but action which constitutes the center from which man undertakes the intelligent organization of reality" (*PSF*, 2:157; *PsF*, 2:158).

In his account of religion Cassirer emphasizes active relationships to the gods: the performance of rites, the observance of festivals. In contrast, Lévi-Strauss concentrates on mythical narratives; nonetheless, one of the basic themes in Lévi-Strauss sheds light on Cassirer's conception of the expressive image: the analogy he draws between myth and music.[33] Lévi-Strauss takes the comparison much further than Cassirer does in his discussion of music and myth, yet they are led to it for the same reason, the similarities between the mythic and musical senses of time. Myth and music, as Lévi-Strauss puts it, are "instruments for the obliteration of time."[34] Both derive this capacity to obliterate time from the expressive image.

The visual connotations of the word *image* are misleading. People speak of the "eye of the mind" because the intellect, like the eye, sees what is distant from the body. The expressive image is not so much "seen" or "looked at" from afar as it is "felt"—even if this feeling occurs through the medium of the eye. We are "struck" by what we see or hear, "moved" emotionally. Synesthetic phenomena such as seeing a "hot color" or hearing a "piercing noise" are phenomenologically the most elementary perceptual phenomena, not sense "data" (*PSF*, 3:73; *PsF*, 3:86). Cassirer's contention that the root of myth is the perception of expression (*LH*, 94) means that in mythic awareness all phenomena appear animate. For mythic thought, "A whispering or rustling in the woods, a shadow darting over the ground, a light flickering on the water: all these are demonic . . . but only very gradually does this pandemonium divide into separate and clearly distinguishable figures" (*PSF*, 3:72; *PsF*, 3:84). We normally think of an image as a fixed depiction of something else, but this is not what Cassirer means by an expressive image.

The comparison between myth and music makes this clearer. In keeping with his emphasis on narrative myths, Lévi-Strauss sees all music in terms of program music and links such musical "narration" and mythic narrations to the common root of language.[35] For Lévi-Strauss, language is prior to myth and to music. This is not Cassirer's view. For Lévi-Strauss, in the beginning was the word, but for Cassirer in the beginning was the act. Myth begins with action, in gesture and ritual in response to the world as expressive, and language too develops in conjunction with action.[36] Lévi-Strauss finds the parallel between myth and music to reside in the experience of the listener rather than in that of the shaman-musician (Cassirer's viewpoint). However, both share the view expressed by Durkheim that myth is fundamentally a social phenomenon reflecting a belief that the world is a "society," an organization of "life" (see *EM*, 80). In music and myth this sense of life is characterized by a particular feeling of time.

Music is not merely perceived with the ear; it is felt viscerally; it is lived. Musicians and listeners experience an acceleration or retardation in heartbeat and breathing rhythm in time with the music. The performance of a rite, like the performance of music, takes time, but neither is experienced as the time of clocks or calendars. In rites of passage or initiation, for example, youth, maturity, and old age are like places that are lived in, entered, or left. In mythic rites, time is arrested. Man can reenter the "original time" of the gods; the cult participates in this time. Cassirer calls the temporality of myth—the festivals, the holy days, the ritual events surrounding birth and death, pregnancy and motherhood, puberty and marriage—"a kind of biological time" (*PSF*, 2:109; *PsF*, 2:146). This time is felt, not thought abstractly. The phases of human life take place in a rhythmic unity of time. Cassirer says that there is no mythic "concept of time," but rather a mythic "feeling of time" (*Zeitgefühl*; PSF, 2:119; *PsF*, 2:146). This time is actually timeless: "For myth there is no time 'as such,' no perpetual duration and no regular recurrence or succession; there are only configurations of particular content which in turn reveal a certain temporal *gestalt*, a coming and going, a rhythmical being and becoming. Thus, time as a whole is divided by certain boundaries akin to musical bars. But at first its 'beats' are not measured or counted but immediately felt" (*PSF*, 2:108; *PsF*, 2:133; cf. *PSF*, 1:222–24; *PsF*, 1:178–80).

The concept of a "temporal gestalt" (*Zeitgestalt*), which Cassirer uses to compare the time of music and myth, has been utilized by others to describe the time of music. The Viennese musicologist Viktor Zuckerkandl calls the musical time of melody a "temporal Gestalt": "The existence of the individual tone in a melody is a being directed toward what no longer exists and what does not yet exist; thus past and future are given with and in the present and are experienced with and in the present; hearing a melody is hearing, having heard, and being about to hear, all at once. But the past is not a part of the future because it is remembered, nor is the future a part of the present because it is foreknown or forefelt. Anyone who thinks back to past tones or anticipates coming tones in imagination ceases to hear a melody."[37] Zuckerkandl's idea of a time experience that is prior to the relational concepts of past, present, and future, that is, a time which is the unity of a vital lived experience, illustrates the kind of "biological time" that Cassirer speaks of in his theory of myth. The subject in such time experience is conceivable only as the bodily subjectivity of a concrete living person. The feeling body rather than a thinking consciousness is the subject in the perception of expression. The unity of feeling is always a kind of temporal gestalt or dynamic image.

The most basic form of subjectivity is characterized by bodily feeling—the perception of expression—and action. Knowledge is not initially "about" the world because the world does not initially appear as an "it," but rather as an expressive community of life. Discourse about the world of things as an "it" depends upon the symbolic function of representation. For expressive awareness there is no such distance or disinterest. Here Cassirer's philosophy of symbolic forms converges, to an extent, with existential thinking.

There is no detached, cool stance possible in mythic thought; the essential feature of mythic awareness is that it is overwhelming. Unlike everyday practical action or scientific thinking, mythic thought stands in awe of what confronts it: mythic thought "has no will to understand the object by encompassing it logically and articulating it with a complex of causes and effects; it is simply overpowered by the object" (PSF, 2:74; PsF, 2:94).

This poses the chief difficulty for a philosophical theory of myth. Myth cannot be explained as an invention, as the creation of certain individuals. As Cassirer puts it: "The problem is not the material content of mythology, but the intensity with which it is experienced, with which it is believed—as only something endowed with objective reality can be believed. This basic fact of mythical consciousness suffices to frustrate any attempt to seek its ultimate source in an invention—whether poetic or philosophical. . . . No one who understands what its mythology means to a people, what inner power it possesses over that people and what reality is manifested therein, will say that mythology, any more than language, was invented by individuals" (PSF, 2:5–6; PsF, 2:9). Cassirer does not propose to explain myth by means of metaphysical, psychological, historical, or social causes, but solely to understand the principle that unifies its diverse configurations. He compares his task at this point with Husserl's descriptive phenomenology, which investigates the meaning of phenomena without regard to the question of the "reality" of the objects in question (PSF, 2:11–12; PsF, 2:15–16).

The explicandum in myth is not so much a type of thinking as a way of living: "What we need here is not an explication of mere thoughts or beliefs but an interpretation of mythical life. Myth is not a system of dogmatic creeds. It consists much more in actions than in mere images or representations" (EM, 79). While Cassirer frequently speaks of mythic "thought," the following passage shows how mythic thought is basically a kind of action.

In totemism the totem animal must in general be spared; but there are also cases where, though not eaten by individuals, it is consumed by the clan as a whole at a sacral feast in which definite rites and customs must be observed. This common eating of the totem animal is looked upon as a means of confirming and renewing the blood kinship which unites the individual members of the clan with one another and their totem. Particularly in times of distress, when the community is endangered and its existence threatened, this renewal of its primordial physical-religious power is necessary. But the true accent of the sacral act is performance by the community as a *whole*. In the eating of the flesh of the totem animal the unity of the clan, its relationship with its totemic ancestor, is restored as a sensuous and corporeal unity; we may say that in this feast it is restored forever anew. . . . Sacrifice is not originally a particular action, sharply distinguished from man's common and profane actions; any action at all, however sensuous and practical its content as such, can become a sacrifice as soon as it enters into the specifically religious "perspective" and is determined by it. In addition to the acts of eating and drinking, the sexual act, particularly, can take on a sacral significance. (*PSF*, 2:227; *PsF*, 2:272)

Mythic "thought" is bound to bodily actions, magical practices intended to equalize or ward off forces in the world of action.

Mythic thought is often a response to a danger threatening the community. Fear and its opposite, hope, combine in the fundamental mythic experience of the sacred. The distinction between the sacred and the profane constitutes the basic opposition in mythic thought. Perception of the sacred arises when "mere bestial terror" becomes the perception of expression (*PSF*, 2:78; *PsF*, 2:99). In his review of the second volume of the *Philosophy of Symbolic Forms*, Heidegger comments that Cassirer is too descriptive, taking myth as something "present-at-hand" (*vorhanden*), without accounting for its presence in a way that shows how it is rooted in man's being in the world. Heidegger traces mythic thought's power to overwhelm man to the "Geworfenheit" (thrownness) of human existence. In particular, the fundamental phenomenon of mana—the nonspecified power that adheres to sacred things or events—can be understood, Heidegger says, by recognizing that "in thrownness there is an openness for whatever may be surprisingly extraordinary."[38] This statement reflects Heidegger's view that language and other forms of meaning depend upon a fundamental type of meaning he calls *Bedeutsamkeit* (significance). This arises as things confront the person as an acting being in the world, as Dasein.[39]

Cassirer's characterization of myth also emphasizes the overwhelming power of myth. Cassirer sees the primary mythic experience in the changing expressive face of the world: "Without transition, an impression of the homelike, familiar, sheltering, and protective can shift into its opposite, the inaccessible, terrifying, monstrous, and gruesome (*PSF*, 3:90; *PsF*, 3:106). According to Cassirer's theory of expression, the world is either basically threatening or friendly in character; human awareness begins with an existential and not an intellectual response to the world. It is not surprising that, as Heidegger reports, he and Cassirer agreed in conversation on the need for phenomenology to engage in existential analysis.[40] There is an obvious existential dimension in Cassirer's analysis of myth, yet the only philosopher to my knowledge to call attention to this aspect of Cassirer's thought is Merleau-Ponty.[41]

Merleau-Ponty approves of Cassirer's desire to avoid the "intellectual 'sublimation' of experience" (*intellektuelle 'Sublimierung' der Erfahrung*) and to understand the world of perception as the structure of the world underlying theoretical scientific knowledge: "Cassirer clearly has the same aim when he takes Kant to task for having most of the time analysed only an 'intellectual sublimation of experience,' when he tries to express through the notion of symbolic pregnancy, the absolute simultaneity of matter and form."[42] But Merleau-Ponty also sees an inconsistency in Cassirer or, at least, in his language: "When Cassirer takes up the Kantian formula according to which consciousness can analyze only what it has synthesized, he is manifestly returning to intellectualism despite the phenomenological and even existential analyses which his book contains" (ibid.). Cassirer's language is, in fact, often "Kantian" and "intellectualistic," yet his doctrine is not.

Cassirer's theory of expression precludes "intellectualism," as Merleau-Ponty calls it. "Where the meaning of the world is still that of pure expression, every phenomenon discloses a definite 'character,' which is not merely deduced or inferred from it but which belongs to it immediately. It is in itself gloomy or joyful, agitating or soothing, pacifying or terrifying" (*PSF*, 3:72; *PsF*, 3:84). An intellectualism would regard expressive phenomena as the result of activities of the mind. A strictly existential theory would attempt to understand expression in terms of man's "being-in-the-world," the course suggested by Heidegger in his review of Cassirer's volume on myth. But Cassirer upholds neither an "intellectualist" nor such an existential approach to expressive meaning. He explains neither myth nor expression by postulating "acts of the mind" that create them, nor does he think that an existential approach can suffice to make such phenomena understandable. Both views fail to make contact with the phenomenon of myth.

The chief problem in the interpretation of myth, Cassirer claimed, is the intensity of belief that it commands, an intensity that can only be explained by the fact that the mythic world is experienced as something objectively real. This objectivity derives for Cassirer from the fact that expressive meaning is a *semiotic* phenomenon. As meaning, expression cannot be understood merely as a psychological or biological phenomenon, nor can it, as a phenomenon of meaning, be derived from an analysis of being in the sense of "being-there." Cassirer emphasizes that expression is not the invention of individuals: "All experience and expression are at first a mere passivity, a being-acted-upon rather than an acting—and this receptivity stands in evident contrast to that kind of spontaneity in which all self-consciousness as such is grounded" (*PSF*, 3:75; *PsF*, 3:88). This "objectivity" of expressive meaning is responsible for the universality of myth and gives it a kind of "usurpatory" character. This is the designation that Kant used for mythic notions (without using the term *myth*).

Mythic notions intrude upon Kant in the *Critique of Pure Reason* who admits them reticently under the name of "usurpatory concepts." In his discussion of the idea of a transcendental deduction, Kant says: "But there are also usurpatory concepts [*usurpierte Begriffe*], such as *fortune, fate*, which, though allowed to circulate by almost universal indulgence, are yet from time to time challenged by the question: *quid juris*. This demand for a deduction involves us in considerable perplexity, no clear title, sufficient to justify their employment, being obtainable either from experience or from reason."[43] For Cassirer the "clear title" of myth is obtained from the expressive function of symbolism.

Cassirer proposes to offer a view of the genesis of myth that is not merely psychological or sociological but "structural" in nature (*PSF*, 2:xv; *PsF*, 2:ix). Cassirer's aim is basically the same as Lévi-Strauss's when the latter rejects explanations of myth that refer to a "myth-making faculty" and, instead, seeks "to show, not how men think in myths, but how myths operate in men's minds without their being aware of the fact."[44]

By taking up the perception of expression as a field for philosophical investigation, Cassirer turns against the general direction of the philosophy of perception that has prevailed since Descartes and Locke. Cassirer agreed that it was of great importance in the history of natural science when Galileo declared sensory properties to be "secondary qualities" incidental to the cognition of nature and proposed that mathematics is the "language of the book of nature."[45] This limited perception to a subordinate role in scientific cognition and changed the epistemological status of sensations. Perception's "secondary" qualities—the feelings of the senses with all their expressive content—were now looked upon as data. Cassirer makes a radical distinction between the perception of expression and the perception of things and correlates each with a different symbolic function. The phenomenon of expression provides Cassirer with an approach to epistemology that is not prejudiced toward viewing perception in reference to scientific knowledge.

The Shift from Expression to Representation

It is commonplace in philosophy to distinguish between the commonsense world of everyday experience on one hand and the world of scientific theory on the other. Cassirer distinguishes among the three symbolic functions of expression, representation, and significance, which permits him to differentiate the world of expression, the perceptual world of things, and the world of theory. In this way Cassirer undercuts one of the most widespread views of myth among philosophers and anthropologists—the view that myth is "primitive science."

Cassirer places myth in the sphere of expressive meaning, *before* the spheres of common sense and theory. "We are in the habit of dividing our life into the two spheres of practical and theoretical activity," he says. "In this division we are prone to forget that there is a lower stratum beneath them both. Primitive man is not liable to such forgetfulness. All his thoughts and his feelings are still embedded in this lower original stratum" (*EM*, 82). Primitive man's basic relationship to the world is neither observational-theoretical nor practical-manipulative; it is simply "sympathetic" (*EM*, 82). By "sympathy" Cassirer means that nature and culture are not perceived as different spheres; the nonorganic and organic, plant and animal, human and nonhuman all appear as one "society of life." Totemistic divisions of the world, an early example of mythic thinking, bear witness to this unified view of things. The astrological belief that the stars are animate is a late example of mythic feeling for nature. Until Kepler showed the nature of the planets' orbits, the "errant stars" were regarded as prime examples of astral beings whose reason set their paths (*PSF*, 2:138–39; *PsF*, 2:167–68; cf. WW, 20–24).

Mythic thinking undergoes extensive development from its earliest forms—animism, totemism, taboo, fetishism, magic, ritual sacrifices—to its late systematization in astrology and other occult sciences. The proliferation in the Renaissance of alchemy, white magic, and Hermetic teachings is discussed in Cassirer's various historical writings, but he develops a systematic interpretation only of astrology.

Cassirer regards astrology as the best illustration of myth's form of causal explanation (*WW*, 29–54; cf. *PSF*, 2:66; *PsF*, 2:85) and alchemy as the clearest illustration of the mythic conception of attributes (*PSF*, 2:66–67; *PsF*, 2:85–86). Cassirer's purpose in examining astrology is not just to show where myth ends and science begins. This could have been as easily accomplished by showing how alchemy precedes chemistry or by explicating anatomy according to the astrological conception of the body's organization in contrast to anatomy as an empirical science in Vesalius.[46] What most interests Cassirer about astrology is not the light it sheds on the demarcation between mythic and scientific cognition, but the fact that in astrology the mythic concept of fate survives. By systematizing the "forces" of mythic thought, astrology is actually a kind of middle thing between myth and science.

Unlike primitive mythic thought, astrology offers an organized, systematic explanation of the world. "Astrology, taken in a purely formal way, is one of the greatest and most daring attempts ever made by the human mind to develop a systematic-constructive view of the world" (*WW*, 35). Astrology is the result of theorizing about the movements of heavenly bodies while retaining mythic conceptions of causality. In mythic thought there are no abstract, impersonal causal "laws," but only acts of will and unique metamorphoses: "The cosmos is fished out of the depths of the sea or molded from a tortoise; the earth is shaped from the body of a great beast or from a lotus blossom floating on the water; the sun is made from a stone, men from rocks or trees" (*PSF*, 2:47; *PsF*, 2:62). Such thinking is completely oriented to concrete substances; for myth, everything is some sort of "body" (*PSF*, 2:55; *PsF*, 2:71). The origin of the cosmos is portrayed as a creation from some kind of body. The relationship between part and whole typical of myths is expressed in the principle *pars pro toto* (*PSF*, 2:50; *PsF*, 2:65). All things can affect all other things because they are substantially one. Objects separated from one another can still affect each other just as the part can affect the whole because of their substantial "belonging together." Magic derives its credibility from this belief. Cassirer says that Hume's analysis of causality, according to which mere contiguity is a sign of causal relationship, unwittingly provides an accurate account of the mythic conception of cause (*PSF*, 2:44–45; *PsF*, 2:59–60. Spatial proximity is enough for the mythic mind to see a force between things. This holds even for astrology, which extends spatial contiguity to the extreme of "belonging" to a particular sign of the zodiac. Because human fate was determined by this mythic link between the individual and the heavens, the astrological conception of the cosmos left little room for freedom. For myth, nothing ever occurs by chance; the principle of sufficient reason finds universal application in myth. Disasters, suffering, sickness, and death are always caused by powers exerting magical influences (see *PSF*, 2:47–49; *PsF*, 2:62–64). Science only explains the general causes of fatal illness, for example, but myth proposes to explain why at some particular time and place a particular person dies. Belief in the distant control of human lives is fundamental in astrology, and such beliefs can persist in even the most enlightened times. Astrology declined not so much due to the rise of astronomy as to its conflict with the Church. When the astrologer Cecco d'Ascoli traced the rise and fall of religions to the effects of the stars and then applied this claim to Christianity, he was burnt at the stake for heresy.[47] Yet, as Aby Warburg showed in his classic study of astrology in the age of Luther, both followers of Luther and opponents within the Church used astrological "proof" to make their case that Luther was sent to bring salvation/destruction.[48] In order to fit with the astrological predictions, Luther's supporters had to (and did) ignore the year on his birth certificate, clear proof of astrology's immunity to "scientific" thinking. The gradual decline in astrology's influence can be attributed not to science but to the new views of human fate proclaimed by the Humanists.

Astrology and the figure of Fortuna were conjoined in Renaissance thought. The belief that man stood completely at the mercy of the ups and downs of Lady Fortune went hand in hand with the belief in astrology. Medieval and Renaissance depictions of Fortuna show her with the wheel of fate, which turns like the stars. Sometimes man is on top, sometimes on the bottom, sometimes on the rise or on the decline. In all of this he had no doing. Drawing upon the work of Warburg, Saxl, and Panofsky about changes in the depiction of Fortuna (*IC*, 76–77), Cassirer points to a new mentality in Renaissance thought: the emergence of the *mente eroica*. Now man's relationship to Fortuna is depicted by the sailboat, not the wheel. The winds of fortune are out of his control, but he sits at the rudder and can set his own course. Even though he cannot be fortune's master, he is not her slave. This new evaluation of humanity, also represented by the Prometheus theme, could not tolerate the astrological conception of destiny. Empirical science developed upon the basis of this new outlook; it did not bring it about. Led by the criticism of the Humanists, figures from many fields brought about this change in attitude (*IC*, 94–98, 118–22).

Cassirer develops these claims in one of his "historical" writings, *The Individual and the Cosmos in Renaissance Philosophy*, but his point is systematic. Cassirer describes a particular shift in attitude that occurred at a particular time (the fourteenth century) and was concentrated in a particular place (Italy), but he does not consider what occurred to be a historical unicum. He points to the unity of action in the "heroic passion" among such diverse figures as the artist and architect Leon Battista Alberti, the political philosopher Machiavelli, the statesman Lorenzo the Magnificent, and, even in the devout circle of Ficino's Platonic Academy, Pico della Mirandola (*IC*, 77). The contemplative spirit of the hierarchical, fixed, medieval worldview, which had developed from the Aristotelian, pseudo-Dionysian, and Neoplatonic writings as expressed politically in the feudal system and visually in medieval church art, was suddenly called into question on many fronts. Following Copernicus, Giordano Bruno asserted that there were no higher and lower spheres, no privileged point in the cosmos. The cosmos, he declared, is "infinite." The feudal system gave way to what Jacob Burckhardt refers to as the idea of "the state as a work of art"; and the artist, no longer the servant of devotion, engaged in what Leonardo—in opposition to Plato's mimetic theory of art—called a "second creation" (*MS*, 132–36; cf. *IC*, 67). In this "new spirit" Cassirer sees something of universal significance.[49] It is nothing less than the reorientation of culture from a mythical, traditional basis to a scientific and humanistic outlook. In an essay on the ancient world and the development of the exact sciences, Cassirer compares Plato and Greek science with Galileo and modern science. Despite all the differences between these two figures, their times, and their solutions to specific questions, he says that they share a common attitude; they chose the same direction, away from sense perception as the object of knowledge. Cassirer observes that "the great thing about all true and deep intellectual decisions is that they only seem to belong to a particular historical moment of thought, whereas in truth mankind is always standing before them again and again in the course of its development."[50]

Changes in beliefs are an important concern in the philosophy of symbolic forms. The shift from mythic to nonmythic thought is the shift from passive to active belief or, rather, from passive to active formation of beliefs. For example, Cassirer compares St. Bonaventure's description of the willingness of the believer to die for a proposition of dogma with the modern individualistic readiness (like Galileo's) to sacrifice oneself for an idea that one alone upholds, in the belief that it is universally valid.[51] This difference in perspective is rooted for Cassirer in irreducible differences between two symbolic forms, religion and science. Mythic and nonmythic thought are radically different even though they can be united in the person. A Renaissance figure like Kepler was a practitioner of astrology and yet a founder of modern astronomy, a believer in mathematical mysticism and yet a theoretical mathematician. Kepler accomplished this by containing his mystical speculations, keeping them separate from his more scientific views.[52] Every person is subject to the power of myth, but mythic and nonmythic, rational thought remain irreconcilable. In his late work, Cassirer proposes a basic conflict within culture between mythic forces and critical forces—"intellectual, ethical, and aesthetic." The mythic forces in culture proclaim fate; the critical forces express and depend upon cultural self-confidence. This cultural conflict makes it impossible for Cassirer to claim that myth can lead to science. Science cannot "develop" from myth because they are entirely antithetical. Science, Cassirer says, leads to the obliteration of every trace of the mythic worldview (EM, 62). Myth, in all its details, denies the scientific conception of things.

Science can only develop by means of the symbolic forms mediating between it and myth: language and technology. The shift from mythic to scientific forms of thought does not take place by a steady development of the one from the other or on the basis of a simple decision. It requires a change in outlook that is made possible by means of other forms of culture. The shift from mythically to critically held belief is not a matter of chance. By necessity it follows a path through language and technical activity. Without these symbolic forms, there would be no way for thought to move beyond myth.

Language and Myth

To understand how language and tool use lead beyond the sphere of myth it is necessary to consider again expressive meaning and symbolism. Cassirer traces myth back to the point where sheer animal terror assumes a "Gestalt." In his attempt to reconstruct the earliest form of mythic experience, Cassirer uses Hermann Usener's notion of Augenblicksgötter (momentary gods) as a foil to his own view. Usener thought that the earliest mythic concepts were images of gods born from the need of a critical moment, in other words, personifications of the feeling of a situation. But, drawing upon more recent anthropological findings, Cassirer points out that Usener's view of these fleeting "gods" depicted them in a way that was too personal and individual. In the earliest stages of mythic thought, man experiences sudden terror or wonder. This feeling is impersonal and anonymous and it serves as the nameless background and basis from which specific demonic or holy images can form. What has been referred to as the "taboo-mana formula as a minimum definition of religion" constitutes for Cassirer the primary stage of mythic thought, a stage in which the perception of a heightened force first assumes mythological form (LM, 64n). A thing possesses mana if it is striking, efficacious, or foreboding. For Cassirer mana represents the crisis in which the sacred is distinguished from the profane. This distinction exemplified what Cassirer regards as the most basic type of predication, Urprädikation (primeval predication). Such "predication" functions at the level of pure expression and is not conceptual.

Cassirer breaks here with the mainstream of philosophical thought. He does not conceive the original form of predication to involve subsuming something under a category; it is "the creation of the category itself" (LM, 88). Preconceptual meaning comes about through imagination, not logic: "All light is concentrated in one focal point of 'meaning,' while everything that lies outside these focal points of verbal or mythic conception remain practically invisible. It remains 'unremarked' because, and in so far as, it remains unsupplied with any linguistic or mythic 'marker' " (LM, 91). To put it differently, Cassirer envisions a thought process that applies to the "intension" rather than the "extension" of concepts. He does not conceive this conceptualization to be the result of an act of comparison or association. No analogy is made. Cassirer points out that all theories of concept formation that require an act of comparison presuppose the function of the concept when they speak of "noticing" qualities or characteristics in things. What Cassirer in Substance and Function called the "function of the concept" is now more explicitly named "radical metaphor" (LM, 87). It is a function of imagination, not logic. The term imagination is most appropriate to designate what Cassirer has in mind because the meaning involved is compressed into an image, something particular, not understood as an "instance" or exemplification of a rule.

At first, reality has a constantly changing face, shifting from horrifying to assuaging; it is demonic in an indeterminate sense, but out of the elementary mythical experiences that arise and then dissolve, personal forces emerge with a unified character. This depends upon the contribution of language: "the god acquires full individuality only through his name and image" (PSF, 3:90–91; PsF, 3:106–07; cf. LM, 18ff.; PSF, 2:199ff., PsF, 2:238ff.).

But mythic language is not rational or argumentative. Mythical language and thought is not quantitative at all, but forms what Cassirer calls "punctiform" units (punktuelle Einheiten) that permit no quantitative distinctions: "Every part of a whole is the whole itself;

every specimen is equivalent to the entire species. The part does not merely represent the whole, or the specimen its class; they are identical with the totality to which they belong; not merely as mediating aids to reflective thought, but as genuine presences which actually contain the power, significance, and efficacy of the whole" (LM, 91ff.). Cassirer's point is that in myth there is no "substitution" of the part for the whole; these are identified immediately with one another. The fact that the Mexican corn goddess Chicomecoatl is perceived to be present in every kernel of corn and in every corn dish illustrates that language in myth serves to establish the identity of felt, perceived qualities—logical punctiform units, not abstract concepts—under which particular entities are subsumed. Cassirer realizes that this thesis goes against long-established views: "the *primary* function of concept formation is not, as most logicians have assumed under the pressure of a centuries-old tradition, to raise our representations to ever greater universality; on the contrary, it is to make them increasingly determinate" (PSF, 1:280; PsF, 1:251–52). In myth, thinking is punctiform rather than quantificational in the sense of formal predicate logic. The "primordial predication" establishes identity pure and simple. This "radical metaphor" is the creation of a category of a basic type, which Cassirer calls a "qualifying concept."

The first function of language is to establish identity by means of such qualifying concepts. A qualifying concept does not subsume a particular under a universal, but rather is named with respect to a property (PSF, 1:282–84; PsF, 1:253–56). The moon is thus called "the measurer" in Greek (μήν), "the radiant" in Latin (luna, luc-na). Cassirer agrees here with Wilhelm von Humboldt that each language has a character of its own, an "inner form," a view that has become known as the "principle of linguistic relativity." On this view, the words of different languages can never be true synonyms since their meaning can never be expressed by a list of the objective characteristics of the object designated (PSF, 1:284; PsF, 1:256). Language is not logic. Logic disregards the human world of action and the fact that culture is historical. The formation of concepts in language is always infused with dynamic factors from the world of man's activities: "What primarily distinguishes linguistic concept formation from strictly logical concept formation [that is, logic of classes] is that it never rests solely on the static representational comparison of contents. . . . It is the reflection not of an objective environment, but of man's own life and action that essentially determines the linguistic view of the world, as it does the primitive mythical image of nature" (PSF, 1:285; PsF, 1:257).

Language represents the world as man lives in it; it is, along with technology, one of the chief means by which man moves from the immediacy of living in a world to having a world. Language objectifies the world so that it can be regarded "from a distance." In a 1932 paper Cassirer designates this difference by adopting Heidegger's terms *Zuhandenheit* and *Vorhandenheit*, "readiness-to-hand" and "presence-at-hand" (STS, 133). The movement from living in to thinking about this world begins with the use of language, the confrontation with the world in the context of the common tasks of the community: "Language arises not in isolated but in *communal* action, it possesses from the very start a truly common, 'universal' sense. Language as a *sensorum commune* could only grow out of the sympathy of activity" (PSF, 1:286; PsF, 1:259). These communal tasks are of two kinds: cult practices and work, that is, myth and "technology." Originally, these are not clearly distinguished—effective action is the "manifestation" of a mythical helper while cult practice centers upon the activity of magic (PSF, 2:203; PsF, 2:243).

Language's close relationship to action can be seen in the variety of particular names for concrete activities among Indian, Eskimo, and other preindustrial societies that have names for *kinds* of hunting, eating, and the like but no general terms for them. The cohesion between language and human activity also asserts itself in advanced languages with the development of technical, "occupational languages" with their specialized terminology (PSF, 1:287; PsF, 1:260).

Social action—physical activities—play the leading role in the development of myth, language, and tool use. Cassirer provides a detailed account of their genealogies, recounting the structural changes that distinguish the feeling of mana and the rites of nature cults from the simplest personal gods of activities, the heroes of classical mythology, and, finally, God in monotheistic religions—a concept with an ideal history of its own. Cassirer's accounts of the development of mythic thought and language are themselves topics of such complexity that an adequate treatment of them would demand an entire book. But for a study on the general outlook of his philosophy of symbolic forms, it is enough to recognize the general function that Cassirer attributes to language and myth in the general framework of human culture. Cassirer sees the representative function of language and tool use as the primary cultural forces that limit the mythical view of the world.

Signs have a representative function when they assert that there is a content which holds "in itself" and is accessible through *perception*, in principle, to everyone.[53] Representation involves existence claims. Only statements with a representational meaning are capable of being true or false. In science there are also purely significative statements,

statements which cannot be decided by reference to the sensory world of objects. These require different methods for testing their truth. The association between "representation" (Darstellung) and the perceptual world of objects is established by the fact that things are experienced as concrete, physical *bodies*.

> Even the terms by which language expresses the "is" of the predicative statement usually preserve a secondary intuitive significance—the logical relation is replaced by a spatial one, a "being-here" or "being-there," a statement of existence. Thus all logical power of determination belonging to language is originally contained in its power of demonstration. The linguistic process of objectivization begins with the demonstrative pronouns, the designation of a definite place, of a "here" or a "there." The object toward which it aims is a τόδε τι in the Aristotelian sense: a something which stands in the presence of the speaker and can be pointed out with the finger. (PSF, 3:450; PsF, 3:527; cf. PSF, 1:313ff., PsF, 1:292ff.; PSF, 3:74–75, PsF, 3:87–88)

The representative use of language depends upon having a world in which things resist sheer expressive desire. Myth follows the logic of dreams; it does not recognize anything as "contrary." Dreams, the mythic worldview of magic, and the experience of the child recognize and are motivated by desire and fear, yet they are not "realistic" because they do not recognize negation. Such realism depends upon representation. The copula *is* provides the clearest example of the function of representation. Even languages that have no copula can be used representatively, but they must employ constructions with a purely material content (for example, "the city big" for "the city is big"; PSF, 1:314ff.; PsF, 1:294ff.). In languages with a copula, etymology shows that its root is always something intuitive or material. In the German language the root of the copula is "dwelling" while in the Romance languages the copula is linked to "standing." Even when the copula is used to designate a purely logical relation rather than to assert actual, tangible existence or being, as can be the case in philosophy, this occurs, Cassirer says, within language, "but at the same time *in opposition to it*" (PSF, 1:315; PsF, 1:296). Representation remains within the bounds of the perceived, commonsense world.

Cassirer concludes the first volume of the PSF the way he began it, with a discussion of the problem of being in the history of philosophy—the attempt in Greek philosophy to formulate the reality of "ideal" being. He again points to Plato's discussion of "being" and "not-being" as the first recognition of the difference between "being" as a designation for existence *and* for the relation of predication (*PSF*, 1:316; *PsF*, 1:296). When nonbeing is grasped as logical negation, not as an ontological assertion, it has a purely significative meaning. Formal logic uses negation in this way, without reference to existence. The strictly relational character of predication is not clearly expressed in the copula of language because natural languages are at once both intellectual and sensory in content. The copula has a representative function as a designation of concrete existence, or it can serve as a logical relation to connect and differentiate concepts. This is the sense of "being" and "non-being" that Plato distinguished from the Eleatic absolutization of ὄν and μὴ ὄν. Plato says in the *Sophist*: "This isolation of everything from everything else means a complete abolition of all discourse, for any discourse we can have owes its existence to the weaving together of forms."[54] The weaving together of forms occurs in the *Urteil* or judgment in which the copula functions as a predicative relation.

The purely significative function of symbolism is more clearly seen in the formal languages of axiomatic systems (for example, Hilbert's axiomatization of geometry) than in natural languages. Pure significance is nonintuitive. Such a use of signs does not refer to observable objects. Concepts in ordinary language, even when they are discussed abstractly in purely logical terms, retain an intuitive character. This can lead to a confusion between the two different dimensions of ideal and referential meaning, or, as Cassirer often puts it, confusion between problems of meaning and problems of being.

Language is initially experienced as an objective reality, as the expression of being itself. This view recedes as different cultures with different languages come into contact with one another and as a result of the internal criticism of language illustrated by Socrates' method of questioning (*PSF*, 1:294; *PsF*, 1:269; on confrontation of peoples, see *AH*, 78–79). The philosophical question "What is . . . ?" comes at the end of the process of differentiation by which man learns consciously to make distinctions. Originally, Cassirer contends, man does not "make" distinctions; rather, mythical and phonetic images "make them visible." The first distinctions are experienced passively; the mythical-phonetic image, Cassirer says, "does not merely reproduce existing distinctions but in the strict sense of the word *evokes* distinctions. Consciousness arrives at a clear division between the different spheres of activity and between their divergent objective and subjective conditions only by referring each of these spheres to a fixed center, to one particular mythical figure. . . . All action seems to be regarded as a mere 'manifestation' of the god" (*PSF*, 2:203; *PsF*, 2:243). With the growth of the pantheon, the classification of divine spheres of influence grows, generating an initial linguistic order of things.

The turning point in this initial view of the world is the use of implements.

It is not possible, Cassirer admits, to indicate a moment in the history of mankind when a change from a magical to a technical approach to practical matters occurred. The purely practical and magical approaches exist side by side in primitive cultures. But the effects of the shift from a predominantly expressive, mythical view of the world to a representational understanding of this world depends upon this physical confrontation with things through the use of tools. As a result of the use of tools "the limits of the world of desire and the world of reality begin to stand out more clearly" (PSF, 2:213; PsF, 2:255). The magic "omnipotence of thought" subsides as negation is learned through the use of tools. The mind can only come to a grasp of negation, in the most basic sense of the word, through the experience of the body and its limitations.

The Place of Technology

Technik, physical effort with implements, is, along with myth and language, one of three basic symbolic forms of culture. Cassirer writes: "Man is a 'reasonable' creature—in the sense that 'reason' stems from language and is indissolubly bound up with it—so that ratio and oratio, speech and thought, are complementary concepts. But at the same time, and not less primordially, he also is a creature who makes tools, 'a tool-making animal', as Benjamin Franklin called him. . . . The intelligent mastery of reality is bound to this double act of 'grasping' [Fassen], to grasping reality in language by theoretical thought and by grasping it by the medium of effort, by giving form through thought and by technics" (STS, 51–52). Cassirer considered physical, technical work to be one of the key elements of culture.[55] Cassirer understood technology, like language or myth, to give man a particular sense of space and time and to make a particular contribution to his conception of the world and of himself. Technik is a way of having a world, not simply an assemblage of instruments employed by man. Cassirer's conception of technology is much like that found in writings on the "philosophy of technology" among such diverse authors as Jacques Ellul, Herbert Marcuse, Martin Heidegger, Max Horkheimer, and Theodor Adorno, although (at least prior to The Myth of the State) Cassirer's thought on technology lacked the negative tone of these writers' works.

The simple tools used for everyday jobs—hoes, fishhooks, spears, axes, or hammers—are not at first regarded as human inventions but seem in mythic thought to be centers of power originated by the act of a cultural hero or god. They themselves can even appear as kinds of gods (LM, 59–61; STS, 65–66). The myth of Prometheus gives classic expression to this feeling that technical mastery is a gift from above.

Tool use gives birth to the discovery of an objective order that, ultimately, takes the place of the magical, mythological world. Tools stand as *Verrichtungen*, ways of accomplishing something, and it is through them that "man comes to recognize an 'objective causality'" (STS, 64). By the use of tools man apprehends how physical things have certain effects on other things and that there are limits to actions; he learns how things resist thoughts and wishes. "As soon as man seeks to influence things not by mere image magic or name magic but through implements, he has undergone an inner crisis. . . . Man now differentiates a set sphere of objects which are designated precisely by the fact that they have a content peculiar to themselves, by which they resist man's immediate desire. It is the consciousness of the means (implements or technical process) indispensable for the attainment of a certain purpose that first teaches man to apprehend 'inner' and 'outer' as links in a *chain of causality* and to assign to each of them its own inalienable place within this chain" (PSF, 2:215; PsF, 2:256). Historically, the magical worldview does not cease to have applicability, but the more man learns that the world cannot be made to respond to wish or magic, the more he learns to recognize its objective regularities and utilize them to his own ends.

In addition to the cognitive gain of recognizing an objective physical world, tool use paves the way for another profound change: the development of the will as opposed to mere wish. Cassirer regards this development as essential for the existence of responsibility and the shift from a mythological to a legal basis for human society. Mythic consciousness is characterized by an absence of reflective self-awareness, but it does not lack the phenomenon of desire. This is manifested in all the forms of magic. Desires stand behind the rituals that precede every great undertaking by a war party, every hunting, fishing, or trapping expedition. These rituals act out the success of the group before it leaves. But these rites represent only a *wish*, not a genuine action of *will* (STS, 59). Desire jumps directly to the goal and believes that desire alone can possess any goal because of the magical sympathy between all things.

Technical activity gradually overturns this view. The practically feasible is distinguished from what is impossible so that, as a result, mere desire is perceived to be arbitrary. This means that man must now deliberate to find the way to ends and must realize that he may fail in the process. Man comes to recognize both the limits and importance of his own efforts in attempts to achieve a goal. This has important consequences for the development of ethics.

In primitive societies all spheres of life are subject to an inflexible system of taboos (EM, 104–08; PSF, 2:76–78; PsF, 2:97–98). Taboo prescribes what is right and wrong without any regard to circumstances or to ideals such as justice. Because customs like rituals derive their validity from an original, divine event that is forever reenacted, the conception of a better, more just future is literally unthinkable. Cassirer observes that "customs [Sitte] and Folkways [Brauch] appear at first as the strictly objective and opposed to this objectivity there is no freedom and no spontaneity" (AH, 78).

In mythic thought there is no individual ethical self-consciousness; every manifestation of personal existence melts into the totality of life surrounding it (PSF, 2:175; PsF, 2:209). In the taboo system no self-responsibility is called for, nor is there any place for it. "There is not a shadow of any individual responsibility in this system. If a man commits a crime it is not he himself who is marked off—his family, his friends, his whole tribe bears the same mark" (EM, 105). In myth, obligation has a purely social character and is experienced as an external force. Deliberation is unnecessary in the rigidly prescribed social sphere of mythic thought. The idea of an open end to action, of different ways to an end, arises with the ability to "will." With the will comes consistency of action and the basis for individual personality. Personality for Cassirer is consistency of action (Folgerichtigkeit des Tuns; AH, 67, 108). Cassirer emphasizes personality because, he says, "by virtue of this persistence of personality we can count on such a person; we rely on his remaining true to himself and on his arriving at a decision not by mood and arbitrariness but by an autonomous law, by that which he recognizes and acknowledges as right" (DI, 204). Technik is essential in the development of the will and, hence, of the personality, but it cannot provide the goals to which the will aspires. Technology is confined to the sphere of the strictly instrumental (STS, 88–89).

Myth, language, and technical activity are the origins of human culture. Cassirer's "phenomenology" of the roots of culture is also an ideal history of the movement from mythic to critical belief. As a theory of the beginning and direction of human cultural development, the PSF leads to the problem of the ends or aims of this development. Does Cassirer believe that the course of history can in any way be predicted? Cassirer does not claim to portray the actual course of the historical development of any particular culture, but only the ideal historical development of "human culture." He traces a movement in all the symbolic forms from mimetic to purely symbolic meaning and an enlargement of the types of meaning from expressive and representational meaning to the purely significative.

Cassirer proposes a theory of the aims of culture, but he does not claim that it is possible to know its outcome, the future course of history; he says flatly, "We are incapable of anticipating the future development of civilization" (LH, 36). In 1936 he wrote an essay in which he argues against all philosophies that purport to be able to predict the future course of history, whether by means of physicalistic, psychological, economic, or metaphysical laws of history. Distinguishing the PSF as a "humanistic" philosophy from these "naturalistic" philosophies, he insists that his attempt to understand the whole of human culture is "no basis for prophecy" (LH, 37, 64). "All that can be said on this score is that culture will advance just to the extent that the truly creative powers, which in the final analysis are only brought into play by our own efforts, are not forsaken or crippled" (p. 37). Cassirer stands in complete agreement here with Karl Popper's rejection of "historicism," that is, philosophical attempts to show that events follow a "law of history." But Cassirer takes a very different view from Popper's on the question "Has history any meaning?"[56] This question is the underlying concern linking Cassirer's philosophy of symbolic forms and his writings on the history of philosophy. Popper argues that history has no "ends" in the sense of objective aims; the ideal of the "Open Society," for example, is presented as desirable, but something which is only chosen by an "act of faith."[57] Such "moral decisions" are, for Popper as for the positivists and the early Sartre, purely subjective matters of choice, inclination, preference, or taste. A principle such as "equality before the law" may be desirable, but on this view it can have no basis that would permit claiming for it any general validity. Cassirer thinks that the philosophy of symbolic forms can show the validity of emerging universal theoretical and ethical norms, which derive from the later symbolic forms of science, history, art, and law (Recht). These develop from the fundamental symbolic forms of myth, language, and technology, but they cannot be considered merely as later stages of these more "primitive" forms. Myth is the origin of culture, but not all culture is a form of myth. Mythic thought overwhelms; language and technical activity make possible the rise of self-critical belief. With this greater reflective distance, a new phase of culture can begin in which myth gives way to the development of science, history, art, law, and philosophical thought.

III

TRUTH

Cassirer approaches the question "What is truth?" through the ideal history of his philosophy of culture. He states fundamental agreement with Hegel's conception of truth in the *Phenomenology of Mind*: "The truth is the whole—yet this whole cannot be presented all at once but must be unfolded progressively by thought in its autonomous movement and rhythm" (*PSF*, 3:xiv; *PsF*, 3:vi). To accomplish this, philosophy must encompass the "totality" (*Totalität*) of cultural forms, a totality which "can only be made visible in the transitions from one form to another" (ibid.). The concept of truth occurs in each symbolic form, but it is not the possession of any one of them. As Cassirer said in his Göteborg inaugural lecture, "Without the claim to an independent, objective, and autonomous truth, not only philosophy, but also each particular field of knowledge, natural science as well as the humanities, would lose their stability and their sense" (*SMC*, 61). But even prior to the organization of different fields of knowledge and any conception of truth as a norm,[1] there is always an understanding of truth.

It is typical of inflected languages that they have a subject-predicate sentence organization. This results, Cassirer thinks, in an understanding of truth that is exemplified in a paradigmatic way in Aristotle. The centrality in Aristotle's metaphysics of *ousia*—substance and its various characteristics—was imposed on Aristotle, Cassirer says, "by the structure of the Greek language." The logical power of language, its ability to distinguish among things and their basic characteristics and so to classify them, provided the basis of science as Aristotle conceived it.[2] Language is the primary medium for formulating an understanding of the world as a world of objects.

The distinction between true and false propositions depends upon the representational function of language, but such Darstellung requires a prior understanding of the world that cannot be obtained from language alone. This is the world of tangible reality, which becomes accessible to us through physical activity. The grasp provided by the manipulation and use of things provides our basic understanding (Verstehen) of the world. For this, no technical production is required. Physical activity per se is a form of understanding, a "bringing forth" (Herausstellen; ex-sistere) of a world.[3] This practical knowledge is a prelinguistic understanding of "truth."

Mythic understanding, based on awareness of the world as threatening or benign, is also prior to disinterested, scientific knowledge. Myth's concern is man's fate and his place in the world, a concern inherited by art, religion, and philosophy. In a world populated with friendly and benign forces, mythic understanding seeks to know the right attitude toward what happens and to know the right thing to do. On practical questions myth is the first source of wisdom. But myth does not have an answer to the moral problem of good and evil, a question which is beyond its ken (MS, 60).

Another quite different understanding of truth emerges in post-Galilean science. When Galileo reinterpreted the "book" of nature in terms of the measurable, mathematically quantifiable, "primary" qualities of things, science attained a new measure of objectivity. For modern science to develop, a change in symbolism was necessary: "The symbols of language have to be superseded by the symbols of mathematics."[4]

The philosophical theory of truth should unify the prelinguistic, linguistic, and postlinguistic conceptions of truth in a way that does not sacrifice their integrity by making one of them into the measure of the others. This approach to truth follows from Cassirer's basic conception of phenomenology and of philosophy as the philosophy of culture.

Cassirer believed that philosophical discussions of truth often fall prey to confusions caused by languages. Yet, while language may mislead, it is not a malin génie. Cassirer says: "Language may be compared with the spear of Amfortas in the legend of the Holy Grail. The wounds that language inflicts upon human thought cannot be healed except by language itself" (ibid., 327). The primary difficulty is caused by formulating the problem of truth in terms of the dichotomy of subject and object. When philosophers conceive truth in this framework they unconsciously, due to their use of language, fall into a "false spatialization" (AH, 41n) that locates truth at one of these poles.

When Cassirer went to Sweden in 1935 he found himself in a very different philosophical climate than he had been used to in Germany; Swedish philosophy was positivistic in spirit, and Cassirer was thought to uphold a kind of subjective idealism. In order to correct this misunderstanding and in reply to the general epistemological position he found in "Scandinavian realism," Cassirer wrote an essay entitled "Was is Subjektivismus?" Cassirer argues that the language of many epistemological discussions is misleading because all talk of the "subjective" and "objective" unwittingly reifies the subject-object dichotomy by making it into a *spatial* opposition. Hence, subsequent discussions all too easily degenerate into an argument for the primacy of one of these two poles. "This mistake is already made when we speak of 'the' subject or 'the' object in the first place as if they were independent substances that then affected one another. Subject and object on our view are neither metaphysical nor are they empirical *things*; they are rather logical categories."[5] Like the categories of inside and outside, up and down, or earlier and later, subject and object are relative concepts that emerge in the course of experience. Cassirer concludes, "Having recognized that it is experience as such that leads to the critical opposition of the 'subjective' and 'objective,' we cannot then apply this opposition, which signifies a specific progressive differentiation of individual aspects, to experience as a whole without thereby falling into a *circulus vitiosus*" (ibid., 128).

The concept of truth is a normative principle and as such it cannot be located spatially in the subject-object dichotomy. The norm of truth has an ideal validity, for it is essentially a phenomenon of meaning. Cassirer concludes his argument by stressing that meaning is not "in the subject" as "a consciousness." "We thereby remain in the sphere of immanence, only this is no longer in the sense of consciousness, but rather is to be understood as the immanence of principles" (ibid., 136). Cassirer uses the term *immanence* here in Kant's sense, to refer to the sphere of possible experience; the opposite of immanence is transcendence in the sense of something *Jenseits*, completely beyond all possible experience.[6] In this sense, meaning is immanent. But the norm of truth also exhibits what Cassirer calls the "transcendence of meaning." Meaning cannot be reduced to consciousness nor to an extended reality like the marble of a statue or the word as a mark on the page. For something to have meaning is for it to be "beyond itself" as a physical thing. This is the essence of Cassirer's idea of symbolic pregnance.

By virtue of symbolic pregnance the fleeting here and now takes its place in different objective orders of meaning. The different perceptual and conceptual orders (temporality, spatiality, number, and other types of objectivity) discussed in the *Phenomenology of Knowledge* are illustrations of the basic phenomenological development that Cassirer calls objectification (*Objektivierung*). This term has spatial connotations, but Cassirer uses *objectification* primarily in another sense. "The central question," he says, "refers not to the objectivity of existence but to the objectivity of meaning" (*PSF*, 3:38; *PsF*, 3:46). The norm of truth is formulated as the criteria for distinguishing among appearance, falsity, and reality in these different symbolic orders.

Perhaps Cassirer's most important statement on truth is given in his inaugural speech as rector of the University of Hamburg in 1929, "Formen und Formwandlungen des philosophischen Wahrheitsbegriffs" (Forms and transformations of the philosophical concept of truth). Cassirer identifies conceptions of truth that constitute different stages in the development of the theory of truth. (This development is more a systematic reconstruction than a historical account, although Cassirer claims that these theories historically have become clearly distinguished from one another.) He calls these the hierarchical, rationalistic, and positivistic conceptions of truth. The hierarchical theory of truth is ontological and theological: it regards the cosmos as a fixed hierarchy in which truth is essentially the ontological relationship between finite beings and their divine origin, absolute primordial being (*Ur-Sein*). In medieval philosophy knowledge of this relationship was conceived as a kind of divine revelation. The rationalistic theory turns this ontological teaching around; the standard of truth becomes the degree of certainty, a measure found in natural reason itself rather than in objective being. Finally, the positivistic theory of truth inverts this subjective standard by taking sense experience, not reason, as its measure. The "factual," which positivism claims can be found in sensation, is taken as immediately evident and certain. Cassirer finds all these theories unsatisfactory because none does justice to the concrete variety of ways in which man has an objective world. Each conceives truth in terms of some single specific measure. But in practice, greatly divergent standards of "truth" are applied in physics, biology, historical research, and art. These different conceptions cannot be forced into a single mold. The first theory finds its fulcrum in the world as a fixed, absolute object; the second claims that the knower has access to certainty in the unshakeable foundation of reason; the third assumes that this absolute certainty resides in the senses. These conceptions of truth not only hold that knowledge and reality are unities but also assume that unity means homogeneousness. They take *Einheit* (unity) to mean "Einerleiheit und Einförmigkeit" (all of one kind and of the same form).[7] Cassirer's theory of truth is a response to this traditional view. To understand Cassirer's theory we must begin with his more specific conceptions of truth in science and in the humanities.

Truth and Science

The Problem of Certainty and the Norm of Truth

The three theories of truth sketched above all seek to establish a metaphysical or epistemological foundation for truth. The ontological, hierarchical view locates truth in the object as eternal substance; the rationalistic theory finds truth in the unerring insight of reason; the positivistic view of truth assumes the absolute certainty of sensation. Cassirer does not believe that the definition of the norm of truth should be allied with the demand for certainty.

For science, no statement is ever absolutely certain nor need it be. Cassirer agrees explicitly with Dewey that a proposition in science is true to a certain degree, the extent to which it succeeds in intellectually organizing and harmoniously shaping originally isolated data and leads to new and fruitful predictions (SF/ET, 318). Cassirer upholds the "instrumental" meaning of scientific hypotheses while at the same time insisting on the purely theoretical nature of the goal of inquiry, that is, knowledge of truth. Science is not constructed simply by convention. Even formal logic and mathematics are no mere "inventions": "the hundredth decimal of the number π is ideally predetermined, even if no one has actually calculated it" (SF/ET, 319). Cassirer combines instrumental, conventional elements with a normative theory of truth. His approach is methodological, not foundational: "The instrument itself which leads to the unity and hence the truth of what is thought, must be firm and secure. If it did not possess a certain stability in itself, no sure and enduring application of it would be possible. . . . We do not need the objectivity of absolute things, but we do require the objective determinancy of the way of experience" (PSF, 3:476; PsF, 3:558; cf. SF/ET, 321ff.).

The norm of truth is inherent in any method of scientific inquiry. It does not guarantee the truth of any given statement but provides the framework without which the notion of the "truth of scientific statements" would be a meaningless phrase. Cassirer defines the norm of truth in science this way: "The One reality can only be disclosed and defined as the ideal limit of the diversely changing theories; but the setting of this limit itself is not arbitrary; it is inescapable, since the continuity of experience is established only thereby" (PSF, 3:476; PsF, 3:557; cf. SF/ET, 321–22). The "inescapability" of this ideal limit is a Kantian element; the norm of truth is the condition of the possibility of the continuity of scientific inquiry. The norm of truth permits conceiving science as progressive in nature and as capable of taking steps backward. Science is fallible. Only methods that admit the possibility of error can recognize the idea of cognitive progress.

Cassirer distinguishes among scientific statements of the first, second, and third order (DI, 40). The first are "statements of the results of measurement"; the second are "statements of laws" (sentences of the "if x, then y" type); the third are "statements of principles" or rules for finding laws, such as the principle of causality. Cassirer rejects the view that inductive logic can explain how we move from statements of the first type to statements of the second type or from these to statements of the third type. His reason for this, which I will only mention at present, is that second-order statements are about classes, which usually consist of infinitely many elements, and no inductive procedure using specific statements can establish such universal statements. Statements of the results of measurements are nevertheless, Cassirer says, "the alpha and omega of physics, its beginning and end. From them all its judgments take their departure and to them they must all lead back again" (DI, 36).

For Cassirer methods of scientific inquiry follow no particular, fixed system of rules, yet they have procedural limits. These are defined by the nature of scientific statements and a basic fallibilistic orientation.

We cannot claim "absoluteness" or ultimacy for any empirical judgment however high in the order of empirical knowledge it may stand, but must always leave open the possibility that an advance in knowledge may lead us to supplement or correct that judgment. But this by no means implies that within empirical knowledge itself all logical differences are to be leveled and obliterated. If such an obliteration were possible, the very process of experience, on which all possible correction depends, could not be carried out. For this process cannot go on except in a definite logical rhythm, in the "three step" of facts, laws, and principles. (DI, 54)

The "steps" involved in empirical inquiry are actually "jumps." Cassirer's theory of scientific method is noninductive (SF/ET, 237–70; DI, 39–40). Scientific discovery, Cassirer maintains, depends upon a kind of instinctive jump to conclusions that must seem wild and farfetched by inductive criteria. When Robert Mayer proposed the principle of conservation of energy in physics he did so on the basis of a single observation, and this observation was made in another field. As a ship's doctor he noticed the much stronger redness of blood taken from the vein on the island of Java and, recalling Lavoisier's theory that body heat comes from a combustion process, he noted that in a southern climate heat loss from bodies is less, so there need not be such a strong process of combustion in order to generate animal heat. In this fact he saw suddenly the general principle of the conservation of energy. Cassirer considered this kind of aperçu the basis of all scientific discovery. It is needed for the move from statements of measurements to statements of laws and for the move from these to statements of principles (DI, 57).

For Cassirer verification of scientific theories is both logically and practically impossible. It is logically impossible because of the character of general "law" statements of the type "if x, then y." They represent classes with an infinite number of contents; to know if a statement of this type is true demands the infinite effort of checking all the cases that fall under it. Thus, "the question always remains open as to what right one has to say anything at all about 'an indefinite number of individual cases,' if each one has not been previously tested and examined" (DI, 41). Verification is also impossible practically because prediction, the basis of the notion of verification, does not work neatly in the real world. If causality is defined as that which can be predicted with certainty, then even classical physics offers problems because "it is not possible in a single instance to predict a physical event really precisely" (DI, 65). For Cassirer, scientific progress does not depend on verification.

Physical science does not aim at a complete knowledge of all facts; it aims at establishing a systematic body of true theories, comprehending the greatest number of phenomena by the fewest possible determining factors. Physical knowledge proceeds by a double process of extension and compression. Theories broaden our knowledge by letting us master new material and, at the same time, compress or simplify it. This striving for simplicity, although economic in purpose, is not just pragmatic; it has a truth content (DI, 66–68). We cannot recognize the truth by means of the impossible comparison of a theory with the world "as such." If we knew the nature of physical reality itself, there would be no need to engage in scientific inquiry. "We never compare the system of hypotheses in itself with the naked facts in themselves, but always oppose one hypothetical system of hypotheses to another more inclusive, more radical system," Cassirer observes, and therefore "we need for this progressive comparison an ultimate constant standard of measurement of supreme principles of experience in general" (SF/ET, 268). One such principle is the principle of causality.

Causality

Causality is not a law, but a principle that permits formulating laws hypothetically. Statements deduced from such hypotheses (predictions) are then compared with statements of laws derived from rival hypotheses. These are then compared with statements of the results of measurements established observationally. In *Determinism and Indeterminism in Modern Physics* Cassirer distinguishes the concept of causality from the concept of continuity. Kant, Cassirer discerns, failed to do this because the schematization of the concept of causality in pure intuition introduces a connection with time and, hence, with continuity in the form of the "succession of the manifold."[8] Causality for Cassirer can only be a regulative idea, a methodological postulate which states that "the phenomena of nature are not such as to elude or withstand in principle the possibility of being ordered" (*DI*, 60). This view permits upholding the principle of causality while also recognizing discontinuities.

With this simple move, the separation of the principle of causality from the manifold of pure intuition, Cassirer radically changes Kant's transcendental theory of knowledge by separating at this point the transcendental aesthetic from transcendental logic. Kant had argued in his transcendental aesthetic that the forms of intuition, space and time, are united with the pure categories of the understanding, a conjunction that Kant termed "schematization." Kant says that "an application of the category to appearances becomes possible by means of the transcendental determination of time, which, as the schema of the concepts of the understanding, mediates the subsumption of the appearances under the category."[9] Time refers here to the pure form of intuition described in the transcendental aesthetic, not the psychological experience of temporality. As in the case of Cassirer's criticism of Heidegger and defense of Kant's conception of reason as the sphere of the infinite (for example, the "ideas" of freedom and truth), Cassirer here defends Kant against himself by insisting on the need to revise the Kantian conception of the role of intuition (*Anschauung*) in causality. Whereas Heidegger used the need to connect the categories with time as a pure form of intuition as an argument for limiting reason, Cassirer thinks that Kant's conception of the schematization of causality results in too strong a claim for reason, one which ultimately would limit it to a particular physical view of the world. Kant could not foresee that the world of Newtonian physics, the pride of the eighteenth-century mind, would appear so different after the reorganization of physics in the twentieth century. In terms of the Kantian architectonic, Cassirer has moved causality as a scientific principle from the sphere of the constitutive understanding into the sphere of regulative ideals of reason. Unlike Kant's strong assertion that "all alterations take place in conformity with the law of the connection of cause and effect" (ibid.), Cassirer's weaker formulation of causality ("the phenomena of nature are not such as to elude or withstand in principle the possibility of being ordered"; DI, 60) permits the conception of deterministic and indeterministic physical theories.

Philipp Frank, an early member of the Vienna Circle, regarded Cassirer's reformulation of the causal principle as a sign of the "disintegration" of the traditional "school philosophy" of idealism, and he welcomed this as a move toward the spirit of logical empiricism.[10] Indeed, as Cassirer himself said, the strictly deterministic conception of nature is "nothing less than the complete expression, the pregnant summary, of that world view from which sprang the great philosophical systems of the seventeenth century, the systems of classical rationalism" (DI, 11). Quantum theory does not permit upholding determinism in some areas of microphysics, but on Cassirer's view this does not mean that causality is denied because the principle of causality concerns the connection between cognitions, not things and events (DI, 65).

Cassirer's weakened version of the causal principle led Carl Friedrich von Weizsäcker to ask: "But may [darf] a philosopher who wants to make the heritage of Kant fruitful for the interpretation of modern physics so easily give up the narrower conception of the causal principle that was appropriate for classical mechanics, and in which Kant himself believed?"[11] Weizsäcker's question here is "Is this permitted?"; darf Cassirer do this? Weizsäcker's objection shows the degree to which Cassirer's thought has been identified with a narrow conception of Kantianism. Cassirer even wrote that he expected Determinism and Indeterminism to be criticized on these grounds, that is, that readers would wonder "whether as a 'Neo-Kantian' I was permitted to draw such conclusions" (DI, xxiii). Weizsäcker is not alone in missing the irony of this statement.

Cassirer begins his essay "Was ist Subjektivismus?" by noting that he has often been called a neo-Kantian, and he takes the occasion to indicate his attitude toward this designation. This label, he says, is often taken to mean a position which he himself completely rejects: "Many of the doctrines that are attributed to neo-Kantianism in present-day philosophical literature are not only foreign to me, but even diametrically opposed to my own conceptions."[12] Among these doctrines, as we have seen, is the primacy of epistemology and of individual consciousness. Cassirer does see justification for calling his thought neo-Kantian in the fact that his work "presupposes the methodological foundation that Kant gave in the *Critique of Pure Reason*," but, he adds, "what is important is not by what name the view upheld by me is labeled" (ibid.). Nonetheless, again and again mistaken conceptions about Cassirer's work have been derived from the belief that he is a neo-Kantian. In addition to the belief that Cassirer's *PSF* must be basically an epistemology and that he must uphold a methodological solipcism, we may now add the assumption that he must strictly adhere to Kant's conception of causality. Cassirer did not follow Kant in such a doctrinal manner. He believed that a reinterpretation of Kant's conception of causality was objectively necessary, but not so much in order to make Kant's philosophy "fit the facts" as to remove the contingent assumptions that infiltrated its conception—no matter how far this deviated from the historical Kant.

The Object of Knowledge in Science

The revision of the concept of causality is not the most radical aspect of Cassirer's revisions of Kant's theory of knowledge. Far more daring is his reinterpretation of the object of empirical knowledge itself. In the first critique, Kant states that "the substratum of all that is real, that is, of all that belongs to the existence of things, is *substance*; and all that belongs to existence can be thought only as a determination of substance."[13] The notion of substance expresses that to which all predicates are attributed. Kant held that this category, *substantia et accidens*, characterized the nature of the object of cognition. This was an assumption in physics until Kant's day and it was even inherent in classical logic. Physically, a thing's characteristics define it as a reality. Logically, characteristics are predicated of the logical subject that names the substance or thing under consideration. Reality is the sum total of these determinations of things. It was assumed that the state of a thing is completely determined in every way and in regard to all possible predicates at any given moment. Kant, Cassirer points out, regarded the concept of "reality" to be interchangeable with that of "*complete* determination," "*durchgängige* Bestimmung."[14] To Cassirer's mind, it was in regard to this category, the thing and its attributes, not in regard to the concept of causality, that quantum theory posed the greatest philosophical problems. In quantum physics it is impossible to completely determine the "state" of a particle. Quantum physics requires that we use the notion of a particle, something discontinuous, and the notion of a wave, something continuous, in regard to the *same object* of knowledge. Quantum physics requires rethinking the semantics of the language we use in describing the object of knowledge. "The 'state' of a physical system no longer exhibits, according to the language of quantum theory, the same form of spatiotemporal connection which it possessed in classical mechanics. . . . For the state takes on entirely different values, according to whether we describe it in one language or the other [i.e., that of classical or of quantum mechanics], and neither can claim to define it unambiguously and exhaustively. It presents itself differently to us according to the different standpoints from which we view it, and it is impossible ever to unite the different perspectives in one glance. The particle and wave pictures must be used side by side, without our ever being able to make them congruent" (DI, 190). Cassirer realized that the solution to the paradoxes of quantum physics resulting from the Copenhagen interpretation required a reinterpretation of the meaning of terms like *state*, which could no longer be understood by the conventional usage for things in the world of perceived objects.

As in the case of causality, Kant conceived the application (schematization) of the category of substance as a determination of time: "The schema of substance is permanence of the real in time, that is, the representation [*Vorstellung*] of the real in time in general, and so as abiding while all else changes" (*Critique of Pure Reason*, 184; A143/B183). Here, as in the case of causality, continuity is introduced, but in the sense of a continuity of place, the notion of something as "abiding" (Kant uses the word *bleibt*). This spatial notion is taken from psychological experience of things in space, but Cassirer indicates that the conceptual terminology of quantum physics was not created for describing "things" or states but rather the behavior of certain physical systems, and therefore we are wrong to speak about its basic concepts, such as that of the material point, as though we were conversing about objects in the world of tangible things. This confuses a semantics of representation with a semantics of pure significance. Physics has had to move toward axiomatization of its basic concepts, which serve as hypothetical constructions from which deductions can be made (DI, 196). Cassirer conceived the method of such hypothetical formulations to be like the use of "implicit definitions" in mathematics.[15]

Physics has left the realm of representability for a more abstract realm of symbolism in which material reality is approached indirectly. Cassirer says: "physics no longer deals directly with the existent as the materially real; it deals with its structure, its formal content" (PSF, 3:467; PsF, 3:547). He describes this transformation in physics in the final chapter of PSF 3, "Symbol and Schema in Modern Physics." The concepts of causality and the object of knowledge undergo a semantic change in contemporary physics that requires a new understanding of space and a further revision of Kant. This problem occupied Cassirer's attention again and again until the end of his life. His solution to the problem of the nature of space is typical of his philosophy of symbolic forms, and it illustrates particularly well how the Cassirerian approach to science differs both from orthodox Kantianism and from the views of the contemporary opponents of Kant's philosophy, the neopositivists.

The Object of Knowledge and the Problem of Space

For common sense, natural science provides knowledge of objective reality, things existing in space. Space itself is the subject matter of a science called geometry. The development of non-Euclidean geometries was incompatible with this commonsense view; even for philosophers, Cassirer says, these new geometries "came as a real shock" (SMC, 276). The shock was especially strong for Kantians. Kant had overturned the empirical view that space is a given, absolute entity, claiming that space was rather a form of *reine Anschauung* (pure intuition), that is, an a priori precondition of experience. Kant had assumed that the structure of the form of intuition could be described by *Euclidean* geometry. This assumption seemed harmless because until Kant's time geometry meant Euclidean geometry, and it seemed clear that space must, even as an a priori form, have some sort of definite structure. The rise of non-Euclidean geometries called both assumptions into question. According to the parallel postulate of Euclidean geometry, only one parallel can be drawn through a point next to a line. In the new geometries this was denied. Depending upon the basic axioms of the geometry involved, it might be possible to draw an infinity of parallels (Lobachevsky, Bolyai) or none at all (Riemann). With this in mind, Moritz Schlick, founder of the Vienna Circle of logical positivism, denied that there is any such thing as Kant's "pure intuition" because the space of geometry turns out to not be fixed or intuitive at all, but a construction.[16] Schlick proposes to replace the Kantian theory of space as pure intuition with a methodological conception based on the idea of the "implicit definitions" used in axiomatic method. In effect, Schlick followed a strategy that Cassirer had developed years earlier. In a discussion of Schlick's main work, the *Allgemeine Erkenntnislehre* (1918, 2d ed. 1925, translated as *General Theory of Knowledge*) published in 1927, Cassirer regards Schlick's work as a vindication of a thesis "that I sought to develop and prove nearly two decades ago in my book *Substance and Function*," namely, that the concept of law replaces the concept of substance in modern physics.[17] Moreover, Schlick uses the same conceptual means to make this point, emphasizing, as Cassirer did, the conceptual role in science of implicit definitions.

The "implicit definition" is a procedure that permits mathematicians and scientists to avoid relying on the supposed certainty of intuition. Basic concepts, such as the geometrical notions of the point or straight line, cannot be defined since they cannot be resolved into more basic or simpler geometrical concepts. They seem to require an appeal to intuition. But the proliferation of geometries had discredited intuition; if the parallel postulate was no longer secure, then nothing else that seemed certain to intuition could be relied upon. David Hilbert's *Foundations of Geometry* dispensed completely with reliance on intuition and made geometry a completely axiomatic science. To this end Hilbert adopted the notion that Gergonne termed an "implicit definition."[18] The meaning of a term defined in this way derives from the place that the concept holds in the system where it finds application. Actually there is no defining in this method, but the procedure functions like a definition. Applied to theoretical concepts in physics as well, the procedure captured the attention of philosophers of science.

Schlick gives the implicit definition a prominent place in his *General Theory of Knowledge*. "To define a concept implicitly is to determine it by means of its relations to other concepts. But to apply such a concept to reality is to choose, out of the infinite wealth of relations in the world, a certain complex or grouping and to embrace this complex as a unit by designating it with a name."[19] Following Poincaré, Schlick termed this procedure "conventionalistic."

Schlick criticizes Kant's theory of space as pure intuition because Kant, he claims, could not help but infer from an (unacceptable) analogy between the space of everyday psychological experience and physical space that the latter is Euclidean. Kant's space as "pure intuition" is therefore really semipsychological because, Schlick concludes, the "sole method" capable of eliminating the psychological element completely from geometry, the method of implicit definitions, was unknown in Kant's day.[20] For this reason Schlick rejects Cassirer's interpretation in *Einstein's Theory of Relativity* that Kant's "pure intuition" is a "method of objectification" (Schlick, ibid.; cf. SF/ET, 451). Schlick fails to distinguish between the role of apologist for the historical Kant and the attempt to develop Kantianism as a philosophy. In the Einstein book Cassirer was concerned with the latter.

Cassirer and Schlick agree on the need to revise Kant's theory of space, but they differ about whether this entails rejecting his basic conception of pure intuition. The point of contention is the extent to which they are prepared to call spatiality, as a form of intuition, "conventional." Cassirer admits that the constructive nature of space, as seen in the different kinds of geometries, involves conventionalism. Indeed, the symbolic character of all physical knowledge always has a conventional aspect. But Schlick, Cassirer says, admits only the negative moment of the "'semiotic' character of all thought and knowledge," the arbitrary and conventional character of signs, whereas it also has another, positive aspect. We become aware of this aspect when we ask how it is possible that meanings are ever assigned to such conventional signs, that is, how it is possible that something sensory ever becomes the carrier of a meaning.[21] This, Cassirer adds, is "one of the most difficult problems of the critique of knowledge, if not the problem of the critique of knowledge itself." Even the problem of the objectivity of "things" is subsequent to it because this question extends to the perceptual world itself. These comments on Schlick raise the central issue of Cassirer's theory of meaning and symbolism: the problem of symbolic pregnance. Without the assumption of the Urphänomen of meaning the idea of a "conventional meaning" does not make sense. Into this dimension of Cassirer's thought Schlick did not enter. But for Cassirer, these questions, which belong to his transcendental "first philosophy" of meaning, are crucial even to problems such as these in the philosophy of science. Even though some aspects of Cassirer's work resemble thinking in the Vienna Circle, it does not vindicate, as Philipp Frank suggested, logical empiricism.

Cassirer grants Schlick that Kant's conception of science was instrumental in the development of his critical philosophy and that Kant's understanding of science was limited to the science of his time. The "analogies of experience" were shaped according to the three fundamental Newtonian laws: inertia, the proportionality of force and acceleration, and the equality of action and reaction (SF/ET, 415). Because of these contingent elements in their conception, Cassirer felt no qualms about completely reinterpreting Kant's first and second analogies, the permanence of substance and succession in accordance with the law of causality. But, unlike Schlick, Cassirer does not regard the need for reinterpretation as a defect in the "transcendental method" itself.

Cassirer does not think that the different geometries pose an insuperable difficulty for transcendental philosophy. Modern mathematical group theory provides a means to reconcile Euclidean and non-Euclidean geometries. It declares no single system to be definitive, but only the "totality of possible geometrical systems" (SMC, 283). Felix Klein's work on the mathematical theory of groups caught

Cassirer's attention as a way to unify the different geometries.[22] The a priori character of spatiality remains unaffected by this variety of geometries. Different physical theories call for different kinds of geometry, but spatiality (of whatever kind) remains a priori—not a given. Cassirer justifies his view by pointing out that "the structures of geometry, whether Euclidean or non-Euclidean, possess no immediate correlate in the world of existence. They exist as little physically in things as they do psychically in our thoughts but all their 'being,' i.e., their validity and truth, consists in their ideal meaning" (SF/ET, 433). In this way Cassirer turns the crisis in the theory of space into an argument in favor of the a priority of space as a form of intuition.

Cassirer regards the development of Einstein's special and general theories of relativity as proof of Kant's thesis of the a priori character of space and time. Einstein's theories illustrate how the pattern of temporal and spatial determinations always follow a "rule of the understanding," namely, that "in the special theory it [the rule] is the constancy of the velocity of light, in the general theory the more inclusive doctrine that all Gaussian coordinate systems are of equal value for the formation of the universal natural laws" (SF/ET, 415). Cassirer treats "pure intuition" functionally.

Cassirer's interpretations of the concepts of space, time, the object, and causality are all functional. Functionalism permits him to regard all the different versions of these concepts as a whole, the "totality" of possible systems of time, space, objectivity, and causality. The functional view permits Cassirer to place these concepts in the broad framework of the PSF. In his lecture "Mythic, Aesthetic, and Theoretical Space," he shows how space exhibits radical and different methods of objectification. In myth, space is defined by atmosphere, that is, an aura of feeling. For example, in mythic thought a geographical conception like "East" (where the sun rises) is felt as the direction of "light" and "life" while "West" (where the sun sets) is the direction of decline, dread, and death. In aesthetic awareness, the emotional character of space becomes a means by which an artist represents an imaginative content of some kind. For example, one need only think of the Surrealists' use of plateaus. In modern physics, space is a nonintuitive, purely significative system of order. In Cassirer's response to questions at this lecture, he describes his position with the typical locutions that space is the "Totalität" of "des möglichen Beisammen" (the totality of possible contiguity; STS, 113, 115). Cassirer distinguishes this from the "realistic view of space," which obliterates the differences between kinds of space, lumping them together in an original substantial "Einerleiheit" (sameness).

It is typical of Cassirer's approach to the problem of the a priori character of space that he does not think it matters whether a type of spatiality is intuitive or nonintuitive. This is because for Cassirer *a priori* does not mean "innate"; it means "not given," neither from without nor from within. Schlick (and Einstein) understood *a priori* to mean "prior to experience" and "fixed."[23] That is, they conceived a priori forms as immune to revision. For Cassirer, the invariants of experience are emergent. The concept of the a priori was more flexible for Cassirer than for Schlick or Einstein. Whereas for Schlick the breach between the psychological experience of space and the ways that space is conceived in modern physics marks the difference between psychological and "pure" space, Cassirer claims that even the most sensuous, most concrete forms of space (that is, the space of myth or of art) depend upon some "method of objectification." The same holds for felt, "physiological" time and for measured, quantitative time as well as for the feeling of warmth and measured temperature (SF/ET, 450). Cassirer does not mean that these "methods" are conscious procedures, but that they are unique directions of symbolic pregnance, ways of having a world. As we saw in chapter 1, for Cassirer "transcendental" philosophy is concerned with a more fundamental question than corrigibility: the theory of meaning (symbolic pregnance)—the condition of the possibility of all truth claims.

Schlick concludes his review of Cassirer's book on Einstein by recognizing and even agreeing with the "high level of the standpoint" that emerges at the end of the book, where Cassirer sketches the idea of the philosophy of symbolic forms and its functional outlook. "But," Schlick adds, "we are left with the impression that this standpoint already transcends the region of critical philosophy proper."[24] Like Weizsäcker, Schlick is concerned whether Cassirer as a neo-Kantian is "permitted" to uphold views that do not fall within the predefined limits of "the school." To Cassirer's mind, it was precisely through moving to a "higher level" of thought, incorporating insights of Hegel and Husserl, that he was able to advance the transcendental method. He felt no compulsion to confine himself to the historical system of Kant or Cohen.

At first glance Cassirer's functionalism might seem to transform transcendental philosophy into conventionalism. This would be compatible with his claim that, at least as far as contemporary physics is concerned, it is necessary to adopt the view that theories can only provide indirect "symbolic" knowledge of reality. Cassirer thinks that philosophers of every school have been forced to agree about the symbolic character of contemporary physical theory.[25] There is no simple isomorphic relationship between the signs used in physics and their referents. Yet the nonintuitive character of the object of theoretical physics did not incline Cassirer toward abandoning the normative concept of truth. He denied that science's symbols were "purely conventional signs" (*rein konventionellen Zeichen*), and he insisted that "the symbols that are the basis of science and which it cannot dispense with, must in the end somehow be adequately applicable (ibid., 461, 460). "Statements of physics may bear a purely symbolic character; but for the totality of these symbols some attachment to reality, some *fundamentum in re* will always have to be demanded. Without the fulfillment of this requirement the truth-value, the logical credit of physics, would be doomed once and for all" (*DI*, 120). Cassirer sees this *fundamentum* illustrated in the historical character of science: "No particular astronomical system, the Copernican no more than the Ptolemaic . . . may be taken as an expression of the 'true' cosmic order, but only the whole of these systems as they continuously unfold in accordance with a certain context." This development, he adds, "must progressively be confirmed in practice, in application to the empirical material" (*PSF*, 3:476; *PsF*, 3:577–78). Cassirer proposes that the philosophy of science must work hand in hand with the study of the history of science.[26] Science moves back and forth between theory formation and empirical research, following the guidelines of simplicity and comprehensibility (*DI*, 66–70). In the history of science Cassirer discerns progress toward a fuller understanding of nature. This progress cannot be measured by an external yardstick. Instead, each individual scientific investigator must apply what Cassirer called an "intensive" measure: the clarity, purity, sharpness, and organizational and predictive power of the theories advanced.[27] Different theories will always be able to explain equally well all the available empirical data. From a strictly logical point of view the choice of one theory is a matter of convention, but in science as a historical reality such choices are not arbitrary. The history of theories in astronomy, for example, is not a history of arbitrary choices or tosses of the coin. Certain theories recommend themselves at particular times in the history of a science "in application to the empirical material." Science is nonetheless unified as a symbolic form, as a way of having a world. Science is the historical quest for truth in the sense of the "ideal limit of the diversely changing theories."[28]

This methodological conception of truth is not determined by the "object" of science. Cassirer rejected such "foundations" for truth, including the one finding favor among positivistically inclined philosophers of science, namely, physicalism. Physicalism, he says, erroneously makes one form of knowledge into the absolute norm and measure of the value of all cognition.[29] The unity of knowledge is dependent upon the unity of meaning, not upon the unity of the object of knowledge. Every attempt to found the concept of truth upon the object of a particular science, be it physics, history, psychology, or logic, limits the concept of the world to a particular interpretation and thereby commits the error of reducing the world as a phenomenon of meaning to a substantial being.

Cassirer pursues a course opposite to that of the positivists in developing his philosophical theory of truth. Instead of reducing the meaning of "truth" to a single substantial reality, physicalism, he insists upon irreconcilable differences between the meaning of this term in the sciences and in the humanities. Only by recognizing these differences is it possible, he thinks, to develop an adequate philosophical theory of truth.

For Cassirer, the true founder of natural science was Galileo and the founder of the *Geisteswissenschaften* or sciences of man was Galileo's countryman, Giambattista Vico. Vico's chief work, *The New Science*, first published in 1725, was named after Galileo's *Two New Sciences* (1638). Vico's book bore its title, Cassirer said, "with good reason" (*LH*, 54). According to Cassirer, Vico provided the first philosophical analysis of historical thought (*EM*, 172); he was the first to conceive the general plan of the study of the Geisteswissenschaften (*WW*, 5); he first recognized and defended—against Descartes—the methodological uniqueness and distinctive value of historical knowledge (*LH*, 52); and, finally, he was the true "discoverer of myth," that is, the one who first grasped that myth was something with a structure all its own, its own language, and its own form of time (*PK*, 296). Cassirer agrees with Vico's conception of the humanities, which interprets art and historical understanding in relation to an original "poetic" understanding of the world. Poetry and historical understanding have one power in common that they share with the original mythico-poetic understanding of the world: personification (*EM*, 153). They bring the world to life for us. This is the chief difference between the humanities and social sciences, which study man "objectively" and statistically. Compared with the knowledge of man we gain by reading a historian or novelist, social scientific knowledge, Cassirer says, is "inert and colorless" because it only deals with man on the "average" (*EM*, 206). Despite the differences between the world of the historian and the world of the poet or artist, their mutual concern for concrete, personal, human experience differentiates their perspective on man from the viewpoint in the social sciences, which model themselves on the natural sciences.

Cassirer claims that the objects of study in the humanities and

Truth and the Humanities

natural sciences can be distinguished by means of "a phenomenological analysis" (*LH*, 97, 101). This analysis shows that there are two basic types of perception, the perception of "things" and the perception of "expression," that is, the perception of the world as containing inanimate things and the perception of the world in terms of expressive qualities—the trustworthy, fruitful, friendly, or terrifying.

A basic tendency of scientific thought, Cassirer says, is that it "strives toward a conception of the world from which the 'personal' has been eliminated" (*LH*, 104). The humanities follow the opposite course: "the science of culture teaches us to interpret symbols in order to decipher their latent meaning, to make visible again the life from which they originally came into being" (*LH*, 158). Cassirer calls this process of interpretation "hermeneutic" (*LH*, 173).

The humanities or human studies cannot be reduced to natural sciences, even though the objects of the humanities cannot be completely divorced from the physical sphere. Their objects are historical artifacts that express human attitudes, beliefs, thoughts, and feelings. The marble in Michelangelo's *David*, the physiological sounds of a poem read aloud, are essential, but they do not provide our understanding of the work as a product of a historical epoch or of the other meanings latent in them. By means of what Cassirer calls a "most difficult, and complex 'hermeneutic,'" it becomes possible to understand, for example, what *David* meant to the citizens of Florence at the time of its creation or to formulate what it expresses artistically.

Because of this interpreted character, works of culture are doubly endangered. They can be physically destroyed or they can lose their meaning through forgetfulness. On the other hand, new meanings can accumulate. The human studies have the endless task of reinterpreting, of recollecting and revitalizing, the works of culture. Here the problem of truth enters.

Cassirer uses the terms *Geisteswissenschaft* and *Naturwissenschaft* to distinguish between the study of human historical life and the study of nature. To this extent he follows Dilthey. It is perhaps not coincidental that Cassirer introduced his notion of symbolic form in "Der Begriff der symbolischen Form im Aufbau der Geisteswissenschaften" (The concept of symbolic form in the structure of the human studies), an essay that recalls the title of Dilthey's chief work, *Der Aufbau der Geschichtlichen Welt in den Geisteswissenschaften*.[30] Cassirer's chief work on the method of the human studies bears the title *Zur Logik der Kulturwissenschaften* (translated as *The Logic of the Humanities*). Cassirer's preference for the term *Kulturwissenschaft* (science of culture) in this title should not be taken to indicate greater agreement with Windelband and Rickert, the main figures of the Baden school of neo-Kantianism that introduced the term *Kultur-wissenschaft*, than with Dilthey's school. Cassirer used *Geisteswis-senschaft* and *Kulturwissenschaft* as interchangeable designations.[31]

In the nineteenth century the accepted scientific picture of the world was mechanistic, revolving around the two notions of force and matter (see *LH*, 71, 164). This mechanistic view was expressed in Germany in naturalistic philosophies ranging from Ludwig Büchner's popular views to Marx and Engels's dialectical and historical materialism. Cassirer regarded historical materialism as the final expression of the naturalistic world view: the belief that all culture and history could be explained in terms of economics (*LH*, 163–64). On this view culture is only a "superstructure" (*Überbau*) erected on the actual driving forces of economic necessity, its *Basis*. For historical materialism "scientific" necessity is all-pervasive, extending naturalism to the origins of human history. In the nineteenth century even thinkers who opposed the subsumption of the Geisteswissenschaften under the natural sciences nonetheless shared in the prevailing mechanistic conception of nature. Dilthey himself distinguished the natural sciences from the Geisteswissenschaften on the basis of the former's use of strict causal explanation and the latter's pursuit of historical "understanding."[32]

A change in the mechanistic outlook occurred in the early twentieth century when what Cassirer called "the armored car of the mathematical-scientific method" suddenly no longer appeared so ironclad. The break came, Cassirer says, because nineteenth-century materialism was so convinced that reality was exhausted by matter and force that it blinded itself to the reality of form (*LH*, 71). Physics, biology, and psychology all underwent far-reaching changes that departed from the mechanistic conception of nature. These changes had one feature in common: they stressed the concept of form over causality (see *LH*, chap. 4). For example, in biology the theory of mutations limited Darwinian theory's predilection for continuity in evolution (the need to find "missing links"; see *LH*, 179–80). Bertalanffy's systems-theoretical biology conceived the organism in a reciprocal relationship with its world (*LH*, 168–69), such that the relationship between the whole system and its parts was inexplicable as a mere summation of forces. In psychology, Gestalt theorists proposed that the structure of the perceptual field could only be understood as a whole, not as atomistic elements (*LH*, 171). Finally, with the advent of electromagnetic field physics, the "material point" turns out to be "an outgrowth of the field" rather than the field being an aggregate of material points. The mechanistic view of nature no longer seemed sufficient.[33]

According to the mechanistic point of view, still shared by Dilthey, the sciences engage essentially in causal explanations. In the new physics, law and property constants were not necessarily explicable as causal invariants. Rejecting panmechanism, Cassirer began with the view that the natural sciences and the human studies both seek to understand structural forms and their transformations. Cassirer called this new way of thinking "structuralism."[34] Because of this common goal, the criterion for distinguishing between the natural sciences and the human studies had to be reconsidered.

Windelband introduced a distinction, then taken over by Rickert, between the natural sciences and human studies according to their generality. According to Windelband, natural science seeks to establish general laws and so is "nomothetic," but the human studies describe particular facts and so are "idiographic."[35] Cassirer disagrees with this view (LH, 89, 120). In some natural sciences, such as geology, the objects of study are concrete, unique events (EM, 186–87). In addition, and more important, every field of study, no matter how particular its objects, aims to relate particular occurrences to a general form or structure. For example, art historians are interested in style; linguists compare the different ways various languages handle the declension of nouns; historians use ideal types like "medieval man" or "Renaissance man." The difference between the natural sciences and human studies therefore lies rather in the *way* in which the particulars are related to universals. The natural sciences, Cassirer says, "subordinate" the particular to the universal, but the human sciences only "coordinate" them, claiming only to be able to "characterize" individuals, never to deduce them from a rule (LH, 140). The constants in the human sciences are entirely different from those in the natural sciences. The latter's invariants are law constants, the former's are constancies of *meaning* (LH, 139–43). The different types of personalities that qualify for the designation "Renaissance man" do so not on the basis of a law but a "common task," which the individuals involved might not themselves recognize as shared because each contributes to this end for different reasons. There is no common trait that permits connecting such contrasting figures as Ficino and Machiavelli or Michelangelo and Cesare Borgia, but they nonetheless all contribute in different ways to the new independence of life and thought and individualism that sets off the Renaissance from the middle ages. The human studies investigate forms that result from human activity, not natural laws. The source of this activity, Cassirer says, is symbolic thought. Symbolic thought "overcomes the natural inertia of man and endows him with a new ability, the ability constantly to reshape his human universe" (EM, 62). Cassirer calls this the "humanistic" conception of culture. By contrast, naturalistic conceptions of culture overlook the human capacity to interpret and restructure life by means of symbolic thought and seek to explain history on the model of natural laws.[36]

The human studies are primarily historical in method. In contrast, the social sciences operate with statistical methods. Statistics have great value for sociology and economics, but Cassirer denies their value in the study of history. The proper place to apply statistics is collective phenomena, Cassirer contends, pointing to the methodological works of Keynes and von Mises (EM, 198); it is wrong to try to use them to understand a single case. Statistics do not permit seeing the individual case for what it is, an *individual* case. The historian does not just describe physical occurrences, but wants rather to disclose the meaning of an event. For example, the statistics on suicides in ancient Rome tell us nothing about the significance of Cato's suicide, as an act of protest to the military victory that gave Julius Caesar dictatorial power. It was, Cassirer says, "a symbolic act" (EM, 198) of a Roman republican against the new order of things. The meaning of such an act cannot be understood statistically. Insofar as the social sciences are statistical and are modeled on the natural sciences, they can tell us little about man as a personality. Cassirer drew upon work in the social sciences—in cultural anthropology, experimental psychology, and linguistics—but he wrote little about the methodologies in these fields. The major exception is his far-reaching essay "Structuralism in Modern Linguistics." Suffice it to say that the social sciences represent a middle ground between the natural sciences and the humanities. Cassirer chose to devote his attention to the extremes. The chief means for the study of man, as distinct from nature, is historical knowledge.

Historical Understanding

Historical awareness is a late product of civilization. The first philosophical analysis of historical consciousness, Cassirer contends, does not arise until the eighteenth century, in the work of Vico. Genuine historical consciousness depends upon a sense of the past as something unique that cannot be repeated. Hence, the discovery of historical time resulted, Cassirer says, in a "new concept of truth" (EM, 173). The historical conception of truth cannot be assimilated to the ideal of truth in science.

From a purely logical standpoint, truth is one, but the aim of science—to find law hypotheses—cannot constitute the meaning of truth for history. On the contrary, to seek law hypotheses for history would be to fall into "historicism" in Popper's sense of the word, that is, to have a "naturalistic" conception of history. History must measure its success by the way it interprets artifacts as "messages from the past" (EM, 177). Cassirer describes the situation of the historian this way: "A new understanding of the past gives us a new prospect of the future, which in turn becomes an impulse to intellectual and social life. For this double view of the world in prospect and in retrospect the historian must select his point of departure. He cannot go beyond the conditions of his present experience. Historical knowledge is the answer to definite questions, an answer which must be given by the past; but the questions themselves are put and dictated by the present—by our present intellectual interests and our present moral and social needs" (EM, 178). From a methodological point of view, the task of the historian is to interpret meanings, not to offer law hypotheses; hence, Cassirer concludes, "history is included in the field of hermeneutics, not in that of natural science" (EM, 195). Cassirer nowhere closely defines his conception of "hermeneutics," nor does he say what is included in this field besides history. But it is clear that hermeneutics has to deal with the interpretation of meaning in order to clarify and expose our "pre-understanding" (Vorverständnis), the outlooks dictated by our often-unconscious intellectual interests, our moral and social needs: "In history the interpretation of symbols precedes the collection of facts, and without this interpretation there is no approach to historical truth" (EM, 196). It is clear too that for Cassirer interpretation never comes to an end. He illustrates this with the many different interpretations given to a philosopher's ideas through the ages: "In the case of Plato himself we can trace the same development. We have a mystic Plato, the Plato of neo-Platonism; a Christian Plato, the Plato of Augustine and Marsilio Ficino; a rationalistic Plato, the Plato of Moses Mendelssohn; and a few decades ago we were offered a Kantian Plato [Paul Natorp's]. We may smile at all these different interpretations. Yet they have not only a negative but also a positive side. They have all in their measure contributed to an understanding and to a systematic valuation of Plato's work. Each has insisted on a certain aspect which is contained in this work, but which could only be made manifest by a complicated process of thought" (EM, 180). The variety of possible interpretations is a problem only if we insist that only one can be valid and that this "definitive" version excludes all others. Cassirer does not hold such a view. Different interpretations are not merely fruitful but also inescapable, since there is a constant need to reinterpret works of culture in order to possess them (EM, 184–85). Only the summation of all the "aspects" of philosophical texts, taken together, can result in what approaches the complete, true interpretation: the totality of acceptable interpretations.

Does this mean that anything goes? The best illustration of Cassirer's conception of the limits of interpretation is his critical review of Heidegger's *Kant and the Problem of Metaphysics*. Cassirer did not believe that fidelity to an author's intention can itself be regarded as the measure of a correct interpretation.[37] An author may not himself be a good witness to his philosophy. Cassirer cites Kant's own remark that a philosopher may, in the attempt to determine a concept, sometimes even speak in opposition to his own intention (*EM*, 180). The history of philosophy shows that the thinker who first introduces a concept is rarely the one to develop it fully (*EM*, 180). To stick to the author's intention would erect a roadblock to the interpretation of his philosophy, which may well involve much more than its author realized. As the author of the *PSF*, Cassirer is in principle committed to the proliferation of interpretations. Despite all this and Cassirer's explicit agreement with the fruitfulness of new interpretations and even his "complete agreement" with Heidegger on many basic theses, he nonetheless rejects Heidegger's interpretation as a whole and calls for a *restitutio in integram* of Kant's philosophy.[38] Upon what criteria does Cassirer base his objection to Heidegger's interpretation? He rejects Heidegger's book for two reasons, both of which reflect Cassirer's standard for an acceptable interpretation: the ideal of doing justice to the whole. Heidegger claims to give an interpretation of Kant's thought as a whole, whereas he bases his argument upon only a small part, the doctrine of the schematism. Cassirer does not find fault in principle with an attempt to interpret the macrocosm in the microcosm; moreover, he agrees enthusiastically with what Heidegger says about the doctrine of the schematism as such. But he rejects Heidegger's claim to interpret Kant as a whole because the conclusions Heidegger draws are inconsistent with the second half of the *Critique of Pure Reason*, with the ethics of the *Critique of Practical Reason*, and with the *Critique of Judgment*. Instead of showing the whole in the part, the whole becomes internally inconsistent. Heidegger gives an interpretation of Kant in which reason becomes bound to sensibility so as to prohibit the transcendence of the idea which Kant characterizes as the nature of reason in the second half of the first critique and upon which depends his ethics and his theory of the beautiful. Heidegger's interpretation makes Kantian idealism into a form of existentialism. In Cassirer's eyes this is not really an interpretation of Kant's philosophy but an attempt by Heidegger to "subdue it and make it serviceable for his problem" (ibid., 149). Cassirer's first criterion for an acceptable interpretation is that it does justice to the whole from the standpoint of "material and systematic correctness" (p. 135).

Heidegger attributes the changes in the second edition of the *Critique of Pure Reason* to Kant's discovering the "common root" of understanding and sensibility in the productive imagination. The resulting realization of finitude, Heidegger claimed, was something from which Kant "recoiled," so that he rewrote the *Critique* in a way that gave less emphasis to the productive imagination. In reality, Kant rewrote the *Critique* because it was misread in the review by Garve and Feder as a form of subjective idealism (ibid., 153). To depict the leading mind of the German Enlightenment as a Kierkegaardean figure recoiling from Nothing in dread is to ignore Kant's character as a thinker, so that this cannot qualify as an acceptable interpretation of Kant's thought. Cassirer protests: "Kant was and remained—in the most noble and beautiful sense of this word—a thinker of the Enlightenment. He strove for illumination even where he thought about the deepest and most hidden grounds of being." In contrast, he adds, "from the very outset Heidegger's philosophy obeys, as it were, a different principle of style" (ibid., 155). Cassirer's second criterion for an acceptable interpretation of a philosopher is that it does justice to the whole from the standpoint of intellectual style.

Whether or not one accepts these two criteria for the evaluation of an interpretation, the point remains that Cassirer envisioned limits to interpretation. He did not sanction a relativistic historicism.

Cassirer's thesis that historical research deals with meaning might appear to be suited to the study of the history of ideas but not to political history. Cassirer denied this. The historian investigating political events is in the same situation as the historian of ideas; both must engage in hermeneutic activity. Practical effects do not give documents or artifacts their *historical* content (*EM*, 196–97). A photograph, an anecdote, a simple quotation may have little effect on history yet might be very helpful for the historical understanding of the character of a person, a nation, an event, or an epoch of political history.

History establishes what Cassirer calls "the ideality of recollection"; it transforms the events of the past into a great drama—full of tensions and conflicts, hopes and illusions, greatness and misery (*EM*, 205). This drama is not invented by the historian; it is reconstructed from records and documents. No matter how much genius the historian brings to his topic or how much his work appears to be like a "good story," his work can nonetheless become "outdated" as historical research progresses. There are better and poorer histories. The criteria for measuring their relative superiority cannot be found, however, simply in the truth value of the specific statements they contain but in the ideal reconstruction of the *whole* drama of events they present.

Art

Like history, art presents us with ideal forms. Artistic form is purely aesthetic yet it is nonetheless cognitive because art is a symbolic form. Prior to Morris, Langer, and Goodman, Cassirer developed the thesis that works of art are symbols.[39] Cassirer is not a defender of *art pour l'art*; he thinks that art provides an indispensable access to the world, a way of understanding reality. At one extreme, the artist—especially the lyric poet and the composer—can revitalize mythic vision and feeling (*SMC*, 188; *EM*, 154–56). On the other extreme, art can be naturalistic, even more "realistic" than any scientific account. Cassirer sees such realism particularly in the comic: "We are perhaps never nearer to our human world than in the works of a great comic writer—in Cervantes' *Don Quixote*, Sterne's *Tristram Shandy*, or Dickens' *Pickwick Papers*. We become observant of the minutest details; we see this world in all its narrowness, its pettiness, and silliness. We live in this restricted world, but we are no longer imprisoned by it. Such is the character of the comic catharsis. Things and events begin to lose their material weight; scorn is dissolved into laughter and laughter is liberation" (*EM*, 150). Art elevates our awareness to a new state because it puts us in a new position. We do not really have the emotions that we do in ordinary experience; otherwise we could not withstand the strains of the outrages, cruelties, and atrocities in a Sophoclean or Shakespearean drama (*EM*, 149; *SMC*, 164). Yet this does not mean that art deceives us with mere phantasmagoria. It introduces us to a world of images through which we gain a perspective on the world we normally live in, the thoughts and emotions we normally have. If art is good, we cannot afterward regard life in the same way as before, because our horizon has been enlarged and we see the world and our place in it differently. In art "the world always seems to be revealed for us in new ways" (*LH*, 83). Even when it is closest to a historical description, as in epic literature, art does more than refresh our memory. Unlike a historical account, which aims primarily at providing us with a reliable chronicle of real occurrences, an epic provides us with "a world-perspective in which we are now able to see the totality of events and the entire world of man in a new light" (*LH*, 83).

How does this let us speak of art in regard to the norm of "truth"? Cassirer says that "every great lyricist gives us knowledge of a new feeling for the world . . . a knowledge which cannot be grasped in abstract concepts. . . . We owe to art the fact that in its particular works it allows us to feel and to know what is objective; that it places all its objective creations before us with a concreteness and individuality which floods them with a life of strength and intensity" (LH, 85). This characterization of art is the extreme opposite of modern physical knowledge, which, as something free from concrete, individual particularities, describes the world "from the standpoint of no one" (PSF, 3:478; PsF, 3:559). Modern physics is a symbolism of pure significance, having no correlate in our immediate sensuous experience. The symbols of art are inseparable from sensuous, expressive content.[40] But works of art are not merely expressive (EM, 146). Like the expressive symbolism in facial expressions and gestures or the perception of physiognomic qualities in natural objects, a work of art is a kind of image, but of a special sort. Cassirer argues against Croce that art is not just expression pure and simple; the artist does not just display his emotions (SMC, 157). Art is an interpretation of reality, opening up a world to us. The artist neither remains in the common reality of empirical, practical things nor withdraws inward, to his private feelings. In art, a medium permits giving expressive meaning an objective form (SMC, 160–62). But working in a medium alone does not make what an artist produces art, nor does the fact that the result might be regarded as "beautiful." The fact that someone succeeds in expressing his emotions in a love letter, Cassirer remarks, does not make the letter's author into an artist. The author as artist must do more than give form to his feelings: he must choose from the infinite potentialities for aesthetic expression a form that says something best. "It is not the degree of infection, but the degree of intensification and illumination which is the measure of the excellence of art" (EM, 148). The artist focuses our attention by intensifying our experience and illuminating it. Works of art do not make assertions like propositions and so cannot be judged in terms of truth value, but they do stand in a dialogical relationship to the spectator, because they have something to say. Addressing Paris artists, Eiffel defined the beauty of his tower by referring to the balance in the way he solved the technical problem of support against high winds. But this, Cassirer points out, has nothing to do with beauty as an expression of a relationship between man and the world (STS, 85–86). Art is not just the aesthetically pleasing nor is it entertainment, a way of evading the truth. It gives us access to knowledge of life as it is otherwise invisible to mere "empirical" observation.

Art has a twofold character for Cassirer. First, it is the creative process in which the whole gamut of human experience is given expression in ideal forms or images. Such images do not merely serve to infect man's feelings or attitudes, as critics of art from Plato to Tolstoi feared. They do not make him a passive slave to his emotions (SMC, 199–202). This is because art also has a second, liberating character. Art allows the spectator to gain distance from his feelings by communicating reality in objective artistic forms (see SMC, 196–215). Art permits the viewer to gain a perspective of the world and the human situation. It broadens the horizon.

One of Cassirer's most profound discussions of this second aspect of art, its liberating character, is found in The Platonic Renaissance in England. There he gives an account of the importance of the comic in Renaissance literature in which he describes how the comic can stand as an "objective criterion of truth and falsehood" (PRE, 168). Cassirer describes the humor of such writers as Cervantes, Boccaccio, Erasmus, Rabelais, Hans Sachs, and, especially, Shakespeare as a "liberating, life-giving, and life-forming power of the soul." It is not sarcasm and so "nothing really genuine and vital need fear its judgment" (PRE, 183). Humor reveals mistaken seriousness, pedantry, and bigotry. "To the pedant, as to the zealot, freedom of thought is an abomination; for the former takes shelter from it behind the dignity of knowledge, the latter behind the sanctified authority of religion. When both entrench themselves behind a false gravity, nothing remains but to subject them to the test of ridicule and so to expose them" (PRE, 184). The comic is a means of bringing the truth to light. Cassirer takes pains to distinguish humor from optimism or an attitude that is blind to tragedy.[41] Humor at its best is a means of revealing the unstated truth about human actions and the human situation. Humor can show what particular attitudes can lead to and thus provide a kind of reductio ad absurdum. The persons in a drama such as Moliere's Miser, although unreal in one sense, show how different human purposes can support or deny freedom or even life itself.

The comic, tragic, and lyrical elements in art together depict what Cassirer calls the Gesamtbild des Lebens, the whole image of life, a constant movement from one constellation of feeling to another, life's ups and downs and turns: "All that which we call life is this kind of transition, from delight and inclination [Lust] to dislike and aversion [Unlust] and vice-versa. Life is therefore neither suffering [Leid] nor delight, neither tragedy nor comedy. Rather, it is both in one."[42] To show this Gesamtbild is an achievement of art to which neither science nor history can attain.

Cassirer contends that neither science, nor history, nor art can ever take the place of one another. Physical science pursues the truth of universal law hypotheses. History cannot pursue this end without falling into naturalism; it depicts historical forces, conflicting human purposes, and the significance of events. This significance can change as later events give new importance to past events. Art confronts us with a world of ideal imaginative forms, in which we can recognize the possibilities and realities of human feeling and experience as a lived, personal reality. This world of feeling is not measured by historical or scientific standards; art can only be judged by standards of artistic truth.

A theory of truth that favors science, history, or art absolutizes one of the dimensions of life, dogmatically elevating it to a position of absolute superiority. The main task for a philosophical theory of truth must be to retain the view that truth is a unity yet correct the mistaken belief that truth is *Einerlei*, of one form. It must avoid falsely compressing different symbolic forms into what Cassirer calls an "ultimate metaphysical unity, into the unity and simplicity of an absolute 'world ground'" (*SF/ET*, 446).

The Unity of Truth   At the conclusion of his work on Einstein's theory of relativity, Cassirer explains how he understands the concept of truth in "systematic philosophy." Instead of searching for an "absolute ground" or "foundation" for truth in a metaphysical principle, the *totality* of the different symbolic forms provides a unifying *methodological* approach to truth. Cassirer concludes that "each particular form would be 'relativized' with regard to the others, but since this 'relativization' is throughout reciprocal and since no single form but only the systematic totality can serve as the expression of 'truth' and 'reality,' the boundary that results appears as a thoroughly immanent boundary, as one that is removed as soon as we again relate the individual to the system as a whole" (*SF/ET*, 447). In other words, the limits of one symbolic form do not limit access to truth absolutely. For Cassirer, the contrary is true; the manifold nature of the symbolic forms is what gives us access to the truth as a totality.

Cassirer's position is that "the manifold character of the meanings of being do not stand in contradiction to the demand for the unity of being. It is this manifoldness that actually fulfills the demand for unity."[43] Keeping this in mind, we can distinguish Cassirer's position from relativism.

Truth and Relativism

The problem of relativism arises when the limits between symbolic forms are confused. Relativism is avoided by recognizing that the different symbolic forms are not arbitrarily interchangeable. By this criterion Paul Feyerabend represents relativism in the philosophy of science. Whereas Schlick's conventionalism permitted upholding the interchangeability of certain scientific theories, Feyerabend is prepared to accept the basic interchangeability of scientific and nonscientific theories. For example, when he discusses astrology in relationship to astronomy, both seem to inhabit a single, homogeneous intellectual space.[44] As we saw, Cassirer has a very positive assessment of astrology, calling it "one of the greatest attempts to achieve a systematic-constructive view of the world ever attempted by the human mind."[45] But he does not conceive astrology to be science. Astrology is the systematization of the forces of myth, and myth is not science (*WW*, 36–37).

Much of Feyerabend's work has a polemical purpose: to expose the narrowness of the scientistic attitudes held by many philosophers of science and to question the wisdom of elevating science to the status of the measure of all culture. But this should not influence the demarcation between myth and science. Feyerabend is not alone in his view of this issue. Cassirer himself points out that "there were always scholars of high authority who were apt to deny that there is any sharp difference between mythical and scientific thought" (*MS*, 7). Feyerabend, however, has read Cassirer and concluded that his radical distinction between myth and science is wrong.

Feyerabend has not himself provided a criticism of Cassirer to justify his conclusion, but rather he claims that there are case studies refuting Cassirer's position that "science and myth obey different principles of formation."[46] The work that Feyerabend refers to, a study of African religious thought by the ethnologist Robin Horton, does not mention Cassirer by name, but Horton's claims directly contradict Cassirer's position.[47] Hence, a comparison of Horton's and Cassirer's views will clearly show what distinguishes Cassirer's position and why his theory of truth is not relativistic; it will also show why the view of the myth-science demarcation advocated by Feyerabend is untenable.

According to Horton, mythical thought and science both transcend common sense by creating a "theoretical" view of the world. They both erect a unified conception of things that places events in a wider context than that provided by common sense. Cassirer and Horton agree in the fact that the function of scientific theory is to provide a more universal understanding of phenomena than the worldview of common sense, that is, the world of particular, concrete objects. They both see the limitations of commonsense thinking in its conception of the objects of knowledge as "things." The difference between their views lies in the fact that Cassirer conceives mythic thought as logically and historically prior to commonsense thought while Horton thinks myth, like scientific theory, belongs to a subsequent level of interpretation, that is, it goes beyond common sense by placing phenomena in a "broader causal context." For Cassirer, our commonsense world of objects and persons and the activities of everyday life depend on the classificatory power of language. The power to perceive the constancy and "identity" of things results from the representative function of language (STS, 10; cf. 126–28), but categorization takes its departure from a basis that is prelinguistic. Myth, in its most primitive forms, is prelinguistic; the ritual act and mute gesture form expressive images without the help of language. *Prelinguistic* does not mean *presemiotic*, however. This is important when we consider the relationship between scientific theory and myth.

Horton does not equate science and myth, but he does regard mythical thinking among primitive peoples as a system of beliefs that, like science, makes it possible to recognize important causal connections in the world.[48] For Horton, a physicist's explanation of some phenomenon by means of nuclear theory and a primitive's explanation of an illness by reference to demons are both attempts to explain a natural effect by means of a natural cause (ibid., 54). He thinks this is proven by the fact that scientists have now recognized the impossibility of tracing all sicknesses to bacteria, viruses, or other such agents because social conditions, such as stress, are also genuine causes of illness. Horton contends that disturbances in social life were already recognized in the mythical "theory" that demons cause sickness. For Horton, the disturbances in social life recognized by primitive societies and those recognized by social psychologists are equally "causal." Horton's standpoint is that "like atoms, molecules, and waves, then, the gods serve to introduce unity into diversity, simplicity into complexity, order into disorder, regularity into anomaly" (ibid., 52). Moreover, he claims that "traditional religious thought is no more or no less interested in the natural causes of things than is the theoretical thought of the sciences. Indeed, the intellectual function of its supernatural beings (as, too, that of atoms, waves, etc.) is the extension of people's vision of natural causes" (ibid., 58).

This organization, which Horton refers to as an "intellectual function," is for him the sufficient condition for speaking here of causality in a scientific sense. The difficulty with this view is that this supposedly "natural order" is not recognized as such in mythic thought. Instead, everything is taken to yield to the power of magic. Horton claims that in myth, as in science, we meet with the intellectual function of causality, the expansion of man's awareness by placing events in a "wider context," that is, a systematic, regular order, but this claim is contradicted everywhere by magical practices. Why is it commonplace in societies that think in terms of myth to attempt at every turn to influence the causes of things by means of magic if these causes are recognized as *natural* causes? Horton admits the existence of magical practices, but he does not seem to recognize the implications of this admission. These practices show that Horton's example of disease and healing is misleading because in mythic thought everything is related to man's social world, whereas the notion of "nature," something *independent* of society and human wishes, is a completely foreign notion. In order to speak of causality in a scientific sense, recognition of this independence is indispensable. Horton, and Feyerabend as well, give this criterion of scientific causal thinking too little attention.

For Cassirer, the recognition of a lawful order independent of human volition is essential for speaking of a cognitive methodology as "science." In the magical practices found everywhere among primitive societies there is no such recognition. Magic is not technology. It does not seek to utilize an objective order; rather it seeks to persuade things to follow man's desires in the belief that gods are in all things, that everything constitutes a community of life. The rituals enacted before a hunting or war party leaves the village anticipate the outcome of the effort in order to gain power from and over the quarry or enemy (*PSF*, 2:181–83; *PsF*, 2:216–18). Magic used to bring about or stop rain does not begin with a concept of nature as something independent of volition; the rain is persuaded to come or go. All those who regard myth as a kind of "primitive science" presuppose a common interest in explaining nature as the connecting factor between myth and science. To have such an interest means having a comparable conception of the object of thought, that is, "nature." This comparison confuses the levels on which myth and science approach nature. Cassirer discussed this confusion in *An Essay on Man*: "We are in the habit of dividing our life into the two spheres of practical and theoretical activity. In this division we are prone to forget that there is a lower stratum beneath them both. Primitive man is not liable to such forgetfulness. All his thoughts and his feelings are still embedded in this lower original stratum. His view of nature is neither merely theoretical nor merely practical; it is *sympathetic*" (*EM*, 82). The whole idea of "nature" is foreign to mythic thought because in myth the world is seen in terms of a living society in which man is a member. The inanimate objects, vegetation, and animals are conceived in animism and totemism to be man's relatives. Hence, magic is the art of persuasion: "The sorcerer, if he is the right man, if he knows the magic spells, and if he understands how to use them at the right time and in the right order, is the master of everything" (MS, 281). This has nothing to do with nor does it give rise to the scientific, causal conception of natural processes. The development of the scientific concept of causality depends, Cassirer says, on the fact that man intervenes with his bodily activities, by means of tool use, into natural processes and so learns that his desires must recognize certain "natural" limits.

In myth and science the notion of causality has radically different meanings. In science, individual events are regarded as expressions of general laws. The mere contiguity of things is unimportant, for example, wisely diverse phenomena such as the free fall of bodies, the motion of the planets, and the actions of the tides are all explained by reference to the law of gravitation. But in myth, spatial and substantial cohesion between things, the fact that things are "related" to one another like members of a community, is all-important. Even where the spatial distance between phenomena is at its greatest in myth—in astrology—the principle of substantial "belonging together" remains operative. Myth does not subsume different things under general rules and so place them in a "wider causal context"; it "brings them together" by finding substantial identities between them. It has a diametrically different directionality than science; it condenses reality to a substantial, thinglike entity, to something like an intellectual point, the very opposite of a wider context of a broad system. Insofar as there are mythical explanations of things, these never place objects in the wider causal context of *universal* rules, but display a unique, *singular* metamorphosis that "explains" their "origin."

Cassirer nowhere denies that in primitive societies people think in a practical as well as a mythical manner; he agreed with Malinowski on this point (EM, 30). He recognized that in the Renaissance it was common for individual thinkers such as Kepler to be engaged both in magic and in scientific research, but such personal conjunctions do not permit inferring that myth and science themselves are therefore the same thing. Horton, Feyerabend, and all those who view myth as "(primitive) science" unjustifiably ignore the radically different conceptions of the object and causality in myth and science. By ignoring these differences, tolerance is proclaimed for a plurality of ways of thinking at the expense of recognizing their autonomy. Either myth is taken to be an early or crude stage of science or the two are simply regarded as interchangeable. On this view there is no real difference between one explanation in terms of natural laws and another in terms of demonic interventions.

The resulting theory of truth is pragmatic in a bad sense. Any view is as good as any other as long as it satisfies us in our dealings with our experience. Quine, for example, was ready to argue this point about abstract mathematical entities: "Epistemologically these are myths on the same footing with physical objects and gods, neither better nor worse except for differences in the degree to which they expedite our dealings with sense experience."[49] On Cassirer's view, scientific thought must regard myth as erroneous because myth does not recognize causal explanation in the sense of natural laws. On the other hand, mythic thinking must regard science as incomplete and unwise because its explanations only treat of what is generally the case, ignoring the concrete. The question of fate so essential to astrology and the—for myth—all-important concern of the significance of death are not scientific problems.

For Cassirer, myth and science do not stand on the same epistemological footing. Science is a phenomenon of pure significance, while myth is a phenomenon of expression. Unless these differences of meaning are kept clearly in mind, the resulting theory of truth must be relativistic, so truth becomes purely a matter of preference.

Cassirer maintains that the unity of truth should not be confused with homogeneity. This is not the same as claiming that truth is a matter of choice. Physical science, history, and art provide distinct types of knowledge. Science provides knowledge of natural laws; history provides knowledge of the actual forces and purposes in human life; art provides ideal understanding of the world as it is experienced through the human imagination. Art seems closest of these three symbolic forms to myth, but here, too, there are radical differences. Myth and art both depend upon the perception of expression, but mythic thought, the more naive of the two, is overwhelmed by this perception. For myth the world is a pan-demonium. Even though poets and artists may have a sentimental longing to return to this sense of things, their work, which stands as an objectification of their awareness of life, prohibits it. Art cannot return to myth and remain art.[50] In mythic experience, human life is "bound and fettered," but in art it becomes "aesthetically liberated" (LM, 98). Instead of merely submerging man in an emotional bath, art provides distance and an awareness of life. The greater the art, the more profound our awareness. This awareness, like mythic awareness, is "sympathetic" (FM, 170). Yet the subject is no longer overwhelmed by this sympathy as in myth—the infection feared by Plato and Tolstoi. Art shows us aesthetic reality; through the senses we are personally confronted with this reality, struck in the way that Cassirer says we are personally affected more by Hölderlin than by Hegel (IG, 155). Depth in art is depth of feeling coupled with the distance accompanying the universality of objectification. Cassirer denies that truth takes only one form.

but nowhere does he suggest that it is immaterial how we consider the world, or that myth, art, science, technology, or an ethical point of view can be equated or interchanged. His point is the opposite; each provides a unique, indispensable understanding of the world.

The closest that any recent philosopher has come to a position like Cassirer's is Nelson Goodman's work on "worldmaking." Instead of symbolic forms, Goodman talks about "world versions." Goodman explicitly follows Cassirer in claiming that having a world depends upon words and other symbols. Faced with the question of the origin of worlds, Goodman simply points out that they are made "from other worlds."[51] Where Goodman is only ready to admit that each "world" is made from another, Cassirer seeks to show that this process of emerging worlds is not arbitrary. It has a beginning—myth—from which all the other worlds develop. Since Goodman objects to Cassirer's emphasis on myth, this approach is closed to him. The interpretative process is metaphysically adrift for Goodman, but Cassirer is brought to the Urphänomene of symbolic pregnance and what he calls Leben. Such metaphysical ultimates seem lacking in Goodman's philosophy of worldmaking.

Cassirer says "the unity and the truth of cognition stems from the living synergy of intellectual forces."[52] This is not so much cooperation or cross-fertilization as a filling-in of what is absent in the other symbolic forms. The different symbolic forms complement one another because "they move in entirely different planes" (EM, 170). Hence, Cassirer proposes that the unity of truth should be conceived as a harmony of oppositions.[53]

The sciences and the humanities cannot be reduced to a common denominator because they do not have an object in common. The unity of truth is not substantial, but functional. Hence, Cassirer adopts what he calls the "funktionale Wahrheitsideal," the "functional ideal of truth." The unity of truth lies in the unity of the discovery of truth. The measure of truth, Cassirer says, is intensive, not extensive, and he expresses it in terms of the notion of "depth" (ibid., 20). Depth is measured within each field, not by a single reality or form of understanding uniting the sciences and humanities. It is possible to speak of understanding in depth in science, history, or art without assuming a common object or substantial reality as a measure for them all. The unity of truth is "functional" because it is expressed differently in each symbolic form. One cannot translate or reduce one symbolic form into another. Explanation by law hypotheses cannot apply to historical understanding; artistic images cannot be measured by the criterion of historical accuracy.

Cassirer did not deny that there is cross-fertilization in culture or interdisciplinarity in science. One need only recall his example of Robert Mayer's application of experience as a doctor to physics. Individuals can move from one field of activity to another, but this does not affect the strict distinctions between the symbolic forms. Cassirer clearly recognized the importance of the interaction between the symbolic forms when he asserted that truth is discovered through the "synergy" of different intellectual activities. By recognizing the integrity of the different symbolic forms it is possible to overcome the dogmatic homogeneousness proclaimed by metaphysical monism, while upholding the functional unity of these forms avoids the relativism of indiscriminate pluralism.

Cassirer said that the problem of truth belongs to a particular *Sinnschicht* or "level of meaning" and that it therefore gains its systematic place in the whole of philosophy only when it is considered in contrast to other levels of meaning.[54] Foremost among these other levels of meaning is that of value. The problem of truth takes its proper place in Cassirer's thought only when we move from the norm of truth to the problem of the ought and the normative questions of moral philosophy and political life.

IV

MORALITY AND LAW

For Cassirer the ethical point of view is a symbolic form. Within this symbolic form he distinguishes between social morality (*Sittlichkeit*) and law (*Recht*).[1] Cassirer's ethical theory includes a theory of moral consciousness that identifies different stages of moral thinking (that is, different levels of criteria by which actions are judged from a moral point of view) and a normative theory of the ought, centering upon the natural law doctrine of inalienable human rights.

It has never been widely recognized in Anglo-American philosophy that a theory of moral development could have philosophical value. The typical approach to ethics has rather been what W. D. Ross called the "time-honored" starting point of reflecting on the moral experience of the philosopher himself.[2] A. C. Ewing once claimed that "the only way in which we can develop a systematic theory of ethics is by starting with the ethical judgments which we find ourselves in our practical thinking constrained to make. To these is often given the name, *common-sense ethics*."[3] In this way philosophy begins and ends with the moral thinking of rational, everyday understanding in an effort to give an account of the nature and foundation of ethics. This approach takes no cognizance of the historical origins of human social conduct—on the grounds that a study of the development of ethics cannot tell us anything about the normative status of moral doctrines.[4] Cassirer's theory of the development of moral consciousness provides what he terms a "phenomenology of moral consciousness" in Hegel's sense of *phenomenology* (AH, 42): it is an ideal history and not a genetic study in an empirical sense. Cassirer does not hold that a philosophical theory of the *validity* of norms can be derived only from a reconstruction of their development, but for him it is nonetheless a grave error for philosophers to believe that the study of ethics can be cut off from study of the cultural reality in which human beings live. The differences between mythic, common-sense, and abstract philosophical criteria of the ethical are important because they are inherent in the cultural world of ethical life—as permanent possible guides for moral action.

Cassirer's approach to ethics begins with the recognition that man is not by nature moral if by "moral" we mean self-responsible conduct based upon deliberation. To assume, even for methodological rea-sons, that the ability to act with reflective moral consciousness is "given" is an unacceptable anachronism. Cassirer stresses rather that "morality, the basic forms of the community and the state—they are all originally tied up with mythico-religious conceptions" (LM, 44). Elementary, mythico-religious forms of morality follow different principles than those of rational ethics. This, Cassirer shows, is an empirical fact. But its significance, he thinks, is not just historical.

This point can be illustrated by reference to recent ethical theory. In A Theory of Justice, John Rawls bases his argument on a methodologi-cal assumption that ignores the original mythico-religious nature of morality. He characterizes the "original position" (the hypothetical starting point from which he constructs his theory) as a situation populated by rational beings who have no foreknowledge of their roles in society. Behind this "veil of ignorance" they would, he argues, rationally select certain principles of justice—"the principles that free and rational persons concerned to further their own interests would accept in an initial position of equality as defining the funda-mental terms of their association."[5] Such agents are not themselves ignorant, but rational and clear-minded.

From Cassirer's point of view this hypothetical approach has two drawbacks. First, it is unrealistic, not just because it depicts an unreal situation, but because it reflects an artificially narrow conception of man as a rational being. Disregard for the origin of morality in mythic thought involves a fundamental disregard of human nature; such disregard leaves us unprepared to deal with or even understand any nonrational form of human action. Second, this approach is based upon too weak a conception of reason. Rawls's argument is ultimately utilitarian, even though it is couched in the language of contract theory, for it begins with a body of reflective individuals who can calculate about what would bring the greatest good to the greatest number. No matter how convincing such an argument for moral principles may be, it will always be a weaker defense than one which characterizes the ought in terms of a categorical imperative, that is, a position that takes "reason" in some sense to guarantee the validity of ethical principles independently of any consensus.

Morality is concerned with social action: "The person that concerns us when we are speaking of ethics is from the outset not merely a psycho-physical individual being but conceived as a social being. He stands in a community and receives the rules for his behavior from it" (AH, 78). As long as society's ways go unchallenged there is no "problem" of ethics. The closed primitive society confronting another society suddenly faces the problem of different customs and moralities (AH, 78–79). The expansion of social contacts historically leads to less narrow but more widely held ethical principles. Philosophy, Cassirer says, completes this process by proclaiming the universal validity of general ethical norms (AH, 79).

Value judgments always presuppose normative criteria of some kind. Philosophy's task is to show the character and universal objectivity of the standards or *Maßstäbe* used in making ethical decisions (AH, 72).

Philosophers did not invent morality; myth and religion provide the first doctrines of human moral conduct. Cassirer seeks to understand these origins through the theory of symbolic forms.

Phases in the Symbolic Form of Morality   Cassirer's discussions of morality differentiate among three phases of moral consciousness, as in all the symbolic forms: the mimetic, analogical, and purely symbolic.

The Mimetic Phase

Myth is first and foremost social practice. "Myth is not a system of dogmatic creeds. It consists much more in actions than in mere images and representations" (*EM*, 79). In other words, myth is a form of life. Rites reinforce and renew the bonds between members of the community. Totemism as a view of the world is based on the feeling of solidarity. In mythic communities life is regulated by rigid, traditional moralities. "Morality [*Sitte*] and custom [*Brauch*] first appear as the only thing that is really objective, and opposed to this objectivity there is no freedom and no spontaneity" (AH, 78). In particular, every sphere of life is subject to an inflexible system of taboos (*EM*, 104–08; cf. *PSF*, 2:76–78; *PsF*, 2:96–100). "The taboo system imposes upon man innumerable duties and obligations. But all of these duties have a common character. They are entirely negative; they include no positive ideal whatever. . . . For it is fear that dominates the taboo system; and fear knows only how to forbid, not how to direct" (*EM*, 107).

In mythic thought there is no room for deliberation of alternatives because the prescriptions for life are countless and specific. Eating, drinking, walking, sexuality, the acquisition of property, even speech, all are subject to detailed taboos. In Polynesia, for example, not only is it forbidden to utter the name of a chief or a deceased person, but even other words that happen to have syllables containing this name may not be used in conversation (*EM*, 108). Taboos must be followed so as not to disturb or incur the wrath of the demonic forces (which may or may not be personalized) that dominate the mythic world. As an impersonal power, which anthropologists call *mana* after the Polynesian word, the mythic forces make themselves felt at certain times in certain places, persons, or things. Taboos prescribe how such things are to be approached or avoided. The reasons for taboos, customs, rites, and totemistic views are provided by myths—narratives that explain the origin of society's ways. Myths tell why things are done; they do not offer moral justifications. Myth does not rely on arguments and hence it has no room for criticism. Its models for action have a sacred nature and exist on a special temporal plateau.

The distinctive quality or original mythic morality results from the particular nature of mythic time. The primordial acts of the gods or divine heroes abide in the original time. Man only has to reenact these original realities. This is not mimesis in the sense of copying but an actual participation. "At the beginning of mythical action stands the mime . . . and nowhere does he have a merely 'aesthetic,' a merely representative, significance. The dancer who appears in the mask of a god or demon does not merely imitate the god or demon but assumes his nature; he is transformed into him and fuses with him" (*PSF*, 2:238; *PsF*, 2:285). Mythic thought is conservative in the extreme. It has no room for innovation or exceptions; actions are sanctioned or forbidden not just by society but by a sacred absolute reality.

Freedom has no positive value in a mimetic morality of this kind. Individual responsibility is uncalled for because responsibility is collective: "There is not a shadow of individual self-responsibility in this system. If a man commits a crime it is not he himself who is marked off—his family, his friends, his whole tribe bears the same mark" (*EM*, 105).

Morality based upon individual responsibility requires a sense of self that is unknown in mythic thinking. A record of such a change in the sense of self is found in the Greek tragedies. Cassirer calls particular attention to the significance of the *Eumenides*, the final play in Aeschylus's *Oresteia*.[6] The furies (Erinyes) become in this play the "kindly ones," Eumenides. The furies are underground demons of vengeance, blindly carrying out vendettas. Athena persuades the furies not to seek vengeance on Athens when Oreste (who killed his mother, Clytaemnestra, for murdering his father, Agamemnon) is acquitted by Athenians, with Athena casting the deciding lot. Oreste is judged by *Dike*, justice, not blind blood revenge. In the *Eumenides* the new gods, Athena and Apollo, subdue the older gods, the Erinyes. Cassirer says of the conclusion of the *Eumenides*: "In man's revolt against the mythic powers he has not only attained himself, but also preserved the image of the divine in his soul. . . . In the moment in which man becomes another, the image of the divine must be transformed and refined."[7] The *Oresteia* dramatizes the struggle for a new morality: "When Clytaemnestra in Aeschylus's *Agamemnon* seeks to shirk the blame for the murder of Agamemnon and declares that it was not her but the old demonic curse on the house which did the deed, the choir opposes her: she alone did the deed and had to be responsible for it" (ibid., 18).[8] The struggle for a morality of self-responsibility is a struggle against myth.

In early mythic-religious life personality is almost totally eclipsed by a feeling of the unity of life. The cultic rites of initiation that usher the individual into the community of adults, unlike a person's twenty-first birthday in modern society, do not mark a person's independence. Instead of becoming legally responsible for his own actions, the initiate in a mythic-religious society gains the identity of the community (*MS*, 39–40). Instead of becoming an individual, self-responsible person, he is perceived as a rejuvenation and reincarnation of the community and the mythic unity of life that is the identity of the tribe. Personality is mimetic.

Underlying this mimetic form of personality is a particular awareness of the world. Cassirer describes how the awareness of an anonymous presence forms the background out of which definite demonic or sacred images take shape in language. (See "The Successive Stages of Religious Thought," *LM*, 62–83; cf. *PSF*, 2:159; *PsF*, 2:190). Human self-awareness also begins with such impersonal feeling. It begins to condense in the experience of the fear of demonic forces. Man's own mind confronts him as an outward, alien force, as demons that attack him from all sides and from within.

A person is felt to have any number of souls that stand in conflict with one another (*PSF*, 2:163–66; *PsF*, 2:194–99). The first form of personal self-awareness, Cassirer says, is the idea of the tutelary spirit, a guardian—something objective that dwells in man but that is not an ego, not the "subject" of his inner life (*PSF*, 2:168–70; *PsF*, 2:200–03). The Greeks have a comparable notion in the *daimon*. Cassirer recounts how in Greek philosophy a transformation of the *daimon* was given expression in Heraclitus, Plato, and Aristotle.[9] The locus classicus of this transformation is *Republic* 617E: "Your genius [*daimon*] will not be allotted to you, but you will choose your genius" (Jowett). Cassirer says of this passage: "We can feel the enormous oxymoron that must have lay in these words for a Greek in the fifth century. For to myth the 'demonic' is precisely that which is beyond all human capability and will. It is something foreign and infinitely superior to him. And it is this completely untransparent, 'irrational' reality which is made subject to choice and hence to *ratio*, the decision of moral reason."[10] What makes possible this radical change in attitude?

Cassirer reconstructs the process by which the impersonal mythic feeling of the self gives way to the awareness of individual freedom and responsibility. He contends that "the most important factor in the growth of the consciousness of personality is and remains the factor of action [*Wirken*]" (*PSF*, 2:199; *PsF*, 2:239). A basic change occurs in the mythic world with the rise of a technical approach to practical things. "For as soon as man seeks to influence things not by mere image magic or name magic but through implements, he has undergone an inner crisis—even if, for the present, this influence still operates through customary channels of magic" (*PSF*, 2:214; *PsF*, 2:256). Man now learns that there is a difference between the inner and outer worlds, that there is a set sphere of objects that resist human desire, and in this man can for the first time recognize a chain of causality. This thesis in the *Philosophy of Symbolic Forms* (*PSF*, 2:213–18; *PsF*, 2:254–61) is developed more fully in the essay "Form und Technik."

This change has both a cognitive and an ethical aspect. Mere wish and desire give way to will: "The will is not just present in the power of a forward driving impulse, but in the way this impulse is guided and controlled. It is not just present in the capacity to reach for a goal, but in a unique capacity to put this goal at a distance and let it remain there, to 'let it stand.' This 'letting-stand' of the goal is what first makes possible an 'objective' view of things, a view of the world as a world of 'objects.' . . . Success in getting what is wanted can never be attained by merely strengthening the self. Rather, this demands that the will intervene [*eingreift*] into an order which, originally, was foreign to it and that the will recognizes and accepts *as* foreign. This recognition [*Erkennen*] is always also a kind of acceptance [*Anerkennen*] of this otherness" (*STS*, 59).

The origin of the will is a fundamental step in the genealogy of moral development. Practical, technical matters stand initially in a close relationship to cult practices. The use of fire and the domestication of animals were first cultic in purpose (*PSF*, 2:204: *PsF*, 2:244; cf. *WW*, 28). In early polytheism the gods that populated the world were recognized through their efficacy (see *PSF*, 2:158–59; *PsF*, 2:189–90). As technical activity gradually shows an objective order in the world, the sphere of action and the mythical view of things begin to separate and human self-awareness grows.

The Analogical Phase

There are two temporal views of the world that became clearly distinguished in mythic thought, that of timeless fate or destiny and that of creation. Destiny, while manifested in time, is atemporal, whereas creation "occurs" and so has an essential temporality (see *PSF*, 2:116–18; *PsF*, 2:142–45). Cassirer recognizes that the idea of a creator is one of the most common, fundamental motifs of myth and that even primitive totemistic societies often trace their origin to a creator who is the original source of things, rites, and the clan itself (*PSF*, 2:206–07; *PsF*, 2:247–48). On closer scrutiny the seemingly abstract notions of "creation" and a "creator" are actually apprehended as particular, concrete varieties of formation (*PSF*, 2:207; *PsF*, 2:247). Ptah in ancient Egyptian religion, Marduk in Babylonian religion, Prajapati in Vedic religion, and numerous other gods are actually cosmic artisans who create by utilizing what is already there. It is only when the idea of creation has been conceived in its purest form as creation ex nihilo that there is a religious notion of a supreme creator god. "The idea of 'creation from nothing' to which pure monotheism ultimately rises and in which the category of creation first acquires its truly fundamental formulation may from the standpoint of theoretical thinking represent a paradox, even an antinomy; but from the religious point of view it nevertheless signifies an ultimate and supreme achievement . . . the being of pure will and pure action, comes to full and unlimited expression" (*PSF*, 2:211–12, cf. 206; *PsF*, 2:253, cf. 247). Consciousness of *action* is raised in the idea of creation ex nihilo to the utmost limit; the being of things is thought away, leaving only the idea of a pure creativity.

This new conception of creation reflects a new nonmythical religious spirit. Religion is connected from the beginning and throughout its historical evolution with mythical thinking, but there is a different directionality in religious thinking than in mythic thought (*SMC*, 86). In the mimetic thinking of mythic societies there is a constant desire to follow and merge with the mythic forces that pervade everything. This desire reflects the decidedly impersonal character of mythic thought. The images and symbols of the cult are experienced as magic realities embodying the sacred itself. They are not "just symbols," and the words and names of these realities are not "just words," but magic utterances that call up benign or malignant forces. Monotheistic religion overcomes the tendency to identify images and symbols with the divinity itself (*PSF*, 2:239; *PsF*, 2:286). In religion, images point to a reality beyond the immediately efficacious; a new relationship can then arise between the members of the religious community and the divine. A personal I-thou relationship arises, which recognizes a distance between this world and the sphere of divinity, a distance unknown in mythic thought. In the prophetic monotheistic religion of Zoroaster, in Judaism, and in Christianity the most important thing in ethical life is recognition of the difference between good and evil (*EM*, 99). In monotheistic religion the prophets who "speak with authority" interpret the will of God as an *ethical* will. Unlike the taboo system, in which the purity or impurity of things is regarded as something substantial adhering to them by mythic forces, religion no longer regards things or actions as such to be tainted. Purity, in religious thought, is purity of the heart (*EM*, 107–08). Religion does not just forbid or inhibit like the taboo system. There is a general change in orientation in the teachings of the great religious prophets: "They discovered in themselves a positive power, a power of inspiration and aspiration" (*EM*, 108). On Cassirer's interpretation, religion is distinguished from myth by a turn away from passive obedience and fear to a positive, active, ethical orientation in which man becomes individually responsible to God.

In religion, conduct assumes a new temporal orientation; the future becomes more important than the past. In myth, the past is the real and the present its repetition. But in religious thinking the individual must prove himself ethically with regard to the future. "Out of the ethical-prophetic idea of the future grows a true discovery of man's individuality, of his personal self" (*PSF*, 2:171; *PsF*, 2:204).

The religious idea of the creator gives prime importance to divine will. Yahweh of Jewish monotheism is first and foremost a personal will: "And God said unto Moses: I Am That I AM" (Exodus 3:13–14). Cassirer emphasizes that this passage marks the watershed between monotheistic religion and Greek philosophy. The idea of the Good in Plato or the unmoved mover of Aristotelian theology are not persons, whereas in Jewish monotheism personality is God's essence. "His essence is his *will*; his only revelation is the manifestation of his personal will. Such a personal revelation which is an ethical and not a logical act is quite alien to the Greek mind" (*MS*, 92). The entire medieval notion of ethical and natural law is marked by this religious conception: "In monotheistic religion the law must always be traced back to a personal source. Without a lawgiver there can be no law" (*MS*, 97). The ethical law in religious ethics is revealed and demands submission to a higher *person*. The ethics of religion is voluntaristic, for it is conceived analogously to lawgiving by a human, personal will: "Religion is and remains a body of belief and of fixed practical injunctions. These statements are held to be true and the commands valid because they have been revealed and announced by God. But their proclamation is realized nowhere except in the souls of the individuals, in the souls of the great founders and prophets of religion" (*LH*, 213). In religion the individual is called upon to be responsible to a divine, personal, ethical will. By contrast, taboos prescribe what must be done in order to avoid infection or impurity, and this impurity is spread, without regard to personal responsibility, from person to person in a family or tribe. There is no need for personal deliberation in taboo morality. The forces of myth are forces in the world; the magic used to assuage these forces is immediately efficacious. But the creator God transcends immediate reality, and the demand that his will be fulfilled reflects an entirely new orientation to ethics; the problem of how to do God's will requires deliberation.

Unlike the oral mythic traditions, religions have sacred texts. With writing, man lives in a much more "logical" world. Language opens up the future through the possibility of "lawgiving" (AH, 103–05). Written law raises the problem of consistency. The Romans' efforts to establish the consistency of ethical claims makes them the first logicians of law (AH, 92). Early customary morality follows "unwritten laws" in the sense that custom is prelinguistic (AH, 103). Custom is a matter of tradition; written laws require a lawgiver. Even the concept of divine law requires a lawgiver. Only the spread of written law permits the rise of the notion of an unwritten law.

This conception of unwritten law was the basis of modern natural law. Cassirer points to Grotius's *De jure belli ac pacis* (*The Law of War and Peace*) as the work containing natural law theory's declaration of independence from either theological or political considerations.[11]

Purely Symbolic Phase

Cassirer describes the purely symbolic phase of a symbolic form this way: "The last semblance of any mediate or immediate *identity* between reality and symbol must be effaced, the *tension* between the two must be enhanced to the extreme, for it is precisely in this tension that the specific achievement of symbolic expression and the content of the particular symbolic form is made evident" (*PSF*, 1:188; *PsF*, 1:137). In the sphere of moral consciousness this tension between reality and symbol is enhanced to its extreme in the philosophical conception of the difference between ought and is. For the theory of natural law, the ought is uncreated—an unchanging, eternal law, independent of even a divine will (MS, esp. 54, 80, 81, 92, 97, 98). Greek philosophers, Socrates in particular, were the first to take this final step in the development of moral consciousness, distinguishing between existing morals (Sitte) and morality (Sittlichkeit) and raising the question, What ought to be and why? (AH, 70ff.).

The demand for objective criteria of truth and the search for objective moral norms are aspects of the same philosophical attitude. Cassirer traces the beginning of philosophical thought to the question of principles—of truth and of morality. "Cognition is not satisfied with the values accepted by the testimony of tradition, custom and authority, but inquires into the meaning of the difference between 'good' and 'evil,' and seeks universally valid, 'objective' norms to justify this distinction" (Encyclopaedia Britannica, 14th ed., s.v. "Truth"). The demand for objective criteria of universally valid norms transfers the discussion of morality from the context of the development of moral consciousness to the philosophical context of justification.

The philosophical conception of natural law does not have recourse to either a human or a divine lawgiver, but to reason in some universal sense.[12] Natural law claims to transcend all positive law and yet remain valid for all mankind. In this philosophical theory the tension between concrete reality and the meaning of law is enhanced to the extreme. Natural law is the "purely symbolic" phase of moral thought. Cassirer is eager to point out that natural law nonetheless was never something foreign to the world. Christian Thomasius's and Beccarias's natural law tracts against torture and the death penalty, Grotius's work on the law of the seas, and the whole doctrine of human rights are examples of the concreteness of natural law (ibid., 18–19).

Cassirer believes that the natural law doctrine of human rights provides the only available universal ethics. His own ethical theory is a justification of the human rights doctrine through the philosophy of symbolic forms. Before examining Cassirer's ethical theory I should add a final word about his phenomenology of moral consciousness. Moral action depends upon the agent's standards or criteria of moral judgment and personal sense of self. In other words, to be able to do what ought to be done a person must be free to choose an act in a self-responsible manner. There is a correlation between the ethical standards and the sense of self that prevails in each of the three stages outlined above. In myth the sense of all-encompassing fate is ubiquitous. In religion there are ever-recurring struggles with the problem of free will in the face of an omnipotent, omniscient God (predestination and grace). Philosophers since Plato have argued that man's self is free to choose his course of action, but even in philosophy this conception has lost ground again and again. For example, Cassirer points to later Neoplatonism, where the self is again regarded as "the demon that is allotted to us" (PSF, 2:173; PsF, 2:206).[13] Cassirer does not claim that the phenomenology of moral consciousness describes a development that must occur, but only that there is such a thing as a purely symbolic form of moral thought and that it is possible for moral consciousness to attain and apply such universal criteria.

Ethics and the Philosophy of Symbolic Forms
In his review of Cassirer's *Myth of the State*, Leo Strauss raised the question of the place of ethics in the philosophy of symbolic forms. Strauss found that Cassirer's treatment of political philosophy demanded more than an analysis of totalitarianism; what it needed was a philosophical theory of ethics: "If Cassirer were correct in his appraisal of the rights-of-man doctrine of the eighteenth century, an adequate answer to the challenge raised by the doctrines favoring the political myth of our time—for example, those of Spengler and Heidegger—would have been not an inconclusive discussion of the myth of the state, but a radical transformation of the philosophy of symbolic forms into a teaching whose center is moral philosophy."[14] What Strauss did not realize, and what is still unrecognized today, is that Cassirer's thought had taken that very turn. Following the publication of *The Philosophy of Symbolic Forms*, the center of his work becomes moral philosophy. He marked the change in his inaugural lecture in Göteborg in 1935; Cassirer admits that he had previously paid too little attention to philosophy's relationship to practical life, and he promises to rectify this (SMC, 60). During the next few years, Cassirer developed his ethical theory in essays, lectures, and, most important, his study on the Swedish philosopher of law, Axel Hägerström. In the preface to that work he declares: "I have used the suggestions that have arisen from my study of Hägerström's main works to more sharply conceive of my own basic outlook, as I presented it in particular in my *Philosophy of Symbolic Forms* (3 volumes, 1923–29), and to apply it to new areas. Hence, my basic interpretation of the problem of ethics and the philosophy of law are more extensively treated [here] than in my earlier writings, which were mostly directed to theoretical philosophy" (AH, 6–7).

But even prior to going to Sweden Cassirer recognized that ethics had to play a central and fundamental role in his philosophy of symbolic forms. At a lecture given in London in 1936 he said: "We cannot build up a philosophy of culture by mere formal and logical means. We have to face the fundamental ethical question that is contained in the very concept of culture. The philosophy of culture may be called a study of forms; but all these forms cannot be understood without relating them to a common goal" (SMC, 81). Cassirer thinks that this common goal, at least in part, is to achieve a universal ethical order.

Philosophy does not invent morality. Social morality, Sittlichkeit, is a part of human culture. Philosophy inquires into the validity of ethical criteria and raises the question of universally valid ethical norms. Kant defined the sphere of ethical obligation by his theory of the categorical imperative. Unlike utilitarian injunctions about how practically to accomplish something or attain some end, an imperative is categorical, Cassirer says in *Kant's Life and Thought*, "when it manifests itself as an unconditional demand that has no need to borrow its validity from some further end, but instead possesses its own validity in that it presents an ultimate, self-evident value" (KLT, 245). Cassirer's historical reconstruction of Kantian ethics remained for decades his longest and most detailed discussion of the problem of ethics. He did not develop his own theory until he encountered an ethical doctrine that denied not just Kant's position, but the validity of any and all values.[15]

The notion of validity is rational, claiming that something which applies to one case logically also applies to another. The emotive theory of value denies that ethical statements, that is, moral imperatives, have any such general, cognitive content at all. Ethical statements are, according to this theory, merely emotional expressions of likes and dislikes (AH, 61). That is, they are purely subjective. From an intellectual point of view, they are meaningless, having no rational content. The emotive theory of value is usually associated with the Vienna Circle of logical positivism and its influence, especially through A. J. Ayer and C. L. Stevenson, but it had already been developed in this extreme form as early as 1911 by Axel Hägerström.[16]

Hägerström was influential as a philosopher of law in formulating the general position known as "Scandinavian realism." Cassirer's opposition to Hägerström's conception of ethics stems from the broader conception of objectivity inherent in the philosophy of symbolic forms than in Scandinavian realism. Jes Bjarup, a philosopher of law, gives the following description of the basic conception of objectivity shared by the philosophers in this school of thought: "For the Scandinavian realists there is only one world, one reality, namely the sum of those phenomena in time and space connected with one another according to the law of causality."[17] This was the conception

Cassirer opposed: "The main reason that Hägerström gives for his rejection of objectivity of any kind in the field of ethics consists, as we have seen, in his view that without a statement of a specific area of objects to which our knowledge of values can relate, such an objectivity becomes meaningless. But such an area cannot be found since the world has been, so to speak, 'given away' to theoretical thinking and judgment. Next to the aggregate of spatial-temporal objects, which provide the content for this kind of thinking, there is no room for another world" (AH, 71). Such a view exemplifies the kind of narrow epistemological philosophy that Cassirer sought to overcome with his philosophy of symbolic forms.

Hägerström's theory of value was put forth with the aim of making ethics and the philosophy of law into a sober investigation that avoided metaphysical assumptions and appeals to subjective "insight" or intuition, and with this aim Cassirer expresses great sympathy (AH, 62–63). He agrees with Hägerström's rejection of metaphysical constructions in the philosophy of law, such as the Hegelian notion of Spirit or the notion of the "spirit of the people" (Volksgeist) in Savigny's historical school of law (AH, 62). At the same time Cassirer rejected all attempts to build up a hierarchy of values on the basis of an intuitive insight into essences (Wesensschau) "as has been attempted in modern phenomenology" (AH, 64). For Cassirer, such attempts are a carry-over from seventeenth-century beliefs that values are capable of mathematical-like proof.[18] Comparisons between natural law and mathematics can be regarded, at best, as an analogy. Like mathematical thinking, the source of natural law is reason—not revelation, tradition, or authoritative command of any kind. But natural law is not abstract; it deals with actions between human beings and any comparison with mathematics must break down here.[19] Hägerström goes further and claims that rationality as such breaks down in the sphere of values.

The emotive theory of values is really a theory of evaluation. It does not deny that people make statements of preference or evaluation; it denies that they have any meaning other than to express a person's emotional reaction to something. Cassirer argues that this thesis simply does not correctly reflect what we in fact experience in making value judgments. He begins with a phenomenological analysis:

Even purely phenomenologically, it seems to me that a definite difference maintains here [between evaluation and mere feeling]. Even if we completely refrain from speaking of "values in themselves," which I concede is and remains a questionable metaphor in any case, when we view values therefore, so to speak, from the I pole, they are something new and unique. For the "I" *participates* in a completely different way in evaluations and when taking a position on something than in mere individual occurrences of emotions or imagining. A feeling of sadness, the feeling of anxiety, and so forth possess me; I give in to them and in this being-given-into-them everything else is forgotten and extinguished. But taking a position on something demands something more; it demands making a comparison, a weighing of one thing against another. And the decision that is made here does not depend only on the conditions given at the time. Rather, it depends on the totality of the "personality," upon the fundamental *direction* of its feelings and will, not upon a single feeling or single impulse . . . evaluation contains a form of review [*Rückschau*], preview [*Vorschau*], and survey [*Überschau*] which feelings, as mere states, lack. (AH, 65).

The problem of objectivity in the sphere of value consists in establishing a universal criterion or standard (*Maßstäbe*; AH, 72–78) for value judgments. Conflicts of will based on different evaluations can be decided either by force or by reason: "divergence cannot, here in the world of will and action, be removed from the world by concepts; it must be settled by struggle [*Kämpfe*]" (AH, 78). Insofar as conflicts are to be decided by reason, the aim is to reconcile different value judgments. This can only be accomplished by a process of unifying and thereby universalizing the norms that stand as guidelines in action (AH, 101–02). Only if there is a unifying norm or standard of judgment can there be, ultimately, an agreement on ethical issues. Philosophy seeks to carry this thinking to its final conclusions and show its final goal (AH, 79); to this end it shows the final norm for judging ethical matters.

Genuine universality of will, an agreement among all human beings on certain values or standards of action, does not de facto exist. Even if it did, such a consensus would not act as a guarantee that what has been agreed upon is morally good. The natural law tradition made use of the notion of consensus in the doctrine of the "contract" that binds everyone in society. Cassirer does not think that the existence of universality of will—for example, mutual agreement in a state of nature—is important to ethics. But he does think that the concept of the universality of will is an indispensable *criterion* for judging an action. As such, this unity is a regulative idea in Kant's sense (AH, 79). Cassirer says, "The idea of a 'unity of will' does not, of course, designate something that is immediately given or realized; it is a kind of 'infinitely distant point' that legal thinking [*Rechtserfahrung*] and social experience refer to. . . . In the sphere of practice the demand for the 'greatest unity' must be posed again and again precisely *because* experience has shown us that it is never adequately met in it, nor can be" (AH, 79).[20]

Cassirer hereby transforms Kant's conception of the "universalizability" of an action: "Act only on that maxim through which you can at the same time will that it should become a universal law," taking it to mean the regulative ideal of a universal agreement of will.[21] Cassirer refers to this "unity of will" as an *Einheit der Zielsetzungen*, a unity in the setting of goals (AH, 78). At this point his argument takes a typically contemporary, but unique, linguistic turn.

Cassirer conceived the language of ethics as performative in character. He makes use of the distinction between the semantic *Darstellungsfunktion* of language and its use in the sphere of action (*im Gebiet des Handelns*) to revitalize the natural law doctrine of human rights (AH, 103–04). This is Cassirer's approach to the problem of ethics and obligation as he derived it from the philosophy of symbolic forms (AH, 85n).

Cassirer presented his interpretation of language as the basis of ethical obligation in "Axel Hägerström."

Here in the sphere of ethics we are no longer in the field of perception or thought about objects, but in the area of action, so our linguistic concepts also attain a new meaning and accomplish something new by being expressed through language. They no longer just have the task of representing given, factual contents. Rather they must reach beyond this into another *temporal dimension*. "Speaking" is not just directed to grasping a state of affairs given here and now as such and bringing it to expression; rather it is directed to the *future*: it becomes a "promise." The presupposition that giving our word is *binding*, that it prescribes a particular direction to our actions, is one of the sources from which a "legal consciousness" flows. (AH, 104)

Cassirer used the language of "speech acts" from time to time, referring to a *Sprachakt* and an *Akt des Sprechens* in the same sense as the English "speech act."[22] He gives special attention to this notion in the case of promising.

It is easy to see that promising involves the norm of keeping one's word, but the problem is how this can be regarded as a *moral* ought and not just a convention or institutional fact. Cassirer considered the speech act of promising from the standpoint of transcendental philosophy. He seeks to show the conditions of the possibility of the linguistic convention of promising and of morality as a social reality. Keeping one's word, Cassirer wants to show, stands as a universally binding point of reference for human action everywhere. His attempt to establish this as a *moral* norm, and not a mere convention, is predicated on the thesis that the act of promising and then keeping one's word bears directly on a person's "humanity" and personality in an ethical sense. It concerns the latter's participation in the former.

The view that man's ethical nature is universal was introduced into philosophical thinking by the Roman stoic philosophers. They contended that all men are fundamentally equal from the ethical point of view. Cassirer cautioned that to claim this does not entail denying that people are born with different temperaments, intellectual abilities, talents, and the like; it asserts only that when we judge actions from the ethical point of view, these differences are of no account (MS, 101). The resulting Roman conception of *humanitas* was a "cosmopolitan ideal" (ibid.). In his reconstruction of the history of political philosophy in *The Myth of the State*, Cassirer shows how this cosmopolitan ideal led to the philosophical doctrine of "human" rights. Cassirer leaves no doubt that for him this doctrine is absolutely crucial for life in the modern secular state. The "catholicity" of the church could not be restored after the Reformation; if there was to be a truly universal ethics it would have to be something that could be admitted by every nation, every creed, and every sect. Cassirer saw the only solution possible in the theory of human rights provided by the philosophy of natural law. "That was the great and, indeed, invaluable service which the theory of natural rights had to render to the modern world. Without this theory there seemed to be no escape from a complete moral anarchy" (MS, 170).

In his 1932 lecture on the essence and development of natural law Cassirer rejected the utilitarian and conventionalistic view that legality (Recht) is only a means to man's self-preservation. For Cassirer, the ability to enter into an agreement with others, the ability to promise and to recognize the ensuing legality of this promise, is "constitutive for man, a necessary precondition for the 'humanitas ipsa.'" "The capacity to rise to the pure thought of legality and legal liability and the capacity to comply at any price with an obligation once it has been entered into, gives us hence the actual origin and the fundament of every specifically human community."[23] Cassirer interprets these capacities as a direct result of what is characteristic in man: "that he gives life a stable and enduring form." One of the chief examples of such form is the idea of law as a "binding and obligatory norm" for action (ibid., 22). The problem is how life is given such form.

On the modern account of natural law, life in society under the rule of law is imagined in terms of a social contract. According to this view, society itself may be conceived as originating in a contractual agreement among the governed by which they submit to rule. In the seventeenth century, Cassirer says, this view was "a self-evident maxim of political thought," not a historical claim but "the 'principle' of the state—its raison d'être" (MS, 173). The early modern philosophers of natural law were so convinced of the logically self-evident character of this theory that they frequently compared their arguments to mathematical proofs. By reducing the legal and social order to the voluntary contractual submission of the governed, the human community had a purely rational basis. "There is nothing less mysterious than a contract. A contract must be made in full awareness of its meaning and its consequences; it presupposes the free consent of all the parties concerned. If we can trace the state to such an origin, it becomes a perfectly clear and understandable fact" (MS, 173). By the nineteenth century, however, this doctrine had become the chief stumbling block for natural law theory. Nineteenth- and twentieth-century philosophers were no longer ready to accept such a fiction as the basis of law. Friedrich Carl von Savigny's "historical school of law" substituted for it the notion of the "spirit of the people" or *Volksgeist* as the basis of the validity of law, thereby emphasizing historical change at the expense of the natural law conception of enduring legal principles.[24] Hegel relegates the notion of the contract to "civil society" (*bürgerliche Gesellschaft*) as a body founded with the purpose of securing certain benefits to individuals. But civil society in Hegel's philosophy derives from the state, which is the ultimate source of the validity of law. Hence, the claim that natural law is a kind of "law above the law" based upon a "social contract" makes no sense in Hegel's *Philosophy of Right*.[25] In a not unsimilar way Marx too rejects the contract theory and natural law doctrine of human rights, claiming that this conception applies to man as a monad and ignores his being as a species.[26]

Cassirer refers to Savigny, Hegel, and Marx as critics of natural law, but the first and last of these thinkers concern him only in passing. Hegel's theory of law and the state occupied Cassirer's attention again and again, from *Freiheit und Form* in 1916 to an article on Schweitzer published thirty years later.[27] Hegel not only represented the opposite *Gesinnung* or attitude on natural law; his philosophical attack was most formidable because it was developed from the German idealistic tradition that Cassirer had credited with providing the metaphysical basis of human rights (LS, 449–58). In his famous "Sollenkritik" (criticism of the "ought"), Hegel accused philosophers who sought to show what ought to be of falling into vacuous abstractions so as to make "unrealistic" claims upon the world. Individuals have moralities of their own (*Moralität*), but ethics (Sittlichkeit) is always social in nature, always the ethics and laws holding in a state. The absolute "world spirit" lives for Hegel in the state and it is only in the state that ethics finds true expression. For Hegel, philosophy gives a verbal expression of the shape taken on by absolute spirit in a historical form in the state, but philosophy cannot do this, Hegel says, "by escaping into the shapelessness of cosmopolitanism, still less into the void of the Rights of Man, or the like void of a league of nations or a world republic."[28] The idea of the "Rights of Man" is a void or *Leerheit* for Hegel because these are not the laws of an actual state but suprastate "unwritten laws." To Hegel's mind this means that they are just the utopian wishes of philosophers as individuals, as "subjective spirits."

Cassirer contradicts Hegel's assertion, pointing out that public conscience (*das öffentliche Gewissen*) has always appealed to other standards than the law of the land, standards it derives from the "unwritten laws."[29] The appeal to the rights of man is not merely the result of an unrealistic attitude among individuals whose desire for personal freedom blinds them to reason; rather, it is a sign of a universal sense of conscience. On the other hand, Cassirer says that Hegel's use of the notion of the Weltgeist in his account of the process by which reason is realized in the world "darkens the simple insight that the medium through which this realization takes place lies solely in the social and ethical efforts that individuals have to undertake" (*FF*, 366). Cassirer agrees with the positivists and sociological theorists in rejecting Hegel's metaphysical theory here. Yet Cassirer is reluctant also to abandon thereby the idea of a reasonable unity in society, that is, to drop the notion of an "objective mind" of any kind along with the "absolute mind" (see AH, 62, 106).

Cassirer stands here before a dilemma. He cannot accept Hegel's attempt to give the social character of ethics a foundation in a metaphysical entity that limits the validity of the "ought" to its particular historical form as the state. But he also cannot regard the normative as either mere individual feeling and preference or social, utilitarian concerns. Hägerström opts for the latter extreme, conceiving the unity of law and society as derivative from a conglomerate of various heterogeneous social factors: different religious beliefs, conflicting social class interests, the so-called "feeling for what's right," the general tendency to adapt to the status quo, the fear of anarchy, and so on (AH, 95). On such a view the resulting "norms" governing society can only be temporary, chance constellations of changing attitudes and decisions made under duress. Metaphysical hypostatizations make mysterious the actual individual processes that govern social life, while the purely sociological conceptions of society give no room to the idea of universal norms or standards for human action. Barring an attempt to revive the older "contract" theory of natural law, the concept of human rights appeared to be a groundless notion.

Cassirer concludes the 1932 natural law lecture by claiming that conscience measures according to the *agraphoi logoi* or unwritten laws and that the justification for philosophy as natural law theory is that it shares with conscience this "respect (*Ehrfurcht*) for the unwritten laws."[30] Thus, philosophy should defend these laws. In order to do this, Cassirer went back to a line of argument developed by Vico. In the *New Science* Vico shows the genesis of natural law philosophy, distinguishing it from the original poetic or mythic and heroic moralities.[31] Vico did not reject natural law, but only the contract theory insofar as it assumed that men and women were originally rational beings capable of forming society by deliberation. Cassirer was familiar with Vico as early as 1902 (see *LS*, 448–49), and in a Yale lecture from 1941 he calls attention to the fact that Vico opposed the rationalism of the Enlightenment in the *founding* of natural law but not its content. Dismissing the social contract, Vico reinterpreted the basis of natural law: each individual has certain rights because he is a representative of a common humanity (*SMC*, 106). It is difficult to say what role Vico's work played in Cassirer's interpretation of the origin of law. In his Hägerström study Cassirer traces law to its origin in mythic thought, the very opposite tendency of the seventeenth-century conception of the contract, but in this work Vico is never mentioned.

Cassirer was struck by the fact that Hägerström, in his study of Roman law, also shows how legal thinking emerges from mythic consciousness (*AH*, 84ff.). But Cassirer and Hägerström see the history of law very differently. For Hägerström, the origin of law in myth is a sociological fact, and the development of society as governed by law is another sociological fact. But for Cassirer natural law theory is the final phase of a "phenomenology of moral consciousness." Its emergence is not coincidental because it completes a process in the development of thought as its logical conclusion. The main point of contention between Cassirer and Hägerström concerns a central tenet of natural law—the acceptability of the concept of a unitary or general will. Hägerström wants to eliminate this concept from the philosophy of law, to show that it is an "idol" in Bacon's sense (*AH*, 106). Cassirer thinks that it is a justifiable and, in fact, an indispensable concept that, when correctly understood, solves the theoretical dilemma of the justification of natural law.

Hägerström expresses his skepticism about the rationality of the general will concept with the following argument:

If a "general will" is assumed, that will must be supposed to be either the will of all or a super-individual will. On the former alternative the theory comes into conflict with the facts; on the latter it leads to absurdities. If the basis of the theory is alleged to be *the will of the holder or holders of de facto power* in a society, the difficulty arises that the law itself is the foundation and the limit of the *de facto* power. If, finally, the *power actually enforcing the law* (the "state will") is taken as the starting point, we are faced with the impossibility of assigning this to an actual will. But this exhausts the possible forms of the theory.[32]

Cassirer seeks to defend the idea of the "unity of will" (*Einheit des Willens*; AH, 79). He agrees with Hägerström's attempt to expose the hypostatizing of any plurality of individual wills such as through the notion of the "state will" (*Staatswillens*; AH, 106). He avoids language that would suggest such a reification, even the phrase "general will." For Cassirer, the unity of will, as we have already seen, is not a de facto consensus, but a criterion by which actions are judged whenever we consider the universalizability of an action (AH, 79). But it is more than this, namely, a temporal orientation to the future: "the direction toward the not-given, the coming future, what has yet to be realized" (AH, 108). This conception of the will is not a substantial metaphysical doctrine in the vein of Schopenhauer: "The 'will' is here no longer a designation for any kind of mysterious original potency of Being, which rules in man and perhaps as an unconscious power, as 'blind will,' also permeates all natural processes."[33] Cassirer's argument against Hägerström is that will as the temporal orientation to the future is necessary for law in any sense: "Legality as a fact of culture [*Kulturfaktum*] is based upon this anticipation, on the ability to take something up in advance so as to anticipate the future in the present" (AH, 105). More specifically, he says "this direction is also characteristic and indispensable for all order according to law because the possibility that a decision made here and now can exceed a particular case and 'prejudice' future cases rests on it. The direction toward something not given cannot be termed a mere illusion or an empty fiction" (AH, 108). The older contract theory of natural law was based upon the notion of a fictional original "act" but Cassirer's theory envisions the rational unity of society in ever-present self-conscious action undertaken with regard to the future. This temporal orientation is a sense of unity of will unlike any of those in Hägerström's "exhaustive" list of possible meanings for the notion of a general will.

Cassirer agrees with Hegel's criticism of the contract as a basis for natural law because, Cassirer says, "a contract has meaning and force only within a state and a medium of laws" (LH, 108). He declares bluntly, "It is impossible to derive the substance of the law and the content of positive legal statutes from any kind of 'original contract' " (AH, 105). Yet there is a unitary origin of all law and the state in the orientation to the future made possible by language (see AH, 102–06). In addition, Cassirer points out, every legal system contains purposes (Zielsetzungen; AH, 78). Philosophy takes the final step of "daring to pose the question of a universal relational system [Bezugssystem]" unifying all of these systems of law (AH, 79). This means that philosophy not only elaborates the unity of will as directness toward the future but also formulates certain norms that give direction to all human action. Cassirer conceived the ethical aspect of this Bezugssystem as the natural law doctrine of human rights.

We should recall the historical context in which Cassirer began to develop his ideas about natural law, namely, the constitutional law crisis in the Weimar Republic. The significance of Cassirer's lecture before the Hamburg Legal Society in 1932, "Wesen und Werden des Naturrechts," cannot be adequately understood unless we keep in mind the theoretical and political controversies it was intended to address. In the legal philosophical discussion in Germany during the Weimar Republic the two extremes of positivism and natural law stood jointly opposed to sociologically oriented approaches.[34] The label "positivism" is a bit misleading here since it was the sociologically oriented theorists who limited their discussions to positive law, that is, to the actual lawgiving and law-enforcement process. The primary representative of legal positivism around whom debate centered was Hans Kelsen (1881–1973). Kelsen developed a normative theory or science of the ought that sought to describe the structure of law but not its contents. By contrast, the founders of the sociological approach to law, Eugen Ehrlich (1862–1922), Max Weber (1864–1920), and Émile Durkheim (1858–1917), conceived the phenomenon of law to be explicable completely in terms of social processes.[35] Hägerström was also an adherent of a sociological approach.[36] From a strictly sociological point of view, law is simply something practical that develops in concrete social processes. On such a basis the claim that natural law is universally applicable can, at best, have only a utilitarian justification.

Natural law postulates definite, although limited, moral norms.

That is, it is a theory of the ought that is not empty. Kelsen's chief work, the *Reine Rechtslehre* (translated as *The Pure Theory of Law*), explicates the structure and essence of *positive* law as a system of norms culminating in the basic norm (*Grundnorm*) that one ought to obey the constitution (whatever it may be). Kelsen's theory of the normative per se has no place for natural law, which he rejects as unacceptable "metaphysics."

In developing his theory, Kelsen claims to follow Hermann Cohen.[37] Kelsen says that his reading of Cohen's *Ethik des reinen Willens* was the decisive influence in his theoretical orientation.[38] Even the title of Kelsen's main work, the *Reine Rechtslehre*, echoes the titles of Cohen's systematic works, all of which contain and emphasize the word *rein*—pure. Kelsen also finds himself in agreement with Cassirer's analysis of scientific concepts in *Substance and Function*, particularly with the idea that concepts like "the state" can be desubstantialized. The state can be conceived as a *Zurechnungspunkt* or *focus imaginarius* of legal theory that provides the notion of the unity of law.[39]

With this, Cassirer would have no quarrel, but it does not mean Cassirer's early work was only amenable to a purely formal theory of law. In 1925 Siegfried Marck published a book critical of Kelsen that bore the title *Substanzbegriff und Funktionsbegriff in der Rechtsphilosophie* (Substance and function in the philosophy of law). It utilized the ideas in the Cassirer work whose title it borrowed in order to show that "precisely the emptiness and absence of content of general conceptions . . . can be overcome."[40] Hence, before Cassirer had himself developed his position on these questions, his ideas had been used for opposing theoretical purposes.

The recurrent criticism directed against Kelsen's doctrine in the Weimar discussion of the theory of law was that it was empty.[41] It was a doctrine of oughtness that permitted *any* content to be given to the basic norm. On such a legal position it was possible politically only to justify the status quo, to follow the constitution. Political opponents of the Weimar Republic—who were legion, on both the right and the left—were naturally dissatisfied with such a view of the legal status of the state. Cosmopolitan ideas were anathema to the prevailing nationalism, and natural law was portrayed as an English or French conception.[42] Cassirer's 1932 lecture on natural law was allied in its aim to his 1928 lecture commemorating the tenth anniversary of the German Weimar Republic. In that address he argued that the idea of a republican constitution was in reality first conceived and developed in the natural law thought of German philosophers, particularly Leibniz, Christian Wolff, and Kant.[43] Neither natural law nor the Republic were "un-German." In a two-part article published in *Inter-Nationes* in 1931 on "Deutschland und Westeuropa im Spiegel der Geistesgeschichte" (Germany and western Europe in the mirror of the history of ideas) Cassirer makes the same argument in global cultural terms.[44] He seeks to demonstrate a common cultural task uniting German, Italian, French, and English thinkers since the Renaissance—the task of enlightenment. This was a doctrine of cultural activism. The significance of Cassirer's argument is that it went completely against the political and intellectual spirit of the times in Germany, which, in the words of Peter Gay, "elevated apathy into a superior form of existence and invidiously compared the traders' mentality of the British and French politicians with the spirituality of the educated German."[45] Cassirer's dedication to the *vita activa*, republican self-government, and cultural cosmopolitanism was also opposition to political passivity, antirepublicanism of the right and left, and cultural chauvinism.[46] He found the justification for this democratic conception in the *Gesinnung* or attitude of natural law.

Even if specific ideas in the natural law tradition could no longer be upheld—such as the notion of society as contractual in origin—Cassirer considered the basic attitude (Gesinnung) of natural law indispensable to jurisprudence and human society itself as a guide in solving problems posed by the historical nature of positive law.[47] Specifically, Cassirer maintained the universal validity of the doctrine of inalienable human rights. These "general binding supra-individual, supra-state, supra-national ethical claims" (SMC, 61) were not empty formal structures, but identifiable universal normative ethical claims. Without such a doctrine, the only alternative was to admit that the state is always a *Machtsstaat* whose every act is by definition legal in every sense, that is, that ultimately right is might.[48]

Neither positivism nor a sociological theory of law can justify the universal validity of the ethical claims of the human rights doctrine. Cassirer never refers to Kelsen specifically, nor does he criticize any particular sociological theory of law until his 1939 study of Hägerström. In his lecture to the Hamburg Legal Society he indicated that he did not really feel competent to speak about the details of the present-day legal controversies.[49] But by defending natural law he supports a position that is equally at odds with both Kelsen and the sociological view of law. He opts for a philosophical conception that had been subjected to severe philosophical criticism throughout the nineteenth and twentieth centuries by the historical school of law, Hegel, Marx, and sociological and positivist theorists. Cassirer marshaled the whole arsenal of the philosophy of symbolic forms to combat these attacks. Later, primarily through his reading of and personal acquaintance with Albert Schweitzer, he came to realize that the attacks on natural law theory were not motivated primarily by technical problems such as the doctrine of the social contract. The attacks on "eternal, immutable, and inalienable rights of man," which had "stirred the eighteenth century so deeply and passionately" (SMC, 58), had a deeper cause. The crisis in natural law theory was a symptom of a more fundamental cultural crisis affecting man's knowledge of himself.

To pose this problem as it appeared to Cassirer we must understand his conception of human rights and the theory of the human upon which it depends.

Human Rights and "Humanity"

Die Erziehung hat ihr Ziel; bei dem Geschlicht nicht weniger als bei dem Einzelnen. Was erzogen wird, wird zu etwas erzogen.—Lessing

Comment redonner un sens au mot Humanisme?—Jean Beaufret

Cassirer's conception of humanity has its origin in German classicism, the late eighteenth-century golden age of German literature. Cassirer had written about the chief figures of this movement—Goethe, Schiller, Herder, Wilhelm von Humboldt—as early as 1918 in *Freiheit und Form* and in numerous subsequent essays, but his most important statement on its philosophical significance is his 1939 essay "Naturalistische und humanistische Begründung der Kulturphilosophie" ("Naturalistic and Humanistic Philosophies of Culture"). In that essay he sees the chief insight of the poets, philosophers, artists, and scholars of German classicism in their recognition that the "fundamental feature of human existence" is the ability to give form (LH, 21–22). Giving form is understood as the setting of limits, and the primary object of this activity is the human personality. "Within the free sphere of one's personality ... checking heightens personality; it truly acquires form only by forming itself" (LH, 25).

In the language of German classicism the formation of the personality is called *Bildung*. *Bildung* is education in a broad sense, the cultivation of all the individual's capacities. Cassirer contrasts the "formation [*Bildung*] of humanity" with mere biological transformation (*Umbildung*; LH, 216). Biological transformations occur throughout the species while the particular organism remains passive. Individual biological changes do not affect the rest of the species; this is what biologists call the "non-transmissibility of acquired characteristics" (LH, 214–15). The formation or Bildung of humanity is not biological but cultural. Cassirer distinguishes radically between the "naturalistic" and "humanistic" conceptions of culture. Man is not a natural being insofar as the formation of humanity occurs in the sphere of meaning (LH, 216). In the sphere of meaning, the creations of individuals leave effects in the human world that extend far beyond their authors' natural lives. This principle holds true no matter whether these creations are "great works of culture" or ordinary "acts of speech" (LH, 216).

Cassirer points out that in classic German humanism the principle of individuality is inseparably linked with the view that humanity is something universal. He says: " 'Humanitas,' in the widest sense of the word, denotes that completely universal—and, in this very universality, unique—medium in which 'form,' as such, comes into being and in which it can develop and flourish" (LH, 22).

Cassirer's account of humanity in German classicism is not purely historical. When Cassirer says that humanitas is the medium in which form comes into being, he means that humanity is symbolism. For Cassirer, as for Peirce, man is a sign. When Cassirer defines man as "animal symbolicum" (EM, 26) he points out that this definition is based on the conception of symbolism as a vinculum functionale, not a vinculum substantiale as in traditional metaphysics (EM, 69). Humanitas is not some substantial "essence" of man, but the medium in which human life attains a form. Cassirer says that, as a name for this medium, "reason is a very inadequate term" since it cannot comprehend the "richness and variety" of human cultural life (EM, 26). The contours of Cassirer's conception of humanity are clearer where he distinguishes it from Heidegger's characterization of man as Dasein. Heidegger emphasizes man's finitude and the individuality of human destiny while he criticizes generality as that lifeless abstraction which he calls "das Man," the "they." The temporality of the finite Dasein is bound to the time that is allotted to it as "factically there" whereas the temporality of the "they" is the public time of the impersonal, the bad infinity of time without end.[50] Cassirer contrasts these personal and impersonal senses of time with the transpersonal (überpersönliche) time of humanity—the time of life in the sphere of meaning. The sphere of meaning is not free from temporality—there is a history of meanings, a history of culture—but the medium of symbolism permits man to overcome the time of his own personal life and live in the time of humanity—which extends far beyond his own life. This fact has fundamental ethical significance for Cassirer.

Cassirer credits Wilhelm von Humboldt with the greatest theoretical contribution to the classic conception of humanity. Humboldt succeeded to a greater extent than Kant, Fichte, Schelling, or Hegel in finding the correct grounding of man's orientation to the infinite (das Unendliche), which is the basis for the transcendence of particular individual existence (*LH*, 23). Humboldt discovered the fundamental importance of language as the origin of human transcendence.

For him [Wilhelm von Humboldt], language is "the clearest evidence and the surest proof that the human being does not possess a self-enclosed individuality; that the words 'I' and 'You' not only mutually support each other; that, as concepts, they are identical; and that, in this sense, there *is* a sphere of individuality, including the weak, needy, and perishing and extending back to the remotest beginnings of mankind." According to Humboldt, without such a rudimentary universality all understanding of others [*alles Einander-Verstehen*], all human life within the medium of speech would be impossible. (*LH*, 25)

Language is the clearest illustration of the unity ("universality") of mankind, that is, of "humanity." Even prelinguistic understanding of others is based upon the understanding of (expressive) meaning. In Cassirer's reconstruction of the development of consciousness of the ego, he shows that understanding of the other is present from the beginning. Language permits giving this feeling of generality a conceptual form; it permits conceiving actions in a way that transcends immediate expediency. Cassirer spoke of such transcendence in "Axel Hägerström" as the temporal direction of will, which includes having a "review, preview, and overview" (*Rückschau, Vorschau, and Überschau*). Giving oneself commands in terms of this temporal orientation is the essence of ethical personality, which Cassirer defines as "the unity, completeness, and inner consistency of a person's character" (AH, 108). The unity of a personality is seen in the "basic *direction* of its feeling and willing, not in a single feeling or impulse" (AH, 65; cf. 67).

Cassirer finds empirical support for his contention that personality is dependent upon symbolic processes in what he calls the pathology of symbolic consciousness. He shows that aphasia and kindred disorders affecting the power of speech result in drastic "changes in personality" (*EM*, 40). There is a disintegration of perspective in which "a teleological structure is replaced by a mere happening, . . . the formation of a purpose is replaced by a mere mosaic of partial acts" (*PSF*, 3:273; *PsF*, 3:319). Only biological needs and immediate practical interests retain importance (*EM*, 41). There is no longer an interest in long-range concerns, no awareness of the whole.

The person is a unity of psychological and physiological aspects. Cassirer follows William Stern in treating the person—the unity of these aspects—as the Urphänomen of psychological study.[51] The person is a phenomenological given, but the personality is not. The personality, as the "basic direction" of a person's sensibilities and actions, is directed to considerations that transcend the immediate situation and even the person's entire life.

Cassirer suggests that the "symbolic future" may be called a "prophetic" future in the sense that, like the biblical prophets, man can orient himself toward a future beyond his own life. "The term 'prudence' (*prudentia*) is etymologically connected with 'providence' (*providentia*). It means the ability to foresee future events and to prepare for future needs. . . . It is more than mere expectation; it becomes an imperative of human life. And this imperative reaches far beyond man's immediate practical needs—in its highest form it reaches beyond the limits of his empirical life" (*EM*, 54–55). Cassirer distinguishes the prophetic orientation to the future from augury. Soothsayers foretell the future so that man can only submit to it, but the prophets call for the opposite of submission. "Prophecy does not mean simply foretelling; it means a promise" (p. 55). We must see the future; we must anticipate what can happen; and we must realize that what we do here and now will bear on the future. A "prophetic" orientation means to promise—with one's own life—a kind of world.[52]

This characteristic of human life, the capacity to affect the whole of humanity, is the source of ethical responsibility. Cassirer's conception of humanity is also the source of his understanding of inhumanity. The doctrine of human rights defines what it would mean to call an act inhuman by establishing limits to actions affecting human beings.

It goes without saying that every human being has a natural right to humanity. Cassirer's most important statement of this right is found in *The Myth of the State*:

If a man could give up his personality he would cease being a moral being. He would become a lifeless thing—and how could such a thing obligate itself—how could it make a promise or enter into a social contract? This fundamental right, the right to personality, includes in a sense all the others. To maintain and to develop his personality is a universal right. It is not subject to the freaks and fancies of single individuals and cannot, therefore, be transferred from one individual to another. The contract of rulership which is the legal basis of all civil power has, therefore, its inherent limits. There is no *pactum subjectionis*, no act of submission by which man can give up the state of a free agent and enslave himself. For by

such an act of renunciation he would give up that very character which constitutes his nature and essence: he would lose
his humanity. (*MS*, 175)

This view clearly reflects the conception of the human personality
found in classical German humanism. It echoes Kant's expression of
the categorical imperative: "Act in such a way that you always treat
humanity, whether in your own person or in the person of any other,
never simply as a means, but always at the same time as an end."[53]
Cassirer claimed that Kant was indebted to Rousseau's theory of
education for this formulation of the categorical imperative, that is, to
Rousseau's claim that "only the free man is the true citizen" (*RKG*,
33). Cassirer's theory of human rights is in its substance a restatement
of eighteenth-century ideas; what is new about it is his justification of
the doctrine. His conception of man as animal symbolicum permits
him to reinterpret the notion of the "general will" (the direction of
consciousness toward the future) as something universal, arising
through the use of language. "Animal symbolicum" is Cassirer's
name for the universal humanity that justifies conceiving of human
rights.

Language is the common ground upon which all social life depends. Without language man could not live in a state any more than
do animals. By this emphasis on the primacy of the language community, Cassirer undercuts Hegel's conception of the supremacy of
the state. Language is the basis of all social organization and the
conditio sine qua non of any contractual agreement. It is the basis
upon which the individual becomes a self-responsible moral agent.
Cassirer does not claim that all people are self-responsible or even
that everyone personally desires freedom. "Freedom is not the natural
inheritance of man. In order to possess it we have to create it. If man
were simply to follow his natural instincts he would not strive for
freedom, he would choose dependence. Obviously, it is much easier
to depend upon others than to think, to judge, and to decide for
himself" (*MS*, 288). Cassirer's point is that as animal symbolicum
man does not live by his natural instincts alone, and though man may
flee from responsibility it is an act of self-destruction.

The right "to maintain and develop one's own personality" is the
only human right that Cassirer explicitly defends, yet he obviously
thinks there are more, for he says that "this fundamental right, the
right to personality, includes in a sense all the others." It is clear that
the right to personality as Cassirer conceives it would include elementary rights concerning the person's mind and body, namely, the
right to life as human life. This would entail freedom from arbitrary

violence to the mind or body. One could define these rights more specifically as the rights to freedom from arbitrary arrest or torture, freedom of movement and speech. Cassirer clearly had such basic rights in mind when he spoke of "all the others." Nowhere does he develop a list of specific rights; he is not concerned with the problem of the limits of human rights, for example, whether they include economic as well as political rights. He seeks only to defend a basic ethical conception of humanity through the idea of human rights. His concern is to show that there are limits to the exercise of political power, limits posed by the nature of humanity itself.

Cassirer's philosophy conceives of culture as something universal, as "human culture," and it would constitute an unacceptable relativism for his theory to admit restrictions to the validity of human rights. There is a common argument that the motion of human rights has meaning only for particular places and times because of the differing historical experiences, religions, or languages in various cultures.[54] To say that therefore no rights have universal application would be tantamount for Cassirer to saying that there is no such thing as humanity. But if there is such a thing, then there are human rights applicable to all human beings and we all have an ethical obligation to defend them.

For Cassirer the doctrine of "eternal, immutable, and inalienable human rights" marks the point where philosophy is "related to the world" (SMC, 58–61). The general tendency of academic philosophy in the twentieth century to become a specialized technical discipline resulted in philosophy's becoming a "stranger to the world" (SMC, 232). Cassirer did not think that the philosopher can, by himself, change history by teaching something new that would make people better or reform the world. In this regard, he says, the philosopher feels like Faust: "Bilde mir nicht ein, ich könnte was lehren, Die Menschen zu bessern und bekehren" ("Do not fancy that I could teach or assert what would better mankind or convert").[55] Cassirer adds, however, that "philosophy as a whole is not allowed to yield to this feeling." Cassirer agrees with Schweitzer that the philosopher must recognize the "duty of philosophy"; he must act as guardian to the values of culture and civilization.[56]

Cassirer argues that Schweitzer had a philosophical insight that had escaped contemporary philosophers. Schweitzer identified a global crisis in nineteenth-century culture extending beyond philosophy to the spiritual condition of the age. Schweitzer finds a general disappearance of the ethical, the erosion of the feeling of acting in a way that contributes positively to the world as it ought to be and, correlatively, a growth of a collective spirit that finds itself swept along by events beyond its control despite an impulse toward action.[57] As a result there is a tendency to sacrifice the question of the ought for the demand of the moment. This crisis in thought had gone unnoticed or at least unheeded by academic philosophy. Confined within its own scholastic concerns, contemporary philosophers, Cassirer says, "all too frequently lost sight of the true connection of philosophy with the world" (SMC, 60). Schweitzer made Cassirer realize that philosophy had become a purely academic discipline, that "it philosophized about everything except civilization" (SMC, 232). Philosophy either had too little or the wrong things to say about the state of civilization. It either insulated itself from the spiritual crisis of the age by its absorption in technical issues or it had a detrimental effect by helping to instill the feeling of helplessness.[58] Cassirer agrees with Schweitzer's assessment of the spiritual condition of man in the twentieth century: "And so we wander hither and thither in the gathering of the dusk formed by lack of any definite theory of the universe, like homeless drunken mercenaries, and enlist indifferently in the service of the common and the great without distinguishing between them. And the more hopeless the condition of the world becomes in which this adventurous impulse to action and progress ranges to and fro, the more bewildered becomes our whole conception of things, and the more purposeless and irrational the doings of those who have enlisted under the banner of such an impulse."[59]

Through his reading of Schweitzer, Cassirer realized that the criticisms of natural law that proliferated in the nineteenth and twentieth centuries and the rise of totalitarianism were both effects of a general cultural crisis—a "crisis in man's knowledge of himself," as Cassirer called it in An Essay on Man. The concept of human rights became problematic because the idea of humanity had lost its meaning. In his last works Cassirer sought to understand this crisis. To this end he reinterpreted the philosophy of symbolic forms as a philosophy of history.

V

HISTORY

Cassirer was a prolific writer on the history of philosophy, but he never wrote a book on the philosophy of history. Not until late in his career did he turn his attention to philosophical questions concerning social and political history. The most prominent such work is *The Myth of the State*. A philosophy of history is inherent, however, in the theory of symbolic forms as a philosophy of culture.[1]

The philosophy of symbolic forms offers two contrasting theoretical perspectives on historical life. First, it interprets history in a universal sense—as the ideal history of human culture. It shows how myth, language, and technology are the basic cultural forms from which religion, written law, history, art, and science develop. It reconstructs the way these symbolic forms move through mimetic and analogical phases before attaining a "purely symbolic" phase of development. In addition to this ideal perspective, the philosophy of symbolic forms is also a theory of conflicting social forces. As concrete social realities, the different symbolic forms generate both concord and conflict. The most fundamental of these conflicts is the antithesis between mythic and nonmythic ways of conceiving the world.

Both of these perspectives are theoretical; each regards historical life from the standpoint of the symbolic forms of culture. The first point of view—the ideal history or "phenomenology" of cultural forms—is prominent in *The Philosophy of Symbolic Forms* and *Essay on Man*. Although it receives less emphasis, the idea that concrete social conflicts are necessarily present in culture was part of Cassirer's conception of the symbolic forms even in its earliest formulation. The symbolic forms are not self-contained ways of having a world; they always stand in relation to—and in conflict with—one another. In the 1921 essay where Cassirer introduces the idea of symbolic forms, he says: "In general, the philosophical study of the 'symbolic forms' can never remain at the stage of describing each of them individually in their specific logical structure and their specific means of expression. Rather, it will have as one of its chief tasks to determine the relationships these forms have to one another—a relationship that results as much from their correlation as from their opposition, from their attraction to one another as from their mutual exclusion" (WW, 192). Part of this opposition is the way the different symbolic forms interact as stabilizing or innovative forces in society. Myth, for example, is conservative to the extreme; art and science favor innovation; language embodies both tendencies. All symbolic forms are social forces acting to unite and to divide people. Religion provides a classic example of this. Although each symbolic form is a means of uniting mankind, "none of them can bring about this unity without at the same time dividing and separating men. Thus what was intended to secure the harmony of culture becomes the source of the deepest discords and dissensions" (EM, 129–30). But the deep divisions caused by different languages and religions are less fundamental than the differences between the symbolic forms themselves, for these differences can never be overcome; they are irreconcilable in principle. I have already discussed the problem of truth as it presents itself in the differences between myth and science and between the sciences and the humanities, but it is a general problem concerning all the symbolic forms. The conflicts between science and religion, religion and secular law, art and technology, or ethical and economic evaluation are all familiar cultural conflicts that are felt again and again in history. Specific instances of such conflicts may become mediated, but the fundamental discrepancies between the symbolic forms remain. The conflicting viewpoints of art, science, religion, and technology cannot be eliminated by pointing out that they all can be philosophically understood as symbolic forms.

In the conclusion of the *Essay on Man* Cassirer calls attention to the oppositions between the individual and society, between conservative and innovative forces, and between the different symbolic forms themselves. Because of these many conflicting forces, Cassirer concludes that culture is "a dialectical unity, a coexistence of contraries" (EM, 222). Culture's unity is dynamic, not static: "it is the result of a struggle between opposing forces" (EM, 223). Cassirer cites Heraclitus on the "hidden harmony" that underlies the discord in the universe:

Harmony in Contrariety

"Men do not understand how that which is torn in different directions comes into accord with itself—harmony in contrariety, as in the case of the bow and the lyre."[2] The *Essay on Man* ends with the words: "The dissonant is in harmony with itself; the contraries are not mutually exclusive, but interdependent: 'harmony in contrariety, as in the case of the bow and the lyre' " (*EM*, 228).

The concluding paragraph of the *Essay on Man* begins with Cassirer's most comprehensive statement of the historical significance of human culture: "Human culture taken as a whole may be described as the process of man's progressive self-liberation" (*EM*, 228). How does this view relate to the notion that the harmony in culture is comparable to that of the bow and the lyre? The idea of "progressive self-liberation" suggests a linear course in the history of culture, a movement from a state of lesser to greater perfection, whereas the notion of contrariety, no matter how harmonious, suggests a stalemate, an impasse to all further progress. The conflict between these two perspectives seems all the more crass when we consider their proximity; they introduce and end the same paragraph, the conclusion of the book.

To begin, we must ask: What does Cassirer mean when he refers to Heraclitus's phrase "harmony in contrariety, as in the case of the bow and the lyre?" A number of interpretations of Heraclitus's meaning have been advanced. G. S. Kirk says that *"harmonia"* "refers primarily to the string of the bow and the strings of the lyre."[3] On this view, the harmony in contrariety that "people do not understand" is being compared to something physical—tension—illustrated by the bow and the lyre. Philip Wheelwright entertains the idea that the conjunction of these two particular objects might metaphorically reflect the conjunction of life and death, but he concludes, concurring explicitly with Kirk, that the fragment "shows no intention of making a comparison between the bow and the lyre."[4] Eugen Fink has suggested that the fragment be read along with fragment 48: "The bow is called life, but its work is death."[5] In Greek the word for "life," βίος, and for "bow," βιὸς, are very close. Fink points to the fact that the bow is an emblem of fighting and death, while the lyre, as the instrument for the celebration of a festive occasion, is a symbol of life.

This more metaphoric reading is further justified by the attempt to read Heraclitus historically, considering the meaning of the "bow and the lyre" to the ancient Greeks. Charles Kahn follows this approach to the text: "The music of Apollo's favorite instrument and the death-dealing power of his customary weapon must be taken *together* as an expression of the 'joining' that characterizes the universal pattern of things."[6] For the Greeks, Apollo appears both as "musagetes," the leader of the muses, and as a deadly archer.[7] Hesiod tells that Apollo, upon his birth, utters the words: "The lyre and curved bow shall ever be dear to me, and I will declare to men the unfailing will of Zeus."[8]

Does Cassirer think that the conflicts in culture find a resolution in a synthesis like that suggested by the image of a reverberating string?[9] Or does he conceive the oppositions to be deeper and more radically disparate than the physical image suggests, something more like the difference between life and death? This inquiry bears directly on how Cassirer conceives human culture to be a process of self-liberation.

The idea of liberation is a basic part of Cassirer's philosophical anthropology. Man as animal symbolicum does not live and die within the confines defined by nature alone. Symbolism permits holding the world "at a distance" and this objectification "liberates" man from the narrowness of existence.[10] This is a basic tenet of the philosophy of symbolic forms. Moreover, culture is cumulative because symbolic communication permits it to be transmitted from one generation to the next. But this is not what is usually meant by speaking of "progress" in history. The idea of progress, usually identified with the Enlightenment, expresses the belief that by applying rational, scientific methods to all aspects of human life, there will be a general improvement in social conditions and even that man will himself thereby be morally bettered.[11] Such thinking is found in Condorcet's Sketch for the Progress of the Human Mind (1794), and Kant himself in the "Streit der Fakultäten" (1798) discerned a tendency to moral progress in history illustrated by the French Revolution ("whether it succeed or fail").[12] I do not think that Cassirer's conception of human culture as man's progressive self-liberation should be interpreted as a theory of progress in this way. The title that Cassirer chose for his book on man, however, immediately calls to mind the eighteenth-century discussions of the question of progress and the doctrine of optimism on which it was based.

Clearly, Cassirer had Alexander Pope's famous work in mind when he titled his "Introduction to a Philosophy of Human Culture" An Essay on Man. In his late work Rousseau, Kant, Goethe, Cassirer discusses the eighteenth-century debate on Pope's poem and rejects the approach to history that both sides adopted. The proponents of optimism and of pessimism both interpret history in purely eudaemonistic terms (RKG, 40). Cassirer holds that history cannot and should not be conceived in terms of happiness; rather it is "the setting in which man is to test and prove his freedom" (RKG, 42). With this, Cassirer dismisses not only "the chimera of a Golden Age and the idyll of a pastoral Arcady" but also the chimera of a future utopic state of perfection. "Man cannot and should not escape pain. For this is the spur to activity. . . . In all social life as well, it is only the opposition of forces, with all the suffering it entails for mankind, that at the same time makes possible the further operation of these forces." For the noneudaemonistic conception of history the value of life lies on a different plane: "The diminution of happiness cannot lessen the value of existence, for this does not consist in what *happens* to a person, but in what a person *does*. Our deeds, not our outward fate, give life its meaning" (RKG, 40–41). The idea of culture as man's progressive self-liberation places an undeniable emphasis on action. The phrase "self-liberation" has an undeniable emotional and evaluative ring, echoing Cassirer's assessment of the value of life. This evaluation has less to do, I think, with the optimism associated with Pope than with the sense of life characteristic of another poet, Goethe.

For an understanding of Cassirer's thought as a whole, Goethe is at least as important as Cassirer's methodological and systematic debts to Kant, Hegel, or Cohen.[13] Cassirer's attraction to Goethe was not simply the usual piety of the educated German for the great man of letters and all-around genius.[14] Cassirer wrote extensively about Goethe, and he adopted many aspects of his thought in his own thinking—the Urphänomen, Goethean cosmopolitanism—but his debt to Goethe goes much deeper than this. Cassirer did not just regard Goethe's work to be of value, as Hegel did, because it can rank as "philosophical."[15] There are no specific problems or issues that Goethe dealt with that Cassirer singles out as his major achievement. Nor does Cassirer agree with Goethe on everything; for example, he agrees neither with his judgment of mathematical physics nor his negative attitude toward historical knowledge (see IG, 33–80; MS, 208–09). And even though he considers Goethe to be unexcelled as a lyric poet, he rates Shakespeare and the Greek tragedians higher as dramatists.[16]

When Cassirer's academic term in Sweden ended, he continued to teach outside the regular academic curriculum and took the opportunity to offer a course he had always wanted to teach, a course on Goethe. In the manuscript of his first lecture he speaks without the usual academic distance, explaining his own lifelong interest in Goethe: "wie von keinem anderen Dichter der Weltliteratur geht nach meinem Gefühl eine solche geistige Befreiung aus, als von ihm" (from no other poet in world literature does there, for my feeling, emanate such a spiritual liberation as from him; ibid.). Cassirer contrasts Goethe's "geistige Befreiung" with liberation in specific spheres of thought. Lessing, for example, was a liberator in the field of theological dogma and rigid conventional criteria of taste, but Goethe was a liberator in every field to which he directed his attention, in his poetry, in his thought, in his scientific research. "Von Philisternetzen, vom geistigem Drucke, geistiger Enge und Befangenheit, von Beschaulichkeit und Vorurteilen wollte Goethe befreien—und das sah er als den Sinn seines Lebenswerkes an" (From the nets of the philistines, from intellectual pressure, intellectual narrowness and timidity, from quiescence and prejudices Goethe wanted to act as liberator—and he saw that as the meaning of his life's work; ibid., 9).

For Cassirer, the objection that Goethe was not politically active does not mean that he was not effective in that sphere as a liberator. On the contrary, Goethe had a definite political attitude, his cosmopolitanism, and its effects were seen in the controversy it wrought. Cassirer cites Goethe's comment to Eckermann explaining why he did not write patriotic songs against the French in the struggle against Napoleon: "between us, I did not hate the French, although I thanked God when we were rid of them. How could I, to whom only culture and barbarism are things of importance, hate a nation that belongs to the most cultivated on earth and to whom I owe such a great part of my own education!" For Goethe, patriotism meant to "fight prejudices, eliminate narrow-hearted views, and contribute to the enlightenment of his people" (ibid., 9–10). Goethe's cosmopolitanism is based upon the recognition that politics deals with people, with individual persons with feelings and unique personalities. Goethe's pronouncements on the cosmopolitan ideas of "world literature" (a term he coined himself), "world culture," and "world communication" were predicated on the view that tolerance enriches culture because it accepts differences.[17]

Time and again Cassirer referred to Goethe's cosmopolitanism as a viable political attitude, for example, in 1918, in reply to the "Völkisch" nationalist views professed by the neo-Kantian philosopher Bruno Bauch—then editor of the *Kant-Studien*—or, in 1930, on the occasion of the French withdrawal from the Rhineland, which had been occupied since the end of the First World War.[18] Cassirer's political sentiments in his address at a convocation celebrating the French withdrawal are comparable in spirit to Goethe's remarks to Eckermann cited above. They express relief at the end of the occupation and sympathy with the solidarity among the people of the area after years of foreign rule. But there is no hate for the French and no chauvinistic, militant language.

For Cassirer, however, the "liberating" character of Goethe's thought lay in something more fundamental than a social attitude, something from which this attitude followed as a correlative point of view. It was Goethe's *Lebensgefühl*, his sense of life. In his 1918 study of Goethe's *Pandora*, an unfinished "Festspiel," Cassirer examines the feeling for life typical of the late Goethe. *Pandora* is one of Goethe's most conceptual dramas; its two main characters, Prometheus and Epimetheus, are allegorical representations of typical forces and attitudes. Both represent a misunderstanding of life. The former exemplifies immediate goal-directed activity and the mere use of things, the latter, an attitude of longing, passivity, and melancholy. Prometheus, a hero to the young Goethe, is a negative figure in this play. Cassirer comments on Prometheus's character in *Pandora* as follows: "In this [Prometheus's] world of exploitation every inner difference, every value inherent in a thing's makeup and every intellectual value distinction disappears. Where the measure [of value] no longer lies in the pure being of something's content, but rather in that which it achieves for some exterior purpose foreign to it itself, there, ultimately, all things are equal in value" (*IG*, 19). Prometheus's inability to take things for what they are prohibits him from appreciating the proclamation of a celebration: "What kind of celebration do you announce to me? I love them not: rest is enough every night for the weary. The true man's celebration is the act." Cassirer says that the view that the true celebration is the act "proves to have a meaning which Prometheus himself did not recognize nor foresee. In Pandora's realm no effort acquires its value through an external purpose which it serves; rather, here activity is itself the outcome of an original and pure will to form and acquires from it its own true and independent value" (*IG*, 22–23). "Pandora's realm" refers to something apart from either Prometheus's boundless activity or Epimetheus's melancholy—the world of "form." Goethe changes the traditional figure of Pandora as the one who brought cares to mankind; now she becomes the bringer of the arts and the sciences—assuming the position of Prometheus as the bringer of culture.

"The world of Epimetheus was that of inactive longing and looking, that of Prometheus was that of formless action, directed only to external results and bound to them" (*IG*, 22). Pandora symbolizes activity in which the act and the celebration are not opposed; "this activity, the only one worth valuing" has its origin in itself, in its "form," understood as "a content that does not reach completely beyond conditioned striving, but rather becomes visible in it." The immanent yet unlimited character of such form characterizes "die menschliche Gemeinschaftsarbeit," mankind's common work (*IG*, 23). "Science and art stand here only at the apex of levels of activity that encompass every form of productive and constructive [gestaltende] activity from the lowest to the highest" (*IG*, 25). In *Pandora*, Cassirer says, form "does not belong to the one who meditates or observes, but to those who grow or create: to the farmers [*Landleuten*] and the shepherds, the vintners, the fishermen, the smiths. Form, in its true essence, only becomes a person's own [*Eigen*] when he daily creates and brings it forth. . . . Only when every particular person in his own narrowly defined sphere seeks and achieves such a fulfillment is the whole fulfilled in him and through him the whole—so that he becomes the vehicle of the genuine and essential form of being."[19]

Because of the element of form, true action cannot be a limitless Faustian striving; it must recognize inner and outer limits. From this grows the attitude that the elder Goethe calls *Entsagung*—forbearance.[20] Whereas "resignation" has the sense of "giving up," of a begrudging abandonment of something, Goethe speaks of the "heiter Entsagenden,"[21] those with a "happy forbearance" who know how to give everything its due. This is the contrary of the view "dass alles eitel ist," that "all is vain."[22] *Entsagung*, Goethe says, is a *resignation* with regard to the temporal that finds something eternal substantiated by the very transience of things (ibid.). Cassirer gives this description at the end of his essay on Goethe's *Pandora*:

Forbearance does not lead to man turning with force against the powers that he feels subjected to, nor to making do in quiet passivity through an abstract and unfeeling stoicism. In suffering itself he experiences yet another necessity and law of existence, which stands above all individual happiness and pain; yet he does not on the other hand subordinate himself to this necessity in dull fatalism but asserts himself in opposition to it even in defeat. Through this basic state of mind, Goethe is able to find salvation in that feeling which would have found complete expression in the second, uncompleted part of the work: in the feeling of the constantly self-renewing totality of life, for which there is no cessation and no growing old. (IG, 30)

This interpretation of forbearance in Goethe is an aspect of the idea of "form" in action—as opposed to unlimited striving or passivity. These Goethean conceptions help to clarify Cassirer's idea of self-liberation. For Cassirer, self-liberation is not concerned with the establishment of some distant, utopian goal, but with self-assertion of a particular kind, namely, self-formation. "Self-liberation" is Cassirer's expression for German classicism's idea of the *Bildung der Humanität*. The symbolic forms of culture are the means to man's self-liberation from ignorance, from injustice (the doctrine of humanity in human rights), and from fear,[23] because they transport the individual from his finite existence into a transpersonal realm of meaning and so enlarge the feeling of self.

Cassirer's interpretation of Goethe's *Faust* is particularly important because it brings together all these aspects of his notion of self-liberation. At the end of *Faust* II Mephisto reveals his philosophy at Faust's entombment:

Why have eternally creation,
When all is subject to annihilation?
Now it is over. What meaning can one see?
It is as if it had not come to be,
And yet it circulates as if it were.
I should prefer—Eternal Emptiness.[24]

Mephisto takes Faust's lifelong striving for naught. But here, Cassirer says, Mephisto's thinking goes wrong. At the end of Goethe's drama, Faust has been blinded. In this state he finally finds satisfaction in the idea of "standing with free people on free ground" (Auf freiem Grund mit freiem Volke stehen) and in the great project of a dike to hold back the sea to make room for them to live: "not safe, but active-free" (ibid., ll. 11580, 11564). Yet Mephisto has played a trick on Faust and the sound of digging that he hears is really the spading of Faust's own grave. Mephisto fails to see any point in Faust's satisfaction; for him this is only Faust's last illusion. But, Cassirer says, "Those of his [Mephisto's] ilk cannot grasp this form of 'abiding' [*Verweilen*]. Where he thought he could lead the human mind astray with pleasure [*Genuß*], Faust discovers an inexhaustible ideal content [*Gehalt*] that he is able to give to life. This content can only be found in perseverance, but the eternal law that this perseverance follows gives back to this striving its inner peace" (*FF*, 266). This striving's content cannot be measured in terms of the pleasure it gives or its external success; it is valuable in itself. Faust's quest leads him to a task that is "objective and unending," the common task of mankind which Cassirer here calls the "Befreiung der Menschheit," the "liberation of mankind" (*FF*, 266). When Cassirer, thirty years later, calls human culture "the process of man's progressive self-liberation," he is speaking in the same Goethean spirit.

The spirit of *Faust* is not utopian. In his last speech, Faust says the highest wisdom is to recognize that "only those earn freedom and life who conquer them each day anew." Cassirer comments that this Faustian perseverance does not guarantee happiness, but bestows dignity (*RKG*, 42–43). The philosopher, Cassirer says, "feels like Faust" because as an individual he has "long ago given up all hopes to reform the political world" (*SMC*, 266) and yet philosophy nonetheless has a role to play in man's self-liberation. The following gloss is representative of Cassirer's belief in the value of philosophy and cultural activity generally: " 'It is not always necessary,' Goethe once said, 'for the true to become embodied; it is enough if it floats about as spirit and brings about agreement, like when the tone of a bell undulates, serious and friendly through the air.' Whoever grasps history spiritually [geistig] and the spirit historically, hears everywhere this serious and friendly tone of the bell. And it is a comforting basic tone that assures him in all the chaotic confusion of external events of the inner harmony in the actual spiritual history of the world" (GGW, 148). Cassirer's reference to the inner harmony of the spiritual history of the world differentiates the history of culture from the history of "external events." The harmony that Cassirer has in mind is not that envisioned by Pope:

All Nature is but Art, unknown to thee;
All Chance, Direction, which thou canst not see;
All Discord, Harmony, not understood;
All partial Evil, universal Good:
And, spite of Pride, in erring Reason's spite,
One truth is clear, Whatever IS, is RIGHT.[25]

In Pope's vision of the world, the idea of self-liberation as the "common task of mankind" would be out of place, because the concept of liberation (Befreiung) is inseparable from the notion of opposition and struggle. Opposition is, of course, an element in the notion that "All Discord" is "Harmony, not understood," but the depth of discord that can be countenanced as harmonious has limits. In the twentieth-century the sentiment is the reverse, so that, to quote Auden, "even the most prudent become worshippers of chance."[26] Cassirer's conception of culture as man's progressive self-liberation is no closer in feeling to this sentiment than it is to Pope. Why then did Cassirer name his book on man after Pope's Essay?

This choice of title reflects Cassirer's sympathy with the eighteenth century in a wide sense and indicates his intention to write An Essay on Man for the present time. His work attempts to show "the inner harmony in the actual spiritual history of the world." The crucial question is, therefore, how does Cassirer conceive this harmony?

We can now consider what Cassirer meant by the "harmony" in culture when he compares it to the harmony in the "bow and the lyre." Conceived as a physical metaphor, the opposition symbolized by the bow and the lyre is harmless, for opposing forces in a taut string are reconciled and at rest when they combine to create a tension. Such a harmony is envisioned in the idea that the symbolic forms all contribute, but in different ways, that is, additively, to man's self-liberation. But as social realities the different symbolic forms do not form a homogeneous whole. The history of religion, of science, and of art as social realities is not merely akin to political history, but part of it.

An example of the political reality of mythico-religious thought is the burning of the library at Alexandria (*LH*, 216). According to tradition, the library was ordered destroyed by the caliph Umar, to whom is attributed the dictum: "No other book but the book of God," that is, the Koran.[27] He justified his act with the argument: "if they contain that which agrees with the Book of God, then having the Book of God we are wealthy without them, and if they contradict the Book of God Almighty then we have no need for them" (ibid., 417). Such thinking precludes finding anything of value in any book but the "Book of God" because the contents of that book are *by definition* what is of value. How is such an event to be philosophically understood?

For a traditional rationalist, the destruction of the Alexandrian library could only count as an accidental failure of reason. Paul Natorp, for example, speaks of the history of knowledge simply as an *unendliche Bahn*, an "unending path." Natorp sees this path as a "tendency toward science" in cultural effort as a whole.[28] For that view, an event like the burning of the library in Alexandria or the National Socialists' book burnings must appear as something "external" to the nature of human culture, an accident which occurred only because scientific thinking had not yet spread far enough. For the philosophy of symbolic forms, such events exemplify the power of mythic thought, a power which is ever-present in culture. Cassirer upholds no global concept of "reason." Reason is the reason of different symbolic forms, the reason of language, the reason of art, of science, of historiography. "For us the word 'reason' has long since lost its unequivocal simplicity even if we are in agreement with the basic aims of the Enlightenment" (*PE*, 6). Cassirer has broken up the global, idealistic view of reason: "The concept of reason is vague, and it becomes clear and distinct only when the right 'differenti specifica' are added" (ibid.). Cassirer was too much of a historian and his conception of reason too differentiated to permit conceiving the harmony in culture in a way that renders events like the burning of the library of Alexandria as a mere accident.

Cassirer provides the way to understand his use of the simile of the bow and lyre when he says that in culture "the dissonant is in harmony with itself" (*EM*, 228). The harmony in culture is compared to something audible. The dissonant may be considered "in harmony with itself" since, to exist, it requires conflicting tone progressions— but is this not to say that dissonance and harmony are the same? Help in understanding Cassirer's meaning can be obtained from another of his late works: his study of Thomas Mann's novel *Lotte in Weimar*.

Pointing to the representation of life and death in Plato's *Phaedo*, to Shakespeare, Cervantes, Molière, and Mann himself, Cassirer claims that it is impossible to portray life as a whole except as a "coincidentia oppositorum." Life is neither tragedy nor comedy; it is both in one.[29] Harmony need not mean "resolution"; it can simply mean a "coincidentia oppositorum."

This conception of the harmony in culture as a coincidentia oppositorum is confirmed by *The Myth of the State*, which Cassirer wrote immediately after the *Essay on Man*. There is a close relationship between the conclusions of Cassirer's last two books. Both end with images depicting Cassirer's philosophical view of history. The *Essay on Man* ends with the figurative image of the tension of the bow and the lyre; *The Myth of the State* ends with an image of a struggle— the ancient Babylonian myth of the combat between the young god Marduk and the ancient monster Tiamat. Cassirer says explicitly that the Babylonian myth is a "simile" of the relation between myth and the "other great cultural powers"—the "intellectual, ethical, and artistic" forces (MS, 297). Surely, therefore, *The Myth of the State* should help to clarify what Cassirer means by the harmony in human culture. Just as Marduk slew Tiamat and created the universe from her limbs, so too the "superior forces" of culture tamed and subdued myth, yet myth survives in civilized culture, no longer commanding the whole but present in each of its parts. There is no final resolution between the primordial forces underlying all culture and the later, critical "intellectual, ethical, and artistic" forces.

I think it is possible to develop further Cassirer's understanding of culture by asking why he chose this particular creation myth to make the concluding point of his book. The choice could hardly have been due to some predilection for Assyriology, since none is in evidence. Cassirer's work on myth generally is not motivated by philological or other particular empirical interests. One obvious reason for introducing the myth of Marduk is its age. Historically, Mesopotamia was the beginning of Western civilization. In the *Essay on Man* Cassirer points to the fact that the Babylonians were the first to develop a theory of the heavens, a theory combining an elaborate astrology with careful observation and a mathematics using a symbolic algebra (EM, 46–47). The Babylonians invented the zodiac and algebra. Cassirer traces this intellectual feat to a heightened awareness of symbolic thinking in Mesopotamia, an awareness which he attributes to the need to translate frequently back and forth between the two radically different languages of Sumerian and Akkadian. This awareness of symbolism and the availability of appropriate sign systems permitted the formulation of the symbolism needed for mathematics.

Cassirer also emphasized the cultural importance of a theory of the heavens in his discussion of the unity of ancient Greek culture in his 1941 essay "Logos, Dike, Kosmos in der Entwicklung der griechischen Philosophie." The three concepts of *Logos*, *Dike*, and *Kosmos* expressed for Greek philosophy a unified order in thought, justice, and nature—especially in the heavens. Cassirer found a similar conception of unity in Mesopotamian culture, formulated not in philosophy but in the Marduk myth.

In the *Logic of the Humanities* Cassirer called attention to the connection in the Marduk myth between the order in the cosmos and the order of justice. "In the Babylonian creation myth we see Marduk waging battle against the shapeless Chaos, against the monstrous Tiamat. Following his victory, he erects those eternal monuments of the cosmic and moral [and legal] orders [Rechtsordnung]: He establishes the signs of the zodiac; he fixes the succession of days, months, and years. And at the same time he sets limits to human action, limits which cannot be transgressed with impunity" (LH, 42–43; Cassirer also refers to this myth in PSF, 2:96, 113–14; PsF, 2:119, 140). Hammurabi, the king of Babylon about 2250 B.C., declares in the prologue to the Hammurabi code (the earliest complete body of written law) that he was sent by Marduk to rule and to this end received and established the law. The stele with the Hammurabi code, discovered in 1901–02, originally stood in the temple of Marduk in Babylon. "While legality's basis in feeling is related to myth, it attains definite intellectual, objective, fixed content by its formulation in [written] language" (AH, 103–04). Making the law public through written language was the first step toward taking the arbitrariness out of the mythical conception of the forbidden. This too is part of the significance of the Marduk myth: the proclamation of a Rechtsordnung or legal cosmos whose limits cannot be transgressed with impunity.

In *The Myth of the State*, however, Cassirer refers to the Marduk myth to explicate a negative side of the history of culture. The Babylonian creation myth does not depict the secure establishment of a lasting human order, as the Frankforts note in a comparison of Egyptian and Mesopotamian myths:

In Egypt creation was reviewed as the brilliant act of an omnipotent Creator disposing of submissive elements. Of the lasting order which he created, society formed an unchanging part. In Mesopotamia the Creator [Marduk] had been chosen by a divine assembly helpless before the threat of the powers of chaos. Their champion, Marduk, had followed up his victory by the creation of the universe. This took place almost as an afterthought, and man was especially designed as a servant of the gods. There was no permanence in the human sphere. The gods assembled on every New Year's Day to 'establish (such) destinies' for mankind as they pleased.[30]

Following his victory over Tiamat and her forces, Marduk took the Tablet of Destinies from her consort, gaining control over fate.[31] Babylonian myth tells that later the tablet was stolen from Marduk by the god Zu. Marduk himself was then captured and confined to a prison without light; he underwent tortuous miseries before the gods were able by trickery to liberate him and restore him to his former position.[32] In the annual Aktu ritual celebration, the most important event in Babylonian life, the recitation of the myth of creation was supplemented by the ritual humiliation of the king as a reenactment of Marduk's trials.[33] There is never a final victory of light over darkness and, hence, Babylonian myth expresses what the Frankforts call "a haunting fear that the unaccountable and turbulent powers may at any time bring disaster to human society."[34] Cassirer, too, says of culture that "we are always standing on volcanic soil and must be prepared for sudden convulsions and eruptions. In the critical moments of man's political and social life myth regains its old strength. It was always lurking in the background, waiting for its opportunity. This hour comes if the other binding forces in our social life, for one reason or another, lose their influence; if they can no longer counterbalance the demonic power of myth" (SMC, 246–47).

Cassirer's conception of the dialectic between myth and the critical forces of culture stands midway between mythic fear and a philosophy of historical optimism.

For the mythic worldview, demonic forces determine the course of events. Such forces are wholly independent. There can be no reckoning with them and they always have the upper hand. For mythic thinking, the only possible attitude toward these forces is fear and submission. For the enlightened, optimistic mind, the shape of history is always man-made; the technical mastery of every event stands as the final goal of history. The intelligent use of the mind can meet every occasion by converting it into a problem to be solved. It is such thinking that, as Walter Benjamin pointed out, was amazed that a cultural catastrophe like the Third Reich was "still possible" in the twentieth century.[35] Cassirer's standpoint differs from either of these extremes. Myth is not something wholly other than the intellectual, ethical, and artistic forces in culture; it is their origin. Even in the present age myth "pervades the whole of man's human existence" (SMC, 245–46). The mythic sense of the world is always present in the ability to experience the expressive, the dramatic, the personified. There can be no elimination of the mythic from life, no elimination of "deification" or "devilization" (SMC, 238). To attempt to eliminate myth from culture would mean forgetting that "man is not exclusively a rational animal, [that] he is and remains a mythical animal" (SMC, 246). When Cassirer compares the creation of culture from myth with the Babylonian myth of the universe from the remains of the monster Tiamat, he means to call attention to the opposition between culture in which myth rules uncontrolled and culture in which myth is subject to critical forces, that is, a "coincidentia oppositorum." Hence, it is a mistake to regard Cassirer's notion of "man's progressive self-liberation" as a belief in or call for an elimination of the mythic from culture and the creation of a world in which private and social life would only follow the dictates of rational organization.

Self-liberation is the struggle for a harmony between the mythic and critical forces in culture, a coincidentia oppositorum. With the mythic forces in check, man can liberate himself from ignorance and fear— this is the positive content of Cassirer's conception of the function of human culture. The philosophy of symbolic forms clearly shares in the spirit of the Enlightenment, but it does not propose a doctrine of progress, only a coincidentia oppositorum between the irrational and rational forces in culture. In doing so, it imposes limits on the belief in progress. At the end of the eighteenth century (1798), the poet Christoph Wieland offered the view that future generations would look back at the "Enlightenment" of that age with contempt because "we shamefully flatter our age, if we claim for it the smallest real advance over all earlier centuries, with the single exception perhaps, that in most European countries neither witches nor heretics are any longer being burned to the greater glory of God."[36] That this was no small achievement could only be realized when it became clear that the tendency to devilization was an integral part of human culture.

Man can only "test and prove his freedom" by engaging in a constant struggle to liberate himself from his own ignorance, barbarism, and fear. Cassirer's conception of history is heroic. Man does not have history at his command, yet he can never be purely a passive spectator. There is something like an "impulse to action and progress" in man, but it is this very impulse that, when frustrated, brings people to enlist in the service of irrational purposes. Cassirer agrees with Schweitzer that this frustration has become universal in the present century because of the "condition of the world." In the *Essay on Man*

Cassirer refers to this condition as "the crisis in man's knowledge of himself."

Myth reasserts itself "in times of crisis," in "an unusual and dangerous situation." Myth enters into society at points of intense feeling, need, or danger. Such an instance occurs, Cassirer says, when the binding forces in man's social life for one reason or another "lose their strength" (MS, 280). When society seems to begin to break apart a call for leadership arises, a call stemming from the collective desire for a renewal of order. A group that seizes upon this collective desire can manipulate these feelings in a way that reunifies society. The "binding forces in man's social life"—"intellectual, ethical, artistic" forces—lose their strength when belief in them begins to fade. When belief in these—whatever they are—begins to decline, the result is a loss in self-confidence, which in turn leads to a feeling of helplessness, the general cause of the return to mythic thought. Myth depicts forces greater than man that threaten and sustain him.

The crisis that Cassirer discusses in the opening chapter of An Essay on Man is not, or at least not directly, a political crisis. It is a crisis in thought. Man's understanding of himself has undergone a gradual, cumulative change since the beginning of the rise of modern science. The steps in this change are well known. Cassirer recounts how the Christian and philosophical notions of a general providence ruling the world and destiny of man were confronted with the new cosmology of Copernicus, according to which man no longer could be regarded as the center of the universe. Gradually, the notion of "purposes" in nature was itself rejected by science. Post-Darwinian biology, finally, holds that even man's existence cannot be regarded as anything more than a coincidence. Cassirer says, "Modern thinkers have held that, after the innumerable fruitless attempts of former times, they have definitely succeeded in accounting for organic life as a mere product of chance" (EM, 19; cf. PK on biology). The real crisis in man's knowledge of himself emerged, however, when it was discovered that now there no longer was even a meaningful way to approach the question of the nature of man. On this question we face today what Cassirer calls a "complete anarchy of thought" (EM, 21). Views and evaluations of human life abound among contemporary thinkers, but there are no longer any generally accepted criteria by which to judge them. Philosophers, psychologists, theologians, sociologists, economists, and other experts disagree with each other and among themselves about the nature of man; there is no longer even a generally accepted way to pose the question, who is man? This is not just a theoretical issue, Cassirer says, but "an imminent threat to the whole extent of our ethical and cultural life" (EM, 22), for "every great crisis in man's thoughts used to be accompanied by a deep crisis in his moral and social conduct" (SMC, 22). The crisis in man's knowledge of himself is not an objective "problem" needing the right solution. It is tantamount to a loss of identity on the part of the questioner himself. This can result in either a loss of self-confidence or in over-confidence bred by the absence of any positive vision of man that can serve as the measure of human action. The view that man's essence is to "make himself"—the central thought of humanist philosophy and the basic thesis of contemporary philosophical anthropology—becomes empty unless there is some general task or purpose, some final end toward which man should strive. The "anarchy of thought" about the nature of man threatens to turn into an anarchy of action.

In the preface to his Philosophy of the Enlightenment, Cassirer calls for a return to the spirit, if not the letter, of eighteenth-century thought. He suggests that the present age can profit by considering itself in the "clear bright mirror" fashioned by the Enlightenment and by emulating its courage in seeking to shape life through reasoned thought (viii–xi). Regarded in the context of Germany at that time (1932), this plea is understandable, but it also shows that Cassirer had not as yet grasped the depth of the crisis in man's knowledge of himself. It was not just a crisis in thinking, but in feeling, in man's sense of self. It does not have its seat in the intellect, but deeper, in what Cassirer later called that "stratum that reaches down to a great depth" (MS, 297), the substratum of feeling in which human beings sustain or lack a sense of purpose.

By the time Cassirer wrote The Myth of the State the Second World War was nearly over, leaving much of Europe in ruins and millions dead. In all of this Cassirer now saw more than a great political tragedy. He regarded the National Socialists to be more than particularly successful propagandists and the Third Reich to be more than an especially ruthless regime. The events leading up to the Second World War, the way this war was fought, and the total dedication that was mustered in this fight had a lasting significance that would have to be dealt with long after the Nazis were gone and the war was history.

After his inaugural lecture in Göteborg in 1935 Cassirer developed his justification of the inalienable human right to "personality." No one had a right to deny another person his autonomy, to deprive him of the freedom to think and decide for himself, a right involving self-responsibility and the duties this entails. In the Third Reich something occurred with which Cassirer had not reckoned. People of every kind, educated and uneducated, young and old, turned away from the values of liberal intellectual culture and became followers of a nationalistic and racist ideology, and in so doing they willingly sacrificed their individuality and blindly did what they were told. The statement "I was only following orders" could stand as the final personal statement of responsibility. Self-responsibility had been eradicated and replaced by a total belief in authority. This came as a great shock to Cassirer, and, he believed, it was a fact that had far-reaching implications. In 1945 Cassirer explained his own reaction this way: "Of all the sad experiences of these last twelve years this is perhaps the most dreadful one. It may be compared to the experience of Odysseus on the island of Circe. But it is even worse. Circe had transformed the friends and companions of Odysseus into various animal shapes. But here are men, men of education and intelligence, honest and upright men who suddenly give up the highest human privilege. They have ceased to be free and personal agents. . . . Methods of compulsion and suppression have ever been used in political life . . . [but] the modern political myths proceeded in quite a different manner. They did not begin with demanding or prohibiting certain actions. They undertook to change the men, in order to regulate and control their deeds. The political myths acted in the same way as a serpent that tries to paralyze its victim before attacking him. Men fell victim to them without any serious resistance. They were vanquished and subdued before they had realized what actually happened" (MS, 286). The National Socialists had discovered something so powerful that it could literally command a whole people. No one was prepared for it. In a sense it was the master weapon. It would miss the point to just call it "propaganda"; it was much more than this.

The National Socialists discovered that it was possible to effectively block critical thinking at its source in the individual mind. They discovered how to implement a kind of mythic consciousness by technical means so that it was possible to "change the men" in a way that rendered the personality subject to outside command. One of the key figures in the Third Reich, Albert Speer, who organized Hitler's great architectural and technical projects, including the famous Nürnberg rallies, read Cassirer's Myth of the State in prison and focused on the above passage. In this passage, he said, Cassirer put his finger on the key to the greatest problem posed by the regime: its eradication of the self-responsible personality.[37]

In The Myth of the State Cassirer emphasizes that philosophy was unprepared to deal with political myth. He makes a judgment about the power of mythic thought that should catch the eye of any philosophically interested reader because it claims to point to the Achilles heel of philosophy, the place where the serpent of myth can always bite and always be victorious. Myth, Cassirer says, "is impervious to rational arguments" (MS, 296). It is impossible to reason with someone possessed by a mythic belief. Is philosophy anything besides rational argument? This statement should have attracted the attention of every philosophical reviewer of the book, but none even mentions it.[38] Indeed, ever since its publication, The Myth of the State has been little studied by professional philosophers.[39]

Philosophers have a disinclination to study myth. This was the point at which Nelson Goodman said that he could not follow Cassirer. Myth is too obscure for philosophers. Cassirer believed that to ignore myth in theoretical philosophy impedes understanding language, knowledge, and the development of culture. But in the area of ethics and social and political philosophy, to have no awareness of the workings of mythic thought is not merely a theoretical flaw; it leaves philosophy in a position where it can no longer do its duty. By ignoring the social function and power of mythic thought, philosophy moves in the rarified atmosphere of academic argument, unable to make contact with or even conceive the deepest forces in political life.

Cassirer says little about the specifically political problems affecting the Weimar Republic, the reparation payments exacted by the Versailles treaty, the devastating inflation of 1923, the worldwide economic crisis of the late 1920s and early 1930s, or the constitutional defect that permitted dozens of political parties to hold seats in the Reichstag, thereby immobilizing the decision-making process. The formation of coalitions was made more difficult as more and more Germans voted for parties of the political extremes until, finally, the Republic was ruled by its enemies. In 1944 Cassirer wrote: "Undoubtedly economic conditions had a large share in the development and rapid growth of the National Socialist movement. But the deepest and most influential causes are not to be sought in the economic crisis which Germany had to endure" (SMC, 236). Unlike the democratic parties, the National Socialists took economic and other problems out of the context of discussion, compromise, and practical decision making and depicted them mythically as a kind of great struggle. The political leaders of the Weimar Republic, Cassirer says, "thought and spoke in terms of economics; they were convinced that economy is the mainspring of political life and the solution of all social issues" (SMC, 236). The sober, empirical way of thinking followed by the leaders of the Republic did not let them realize the significance of the fact that they and the National Socialists did not speak the same language. The democratic parties could not win the confidence of the people. The National Socialists were successful, Cassirer believed, because they created something new that was the key to their triumph at the polls and afterward: "The invention and the skillful use of a new technical instrument—of the technique of political myths—decided the victory of the National Socialist movement in Germany" (SMC, 236).

This view has the benefit of hindsight. Cassirer had at first hoped that liberal humanism and intellectual culture could be mustered to turn back the irrational forces that had gained control of political discussion in the Weimar Republic. Like Thomas Mann, Cassirer sought to make the Republic more accepted by appealing to reason, arguing that it was based on the ideas of Leibniz, Wolff, and Kant and so was a child of German philosophy and nothing "un-German." Mann too proffered such arguments, tracing the Republic to the idea of Humanität in German classicism.[40] But an irrational ideology that led large numbers to street violence could not be met by a rational form of politics that promised to secure what Mann called "civil demands for happiness like freedom, intellectuality, culture."[41] A rational form of politics could hardly provide anything more than this.

Cassirer's surprise at the success of the National Socialists was not caused by the fact that it was possible to have an oppressive regime accepted in the enlightened twentieth century, but by their successful use of a technique of myth. This, he argued, was something entirely new in the history of politics. It was new because it depended upon and required the development of modern technology, especially in the field of communications. But, most of all, it was new because the new means of communication—radio, film, illustrated periodicals—were used to create another new technology: myth as a tool for the control of thought. "It has been reserved for the twentieth century, our own great technological age, to develop a new technique of myth. Henceforth myths can be manufactured in the same sense and according to the same methods as any other modern weapon—as machine guns or airplanes. That is a new thing—and a thing of crucial importance" (MS, 282).

The Technique of Myth

Totalitarian government is characterized by its power over individual lives, that is, by the lack of limits to governmental authority. With the Ermächtigungsgesetz (law of empowerment) of March 24, 1933, the German legislature's power to make law was transferred to the Führer, who now was declared to be the final authority in the government of the country. Neither the legislature nor the constitution was eliminated; they were simply no longer effective aspects of government. The Führer was the state. The state no longer derived its legitimacy from legality because, in reality, *Recht* had become whatever served the will of the Führer, who stood above the law. Such a totalitarian state could no longer derive its legitimation from legality, but it could derive it from myth.

Primitive, mythic societies are not based upon rule by law, but on custom, taboo, tribal beliefs, and faith in the wisdom of those entrusted with the power of augury. In mythic society everyone "knows his place" and someone who fails to recognize this is perceived as a threat to the community. It would be an anachronism to say that open discussion as a forum for government is repressed in such primitive societies; it simply does not yet achieve a place of prominence. So, too, repression of discussion is nothing new in politics, but it takes on a new form in totalitarianism. Criticism became so ineffective during the Third Reich that the only alternative to cooperation was to leave or withdraw into "inner immigration." This was due not only to the uninhibited use of repression but also to the strength of dedication among the people. It was the citizenry's willingness to follow orders that gave the Third Reich its strength. The source of this tenacity of belief did not lie in the content of National Socialist ideology per se. The doctrines it propagated were, as ideas, neither new nor intelligent.[42] Its ideology thrived because it was given a mythic form that made it immune to rational criticism, and it was given this form by a deliberate process, using specific techniques. That is Cassirer's thesis in *The Myth of the State*.

When Cassirer wrote *The Philosophy of Symbolic Forms*, he regarded myth as something purely traditional in character, something that could no more be invented and spread among a people than could this people's language (*PSF*, 2:6; *PsF*, 2:9). In 1945 he revises his earlier view: "Myth has always been described as the result of an unconscious activity and as a free product of the imagination. But here [among the National Socialists] we find myth made according to plan. The new political myths do not grow up freely. . . . They are artificial things fabricated by very skillful and cunning artisans" (*MS*, 282).

The technique of myth has four parts, all of which serve the same end: the prohibition of independent thought and critical discussion. These techniques are (1) the manipulation of language to prevent or limit communication, (2) ritualization of action so as to eliminate the difference between the public and private sphere, (3) the elimination of all ideal values and their replacement by concrete images of good and bad in order to prejudice all decisions, and (4) the reinterpretation of time and history as "fate," which provides the ultimate justification of personal submission. The first two techniques limit the spontaneity of thought and action; the latter two provide a substitute for them.

A "myth of the state" as propagated by the leaders of a government is not substantially the same as the spontaneous occurrence of mythic beliefs in culture, but its function and power—and this is Cassirer's point—derives from myth as an elemental social phenomenon.[43] In mythic thought the mind is captivated by the strength of its own beliefs, beliefs that are not private but communal, uniting the believer with a group.

Technique 1. Language is ordinarily both emotive and propositional in nature. Both functions contribute, Cassirer says, to the aim of "social communication and mutual understanding" (SMC, 254). By shifting the emphasis far enough away from descriptive language toward emotive speech, the words used for designating things or ideas can be made to bristle with contempt, hatred, and mistrust (see MS, 282–84; SMC, 253–55). In order to manipulate language this way on a national scale, technical means of communication must be available.[44] Gradually, the continual use of carefully slanted language can block disinterested discussion. Such discussion requires putting a stop to the feelings that accompany the emotive words. In strongly emotive language, such distance is unattainable.

Technique 2. The ritualization of life serves, Cassirer says, to "take away our feeling of personality and individual responsibility" by the introduction of constant public displays of "belonging" (MS, 284–85; SMC, 255–58). The goal is for there to be "no longer any separation between private and public life" (SMC, 256). This too is part of the manipulation of language; the ubiquitous Hitler greeting and raised hand salute brought constant, daily declarations for the Reich. This practice extended to the creation of groups—youth groups, worker's groups, mother's groups—all with their own special signs, badges, uniforms, and rites.[45] The effect of this ritualization of life, Cassirer says, was to reduce the feeling of human spontaneity: "Nothing is more likely to lull asleep all of our active forces, our power of judgment and critical discernment, and to take away our feeling of personality and individual responsibility than the steady, uniform, and monotonous performance of the same rites" (MS, 284–85).

Technique 3. To unite all the members of society, a single, simple, supreme value is proclaimed, a value that permits none other next to it. This was "the myth of the race" (MS, 287; cf. 224–47). The Aryan or master race is not a value at all; values are ideal standards or norms. A race, like any group of people, is something concrete, unlike the "good," the "just," the "true," or the "beautiful." A genuine value provides a normative standard for judging what is, but the conception of the master race works the other way around; what ought to be is measured by what is. The transformation of value by this technique of myth inverts the normal sense of "ought" and "is" so that "ontology precedes morality and remains the decisive factor in it" (MS, 238). According to the ideology of the master race, a person is noble or virtuous not on account of his actions, but by virtue of his blood. What a person of a noble race does is by definition good. Virtue is, therefore, "a gift of the earth" (MS, 237).

Cassirer shows how this kind of circular reasoning is used in Gobineau's *Essai sur l'inégalité des races humaines* to establish the supremacy of one race. The standard for establishing what race is the highest is the judgment of the highest race. "What they *call* noble, good and virtuous *becomes* virtuous by this token" (MS, 238). The highest race, Gobineau says, is the Aryan race. Since Gobineau is an Aryan, this cannot be wrong. For rational thought this is an obvious petitio principii. To reason, Gobineau's argument looks hopelessly naive, but "it was precisely this naiveté that gave Gobineau's theory its great practical force and influence. By this circular definition the theory became, in a sense, invulnerable. You cannot argue with an analytical judgment; you cannot refute it by rational or empirical proofs" (MS, 238). The image of the Aryan master race as the highest good is very simple; anyone can understand it. It owes this simplicity to its form, not its content. Any content could be proclaimed this way, any race defined as the master race, any religious, political, or other content declared the measure of all other things. This kind of thinking imagines the world in a particular way. The image is an absolute, admitting no other one. On such a view, there can be no hope of the nonnoble becoming noble, no hope of change. This is the logic of myth: "there is no time for invention, either by individuals or by a people, no time for artificial disguises or misunderstanding" (PSF, 2:6; PsF, 2:9); things are as they are and always have been and always will be. Whoever is possessed by such an image of things is incapable of criticizing his belief because he is predisposed to regard all criticism as conspiracy. He is incapable of conceiving a point of view that would allow an outside standard for criticizing his belief because his belief is, by definition, the supreme point of view.

Technique 4. Finally, the technique of myth draws upon the mythic conception of time and history as "fate." This is done by various means, most prominently by the introduction of prophecy (in the sense of augury) into politics: "We no longer have the primitive kind of sortilege, the divination by lot; we no longer observe the flights of birds nor do we inspect the entrails of slain animals. We have developed a much more refined and elaborate method of divination—a method that claims to be scientific and philosophical. . . . Our politicians know very well that great masses are much easier moved by the force of the imagination than by sheer physical force. And they have made ample use of this knowledge. The politician becomes a sort of public fortune teller. Prophecy is an essential element in the new technique of rulership" (MS, 289; cf. SMC, 258–63). The constant references in National Socialist literature and Hitler's speeches to Vorsehung or providence that intervenes as Schicksal or fate in history is one of the most striking aspects of the National Socialist regime.[46] The political function of the notion of fate (the notion of a "law of history") is to justify the elimination of democratic procedures. An elite who knows what "must" be and so, too, what must be done can infallibly interpret providence to the people and so justify any action that is taken by appealing to necessity. The prophetic conception of history was not just a part of Nazi political ideology, but a doctrine that enjoyed academic respectability and gained a wide acceptance among the educated even prior to its achieving official status in the Third Reich. Cassirer points to the extraordinary success of Spengler's Untergang des Abendlandes, a work which proclaims that history has no purpose and that man can do nothing but accept it as fate (SMC, 226–29; MS, 289–92). Furthermore, Heidegger's conception of Geworfenheit, man's "thrownness" into the world, is a paradigm for Cassirer of how philosophical thinking can proclaim the need to submit to "fate" (SMC, 229–30; MS, 292–93). Spengler and Heidegger, he says, encourage a passive attitude; their doctrines "cannot teach man how to develop his active faculties in order to form his individual and social life" (SMC, 230).

The technique of myth is presented in The Myth of the State as an invention. Cassirer's analysis of this technique refers to its application by its inventors, but it is not just a historical description. In Cassirer's interpretation, the technique of myth is quite literally a technique, something capable of application in different places and at different times for different ends. The Myth of the State is therefore not a book about German National Socialism; rather it is about the new form of politics that the National Socialists invented and employed. Cassirer makes clear that this form of politics is itself a technique, a product of "our own great technical age" in the sense that it required the existence of other techniques, primarily those of mass communication. But Cassirer says nothing in The Myth of the State about the reason for its effectiveness in the twentieth century, only that myth can reassert itself when a culture's intellectual, ethical, and artistic forces lose their power in a time of crisis. Cassirer offers an explication of the *effectiveness* of the technique of myth, but not of the *susceptibility* of a people in the enlightened twentieth century to become true believers in an irrational ideology. What is it in post-Enlightenment European history that could make attractive the doctrine that history is fate? This was Leo Strauss's main question in his review of *The Myth of the State*. That the readiness to accept such a view was already present for the National Socialists to capitalize upon is clear from Cassirer's own remarks on the popularity of a writer like Spengler.

The intellectual "crisis in man's knowledge of himself" that Cassirer described in the *Essay on Man* cannot be denied, but was it the crucial factor in the effectiveness of the technique of myth? Was it the source of a *general* loss of self-confidence? The intellectual concerns that Cassirer discusses in the *Essay on Man* point to a general deterioration of the conception of final ends of human activity. But Cassirer's presentation of this problem in the *Essay on Man* is intellectual in conception; it is presented in terms of the "theory of man." A further example of this is his discussion of the determination of the will in *Determinism and Indeterminism in Modern Physics*. Although his analysis of the difference between physical and volitional "indeterminacy" is well informed and philosophically penetrating, the problems of quantum physics are far removed from political life and, although they may be part of a general intellectual crisis, cannot account for the popular feelings of such a crisis.

Cassirer's treatment of the background of National Socialist ideology in *The Myth of the State*, the role of myth in political thought from the Greeks to the present, is subject to similar criticism. Commenting on Cassirer's special consideration of Carlyle, Gobineau, and Hegel, George Sabine wrote that "it is hard to believe that the three men mentioned were a solvent of sufficient force to bring about the disruption of European culture, when it suffered the stresses and strains of the period after the first World War."[47] This can be said for the entire intellectual movement that Cassirer discusses. Of course, Cassirer does not claim that these thinkers *caused* what occurred; his point is that they were an important contributing factor to the weakening of man's active powers. Yet they were effective because their words did not fall on deaf ears. The question remains, what accounts for this susceptibility to the irrational in the twentieth century?

As I mentioned above, Cassirer comments on the destructive social forces in the Weimar Republic only in passing. He refers to the inflation and unemployment that plagued the Republic, and he seems to suggest that the economic chaos and the social distress resulting from it made people susceptible to the mythic ideology that brought the National Socialists into power. Sabine wondered how these economic matters fit in with the philosophy of symbolic forms: "But these are simply sociological and economic causes, such as even a Marxist might appeal to. They hardly move on the same plane with the 'forces intellectual, ethical, and artistic' which are supposed to tame myth and create culture. But if adverse economic conditions can tear down a culture, can it be supposed that favorable conditions are irrelevant to its creation? Professor Cassirer's symbolic forms exist as a rule in a highly rarified atmosphere of art and theory. It is a little disconcerting to find them consorting with vulgarities like inflation and propaganda" (ibid., 317–18).

These observations are correct in that Cassirer cannot take an economic view of the decline of culture without contradicting his view that the chief powers in culture that hold myth in check are intellectual, ethical, and artistic. This would mean that Cassirer had moved toward a more naturalistic conception of history and culture, making economics and man's natural instincts—the need to eat and the like— into the prime movers of culture. This problem was known in German discussion of Marxian views of history as *die Magenfrage*, the question of the stomach.[48] For Cassirer, as for Hermann Cohen, this problem is a preliminary consideration to ethics, but not a part of it. Economic well-being is a necessary but not a sufficient condition for civilization. It does not guarantee ethical virtue nor does its lack necessitate the return to barbarism. Cassirer denies that economic causes were responsible for the success of National Socialism (*SMC*, 236).

Sabine was right in pointing out that Cassirer could not embrace an economic, causal explanation of the rise of totalitarianism. The philosophy of symbolic forms is a philosophy of meaning. Material hunger cannot by itself explain a readiness to accept a totalitarian ideology or to believe in a law of history. The National Socialists realized that, by blaming a specific group of people for Germany's economic misery, they could capitalize not only on the material hunger but also on the desire for its explanation. Instead of appealing to economic principles, they pointed to an enemy.

Sabine was incorrect, however, in associating the symbolic forms exclusively with theoretical and artistic meaning. It is not economics that Cassirer appealed to as a "materialistic" explanation of the rise of totalitarianism; it was technology: the technique of myth. Cassirer did not hold that the economic situation as such was capable of explaining the historical rise of totalitarianism; it was rather a raw material used by the practitioners of the technique of political myth. Of course, *Technik* is not simply a material aspect of cultural life, but a way of understanding the world—a symbolic form.

Cassirer's conception of *Technik* provides yet another way to understand the rise of totalitarianism. When Cassirer says that the invention of the technique of myth was something reserved for our technological age, this can mean more than that our communication media provided the equipment for the development of this technique. In "Form und Technik," Cassirer also pointed out that the rise of modern technology was responsible for a cultural crisis that goes to great depth, affecting the general perception of society.

"Technik" as a Cultural Crisis Cassirer's most specific discussion of the conflicts between the different symbolic forms is found in his essay "Form und Technik." The primary conflict between symbolic forms in contemporary social life, he says, is caused by the growing influence of Technik. "In the course of its [Technik's] development, it does not simply take its place *next* to the other basic directions of culture nor peacefully and harmoniously order itself among them. By differentiating itself from them, it cuts itself off from them and opposes them" (STS, 78). This can be said of all symbolic forms, but Technik in the twentieth century is not one cultural force among many: Technik "does not adhere to its own norm. Rather it threatens to absolutize this norm and force it upon all other areas [of cultural life]."[49] Cassirer claims in "Form und Technik" that technology is the most powerful force in twentieth-century culture.

In his classic study of modern technology, *Mechanization Takes Command*, Siegfried Giedion, who was associated with the Bauhaus during the Weimar Republic, called the twenty years between the two world wars the era of "full mechanization" in which technology had its greatest initial impact on everyday life.[50] Cassirer's essay was written in the middle of this era. The impact of Technik was felt strongly in Germany, one of Europe's most industrialized nations. The awareness that Technik was causing deep changes in social life was prominent in the arts in the Weimar Republic. The Bauhaus sought to find an aesthetic appropriate to mass production techniques. German theaters produced a genre of dramas depicting present or future technical ages either as glorified or dark and sinister. The most frequently performed play during the Weimar Republic was Georg Kaiser's *Gas*, a tale of technology out of control.[51] The opposite feeling is expressed in Brecht's radio play *Der Ozeanflug* (The ocean flight), which magnifies popular excitement about the combination of technology and individual daring in Lindberg's 1927 solo flight across the Atlantic, creating a heroic vision of Technik and man.[52] The consciousness of technical function inspired the neue Sachlichkeit as a style in architecture and design.[53] In the 1920s Technik was a theme of popular culture from cabaret songs to films.[54] In short, consciousness of Technik as a phenomenon was a matter of widespread concern in German culture in the 1920s.

Under these circumstances it is not surprising to find theoretical interest in Technik. The volume Kunst und Technik (Art and technology), in which Cassirer's "Form und Technik" is the lead essay, is an example of such theoretical interest. The volume contains studies of specific theoretical and practical problems created by the proliferation of radio, films, and recordings, for example, "Der schaffende Musiker und die Technik der Gegenwart" (The creative musician and the technology of the present) by the composer Ernst Krenek.[55]

Cassirer himself was at this time in a position that made him acutely aware of the changes being wrought in daily life by the advancement of technology. During his tenure as rector of the University of Hamburg (November 1929 to November 1930), his office required him to attend events like electric utility conventions, to open and visit automobile exhibitions, and to come into frequent contact with the business world.[56] During the 1920s, a literature on the philosophy of technology grew in Germany (written by such figures as Friedrich Dessauer and Max Eyth) and Cassirer refers to this literature in "Form und Technik."[57] Cassirer's essay was in part systematic, a further development of the theory of symbolic forms, but it was also a sign of the times, particularly parts 3 and 4, which address the question of the cultural value and impact of modern technology.

Among the questions that can be raised about the effects of technology on society, the ultimate one, Cassirer says, is whether technology is a form of man's self-liberation or actually a phenomenon of alienation (Entfremdung; STS, 68) from man's "true nature." Cassirer takes this formulation of the question from the contemporary discussion of technology. He uses the term alienation in the sense given to it by Simmel, who thinks that culture as a whole must necessarily become solidified into an objective reality alien to man. Simmel argues that, since culture is inherently cumulative, it leads man, its creator, away from his personal self-realization.[58] This situation is tragic for Simmel because it is innate to culture itself, that is, there is no escaping it.

Simmel associates his conception of alienation with Marx's description of the alienation of labor.[59] For Marx, labor becomes alienated when its products become commodities. When the worker sells his labor, what he produces is no longer his own and appears to him as a foreign, thinglike reality (he calls this "fetishism"). Marx's analysis in *Capital* is offset by the thesis that this occurs in a historical phase in which man is dispossessed, exploited by his fellow man. Because he attributes its origin and termination to changes in economic systems, Marx thinks that this historical situation can be alleviated by social action. This is not so for Simmel: "The 'fetishism' which Marx assigned to economic commodities represents only a special case of this general fate of contents of culture. With the increase in culture these contents more and more stand under a paradox: they were originally created by subjects and for subjects: but in their intermediate form of objectivity . . . they estrange themselves from their origin as well as from their purpose."[60] The unintended consequence of all cultural activity is that it becomes self-propagating. It develops by its own logic, creating demands and desires in man and overwhelming him with more complexity than he as an individual can ever hope to master or even understand. The division of labor in complex societies is responsible for this: "Through the cooperative effort of different persons, then, a cultural object often comes into existence which as a total unit is *without a producer*, since it did not spring forth from the total self of any individual" (ibid., 41). Man as an individual becomes lost in such complex societies. The situation is tragic: "even in its first moments of existence, culture carries something within itself which, as if by an intrinsic fate, is determined to block, to burden, to obscure and divide its innermost purpose, the transition of the soul from its incomplete to its complete state" (ibid., 46). Simmel contrasts this alienation with the freedom of the early Franciscan monks who had nothing to divert them from the "path of their souls" (ibid., 44). In comments like these Cassirer sees a mystic's desire for immediacy (*KW*, 107). Cassirer rejected this irrationalistic tendency in Lebensphilosophie.[61] But he grants Simmel the thesis that there are consequences to cultural activity that are far removed from those originally intended. Cassirer does not challenge the sociological correctness of Simmel's observations of the stultifying results of the growth of modern society. He even grants that nowhere is Simmel's analysis more appropriate than in regard to modern technology (*STS*, 76–77). More specifically, Cassirer agrees with Simmel's account of how the methods of modern mass production constantly generate new products that increase the level of consumption. New products do not act so much to fill needs as to create them.[62] Cassirer takes this theme to even greater extremes, attributing a shrinking horizon of the individual will to the increase in a desire for material goods. "Every satisfied need only serves to bring forth more needs in an increased measure—and for the one who is caught in this vicious circle there is no escape. Even more unrelenting than the treadmill of work, man is confined in the machinery of what is made and produced by the technical culture in which he finds himself and in which, in a never-ending frenzy, he is thrown from desire to gratification and from gratification to desire" (STS, 87–88).

For Cassirer, what makes technology such a volatile social force is that it knows no natural bounds. This applies also to the actual process of working with advancing technology. "The feeling of solidarity [with his work] is what enlivens the genuine hand craftsman. The particular individual work that comes into being under his hands is not a mere thing before him; rather he sees himself and his own personal effort in it. The further that technology progresses and the more that the law of the 'emancipation from organic boundaries' develops in it, the more this original unity loosens until it finally breaks up completely. The relationship between a person's labor and what is made is no longer in any way an *experienceable* relationship" (STS, 76). Cassirer calls the process in which machines overcome the organic limits of the body and manual work "the emancipation of work from organic boundaries." He borrows this designation from Marx's analysis of "Machinery and Modern Industry," but Cassirer's meaning for this phrase is radically different from Marx's.[63]

Marx was a naturalist; for him, nature, man, and technology can all be regarded as following natural laws. For Cassirer, culture cannot be understood in naturalistic terms. The final stage of technology is therefore not simply, as Marx conceived it, one of greater productivity exceeding the limits inherent in manual labor.[64] Technology brings an emancipation from nature in a radical sense. The cumulative development of technologies results in the creation of unheard-of practical possibilities: "What distinguishes the instruments of completely developed technology is just this, that they have freed themselves from the model that nature immediately presents to them and, so to speak, leave it behind" (STS, 73). When Cassirer speaks of an "emancipation from organic boundaries," therefore, he is not thinking of a mere quantitative increase in productivity, but a departure from the natural order. The changes that technology is capable of bringing about are therefore not circumscribed by anything outside of technology itself.

Cassirer presents his observations on technology's impact on society as descriptions, as characterizations of a situation that has developed historically. To say that technology is at present the primary force in cultural change does not mean that it must be so. The situation is not "tragic" for Cassirer because it is not necessary. Even if technology, at the moment, seemed to be a means not of self-liberation but rather of self-alienation (which he was ready to admit), Cassirer was unwilling to see in this something more than a temporary phase. He thought that Technik could be a means to the development of humanity (STS, 86). Man was not prepared for the great changes that the growth of technology had brought to his life, and man had yet to orient himself. More than ever before, people stood under the technological principle of the *Sachdienstgedanke*, the notion of "serving some purpose" (STS, 89). The problem is that this "purpose" did not have an ethical form; a society had arisen in which there was tremendous external cooperation and unheard-of organization, but Technik could not, by its very essence, provide the *final* ends or purpose for this society. Given an end, Technik provides means. Ethical imperatives are not instrumental. "As little as Technik can immediately create ethical values itself or draw them from the sphere in which it is effective, so little is there an alienation and conflict between such values and its specific direction and basic attitude." The result of the technical organization of society was therefore the creation of a new "solidarity of work in which, finally, all are active for one and one for all" (STS, 89).

Cassirer's view in 1930 was that this cooperation has only to be raised to ethical consciousness. Man had not yet recognized the cooperative aspect of life in a technical society; instead, man had become alienated from his work and, by his hedonistic attitude as a consumer, had lost sight of society as an ethical institution. Cassirer sums up his understanding of the situation this way: "It [Technik] creates, prior to a truly free community of will [*Willensgemeinschaft*] a kind of community of fate [*Schicksalsgemeinschaft*] between all those who are active on its works" (STS, 89).[65] To be active on Technik's works means to be alienated from one's own activity. Social life is more highly organized than ever before, but this organization does not seem guided by a unified political will. Modern technical society is experienced as a fate, not as the result of human will.

Despite this negative characterization of modern society, Cassirer closes "Form und Technik" on a hopeful note: perhaps the increased interdependence among persons in a technological society, once raised to ethical consciousness, would make everyone aware of how each person is responsible for the lives of others (STS, 89–90). "Form und Technik" ends with an open question: Will Technik prove to be the vehicle of human self-liberation or serve further to alienate man from what is most essentially his own, the human community as the result of human will, as a *Willensgemeinschaft*?

To serve as a vehicle of human self-liberation, Technik must do more than serve to make man the "master and possessor of nature"; it must, Cassirer says, give man control over what is chaotic in himself (STS, 89; cf. D, 109). While hoping that Technik would contribute to the formation of human personality by increasing the feeling of responsibility for the whole, Cassirer ignored another aspect of Technik that fosters the very opposite feeling. In "Form und Technik" Cassirer pointed out that Technik is always anonymous (STS, 86). In keeping with technical efficiency, improvements, once adopted, become universally applied. Such improvements do not carry the stamp of the personality of their inventors because Technik is essentially determined by the purpose it serves. In fact, technical progress is usually the result of joint research rather than the result of a single person's efforts. Technical organization is always impersonal. As society comes under the influence of technology, life becomes increasingly depersonalized. This is part of the reason for calling it a "community of fate." But this is really an oxymoron, for it is not experienced as a "community" or Gemeinschaft at all.

In his review of The Myth of the State, Leo Strauss asked what could account for the weakening of the intellectual, ethical, and artistic forces in culture in the twentieth century that permitted mythic thought to again permeate social life. As Strauss pointed out, The Myth of the State gives no answer to this question. Cassirer was convinced that such an account had already been given long before by Albert Schweitzer in lectures originally presented in 1922.[66] In a 1944 lecture Cassirer said that Schweitzer had given "a perfect diagnosis of the present crisis of human culture" (SMC, 231).

This crisis in its essence is characterized by a feeling of loss of self. Cassirer quotes from Schweitzer: "The modern man is lost in the mass in a way which is without precedent in history, and this is perhaps the most characteristic trait in him. . . . Since, over and above this, society, with its well-constructed organization, has become a power of as yet unknown strength in the spiritual life, man's want of independence in the face of it has become so serious that he is almost ceasing to claim a spiritual existence of his own. He is like a rubber ball which has lost its elasticity, and preserves indefinitely every impression that is made upon it. He is under the thumb of the mass, and he draws from it the opinions on which he lives, whether the question at issue is national or political or one of his own belief or unbelief" (SMC, 231–32). Cassirer expresses wholehearted agreement with Schweitzer. It is clear that such a lack of independence and individuality in a majority of persons makes them ready prey for the technique of myth. Schweitzer's observations antedate the popularity of the National Socialist movement, just as do the somber apocalyptic prophecies of Oswald Spengler to which Cassirer also refers (MS, 289–92; SMC, 226–29,

259–63). In a spirit totally antithetical to Schweitzer's *Philosophy of Civilization*, Spengler's *Decline of the West* (*Der Untergang des Abendlandes*, originally published in 1918) urged submission to history, conceived as a mysterious fate. And yet Spengler's book, which Cassirer calls "an astrology of history and the work of a fortune-teller" (*SMC*, 262), was enormously popular. Cassirer explains Spengler's literary success by his book's title, which Cassirer says gave expression to the "general uneasiness" of Europeans after the First World War (*SMC*, 260).

Neither Spengler nor Schweitzer was an academic philosopher, but Cassirer was. If the philosophy of symbolic forms is a viable philosophy of culture, one should be able to expect from it insights into the cultural crisis that Schweitzer and Spengler discuss in general terms. For this, one must look particularly to the analysis of Technik as a symbolic form.

In keeping with the general plan of the philosophy of symbolic forms, a complete analysis of Technik as a symbolic form would show how it comprises a particular way of having a world—a way of informing temporal and spatial perception, the conception of the object and the subject, and so forth. Insofar as Technik dominates contemporary life, its structuring of experience will also be predominant. Cassirer does not carry out his analysis of Technik as fully as he does the other two basic symbolic forms of myth and language, to which he devotes whole volumes, but even a sketch of the basic characteristics of perception as it is informed by Technik will show how the primacy of a technical perception of the world can effect a major change in man's sense of life. This major change derives from the way Technik determines the perception of time.

In lived time, as we normally conceive it, the passage from one moment to the next has a wholeness reminiscent of music because it seems dynamic and yet whole at every moment. Lived time seems to move quickly in excitement and slowly in boredom. It has rhythms, such as that of sleeping and waking. In mythic thought time has a different character, appearing to be substantial in nature, so the ages of life—youth, maturity, and old age—are occupied like places. The entry or departure from these places is marked by special rites in which time is arrested. Other rites recreate the acts of the gods, and the performance of such rites is taken to involve a return to the original great time of these events, a time which is the locus of true reality. Both ordinary lived time and mythic time differ from the measured time of clocks. Clock time progresses constantly without any reference to human feelings. Such a conception of time is foreign to mythical thought, as foreign as the Newtonian system of physics of which it is a central part. Yet another form of time is found in historical consciousness or calendar time, which, unlike clock time, has a distinct beginning. In the case of technology we are confronted with another kind of time. In technology we experience a kind of action time in which things that would otherwise be inaccessible to us are *made present*.

Presence brought about by technology is quite different from presence without any technical mediation. The latter is continuous with what comes before and after, but presence mediated by some technique has the character of an *event*. It lacks the continuity of lived time in the ordinary sense. Cassirer distinguishes three stages of Technik—mimetic, analogical, and purely symbolic. These are characterized by their relative divergence from immediate, lived experience. Illustrations of this development can be readily found. For example, Wolfgang Schivelbusch writes: "pre-industrial transport movement is a mimesis of outer nature. Ships move with the flowing stream of water and wind, movements on land follow the natural irregularities of the landscape and are bound by the natural pulling capacities of the animals."[68] But this organic unity disappeared when steam power introduced sustained, straight-line movement on water and land at speeds impossible by animal power or sails. The effect of rapid movement is that "from now on places are no longer spatially individual or autonomous, but instances" (ibid., 174). In my view, the key word here is "instances" (*Momente*), indicating both interchangeability—due to easy accessibility—and a form of time (and space) awareness: the event or happening. Walter Benjamin points out a similar phenomenon. The technical media of film and photography only present us with "instances" of an image; the notion of an "original," as applied to a work of art, has no place in these media, that is, in the sense of something that exists only here and now. Modern reproductive techniques make works of art available to everyone everywhere, but at the expense of losing what Benjamin terms the "aura" of their originality, that uniqueness adhering to something that is one of a kind and which cannot be reproduced.[69] The composer Ernst Krenek applied Benjamin's analysis to broadcast and recorded music. The performance is made present; but it is cut off from an organic context, the visit to the concert hall.[70] In all these cases media function to make something present by reproducing the original as an instance or event. The sense of time involved in these examples is more obvious in electronic communication. Modern information distribution, unlike person-to-person discussion, is frequently anonymous. Countless sources provide reports on current events. The constant influx of information provides no feeling for the continuity or resolution of these events. As a result, current events appear chaotic; in the words of Jacques Ellul, they seem to be "a negation of what man heretofore has called law or politics—the creation of a stabilized universe, an artificial universe . . . made by the skill of man."[71] These words describe the same feeling of impotence that Cassirer identifies when he characterizes technical society as a "community of fate." This perception of society derives from regarding it in terms of events.

Examination of the sense of time inherent in Technik shows that this felt lack of continuity goes deeper than the conception of society, affecting even the individual's sense of self. In the nineteenth century Hegel claimed that the state was the fundamental social reality; it could not be reduced to a mere "civil society" (*bürgerliche Gesellschaft*), which Hegel defined as an organization of individuals living only for their private ends.[72] With the primacy of Technik something new occurs in social life that cannot be compared to the privatization that Hegel had in mind. Even the life of the individual person appears, in the context of Technik, to be a series of events or happenings. Hegel conceives civil society to be an association for the protection of the individual and so to reflect a common will. But insofar as life is perceived to consist of events that just happen, society, in the sense of a general will (as Cassirer uses the term—a common direction toward the future) seems to be a nonentity. The reason for this is that when life is perceived as mere events, even the personal identity of the individual appears fragmented. In this case, chance—what Hegel held to be the complete negation of reason—seems to be the ultimate principle guiding events.[73] Will appears only as *Willkür*, arbitrariness. The sense of time inherent in Technik, the event of making something present, can be called tychastic time, using *tyche* as defined by C. S. Peirce to stand for absolute chance.[74] It is the time of the chance event; it is whatever occurs. Fully "emancipated" Technik is based upon will as *Willkür*. In its final phase, Technik is guided by no model in nature and, at this stage, becomes autonomous.

Cassirer said that Technik first creates a community of fate prior to establishing a community of will. He does not elaborate on what he means by "Schicksal" in *Schicksalsgemeinschaft*, but it would clearly be wrong to interpret it to mean fate in the ancient Greek sense of *moira*, which means providential destiny.[75] *Schicksal* is meant here in a distinctly contemporary sense of whatever happens: chance. No higher order is perceived in society unless it be Technik itself, not human will, not providence.

In tychastic time experience the world seems to take on the form of mere events or happenings. Whereas mythical thinking spatializes time, technology results in a kind of temporalization of space in which fixed orders and continuity are replaced by events. Time in Technik has the opposite character of time in mythic thought. In his discussion of the "Pathology of Symbolic Consciousness" Cassirer describes how an individual can suffer a restriction of symbolic thought and action through aphasia and kindred disorders. The result of such impairments on human activity, he says, is that "a teleological structure is replaced by a mere happening, . . . the formation of a purpose is replaced by a mere mosaic of partial acts" (PSF, 3:273; PsF, 3:319). This phenomenon can be seen on the social level when Technik is the predominant way of having a world. In such a case the world seems to consist of events, without continuity. From a purely technical point of view, people and things temporarily fill functions that in a fast-changing world are themselves only temporary. Technik is innovative to the extreme. The capacity to understand and formulate long-term purposes and a social telos requires a different perspective than the merely technical. Insofar as Technik is the predominant symbolic form, man and the world are then perceived primarily in terms of technical principles and those of the other symbolic forms appear subordinate or inapplicable.

Hannah Arendt wrote that "what prepares men for totalitarian dominion is that the fact of loneliness, once a borderline experience . . . has become an everyday experience of the growing masses of our century."[76] Using the above analysis, a further dimension of this isolation can be seen. Loneliness as a sense of isolation becomes most extreme when it does not just mean isolation from society but something internalized. At its extreme, it applies to the sense of time that Kant calls "inner sense" (innerer Sinn), that is, consciousness of my existence in time.[77] Unlike solitude, which involves not communicating with others, such isolation includes an inability to even "commune" with oneself. This psychological state may be understood in terms of the tychastic time experience, in which the inner sense of self seems to consist only of happenings or events without direction or purpose. It goes without saying that this absence of a holistic perspective inhibits the kind of reflective, self-critical thinking and planning essential to ethical self-responsibility—what Cassirer calls a Vor-, Rück- and Überschau. Such an internal breakdown of dialogue at the level of personal reflection poses a social threat. The breakdown in self-communing means the loss of conscience. From the standpoint of the philosophy of symbolic forms, even communicative competence is a task and not a given.

Cassirer expressed the hope that technology's impact on society would heighten ethical awareness of interdependence in society, but, if the above analysis is correct, it resulted instead in a fundamental loss of the individual's relationship to himself, without which one cannot be a self-responsible member of society. This is the point of weakness in contemporary society where political myth has shown its greatest power. A mythic depiction of history as an irreversible "fate," a "law of history" to which the individual can only submit, allows each person a place in the march of events without the burden of individual responsibility. The mythic notion of fate justifies the individual's feeling of helplessness, and at the same time it can seem to give a person's existence a higher purpose than that of his ephemeral life as an employee and consumer. The ideology justifying this belief in fate may be absurd or fantastic, but, as Cassirer points out, even the strangest and most extravagant motivation to action is better than no motivation at all (SMC, 249).

Cassirer agreed with Schweitzer that as the modern conception of things becomes more bewildered the impulse to action engages in ever more irrational and purposeless pursuits. When people collectively become eager for something to motivate them at a fundamental level so that their lives seem to serve something more than a private purpose, myth enters. Such an ideal need is intensified by a material crisis. No strictly scientific explanation of the economic fluctuations responsible for an economic crisis can assuage the frustrated feelings of those affected by material want. But with the technique of myth it becomes possible for a political leadership effectively to channel such rage and to fuel it so as to create a tremendous political force. The image of a devilized enemy, although it is a purely negative object of action, appeals to the imagination in direct proportion to the lack of any other motivating ideals. Just as the rise of technical society acts to erode the feeling of community and humanity, so, too, modern technology provides means—the technique of myth—by which skillful leaders can create an Ersatz for this lost feeling of community. This new communal feeling is a response to a threat, and hence it too is a Schicksalsgemeinschaft (a community of fate), not a true Willensgemeinschaft (community of will), but, by giving the helplessness a common objective focus, the sense of isolation is removed; the experience of suffering a fate becomes a Gemeinschaftsgefühl, a shared feeling.

Philosophy and History Cassirer was not essentially a political or social philosopher. His interest in the modern period from the Renaissance to the Enlightenment focuses indirectly on the sociopolitical, while his main concern is with the intellectual energy of the time. He was attracted to what he called "that whole intellectual development through which modern philosophic thought gained its characteristic self-confidence and self-consciousness" (PE, vi). In the preface to The Philosophy of the Enlightenment he points out that "in former works, especially The Individual and the Cosmos in Renaissance Philosophy (1927) and The Platonic Renaissance in England (1932), I have tried to present and evaluate other phases of this great movement" (PE, vi). This trilogy of historical works shows how ideas developed in the Renaissance were handed down via the Cambridge Platonists to the Enlightenment, which brings them to fruition. Philosophy is not pure thought for the Enlightenment: "the fundamental tendency and the main endeavor of the philosophy of the Enlightenment are not to observe life and to portray it in terms of reflective thought. This philosophy believes rather in an original spontaneity of thought; it attributes to thought not merely an imitative function but the power and task of shaping life itself" (PE, viii). Cassirer's presentation of the philosophy of the Enlightenment portrays it as a story of self-liberation on all fronts, of new toleration in religion (Lessing, Mendelssohn), of cosmopolitan universality in ethics (the human rights doctrine), and of expanding horizons of knowledge (the flourishing of science, history, aesthetics). The whole modern age in Cassirer's interpretation moves toward the Enlightenment. Something important gets lost on the way: the negative aspects of the intellectual history of this period, which were formidable.

An important example of Cassirer's disregard of the negative in history is found in his book on the Cambridge Platonists. Henry More appeals in his arguments against Hobbesian materialism to beliefs about witchcraft. Cassirer treats Henry More's relationship to occultism as a curiosity that he notes in passing and dismisses with the following negative judgment: "Hence we have the strange spectacle that the Cambridge Platonists, who in the sphere of religious doctrine stood for the inalienable prerogative of reason, renounce and betray reason just at the point where they undertake an explanation of nature" (PRE, 131). Cassirer says that this readiness to incorporate "stories of ghosts and apparitions" into serious thought is "the real systematic weakness of this school and the historical explanation of its ineffectiveness in its own time" (PRE, 132). Yet this readiness is hardly the weakness of a particular school of thought, for the belief in witchcraft even found an adherent in the scientist Robert Boyle, the most prominent member of the Royal Society, to which More also belonged.[78] The belief in witchcraft had swept through Europe in the sixteenth and seventeenth centuries, capturing the imagination of the educated and uneducated. Conservative estimates of the death toll resulting from the witch trials during this period exceed 200,000.[79] The grotesque logic of these trials, at which attempts by the accused to prove innocence were construed as proof of guilt, even caught Hegel's attention.[80] Yet Cassirer, the theoretician of myth, avoids discussing the recurrence of mythic belief in the seventeenth century in a book published as late as 1932.

Even his discovery of the theoretical importance of myth was at first conceived in purely intellectual terms, as the problem of the "form of the concept in mythic thought" ("Die Begriffsform im mythischen Denken" was Cassirer's first study of myth). Walter Benjamin once observed about this early work of Cassirer's that "it is questionable whether it is possible to present mythical thought only in conceptual terms."[81] Although Cassirer did go on to broaden greatly the scope of his studies of myth and although he was ready in *The Myth of the State* to grant that the irrational forces in mythic thought are ever-present, he did so, the reader must conclude, with reluctance. This reluctance to accept the negative is perhaps a reflection of Cassirer's personality, but it is not an indication of limits inherent in the philosophy of symbolic forms, as Cassirer himself showed in *The Myth of the State*.

Cassirer believed that philosophy could make history understandable and so contribute to a resolution of the cultural crises of the time. Beginning with his Göteborg inaugural lecture, Cassirer actively took issue with the view that philosophy could only be a spectator to world history. Here he found himself particularly opposed to Hegel: "Hegel was firmly convinced that no individual thinker could go beyond his own time. Philosophy is its own time apprehended in thoughts. . . . That is the most characteristic difference between the spirit of the Enlightenment and the new spirit of the nineteenth century. Neither Kant nor the French Encyclopedists were afraid to think *against* their time. They had to combat the *ancien régime*; and they were convinced that in this struggle philosophy had its share as one of the most powerful weapons. But Hegel could no longer assign this role to philosophy. He had become the philosopher of *history*" (*MS*, 269; cf. *SMC*, 226). In Hegel's conception of history, freedom becomes the privilege of absolute spirit. The philosopher can only describe this spirit.[82] This view, Cassirer says, condemns philosophy to a kind of "speculative idleness" (*MS*, 296). Cassirer sees in Hegel the "verdict of the Romantic Movement on the Enlightenment" (*PE*, xi).

Cassirer affirms in his own thought the principle that he attributes to the philosophy of the Enlightenment, a belief that philosophy has "the power and task of shaping life itself." Because this attitude is visible in all of Cassirer's writings, some critics have claimed that his thought reflects the very crisis in culture that he critically examines in *The Myth of the State*. Charles N. R. McCoy claims that Cassirer overlooked the deeper cause of the political catastrophe analyzed in *The Myth of the State*: man has lost the awareness that Cassirer attributes to myth in the early chapters of the work, namely, "that which lies beyond the proper competence of man." He asks, "Is there any other possibility now but that the modern superman should assume the role of Providence, foreseeing, ordaining, ordering all things according to the free designs of his own mind?"[83] McCoy attributes to Cassirer's thought the same lack of a sense of limits. In John J. Schrems's work on Cassirer's political thought we find the same argument: without a "substantial" view of man there can be no barriers to the symbolic process of culture, so that "complete enslavement seems to be the proper fulfillment of the creative life."[84] Cassirer's assertion in *The Myth of the State* that there are (natural) "laws that cannot be broken with impunity" is no solution, Schrems says, because the laws are actually "man-made" since they are conceived in terms of a social contract.[85]

Cassirer presents the idea of the social contract in *The Myth of the State* as something man-made, but he does not think that its basis is conventional. Contracts are only possible on the basis of the Urphänomen of language and meaning. Contracts are made, but *Recht* as a symbolic form is not a convention. Man does not "make" human rights himself any more than he makes himself animal symbolicum. Hence, for Cassirer, there is something called "humanity" which contains certain limits that cannot be violated with impunity. These critics overlook Cassirer's emphasis on the Goethean Urphänomen and his adherence to the *Humanitätsideal*. Cassirer can act as a critic in *The Myth of the State* because his concept of action distinguishes between unlimited activity (as represented by the Prometheus of Goethe's *Pandora*) and action that recognizes the form of humanity as a goal and limit. The political leaders of the Third Reich sought to "change the men" in order to gain control over them, but where they succeeded the result was debasement. The mere use of power cannot succeed in furthering the aim of the state, Cassirer says, because sheer economic or military power cannot succeed in "making the souls of the citizens better" (MS, 76). Under no circumstances for Cassirer can an overconfidence in power be construed as "reason," for it reveals a failure to recognize limits. Such overconfidence is not rational, but rather a sign of a belief in magic (see STS, 55–61; MS, 282–83).

Cassirer's most important theoretical discussion of the rational limitation of the will is found in his late book *Descartes: Lehre–Persönlichkeit–Wirkung* (1939). Cassirer attempts to understand the unity of Descartes' thought through the idea of the "heroic will." The notion of heroic will provides what Cassirer calls the "historische

Substanz des Zeitalters," the historical substance of the age (that is, the seventeenth century; *D*, 266). Cassirer's interpretation links Descartes' *Passions de l'âme* and Corneille's heroic dramatic personae, a connection which had first been made forty years earlier by Gustave Lanson and was subsequently much discussed.[86] But Cassirer adds a new historical dimension to this theoretical relationship—the life of Queen Christina of Sweden. Queen Christina, daughter of King Gustav Adolph II who defended Protestant northern Europe from the Counter-Reformation in the Thirty Years' War, gave up her throne to convert to Catholicism. Cassirer was not concerned to show the historical influences among these figures, that is, whether Descartes' instruction to Queen Christina in Stockholm was instrumental in her conversion or if she had been influenced by figures in Corneille's dramas or if there were an indirect connection, such as Corneille's heroes serving as models for Descartes' conception of *Generosité*. For Descartes, *Generosité* is the self-esteem coming from the realization that the "free disposition of the will" is what truly pertains to a person and that it alone is subject to praise or blame.[87] Cassirer considers Christina to be such a "homme genereux" (*D*, 219), like the heroes in Corneille's dramas. Cassirer treats Corneille's writings as an "Organon der historischen Erkenntnis" (*D*, 256), an organon of historical knowledge of the period to aid in understanding the common spirit of the age.

Descartes' view of the passions is part of the seventeenth-century conception of heroic will which, though passionate, is rational. For Descartes, the passions are not something to be feared or denied as they were in the Christian tradition, nor are they to be held in disdain as the stoics did. They must be accepted for what they are—natural phenomena. This will permit recognizing that they serve an important purpose. Instead of *apatheia*, the heroic will must have pathos because passion is necessary to furthering ethical ends (*D*, 242).[88] The heroism of Corneille, Christina, and Descartes is rational because, unlike the heroic will in the usual sense of the warrior who fights for some common cause, it is a heroism of conscience. Like Queen Christina, the figures in Corneille's dramas act as solitary individuals, forfeiting personal gains, friendships, and even their lives in order to meet ethical demands made upon them. The heroic ideal of the seventeenth century consists in the ability to say no. "According to its ethical-aesthetic imperative this epoch did not see true human greatness in the unbounded exaggeration of human striving and activity. It demanded the capacity and courage to stand still at a certain point and take pause. It did not worship the mere expression and uncontrolled outbreak of power; rather it demanded the true power of self-limitation and self-moderation. Here there was not just a heroism of activity, but also a heroism of renunciation" (D, 275). Accordingly, when Cassirer says that Descartes' famous proposal that man should become the "ruler and possessor of nature" (maître et possesseur de la nature) applies "even more strongly" to man himself (D, 109), this self-mastery should not be construed to mean an unlimited "Will to Power." Self-liberation "stands everywhere under the law of forbearance [Entsagung]: under the command of a heroic will, which knows that to achieve its goal, that even to propose it, requires giving up the naive-affective demand for happiness" (STS, 77–78). Cassirer refers specifically to the wish to return to the "idyll of a pretechnical 'state of nature'" (ibid.), but his point has a general significance: his conception of self-liberation has nothing to do either with hedonism or the supremacy of the will.

Cassirer's final position on the cultural crisis he describes in The Myth of the State can be summarized as follows. The forces of mythic thought are subjected to critical control by the intellectual, ethical, and artistic forces of higher culture. If these are weakened, primitive mythic forces reassert themselves. But the next step is problematic. Cassirer does not say how the intellectual, ethical, and artistic forces in culture regain their position. In the case of the Third Reich this occurred by default when the mythic conceptions led to social ruin. Yet the myth of the master race was not refuted. Myth can always return in its primitive, demonic form. This moment of the dialectic in the history of culture remains open for Cassirer.

The critical forces of culture are transformations of the primitive forces. About the reconstruction of these critical forces Cassirer said little. Of the intellectual forces he pointed to philosophy only, he remarked only briefly on the ethical, and of the artistic he said nothing. His comments about philosophy and about ethics are interrelated, for both are influenced by the same figure, Albert Schweitzer. To Cassirer Schweitzer's thought and Schweitzer the man seemed to point the way for the regeneration of culture. Schweitzer's Philosophy of Civilization, with its claim that philosophy had a duty to civilization, seemed to express an important truth unrecognized by those who practiced academic philosophy, which had become a specialized technical discipline. Schweitzer himself seemed to be a perfect representative in the twentieth century of the kind of ethical hero whose very life raised the question of the "ought."[89]

The Myth of the State was published after Cassirer's death. Along with the related essays from the last years of his life, it remains the last word of Cassirer's philosophy. Yet it would be wrong to ascribe too great a concern for the political to Cassirer even at this stage of his career.[90] He believed that politics was shaped by something more fundamental, the cultural forces—intellectual, ethical, and artistic. These cultural forces determine the political.[91] In all of Cassirer's writings, from his first book, in which Leibniz was portrayed as the metaphysician of the concept of Humanität (LS, 446, 456–58), to his last, in which the problem was the loss of humanity, Cassirer's chief concern was the same: "the formation of humanity." The philosophy of symbolic forms was to provide the systematic justification of the thesis that human culture is man's progressive self-liberation.

At the beginning of The Myth of the State, Cassirer refers to Goethe's Faust to compare the Romantics' feeling of rejuvenation through their rediscovery of myth with the sober views of the mythical current in the Enlightenment: "There is a scene in Goethe's Faust in which we see Faust in the witch's kitchen waiting for her drink by virtue of which he shall regain his youth. Standing before an enchanted glass he suddenly has a wonderful vision. In the glass appears the image of a woman of supernatural beauty. He is enraptured and spellbound; but Mephisto, standing at his side, scoffs at his enthusiasm. He knows better; he knows that what Faust has seen was not the form of a real woman; it was only a creature of his own mind" (MS, 5). Cassirer's philosophy also bears such a comparison. In an age when from all sides voices warn of the loss of culture, control of opinion, growing collectivism, and a loss of the personal and human, Cassirer's efforts to reconstruct philosophy in the spirit of the Enlightenment might seem like an enchanted image. In a historical epoch that otherwise bears little resemblance to the eighteenth century, Cassirer's thought might seem to be only a creature of his own mind. Yet Cassirer no less than Goethe conceived self-liberation as the vital essence of human life, not a utopian ideal. Historical life is and always will be bound to the conflicting forces of culture, so liberation from fear, injustice, and ignorance will remain an endless task requiring endless effort. The philosophy of symbolic forms is Cassirer's attempt to show that although this task is never complete, it is still possible to give a positive answer to the question whether history has any meaning. History is not without direction. The origin and ends of historical life endure throughout time in the Urphänomen of the symbol. The symbolic forms are the means for the process of human self-liberation; the philosophy of these forms provides the theory of their origin and of their phenomenological development.

Cassirer's philosophy of symbolic forms was conceived at least as much in the spirit of Hegel and Goethe as in that of Kantianism. Unlike so many of the latter's followers, Cassirer was unwilling to restrict philosophy to epistemology or the philosophy of science. He shared the Life-philosophers' dissatisfaction with the idealists' claim to comprehend logically reality as a whole, and he also agreed with them that lived experience could not be reduced to scientific knowledge. Cassirer sought to provide a systematic understanding of both lived experience and scientific knowledge. The philosophy of symbolic forms attempts to relate these two dominant directions of contemporary philosophy. This is a reflection, at the level of philosophy, of Cassirer's attempt to find in all culture a harmony in contrariety.

NOTES/BIBLIOGRAPHY/INDEX

NOTES

INTRODUCTION

1. Raymond Klibansky and H. J. Paton, eds., *Philosophy and History* (1936; rev. ed., New York: Harper & Row, Harper Torchbooks, 1963).

2. Only two of the twenty-one contributions came from authors still living in Germany, Theodor Litt and Ernst Hoffmann.

3. Hans J. Morgenthau, review of *The Myth of the State* by Ernst Cassirer, *Ethics* 57 (1947): 142.

4. Iredell Jenkins, review of *The Philosophy of Ernst Cassirer* ed. Paul Arthur Schilpp, *The Journal of Philosophy* 47 (1950): 47. Nonetheless, the *PEC* is valuable in that it provides a clear and detailed picture of the state of Cassirer studies.

5. Carl Hamburg, *Symbol and Reality: Studies in the Philosophy of Ernst Cassirer* (The Hague: Martinus Nijhoff, 1956).

6. Seymour Itzkoff, *Ernst Cassirer: Scientific Knowledge and the Concept of Man* (Notre Dame: University of Notre Dame Press, 1971).

7. Seymour Itzkoff, *Ernst Cassirer: Philosopher of Culture*, Twayne's World Leaders Series, no. 61 (Boston: Twayne Publishers, 1977), 77–78.

8. David R. Lipton, *Ernst Cassirer: The Dilemma of a Liberal Intellectual in Germany, 1914–1933* (Toronto: University of Toronto Press, 1978). See my review in the *Journal of the History of Philosophy* 20 (1982): 209–13.

9. This interest is evident in *The Myth of the State* and in his pivotal essay "Form and Technik," discussed below; see chap. 5.

10. The only major German-language publication on Cassirer's philosophy is a translation of Schilpp's *Philosophy of Ernst Cassirer* under the title *Ernst Cassirer*, trans. Wilhelm Krampf, in the Philosophen des 20. Jahrhunderts series (Stuttgart: Kohlhammer Verlag, 1966). Toni Cassirer's memoirs offer valuable information about her husband's life and career but cannot be counted as a study of his thought. These recollections, which were circulated for years in a privately published version (New York, 1950), have now been published as *Mein Leben mit Ernst Cassirer* (Hildesheim: Gerstenberg Verlag,

1981). A doctoral dissertation on Cassirer, University of Saarbrücken, 1980, has been published: Jens-Peter Peters, *Cassirer, Kant und Sprache*, European University Studies, vol. 121 (Frankfurt am Main: Peter Lang Verlag, 1983). Peters investigates the relationship between Cassirer's philosophy of language and earlier as well as more recent treatments of the philosophy of language.

11. In the opening lecture given at the Hamburg conference in celebration of Cassirer's hundredth birthday in 1974, Hermann Lübbe calls attention to this fact, which he attributes to the "academic" character of Cassirer's writings. See Lübbe, *Cassirer und die Mythen des 20. Jahrhunderts*, Veröffentlichung der Joachim Jungius Gesellschaft der Wissenschaften (Göttingen: Vandenhoeck & Ruprecht, 1975), 1–5.

12. It is difficult to assess Cassirer's influence in these fields, but for indications see, on linguistics, Robert L. Miller, *The Linguistic Relativity Principle and Humboldtian Ethnolinguistics: A History and Appraisal* (The Hague: Mouton, 1968), 42n; on semiotic, see Reto Luzius Fetz, "Genetische Semiologie: Symboltheorie im Ausgang von Ernst Cassirer and Jean Piaget," *Freiburger Zeitschrift für Philosophie und Theologie* 28 (1981): 434–70; on anthropology: see references in A. L. Kroeber and Clyde Kluckhohn, *Culture: A Critical Review of Concepts and Definitions* (New York: Vintage Books, n.d.), and Leslie White's review of *An Essay on Man* in *American Anthropologist* 48 (1946): 461–63; on art history, see Michael Ann Holly, *Panofsky and the Foundations of Art History* (Ithaca: Cornell University Press, 1984), chap. 5; on education, see Theodore Brameld, "Philosophical Anthropology: The Educational Significance of Ernst Cassirer," *Harvard Educational Review* 26 (1956): 207–32; on psychology and psychoanalysis see below, chap. 2. According to one history of psychoanalysis, C. G. Jung was influenced by Cassirer for his concentration on symbols: "Jung bezieht sich in seiner Interpretation des Symbols vor allem auf Cassirers 'Philosophie der symbolischen Formen'"; see Dieter Wyss, *Die tiefenpsychologischen Schulen von den Anfängen bis zur Gegenwart*, 2d ed. (Göttingen: Vandenhoeck & Ruprecht, 1966), 250.

Cassirer's historical works continue to be highly regarded. Nearly fifty years after its publication, M. S. Anderson writes that Cassirer's *Philosophy of the Enlightenment* "remains today the most penetrating and satisfactory work on its subject" (*Historians and Eighteenth-Century Europe, 1715–1789* [Oxford, Oxford University Press, Clarendon Press, 1979], 95). Cassirer's historical method and contribution to historiography have yet to be investigated in detail, but see the brief study by Peter Gay, "The Social History of Ideas: Ernst Cassirer and After" in Kurt H. Wolff and Barrington Moore, Jr., eds., *The Critical Spirit: Essays in Honor of Herbert Marcuse* (Boston: Beacon Press, 1967).

13. Cassirer traces the philosophy of myth to Vico ("the real discoverer of myth," *PK*, 296–99). The philosophy of myth was given fuller and more systematic development by the Romantics, especially Schelling (*PSF*, 2:3–4) but it was hardly the subject of serious philosophical interest in the twentieth century.

14. This idea has been applied by Nelson Goodman in his *Ways of Worldmaking* (Indianapolis: Hackett Publishing Co., 1978).

15. For different but complementary statements of this feature of contemporary philosophy, compare the introduction in Richard Rorty, ed., *The Linguistic Turn: Recent Essays in Philosophical Method* (Chicago: University of Chicago Press, Phoenix Books, 1967) and the introduction in Karl-Otto Apel's *Transformation der Philosophie*, 2 vols. (Frankfurt am Main: Suhrkamp Verlag, 1973), 2:9–76. The English edition of the latter, *Towards a Transformation of Philosophy*, trans. Glyn Adey and David Frisby (London: Routledge & Kegan Paul, 1980), does not include this introduction.

16. See, e.g., I. M. Bochénski, *Contemporary European Philosophy*, trans. Donald Nicholl and Karl Aschenbrenner (Berkeley and Los Angeles: University of California Press, 1969), 95; Emile Bréhier, *The History of Philosophy*, vol. 7, *Contemporary Philosophy*, trans. Wade Baskin (Chicago: University of Chicago Press, 1969), 174ff.; A. Robert Caponigri, *A History of Western Philosophy*, vol. 4 (Notre Dame: University of Notre Dame, 1971), 234–39; Frederick Copleston, *A History of Philosophy*, vol. 7, *Modern Philosophy: Schopenhauer to Nietzsche* (New York: Doubleday and Co., 1963), 140–41.

17. For examples see Leon Rosenstein, "Some Metaphysical Problems of Cassirer's Symbolic Forms," *Man and World* 6 (1973): 318; Wolfgang Marx, "Cassirers Symboltheorie als Entwicklung und Kritik des Neukantischen Grundlagen einer Theorie des Denkens und Erkennens," *Archiv für die Geschichte der Philosophie* 57 (1975): 312ff.

18. See, e.g., the following passages in contributions to Schilpp, PEC: Baumgardt, 577–79; Bidney, 535–41; Gutmann, 457–60; Hamburg, 84–91; Holborn, 43; Felix Kaufmann, 185–94; Fritz Kaufmann, 812–15; Kuhn, 549–74; Langer, 385; Smart, 264–66; Solmitz, 736–37, 750–52; Stephens, 152–60; Swabey, 123–24; Urban, 404–05; Werkmeister, 759–98.

19. Helmut Kuhn, review of *An Essay on Man* by Ernst Cassirer, *Journal of Philosophy* 42 (1945): 499–500.

20. Fritz Kaufmann, review of *An Essay on Man* by Ernst Cassirer, *Philosophy and Phenomenological Research* 8 (1948): 283.

21. *Scientific Knowledge and the Concept of Man*, 1–20.

22. Iredell Jenkins, "Logical Positivism, Critical Idealism, and the Concept of Man," *The Journal of Philosophy* 47 (1950): 677–95.

23. Quoted in the *Encyclopedia of Philosophy*, s.v. "Neo-Kantianism."

24. Karl Neumann, "Ernst Cassirer: Das Symbol" in Josef Speck, ed. *Grundprobleme der grossen Philosophen: Philosophie der Gegenwart* (Göttingen: Vandenhoeck & Ruprecht, 1973) 2: 104.

25. Hermann Cohen, *System der Philosophie*, Teil 1, *Logik der reinen Erkenntnis*, vol. 6 of *Werke* (1914; reprint, Hildesheim and New York: Georg Olms Verlag, 1977), 594–97.

26. Jürgen Habermas, *Knowledge and Human Interests*, trans. Jeremy J. Shapiro (Boston: Beacon Press, 1971), 331–32.

27. Apel, *Transformation of Philosophy*, 99–100.

28. Klaus Oehler, "Zur Logik einer Universalpragmatik," *Semiosis* 1 (1976): 14.

29. Kuhn, PEC, 573–74; for other remarks in PEC in a similar vein, see Fritz Kaufmann, 837–44; Leander, 352–57; Slochower, 656; Werkmeister, 798.

30. Nathan Rotenstreich, "Schematism and Freedom," *Revue Internationale de Philosophie* 28 (1974): 473.

31. Leo Strauss, review of *The Myth of the State* by Ernst Cassirer, *Social Research*, 14 (1947): 128.

32. See especially "The Concept of Philosophy as a Philosophical Problem" in *SMC*.

33. See Heinz Paetzold, "Ernst Cassirer und die Idee einer transformierten Transzendentalphilosophie," in Wolfgang Kuhlmann and Dietrich Böhler, eds., *Kommunikation und Reflexion: Zur Diskussion der Transzendental pragmatic, Antworten auf Karl-Otto Apel* (Frankfurt am Main: Suhrkamp, 1982), 146–47.

34. See John Herman Randall, Jr., review of *The Logic of the Humanities* by Ernst Cassirer, trans. Clarence S. Howe, in *History and Theory*, 2 (1962): 67; see also the translator's foreword to *Logic of the Humanities*, x–xviii. Another indication that Cassirer was well acquainted with Dewey's thought is found in the preface to a comprehensive study on Dewey by Folke Leander, a contributor to the *PEC*. Leander indicates in the preface to his study that he profited most in preparing the work from "generous assistance" by Ernst Cassirer. See Folke Leander, *The Philosophy of John Dewey*, Göteborgs Kungl. Vetenskaps och Vitterhets-Samhälles Handlingar, series A, vol. 7, no. 2 (1939).

35. Cassirer's references to American Pragmatism go back to his earliest systematic work, *Substance and Function*, and they are scattered throughout his writings.

36. John Passmore, *A Hundred Years of Philosophy* (Middlesex: Penguin Books, 1968), 315.

37. See Ernst Cassirer, "Erkenntnistheorie nebst den Grenzfragen der Logik," *Jahrbücher der Philosophie* 1 (1913): 32–34.

38. Brand Blanshard, review of *An Essay on Man* by Ernst Cassirer, *Philosophical Review* 54 (1945): 510.

39. The idea of man's progressive self-liberation is pivotal for Cassirer's philosophy. See below, chap. 5.

40. Helmut Kuhn takes this view, i.e., that the *Essay on Man* is really a "rigorous condensation" of *The Philosophy of Symbolic Forms*; see *Journal of Philosophy* 42 (1945): 498.

41. *Ways of Worldmaking* (see n. 14), 5.

42. Susanne K. Langer, *Philosophical Sketches* (New York: Mentor Books, 1964), 56.

43. See "Kurt Goldstein, 1878–1965" in Marianne L. Simmel, ed., *The Reach of the Mind: Essays in Memory of Kurt Goldstein* (New York: Springer Co., 1968), 3.

44. The main biographical works on Cassirer are Toni Cassirer, *Mein Leben mit Ernst Cassirer* (see note 10 above) and Dimitry Gawronsky, "Ernst Cassirer: His Life and Work," in Schilpp, *PEC*, 3–37.

45. Ernst Cassirer, "Hermann Cohen, 1842–1918," *Social Research* 10 (1943): 220–21.

46. Cassirer's doctoral thesis was subsequently published as the introduction to his book *Leibniz' System* (1902; reprint, Darmstadt: Wissenschaftliche Buchgesellschaft, 1962).

47. For an account of the Cassirer family's role in cultural life in Berlin during this period, see Peter Letkemann, Klaus P. Mader, and Günter Wollschlaeger, "Cassirer und Co.: Ein Beitrag zur Berliner Kunst- und Kulturgeschichte," *Mitteilungen des Vereins für die Geschichte Berlins* 69 (1973): 233–44.

48. Ernst Cassirer, ed., *Immanuel Kants Werke*, 10 vols. (Berlin: Bruno Cassirer, 1912).

49. See Peter Gay, *Freud, Jews and Other Germans* (New York: Oxford University Press, 1978), 159.

50. Peter Paret, *The Berlin Secession: Modernism and Its Enemies in Imperial Germany* (Cambridge: Harvard University Press, Belknap Press, 1980), 239.

51. I am indebted to Peter Paret for this information.

52. See "Toward a Pathology of the Symbolic Consciousness," *PSF*, 3:205–78.

53. Gottfried Wilhelm Leibniz, *Hauptschriften zur Grundlegung der Philosophie*, 2 vols., edited with introductions by Ernst Cassirer (1st ed. 1904 and 1906, 2d ed. 1924; reprint, Hamburg: Felix Meiner Verlag, 1966); *Neue Abhandlungen über den menschlichen Verstand*, translated with introduction by Ernst Cassirer (1915; reprint, Hamburg: Felix Meiner Verlag, 1971).

54. See *Leibniz' System*, xii, 446–49, 455–58; cf. *Hauptschriften*, 2:32–33, 116–22. Forty years after *Leibniz' System*, Cassirer returned again to this point in a lecture on "Descartes, Leibniz, and Vico" in *SMC*, 100–02.

55. Cassirer, "Der Kritischer Idealism und die Philosophie des 'gesunden Menschenverstandes,'" *Philosophische Arbeiten* 1(1906): 34–45.

56. See *LH*, chaps. 1, 3, and 4. See also Cassirer, "Remarks on the Originality of the Renaissance," *Journal of the History of Ideas* 4 (1943): 49–56.

57. See Toni Cassirer, *Mein Leben*, 99–101; Gawronsky, *PEC*, 16–17.

58. Cassirer, "Kant und die moderne Mathematik," *Kantstudien* 12 (1907): 1–49.

59. *SF/ET*, 268. The Swabey translation has been altered; cf. *SF/ET*, 356.

60. *SF/ET*, 318; cf. the discussion of James and Dewey in Cassirer, "Erkenntnistheorie nebst den Grundfragen der Logik," *Jahrbücher der Philosophie* 1 (1913): 35–40.

61. But Cassirer does attribute to Judaism a special critical contribution to human culture; see "Judaism and the Modern Political Myths," *SMC*, 233–67. Cassirer was by no means unfamiliar with nor unsympathetic to the many criticisms made by socialist theoreticians. He lectured on Georg Lukács's *Geschichte und Klassenbewußtsein* at Hamburg, summer semester 1927. See Ms 131, Cassirer Papers Deposit, Beinecke Rare Book and Manuscript Library, Yale University. Cassirer remarks about consumer society in "Form und Technik" (*STS*, 87).

62. Paul Natorp, "Das akademische Erbe Hermann Cohens: Psychologie oder Philosophie?" *Frankfurter Zeitung*, October 12, 1912, 1.

63. Gawronsky, *PEC*, 22; see also the comments commemorating this occasion by Hans Blumenberg, "Ernst Cassirers Gedenkend: Bei Entgegennahme des Kuno Fischer—Preises der Universität Heidelberg im Juli 1974," *Revue Internationale de Philosophie* 85 (1974): 456–63.

64. See the discussion of *Freiheit und Form* in Ernst Troeltsch, "Humanismus und Nationalismus in unserem Bildungswesen" [1916], in *Deutscher Geist und Westeuropa*, ed. Hans Baron (1925; reprint, Aalen: Scientia Verlag, 1966), 231–35.

65. See E. H. Gombrich, *Aby Warburg: An Intellectual Biography* (London: Warburg Institute, 1970).

66. See especially Aby Warburg, "Dürer und die italienische Antike." This paper from 1906, which gives a summary of his views, is available with other key works by and about Warburg in Aby M. Warburg, *Ausgewählte Schriften* ed. Dieter Wuttke (Baden-Baden: Verlag Valentin Koerner, 1980), 125–36.

67. See the excellent article on these topics by Edgar Wind (who was also Cassirer's first doctoral student at Hamburg), "Warburgs Begriff der Kulturwissenschaft und seine Bedeutung für die Aesthetik," Vierter Kongress für Aesthetik und Allgemeine Kunstwissenschaft, October 7–9, 1930, in *Beiheft zur Zeitschrift für Aesthetik und Allgemeine Kunstwissenschaft* 25 (1931) 163–79.

68. Fritz Saxl, "Warburgs Besuch in Neu-Mexico," in Warburg, *Schriften* 321.

69. 1 (1923): 11–39; reprinted in *WW*, 169–200. See *WW*, 175 for Cassirer's formal introduction of the term *symbolic form*.

70. Originally published in *Studien der Bibliothek Warburg* 1 (1922) reprinted in *WW*, 1–70.

71. First published in *Studien der Bibliothek Warburg* 6 (1925); reprinted in *WW*, 71–167.

72. Originally published in the *Zeitschrift für Ästhetik und allgemeine Kunstwissenschaft* 21 (1927): 295–312; trans. John Michael Krois, *Man and World* 11 (1978): 411–28.

73. *Jahrbücher der Philosophie* 3 (1927): 31–92.

74. "Zur Theorie des Begriffs," *Kant-Studien* 33 (1928): 130.

75. *Die Idee der Republikanischen Verfassung: Rede zur Verfassungsfeier am 11. August 1928* (Hamburg: Friederichsen, 1929); cf. Toni Cassirer, *Mein Leben*, 159.

76. *Zeitschrift für Rechtsphilosophie* 6 (1932): 1–27.

77. See Toni Cassirer, *Mein Leben*, 149; see also Aby Warburg, "Ernst Cassirer: Warum Hamburg den Philosophen nicht verlieren darf," *Hamburger Fremdenblatt*, no. 173, June 23, 1928, 1–2.

78. "Formen und Verwandlungen des philosophischen Wahrheitsbegriffs," *Hamburger Universitätsreden* gehalten beim Rektoratswechsel, 1929 (Hamburg, 1931), 17–36.

79. See Toni Cassirer, *Mein Leben*, 189–90.

80. At the University of Hamburg's celebration of Cassirer's 100th birthday, the president of the university gave a biographical lecture on Cassirer in which he indicated that Cassirer received his notice in a letter dated July 28, 1933. See Peter Fischer-Appelt, "Zum Gedenken an Ernst Cassirer," Ansprache zur Eröffnung der Wissenschaftlichen Tagung "Symbolische Formen" am 20. Oktober, 1974 (Hamburg: Pressestelle der Universität, 1975), 15; cf. Toni Cassirer, *Mein Leben*, 172–87.

81. See Toni Cassirer (*Mein Leben*, 235–39) for a description of Cassirer's relationship to Schweitzer.

82. "Schiller und Shaftesbury," *Publications of the English Goethe Society* 11 (1935): 49–50.

83. *Theoria*, respectively, 2 (1936): 207–32; 4 (1938): 145–75; and 5 (1939): 111–40.

84. Ernst Cassirer, "Science and Ethics: Equal Partnership," *Saturday Review*, March 2, 1957.

85. *Göteborgs Högskolas Arsskrift* 47 (1941): 1–31.

86. Toni Cassirer's description of the crossing in her *Mein Leben* (274, 282–

88) is also substantiated by Jakobson, who worked during the voyage on his "Notes on Gilyak." See Roman Jakobson, *Selected Writings* (The Hague and Paris: Mouton, 1971), 2:97n. See also note 88 below.

87. Published in *Word*, Journal of the Linguistic Circle of New York, 1 (August 1946): 99–120.

88. Letter to Paul Arthur Schilpp, June 3, 1943, in Library of Living Philosophers Archive, Southern Illinois University, Carbondale. In this letter Cassirer mentions his long discussions with Jakobson on their voyage to New York and emphasizes the close philosophical agreement between them. For whatever reason, no article by Jakobson appeared in *PEC*.

89. See Gawronsky, *PEC*, 32; cf. Charles W. Hendel, *PEC*, 58.

90. This paper appeared in the *Albert Schweitzer Jubilee Book*, ed. A. A. Roback (Cambridge: Sci-Art Publishers, 1946), 239–58. Other papers on this theme are published in *SMC*.

91. Ernst Cassirer, Paul Oskar Kristeller, John Herman Randall, Jr., *The Renaissance Philosophy of Man* (1948; reprint, Chicago: University of Chicago Press, Phoenix Books, 1967).

92. Letter to Paul Arthur Schilpp, May 13, 1942. Library of Living Philosophers Archive, Southern Illinois University, Carbondale. Cassirer says: "Schon im ersten Entwurf der Phil. d. s. F. war ein besonderer Band über Kunst vorgesehen die Ungunst der Zeiten hat aber seine Ausarbeitung immer wieder hinausgeschoben." (Even in the original plan of the *PSF* a volume on art was proposed—but the unfavorableness of the times postponed its preparation again and again.)

93. Ms 184b, Cassirer Papers Deposit, Beinecke Rare Book and Manuscript Library, Yale University. In addition, two other manuscripts, 184a and 184c, contain other material, some written out, some in outline form, as well as notes for further parts of the planned fourth volume.

94. Originally published in *Germanic Review* 20 (1945): 166–94; reprinted in Helmut Koopman, ed., *Thomas Mann*, Wege der Forschung, vol. 335 (Darmstadt: Wissenschaftliche Buchgesellschaft, 1975), 1–34.

95. Ernst Cassirer, *Rousseau, Kant, Goethe* (1945; reprinted with an introduction by Peter Gay, New York: Harper & Row, Torchbook, 1963).

CHAPTER I. CASSIRER'S TRANSFORMATION OF PHILOSOPHY

1. On this movement as a whole see Frederick Gregory, *Scientific Materialism in Nineteenth-Century Germany*, Studies in the History of Modern Science, no. 1 (Dordrecht and Boston: D. Reidel, 1977).

2. "Es muß auf Kant zurückgegangen werden." Otto Liebmann, *Kant und die Epigonen* (Stuttgart, 1865), reprint by the Kantgesellschaft (Berlin: Verlag von Reuther & Reichard, 1912), 216.

3. Frederick Albert Lange, *The History of Materialism*, 3d ed., three volumes in one, translated by Ernest Chester Thomas with an introduction by Bertrand Russell (New York: Harcourt, Brace and Company, 1925), book 2, 154n.

4. Cohen edited Lange's last work, the *Logische Studien* (1877), and contributed a biographical preface and a 125-page introduction to the ninth printing of the third German edition of *The History of Materialism*.

5. See Hermann von Helmholtz, *Die Tatsachen in der Wahrnehmung* (1878; reprint, Darmstadt: Wissenschaftliche Buchgesellschaft, 1959), 13–14.

6. Eduard Zeller, "Ueber Bedeutung und Aufgabe der Erkenntnistheorie" (1862) in *Vorträge und Abhandlungen*, zweite Sammlung (Leipzig: Fues's Verlag [R. Reisland]. 1877), 1:479–95. See Cassirer, *PK*, 4. Klaus Christian Köhnke has shown that the term *Erkenntnistheorie* occurs some thirty years before Zeller's lecture in writings by different authors, viz., Immanuel Hermann Fichte, Christian Hermann Weisse, Ernst Reinhold, and Friedrich Eduard Beneke. Köhnke holds, however, that Zeller's lecture is historically important as an early formulation of the position that came to be known as neo-Kantianism. See Köhnke, "Über den Ursprung des wortes Erkenntnistheorie—und desen vermeintliche Synonyme," *Archiv für Begriffsgeschichte* 25 (1981): 185–210. For a discussion of Zeller (1814–1908) see Thomas E. Willey, *Back to Kant: The Revival of Kantianism in German Social and Historical Thought, 1860–1914* (Detroit: Wayne State University Press, 1978), 68–78.

7. A German reader on neo-Kantianism—the first such volume in any language—focuses on the theory of knowledge; see Werner Flach and Helmut Holzhey, eds., *Erkenntnistheorie und Logik im Neukantianismus*, Seminar Textbücher 1 (Hildesheim: Gerstenberg Verlag, 1979). Neo-Kantianism has experienced a renaissance among historians of philosophy. See Hans-Ludwig Ollig's *Der Neukantianismus* (Stuttgart: Metzler, 1979) and his collection of texts, *Neukantianismus* (Stuttgart: Philipp Reclam, 1982). For the Marburg school, see the magistral study by Helmut Holzhey, *Cohen und Natorp*, 2 vols. (Basel/Stuttgart: Schwabe & Co., 1986). A comprehensive overview is given by Klaus Christian Köhne, *Entstehung und Aufstieg des Neukantianismus* (Frankfurt am Main: Suhrkamp Verlag, 1986).

8. Ms 184b, Cassirer Papers Deposit, Beinecke Rare Book and Manuscript Library, Yale University, contains two finished chapters: the first is " 'Geist' und 'Leben,' " the second, "Das Symbolproblem als Grundproblem der philosophischen Anthropologie." The material on the *Urphänomen* is contained in 184c. Introductory material is contained in 184a. The manuscript for the fourth volume of *The Philosophy of Symbolic Forms* is being edited by John Michael Krois and Donald Phillip Verene, to be published by Yale University Press.

9. In Marburg neo-Kantianism, as I. M. Bochénski points out, every irrational element, even sensation, is excluded, making the school's position a pure "panlogism"; *Contemporary European Philosophy*, trans. Donald Nicholl and Karl Aschenbrenner (Berkeley and Los Angeles: University of California, 1969), 93. On Marburg panlogism see also Gerd Wolandt, "Cassirer's Symbolbegriff und die Grundlegungsproblematik der Geisteswissenschaften," *Zeitschrift für philosophische Forschung* 18 (1964): 614–26.

10. Walter Benjamin, *Gesammelte Schriften*, vol. 3, ed. Hella Tiedemann-Bartels (Frankfurt am Main: Suhrkamp Verlag, 1972), 565.

11. See Cassirer, "Hermann Cohen, 1842–1918," *Social Research* 10 (1943): 220–23.

12. Hermann Cohen, *Kants Theorie der Erfahrung* (Berlin: Bruno Cassirer Verlag, 1871), 93–110.

13. A history of the term *transcendental method* is given in the *Historiches Wörterbuch der Philosophie*, s.v. On the origins of the concept of the transcendental in Kant's thought, see Norbert Hinske, *Kants Weg zur Transzendentalphilosophie* (Frankfurt am Main: Kohlhammer, 1970). A helpful brief discussion is provided by Ignacio Angelelli, "On the Origins of Kant's 'Transcendental.'" *Kant-Studien* 63 (1972): 117–22.

14. Immanuel Kant, *Prolegomena to any Future Metaphysics*, trans. Mahaffy-Carus, rev. Lewis White Beck (Indianapolis: Bobbs-Merrill, 1950), 122n.

15. Immanuel Kant, *Critique of Pure Reason*, trans. Norman Kemp Smith (New York: St. Martin's Press, 1961), 59.

16. See Hans Vaihinger, *Kommentar zu Kants Kritik der reinen Vernunft*, 2 vols. (1881, 2d ed. 1922; reprint, Aalen: Scientia Verlag, 1970), 1:467–71.

17. Cohen, *Kants Theorie der Erfahrung*, 108.

18. Hermann Cohen, *Ethik des reinen Willens*, 2d ed. (Berlin: Bruno Cassirer Verlag, 1907), 65.

19. See Hermann Cohen, *Das Prinzip der Infinitesimal-Methode und seine Geschichte* (1883; reprint, Frankfurt am Main: Suhrkamp Verlag, 1968), 24, 49.

20. Ernst Cassirer, "Hermann Cohen," *Korrespondenzblatt des Vereins zur Gründung und Erhaltung einer Akademie des Judentums* 1 (1920): 5.

21. See Ernst Cassirer, "Hermann Cohen," *Korrespondenzblatt*, 6; s.v. "Neo-Kantianism," *Encyclopedia Britannica*, 14th ed.; "Hermann Cohen und die Erneuerung der Kantischen Philosophie," *Kant-Studien* 17 (1912): 254; "Hermann Cohen, 1842–1918," *Social Research* 10 (1943): 223–25.

22. Cassirer, "Hermann Cohen und die Erneuerung der Kantischen Philosophie," 257.

23. Cassirer, "Was ist Subjektivismus?" *Theoria* 5 (1939): 114.

24. Toni Cassirer, *Mein Leben mit Ernst Cassirer*, 94.

25. The neo-Kantian philosopher Bruno Bauch (1877–1942), while an editor of the *Kant-Studien*, went so far as to question Cohen's ability to understand Kant on the grounds that Cohen was a Jew. See below, chap. 5, note 18.

26. The protocol of this debate was written by Joachim Ritter, a student of Cassirer, and Otto Friedrich Bollnow, a student of Georg Misch invited by Heidegger to attend the courses. Although the protocol is not a word-for-word transcript of the exchange between Cassirer and Heidegger, its accuracy is attested to by the fact that Heidegger himself was willing to include it as an appendix ("Davoser Disputation zwischen Ernst Cassirer und Martin Heidegger") to his book *Kant und das Problem der Metaphysik*, 4th ed. (Frankfurt am Main: Vittorio Klostermann, 1973), 246–68. An abbreviated version of the protocol was duplicated and distributed at the conclusion of the meetings. This abbreviated version was published by Guido Schneeberger, *Ergänzungen zu einer Heidegger-Bibliographie* (Bern, 1960), 17–27. Two English translations of the abbreviated protocol are available: Carl H. Hamburg, "A Cassirer-Heidegger Seminar," *Philosophy and Phenomenological Research* 25 (1964–65): 213–22 (pp. 208–13 give Hamburg's comments on the debate); Francis Slade, "A Discussion between Ernst Cassirer and Martin Heidegger," in Nino Langiulli, ed., *The Existentialist Tradition* (New York: Doubleday & Co., Anchor Books, 1971), 192–203. The original, complete version of the protocol first appeared in print in a French translation by Pierre Aubenque in Ernst Cassirer and Martin Heidegger, *Débat sur le Kantisme et la Philosophie* *et autres Textes de 1929–1931*, trans. P. Aubenque, J.-M. Fataud, and P. Quillet (Paris: Éditions Beauchesne, 1972), 28–51. No English translation of the complete protocol is presently available. The unabridged version is nearly twice as long and more detailed than the abridgment. Therefore I refer only to the full-length version, giving my own translations of the passages cited. (For information about errors in the shorter version, see Aubenque, Fataud, and Quillet, p. 10n.) A complete documentation of the Davos debate is under preparation by Karlfried Gründer, Free University of Berlin.

27. "Davoser Disputation" in Heidegger, *Kant*, 246.

28. Max Scheler, "Erkenntnis und Arbeit," *Die Wissensformen und die Gesellschaft*, vol. 8 of the *Gesammelte Werke* (Bern: A. Franke Verlag, 1960), 201.

29. "Davoser Disputation" in Heidegger, *Kant*, 262.

30. See Maurice Merleau-Ponty, *The Phenomenology of Perception*, trans. Colin Smith (London: Routledge and Kegan Paul, 1962), 235.

31. I have given an account of the differences between Cassirer and Heidegger in a discussion of Cassirer's criticisms of *Being and Time*; see "Cassirer's Unpublished Critique of Heidegger," *Philosophy and Rhetoric* 16 (1983): 147–59.

32. "Davoser Disputation" in Heidegger, *Kant*, 266–67.

33. In Cassirer's critical treatment of Lebensphilosophie in the manuscript of the fourth volume of the *PSF*, he focuses on the isolatedness of Dasein in Heidegger's *Being and Time*. This portion of Cassirer's manuscript, along with a translation, has now been published. See Ernst Cassirer, " 'Mind' and 'Life': Heidegger," *Philosophy and Rhetoric* 16 (1983): 164–66; the original German appears as " 'Geist' und 'Leben': Heidegger." Although Heidegger speaks of *Mitsein* (Being-with) as fundamental, the existential view of the "authentic" predominates. On discourse see *Being and Time*, trans. John Macquarrie and Edward Robinson (New York: Harper & Row, 1962) H 163.

34. Ernst Cassirer, "Erkenntnistheorie nebst den Grenzfragen der Logik und Denkpsychologie," *Jahrbücher der Philosophie* 3 (1927): 34.

35. I use the phrase "critique of meaning" in the sense given to it by Karl-Otto Apel in his characterization of the transformation of philosophy in contemporary thought from theory of knowledge to theory of meaning. See Apel's "Wittgenstein und Heidegger: Die Frage nach dem Sinn von Sein und die Sinnlosigkeitsverdacht gegen alle Metaphysik," *Transformation der Philosophie*, 1:225–75.

36. The most important of Cassirer's discussions on the central topics of meaning—"symbolic form" and "symbolic pregnance"—are found in the third volume of *The Philosophy of Symbolic Forms* and the essays "Der Begriff der symbolischen Form in dem Aufbau der Geisteswissenschaft" (1922; The concept of symbolic form in the construction of the human sciences), "Das Symbolproblem und seine Stellung im System der Philosophie" (1927; translated as "The Problem of the Symbol and Its Place in the System of Philosophy"), and "Zur Logik des Symbolbegriffs" (1938; On the logic of the symbol concept). A summary description of Cassirer's theory and its relation to semiotics is given in my essay "Ernst Cassirers Semiotik der symbolischen Formen," *Zeitschrift für Semiotik* 6 (1984): 433–44.

37. Cassirer refers to Peirce briefly as quoted by another author in *DI*, 90. Edgar Wind mentions Peirce in his contribution to the festschrift given to

Cassirer on his sixtieth birthday (*Philosophy and History*, ed. Klibansky and Paton), but there is no indication that Cassirer read any of Peirce's writings on the theory of signs.

38. Cassirer, "Structuralism in Modern Linguistics," *Word*, Journal of the Linguistic Circle of New York, 1 (August 1946): 119.

39. Cassirer, "Erkenntnistheorie nebst den Grenzfragen" (1927): 78ff.

40. I have discussed this point in a paper, "Peirce and Cassirer: The Philosophical Importance of a Theory of Signs," *Proceedings of the C. S. Peirce Bicentennial International Congress*, ed. Kenneth L. Ketner et al. Lubbock: Texas Tech University Press, 1981), 99–104.

41. Cassirer, "Kant und die moderne Mathematik," *Kant-Studien* 7 (1907): 10.

42. See W. V. O. Quine, *Methods of Logic*, 3d ed. (London: Routledge and Kegan Paul, 1974), 137–43.

43. When Cassirer cites Frege, he usually refers to the *Foundations of Arithmetic*, never the Begriffsschrift, "Function and Concept," "Sense and Meaning," or any other work where Frege explicates his application of the mathematical notion of function to predicative relations. Cassirer says that for Frege "the concept itself is essentially understood and defined as a function" (*PsF*, 3:342; *PSF*, 3:293). See *SF/ET*, 28–30, 43, 45ff, 52; *PK*, 56–58, 63–65; *PsF*, 3:342, 402–03; *PSF*, 3:293, 345.

44. *PsF*, 3:342; *PSF*, 3:293. The passage that Cassirer refers to is found in Frege's "Critical Elucidation of Some Points in E. Schröder, *Vorlesungen über die Algebra der Logik*," in Gottlob Frege, *Collected Papers on Mathematics, Logic, and Philosophy*, ed. Brian McGuinness (Oxford: Basil Blackwell, 1984), 228.

45. See Burkamp, *Begriff und Beziehung* (Leipzig: Felix Meiner Verlag, 1927), 210. Burkamp even claims (p. 199) that Frege in the *Begriffsschrift* interprets the affirmation and negation of a general concept in an existential sense as "es gibt kein" and "es gibt ein" because this was also needed for his attempt to deduce numbers as quantities from logic. However, in a letter to Husserl dated December 9, 1906, Frege clearly says, "Now I use the expressions containing 'all' in such a way that existence is neither part of what I mean nor something I presuppose as having been admitted." Gottlob Frege, *Philosophical and Mathematical Correspondence* trans. Hans Kaal, ed. Gottfried Gabriel, Hans Hermes, Friedrich Kambartel, Christian Thiel, Albert Veraart (Chicago: University of Chicago Press, 1980), 71.

46. Frege says: "I do not start from concepts in order to build up thoughts or propositions out of them; rather, I obtain the components of a thought by decomposition (*Zerfällung*) of the thought. In this respect my *Begriffsschrift* differs from the similar creations of Leibniz and his successors—in spite of its name, which perhaps I did not choose very aptly." In Jean van Heijenoort, ed., *Frege and Gödel: Two Fundamental Texts in Mathematical Logic* (Cambridge, Mass.: Harvard University Press, 1970), 1n.

47. Frege, *Begriffsschrift*, in Heijenoort, *Frege and Gödel*, 22.

48. See "Function and Concept" in Frege, *Collected Papers*, 140.

49. See "Zur Theorie des Begriffs," 130–31.

50. Helmholtz's notion of language as "energia" (discussed below) and Hertz's notion of the essential cognitive contribution of signs (see *SF/ET*, 1) were important for Cassirer's intellectual grasp of the sign, but Goethe's metaphysical idea of the symbol captured Cassirer's philosophical imagination. Ferdinand Weinhandl's book, *Die Metaphysik Goethes* (1932); reprint, Darmstadt: Wissenschaftliche Buchgesellschaft, 1965) claims that the notion of the symbol was Goethe's central metaphysical idea.

51. Humboldt says: "Properly conceived of, language is something persistent and in every instant transitory. Even its maintenance by writing is only an incomplete, mummified preservation, necessary if one is again to render perceptible the living speech concerned. In itself language is not work, i.e., not a work [*kein Werk*], but an activity [*energia*]. Its true definition may therefore only be genetic. It is after all the continual intellectual effort to make the articulated sound capable of expressing thought." Wilhelm von Humboldt, *Linguistic Variability and Intellectual Development*, Miami Linguistics Series no. 9, trans. George C. Guck and Frithoj A. Raven (Coral Gables: University of Miami Press, 1971), 27.

52. See Leon Rosenstein, "Some Metaphysical Problems of Cassirer's Symbolic Forms," 318.

53. Carl Hamburg and Heinz Paetzold have presented Cassirer's theory as dyadic. See the former's *Symbol and Reality*, 72ff.; cf. Heinz Paetzold, "Ernst Cassirers 'Philosophie der symbolischen Formen' und die neuere Entwicklung der Semiotik," in *Zeichenkonstitution. Akten des 2. Semiotischen Kolloquiums Regensburg, 1978*, ed. A. Lange-Seidl (Berlin: Walter de Gruyter, 1981), 1:90–100. Paetzold and Hamburg refer to frequent locutions of Cassirer's about *Sinn in dem Sinnlichen*, but neither discusses his *definition* of symbolic form (*WW*, 175), which is clearly triadic. Paetzold, in the spirit of German criticisms of Cassirer, points to Peirce's triadic theory of the sign-relation as a step beyond Cassirer.

54. Ferdinand de Saussure, *Course in General Linguistics*, trans. Wade Baskin, ed. Charles Bally, Albert Sechehayne, and Albert Riedlinger (New York: McGraw-Hill, 1966), 117.

55. Martin Heidegger, "Review of Ernst Cassirer's Mythic Thought" in *The Piety of Thinking: Essays by Martin Heidegger*, trans. James G. Hart and John C. Maraldo (Bloomington: Indiana University Press, 1976), 45. The review originally appeared in the *Deutsche Literaturzeitung* 21 (1928): 1000–12.

56. Jacques Derrida, "Structure, Sign, and Play in the Discourse of the Human Sciences" in Richard Macksey and Eugenio Donato, eds., *The Structuralist Controversy* (Baltimore: Johns Hopkins University Press, 1972), 247–65, esp. 264.

57. See Feruccio Rossi-Landi, *Semiotik Ästhetik und Ideologie*, trans. Burkhart Kroeber (Munich: Carl Hanser, 1976), 22–32.

58. See Günther A. Saafeld, *Fremd und Verdeutschungswörterbuch* (Berlin: Oswald Seeligens Verlag, 1898), s.v. "Pregnänz," 340.

59. Kurt Koffka, *The Principles of Gestalt Psychology* (London: Routledge and Kegan Paul, 1935), 110.

60. George W. Hartmann, *Gestalt Psychology: A Survey of Facts and Principles* (New York: Ronald Press, 1935), 48.

61. He used this device repeatedly to make his point. Cf. "Das Symbolproblem und sein Stellung im System der Philosophie," *STS*, 5–6 ("The Problem of the Symbol and Its Place in the System of Philosophy," trans. John Michael Krois, *Man and World* 11 [1978]: 414); *WW*, 211–18; and *PSF*, 3:191–204.

62. See William Hogarth, *Analysis of Beauty* (1753; reprint, Hildesheim: Georg Olms Verlag, 1974), 38–39.

63. This objection—and Cassirer's reaction to it—are illustrated in the exchange between Schmied-Kowarzik and Cassirer in the discussion following his lecture on the "Symbolproblem." See *STS*, 30, 32–35.

64. "Leib und Seele also philosophisches problem" (Body and soul as a philosophical problem), Ms 132, Cassirer Papers Deposit, Beinecke Rare Book and Manuscript Library, Yale University, 37 numbered pages.

65. Merleau-Ponty, *The Phenomenology of Perception*, trans. Colin Smith (London: Routledge and Kegan Paul, 1962), 28, 53, 58, 124–25, 127n, 148, 152, 182, 192, 235, 290–91, 297, 410, 429, 433.

66. *PSF*, 3:39; *PsF*, 3:46. This point is confused in the translation, which reads: "the necessary condition for both the existence of the I and its knowledge of itself."

Another basic difference between Merleau-Ponty's *Phenomenology of Perception* and Cassirer's *Phenomenology of Knowledge* can be seen in the ways they use the word *phenomenology* in their titles. Merleau-Ponty refers to the kind of descriptive study associated with Husserl. He centers on the sphere of expressive meaning as it is manifested in perception. Cassirer uses the term in two senses. He, too, engages in such pure phenomenological description, and he acknowledges that his descriptive approach to myth was inspired by Husserl's phenomenology (*PSF*, 2:12n; *PsF*, 2:17n). But the primary meaning of *phenomenology* in his title is Hegelian. Cassirer wants to show the way from one dimension of meaning to another, from the expressive world of perception to the world of representation and, finally, the world of pure significance.

67. Martin Heidegger, *Sein und Zeit*, 12th ed. (Tübingen: Max Niemeyer Verlag, 1972), §18, §31. The English translation by John Macquarrie and Edward Robinson, *Being and Time* (New York: Harper & Row, 1962) and the German edition are cited according to the German pagination, which also appears with the text of the translation.

68. Heidegger, *Being and Time*, H 151; cf. 324.

69. *Goethes Werke*, sect. 2, *Goethes Naturwissenschaftliche Schriften* (Weimar: Herman Böhlau Nachfolger, 1890), 1:72–74 §175–77. cf. *IG*, 49.

70. The first two chapters on the concepts of Geist and Leben and on philosophical anthropology (Ms 183b) are clearly dated 16 IV 1928. The material in 183c dealing with the problem of the Urphänomen is most likely the part of the work written in Sweden in 1940 discussed in Toni Cassirer's memoirs, *Mein Leben*, 267–70.

71. On the importance of Goethe for Dilthey as the source of Lebensphilosophie, see the editors' introduction to Wilhelm Dilthey, *Selected Works*, vol. 5, *Poetry and Experience*, ed. Rudolf A. Makkreel and Frithjof Rodi (Princeton: Princeton University Press, 1985), 19–22.

72. Isabel Stearns, review of *The Problem of Knowledge* by Ernst Cassirer, *The Review of Metaphysics* 5 (1951): 119.

73. Stearns, 119. Cassirer says that Goethe created a theory of the relationship between particular and universal "such as can hardly be found elsewhere in the history of philosophy or natural science" (*PK*, 145). For Cassirer's account of Goethe's theory, see *FF*, 240–41.

74. See *EP*, 2:751ff.; cf. "Was ist Subjektivismus?," 134ff.

75. See especially the discussions of myth (*PSF*, 2: pt. 3; *PsF*, 2: pt. 3) and technology (*STS*, 84–90). The philosophy of culture developed in the *Essay on Man* is basically a philosophy of social reality.

76. Hegel says: "Enjoying however an absolute liberty, the Idea does not merely pass over into life, or as finite cognition allow life to show it: in its own absolute truth it resolves to let the 'moment' of its particularity, or of the first characterization and other-being, the immediate idea, as its reflected image, go forth freely as nature." *Hegel's Logic*, part one of *The Encyclopedia of the Philosophical Sciences* (1830), trans. William Wallace (Oxford: Clarendon Press, 1975), 296. Cassirer also quotes from the greater logic to make his point. See *EP*, 3:374–75.

77. See Heinrich Rickert, *Die Philosophie des Lebens: Darstellung und Kritik der philosophischen Modeströmungen unserer Zeit* (Tübingen: Verlag J.C.B. Mohr [Paul Siebeck], 1920).

78. On vulgar Lebensphilosophie as a political force, see Kurt Sontheimer, *Anti-Demokratisches Denken in der Weimarer Republik* (1968; reprint, Munich: Deutscher Taschenbuch Verlag, 1978), 56–61.

79. Ms 184b, 232–34.

80. See especially the late work "Leben und Erkennen" (c. 1892/93, in Wilhelm Dilthey, *Grundlegung der Wissenschaften vom Menschen, der Gesellschaft und der Geschichte*, ed. Helmut Johach and Frithjof Rodi, vol. 19 of the *Gesammelte Schriften* (Göttingen: Vandenhoeck & Ruprecht, 1982), 333–88. Dilthey traces the genesis of concepts to the process of Leben. Cassirer describes the genesis of the concept of causality from Leben, the interaction between man and the world in his essay "Form und Technik"; see below, chap. 2. Since Dilthey's essay was not published until 1982, Cassirer could not have been familiar with it. He notes that the early Dilthey still treated the notion of an analogical inference (*Analogieschluß*) to the external world and other minds almost as an axiom (*PSF*, 3:82; *PsF*, 3:96).

81. Ms 184a, 16.

82. Here, again, his outlook is virtually identical with Dilthey's conception of the unfathomableness of life. See *Gesammelte Schriften*, 19:346–47; cf. *LH*, 176–81; *KW*, 99–102.

83. Ms 184b, 18ff.

84. Georg Simmel, "Transzendenz des Lebens," in *Lebensanschauung: vier metaphysische Kapitel* (Munich and Leipzig: Duncker & Hunblot, 1918), 1–27.

85. Cassirer wrote on Simmel's conception of the "tragedy of culture" in *LH*, 182–217 (*WW*, 103–27). See below, chap. 5.

86. Simmel, *Lebensanschauung*, 39.

87. Heidegger, *Being and Time*, H 156.

88. Cassirer, "Henri Bergson's Ethik und Religionsphilosophie," *Der Morgen* 9 (1933): 27–29.

89. Ibid., 21; a similar, more detailed discussion is found in the manuscript of *PSF* 4 (Ms 184b, 247–50).

90. Cassirer refers to "trans-personal meaning" (*überpersönlichen Sinn*) in his criticism of *Being and Time*. Cassirer, " 'Mind' and 'Life': Heidegger," trans. John Michael Krois, *Philosophy and Rhetoric* 16 (1983): 161.

91. Cassirer, " 'Mind' and 'Life': Heidegger," 162.

92. Heidegger, *Being and Time*, H 227.

CHAPTER II. PHILOSOPHY AND CULTURE

1. Kant, "Idea for a Universal History from a Cosmopolitan Point of View" in Lewis White Beck, ed., *On History* (Indianapolis: Bobbs-Merrill Co., 1963), 12.

2. See Kant, *The Doctrine of Virtue*, part 2 of the *Metaphysics of Morals*, trans. Mary J. Gregor (New York: Harper & Row, 1964), § 19.

3. Natorp speaks of the "Wissenschaftstendenz der gesamten Kulturarbeit" (tendency toward science of the complete effort of culture); see Paul Natorp, *Philosophie: Ihr Problem und ihre Probleme*, 4th ed., Wege zur Philosophie, Ergänzungsreihe: Einführung in die Philosophie der Gegenwart, no. 1 (Göttingen: Vandenhoeck & Ruprecht, 1929), 26. The philosophy of science is not the only kind of philosophy but, Natorp says, it is "first" philosophy (ibid., 28).

4. Wilhelm Windelband, *Präludien: Aufsätze und Reden zur Philosophie und ihrer Geschichte*, 2 vols. (Tübingen: J.C.B. Mohr [Paul Siebeck], 1921), 2:287. The essay is from 1910.

5. Windelband makes this declaration in his 1910 lecture "Die Erneuerung des Hegelianismus" (The renewal of Hegelianism), *Präludien* 1: 283. This lecture and the Kulturphilosophie essay are landmarks in the transformation of neo-Kantianism into neo-Hegelianism.

6. On Cohen, see *PSF*, 1:71; *PsF*, 1:VII. On Dilthey, see Cassirer, "Structuralism in Modern Linguistics," 111.

7. Willard van Orman Quine, *Word and Object* (Cambridge, Mass.: MIT Press, 1960), 3.

8. See Cassirer, "Structuralism in Modern Linguistics," passim; see also *LH*, 171–72, *EM*, 68–69, 119–24, 172.

9. See David Robey, "Introduction" to *Structuralism: An Introduction*, ed. David Robey (Oxford: Clarendon Press, 1972), 2; Peter Caws, "The Recent Literature of Structuralism," *Philosophische Rundschau* 18 (1972): 64.

10. See the following comparative studies; Roger Silverstone, "Ernst Cassirer and Claude Lévi-Strauss: Two Approaches to the Study of Myth," *Archives de Sciences Sociales des Religions* 21 (1976): 25–36 and Reto Luzius Fetz, "Genetische Semiologie?: Symboltheorie im Ausgang von Ernst Cassirer und Jean Piaget," *Freiburger Zeitschrift für Philosophie und Theologie* 28 (1981): 434–70; Edward Seltzer, "The Problem of Objectivity: A Study of Objectivity Reflected in a Comparison of the Philosophies of E. Cassirer, J. Piaget, and E. Husserl" (Ph.D. dissertation, New School for Social Research, 1969). A parallel between Cassirer and Lévi-Strauss not mentioned in Silverstone's essay is their use of the notion of the "totality of versions" as a way to define the unity of cultural phenomena. Lévi-Strauss defines the structural law of a myth as consisting of "all of its versions"; none alone is the "true" version. See Claude Lévi-Strauss, "The Structural Study of Myth," in *Structural Anthropology*, trans. Claire Jacobson and Brooke Grundfest Schoepf (Garden City: Doubleday and Co., Anchor Books, 1967), 213–15. Cassirer, too, refers to the "totality of versions" in his theory of scientific truth. See below, chap. 3.

11. See *LH*, 159–81. On the importance of transformations in structuralism, see Jean Piaget, *Structuralism*, trans. Chaninah Maschler (London: Routledge & Kegan Paul, 1971), 10–13. Perhaps the most striking parallel between

Cassirer's and Piaget's treatment of transformations in structuralism is their emphasis on the method of structuralism in the mathematical theory of groups as a way to understand transformations in other spheres. Piaget points in particular to Felix Klein's Erlanger Program as a prime example of the systematizing power of transformations, here permitting the unification of different geometries (17–22). Cassirer makes the same point in the same way, even claiming that Klein's work was the chief inspiration for his conception of structuralism. See "Reflections on the Concept of Group and the Theory of Perception" (SMC, 271–85); cf. "The Concept of Group and the Theory of Perception," *Philosophy and Phenomenological Research* 5 (1944): esp. 6–8. This article, translated by Aron Gurwitch, originally appeared in 1938 in French. Fetz's otherwise detailed comparative study of Piaget and Cassirer (see note 10) does not treat of this or their general views of structuralism as a method although he terms Cassirer a structuralist (p. 438). For other discussions of Klein in earlier work, see PK, 24–25, 28–36, 50–52; PSF, 3:353ff.; PsF, 3:412ff.; SF/ET, 86, 90.

12. See, e.g., Joseph E. Doherty, *Sein, Mensch und Symbol: Heidegger und die Auseinandersetzung mit dem Neu-Kantischen Symbolbegriff*, Münchner Philosophische Forschungen, vol. 6 (Bonn: Bouvier Verlag Herbert Grundmann, 1972). By treating Cassirer purely as an epistemologist, this study, instead of confronting Cassirer's and Heidegger's thought, provides only a caricature of the PSF, which serves the function of a straw man.

13. Willard Van Orman Quine, *Ontological Relativity and Other Essays* (New York: Columbia University Press, 1969), 15–16.

14. Cassirer, "The Problem of the Symbol" (1927), 427.

15. Cassirer, "Die Philosophie der Griechen von den Anfängen bis Platon" in Max Dessoir, ed., *Lehrbuch der Philosophie*, vol. 1, *Geschichte der Philosophie* (Berlin: Ullstein, 1925), 83–84.

16. Plato, *Sophist*, 241d, in Edith Hamilton and Huntington Cairns, eds. *The Collected Dialogues of Plato* (Princeton: Princeton University Press 1961); cf. EP, 3:307.

17. Cassirer, "Giovanni Pico della Mirandola," *Journal of the History of Ideas* 3 (1942): 331–32.

18. Cassirer, "Erkenntnistheorie nebst den Grenzfragen der Logik und Denkpsychologie," 32.

19. On action as the center of interest in post-Hegelian philosophy, see Richard J. Bernstein, *Praxis and Action: Contemporary Philosophies of Human Activity* (Philadelphia: University of Pennsylvania Press, 1971).

20. Cassirer, "Structuralism in Modern Linguistics," 113–14.

21. *Hegel's Science of Logic*, two volumes in one, trans. A. V. Miller (London: George Allen & Unwin, 1969), 781–82; G. W. F. Hegel, *Wissenschaft der Logik*, zweiter Band, ed. Friedrich Hogemann and Walter Jaeschke, vol. 12 in *Gesammelte Werke* (Hamburg: Felix Meiner Verlag, 1981), 198.

22. G. W. F. Hegel, *The Phenomenology of Mind*, trans. J. B. Baillie (New York: Harper & Row, 1967), 135; cf. G. W. F. Hegel, *Phänomenologie des Geistes*, ed. Wolfgang Bonsiepen and Reinhard Heede, vol. 9 in *Gesammelte Werke* (Hamburg: Felix Meiner Verlag, 1980). 55. "Erscheinendes Wissen" is translated "phenomenal knowledge."

23. See the introductory discussion in "Der Begriff der symbolischen Form im Aufbau der Geisteswissenschaften," WW, 178–83.

24. On language, see *PSF*, 1:186–97; *PsF*, 1:137–48; on myth and religion, *PSF*, 2:237–39, 255–61, *PsF*, 2:284–86, 304–11; on art, *WW*, 182–87; on technology, *STS*, 61–74; on science, *PSF*, 3:453–59, *PsF*, 3:530–37.

25. Cassirer, "The Problem of the Symbol," 418.

26. See Sigmund Freud, *The Interpretation of Dreams* (part 2), vol. 5 of *The Standard Edition of the Complete Psychological Works of Sigmund Freud*, trans. James Strachey (1953–66; London: Hogarth Press, 1978), 318. Cf. "Negation" (1925) in vol. 19, 235ff.

27. Paul Ricoeur, *Freud and Philosophy: An Essay on Interpretation*, trans. Denis Savage (New Haven: Yale University Press, 1970), 12.

28. R. H. Hook, "Phantasy and Symbol: A Psychoanalytic Point of View" in R. H. Hook, ed., *Phantasy and Symbol: Studies in Anthropological Interpretation* (New York: Academic Press, 1979), 277n.

29. Alfred Lorenzer, *Kritik des psychoanalytischen Symbolbegriffs* (Frankfurt am Main: Suhrkamp Verlag, 1970), 50–51.

30. Leon Wurmser links Cassirer's theory of myth and Freud's "primary process" thinking in his article "Is Psychoanalysis a Separate Field of Symbolic Forms?" *Humanities in Society* 4 (1981): 270. Wurmser, who considers only Cassirer's relationship to Kant but thinks Goethe would be a better guide to psychoanalysis as a symbolic form (281–83), is unaware of Cassirer's debt to Goethe. On ethnopsychoanalysis, see Ariane Deluz's discussion of George Devereux in Hook, *Phantasy and Symbol*, 11–18.

31. See Susanne Langer, "On Cassirer's Theory of Language and Myth," *PEC*, 398; cf. Langer, "De Profondis," *Revue Internationale de Philosophie* 28 (1974): 449–55. The latter is devoted to Cassirer's view of Freud's thought.

32. Cassirer's discussion of the psychoanalytic theory of myth (*MS*, 28–34) has polemical overtones: "Freud stood at the sickbed of myth with the same attitude and the same feelings as at the couch of an ordinary patient" (p. 29).

33. This comparison has been made before; Carl Kérenyi made a point of it. Kerényi and C. G. Jung, *Essays on a Science of Mythology: The Myth of the Divine Child and the Mysteries of Eleusis*, trans. R. F. C. Hull (Princeton: Princeton University Press, 1969), 3–4, 58.

34. Claude Lévi-Strauss, *The Raw and the Cooked: Introduction to the Science of Mythology*, trans. John and Doreen Weightman (New York: Harper & Row, 1969), 16. The analogy between myth and music is a leitmotiv in *The Raw and the Cooked* and recurs in *The Naked Man*, trans. John and Doreen Weightman (New York: Harper & Row, 1981), 646–67.

35. Claude Lévi-Strauss, *Myth and Meaning: Five Talks for Radio* (New York: Schocken Books, 1979), 44–54.

36. Roger Silverstone also brings out this difference in his essay "Ernst Cassirer and Claude Lévi-Strauss: Two Approaches to the Study of Myth," *Archives de Science Sociales des Religions* 21 (1976): 25–36, esp. 27.

37. Viktor Zuckerkandl, *Sound and Symbol: Music and the External World*, trans. Willard R. Trask (Princeton: Princeton University Press, 1956), 234, 235.

38. Heidegger, review of *Mythic Thought* (vol. 2 of the *PSF*) by Ernst Cassirer, in Heidegger, *The Piety of Thinking*, trans. James G. Hart and John C. Maraldo (Bloomington: Indiana University Press, 1976), 43.

39. Heidegger, *Being and Time*, 83, 87. Heidegger later developed the notion of the "overpowering" character of "Being" along the lines presented in his review of Cassirer's *Mythic Thought*; see the discussion of *Not* (distress, need) in Heidegger, *Introduction to Metaphysics*, trans. Ralph Manheim (New Haven: Yale University Press, 1959), 162–63.

40. Heidegger, *Being and Time*, 51n.

41. In one place Merleau-Ponty says that many of Cassirer's analyses in the third volume of the *PSF* are "existential" (*Phenomenology of Perception*, 127n); he treats Cassirer's work as a whole in light of an existential interpretation.

42. Ibid., 127; cf. *PSF*, 3:10; *PsF*, 3:14.

43. Kant, *Critique of Pure Reason*, trans. Norman Kemp Smith (New York: St. Martin's Press, 1961), 80 (A84).

44. Lévi-Strauss, *The Raw and the Cooked*, 12.

45. Cassirer, "The Influence of Language upon the Development of Scientific Thought," *Journal of Philosophy* 39 (1942): 316ff.

46. See Cassirer, "The Place of Vesalius in the Culture of the Renaissance," *Yale Journal of Biology and Medicine* 16 (December 1942): 109–19.

47. See *IC*, 107. Religion, Cassirer thinks, is engaged in a constant struggle with its own mythic roots (*PSF*, 2:248ff.; *PsF*, 2:296ff.).

48. See "Heidisch-antike Weissagung in Wort und Bild zu Luthers Zeiten" (1919), in Aby M. Warburg, *Ausgewählte Schriften und Würdigungen*, vol. 1, ed. Dieter Wuttke with Carl Georg Heise Saecvla Spiritalia (Baden-Baden: Verlag Valentin Koerner, 1980), 199–304, esp. 208–21. Cassirer discusses Warburg's essay in *IC*, 105, 169ff.

49. See Cassirer, "Galileo: A New Science and a New Spirit," *American Scholar* 12 (1942): 5–19.

50. Cassirer, "Die Antike und die Entstehung der exakten Wissenschaften," *Die Antike* 13 (1932): 291.

51. Cassirer, "Galileo: A New Science and a New Spirit," 19.

52. See Cassirer's discussions of Kepler in "Mathematische Mystik und mathematische Naturwissenschaft," *Lychnos* (1940): 264. See also *IC*, 102; *EP*, 1:209.

53. Cassirer, "The Problem of the Symbol," 418.

54. Plato, *Sophist*, 259 ef.; see Cassirer, "Die Philosophie der Griechen," 128–31.

55. See *LM*, 58–62; *PSF*, 2:213–18, *PsF*, 2:255–61; *PSF*, 3:276–77, *PsF*, 3:323–25; and esp. "Form und Technik," *STS*, 39–90.

56. See Karl R. Popper, *The Open Society and Its Enemies*, vol. 2, *The High Tide of Prophecy: Hegel, Marx, and the Aftermath* (1945; London: Routledge & Kegan Paul, 1966), 269–80.

57. Popper, *The Open Society and Its Enemies*, vol. 1, *The Spell of Plato*, (1945; London: Routledge & Kegan Paul, 1966), 231.

CHAPTER III. TRUTH

1. The terms *norm* and *normative* occur frequently in Cassirer's writings, usually to refer to the norm of truth or ethical norms. For examples of the former, see Cassirer's article in the *Encyclopaedia Britannica*, 14th ed., s.v. "Truth"; his lecture "Formen und Formwandlungen des philosophischen Wahrheitsbegriffs," *Hamburger Universitäts-Reden* gehalten beim Rek-

torswechsel 1929 (Hamburg, 1931), 20; and "The Influence of Language upon the Development of Scientific Thought" (1942), 324; for examples of the latter, see "Wesen und Werden des Naturrechts," *Zeitschrift für Rechtsphilosophie* 6 (1932): 3, 6. The question of objective standards or a *Maß* has a systematic and topical importance for Cassirer. The next two chapters deal with the problem in systematic terms; chap. 5 addresses the problem as part of what Cassirer conceived as a general crisis in culture.

2. "The Influence of Language on the Development of Scientific Thought," 312. Cassirer says that the basic concepts of Aristotle's physics "scarcely go further in their function and achievement than the attributive concepts of language" (*PSF*, 3:453–54; *PsF*, 3:531. See also "Die Sprache und die Aufbau der Gegenstandswelt," *STS*, 121–51.

3. Ms 184a, pp. 78–79 (β 18–19). This discussion occurs in remarks on the philosophy of technology in material for the concluding chapter of *PSF* 4. *Techne*, Cassirer says, is a "Durchgangspunkt des *Verstehens*," an avenue of understanding.

4. "The Influence of Language on the Development of Scientific Thought," 316.

5. "Was ist Subjektivismus?", *Theoria* 5 (1939): 134.

6. Kant, *Critique of Pure Reason*, trans. Norman Kemp Smith (New York: St. Martin's Press), 299; A296ff/B351ff.

7. "Formen und Formwandlungen des philosophischen Wahrheitsbegriffs," 17–18.

8. Kant, *Critique of Pure Reason*, 218; B232ff.; *DI*, 162–63.

9. Kant, *Critique of Pure Reason*, 181; A139/B178.

10. Philipp Frank, *Modern Science and Its Philosophy* (Cambridge, Mass.: Harvard University Press, 1949), 174–75. Chapter 9 (172–85) is devoted to Cassirer.

11. Carl Friedrich von Weizsäcker, review of *Determinismus und Indeterminismus in der modernen Physik* by Ernst Cassirer, *Physikalische Zeitschrift* 38 (1937): 861.

12. "Was ist Subjektivismus?", 114.

13. Kant, *Critique of Pure Reason*, 213; B225.

14. *DI*, 189; cf. *Critique of Pure Reason*, 488; A571/B599.

15. See *DI*, 195; *PSF*, 3:429; *PsF*, 3:501–02; *SF/ET*, 3–94, 123–24. This is much like the view developed by Moritz Schlick, founder of the Vienna Circle. See, for example, *WW*, 226–27.

16. Moritz Schlick, *General Theory of Knowledge*, 2d ed., trans. Albert E. Blumberg (1927; reprint, New York and Vienna: Springer-Verlag, 1974), 352.

17. Cassirer, "Erkenntnistheorie nebst den Grenzfragen der Logik und der Denkpsychologie" (1927), 75.

18. Joseph Diaz Gergonne (1771–1859) introduced the notion of "implicit definitions" in his essay "Considérations, philosophiques sur les élements de la science de l'étendue," *Annals de mathématiques pure et applique* 18 (June 1826): 125ff.

19. Schlick, *General Theory of Knowledge*, 71.

20. Schlick, "Kritische oder empirische Deutung der neuen Physik?" *Kant-Studien* 26 (1921): 108. This article, a review of Cassirer's *Einstein's Theory of Relativity*," is available in translation as "Critical or Empiricist Interpretation of Modern Physics?" in Moritz Schlick, *Philosophical Papers*, vol. 1 (1909–

22), ed. Henk L. Mulder and Barbara F. B. Van de Velde-Schlick and trans. Peter Heath (Dordrecht: D. Reidel, 1979), 331.

21. Cassirer, "Erkenntnistheorie nebst den Grenzfragen der Logik und Denkpsychologie," 78–79.

22. See above, chap. 2, note 11.

23. In a study of the Schlick-Einstein correspondence, Don Howard summarizes the point of contention with Kantianism: "For both Schlick and Einstein, the basic issue at focus of debate with the Neo-Kantians was this: are the fundamental principles guiding inquiry fixed, *a priori*, as the Neo-Kantians maintained, or are these principles conventional, and thus capable of being changed as science progresses?" "Realism and Conventionalism in Einstein's Philosophy of Science: The Einstein-Schlick Correspondence," *Philosophia Naturalis* 21 (1984): 626.

24. Schlick, "Critical or Empiricist Interpretation," 332.

25. Cassirer, review of *An Introduction to the Philosophy of Science* by A. Cornelius Benjamin, *Lychnos*, Annual of the Swedish History of Science Society (1938): 460.

26. Review of Benjamin's *Introduction*, 458.

27. "Formen und Formwandlungen des philosophischen Wahrheitsbegriffs," 20–21.

28. On science as a symbolic form, see *EM*, 207–21.

29. AH, 119. One of Cassirer's unpublished manuscripts (Ms 119, an untitled discussion of the *Darstellungsfunktion*) contains an analysis of basic doctrines of the Vienna Circle, including physicalism and the criterion of "meaning" and "meaningless" as used in the Circle's criticisms of metaphysics. Physicalism continues to have adherents. Quine appeals to the physicalist conception of the unity of the world in his criticisms of Goodman's theory of worldmaking, declaring that "nothing happens in the world, not the flutter of an eyelid, not the flicker of a thought, without some redistribution of microphysical states." See Willard van Orman Quine, "Otherworldly," review of *Ways of Worldmaking* by Nelson Goodman, *New York Review of Books*, November 23, 1978, 25.

30. Dilthey's *Aufbau* first appeared in the *Abhandlungen der preussischen Akademie der Wissenschaften*, Philosophisch-Historische Klasse, Jahrgang 1910: 1–123. Cassirer does not mention Dilthey in his essay.

31. For a discussion of the different schools of thought behind these designations, see Rudolf A. Makkreel, "Wilhelm Dilthey and the Neo-Kantians: The Distinction between the *Geisteswissenschaften* and the *Kulturwissenschaften*," *Journal of the History of Philosophy* 7 (1969): 423–40. I cannot agree, however, with Makkreel's view that Cassirer's inclusion of the *Kulturwissenschaften* and the *Naturwissenschaften* in the framework of his philosophy of symbolic forms attributes any greater continuity to them than does Dilthey.

Cassirer uses *Geisteswissenschaften* and *Kulturwissenschaften* as equivalent terms (see KW, 23). Cassirer's study of Axel Hägerström (1939) includes a chapter entitled "Zur 'Logik der Geisteswissenschaften'" (AH, 109–19). Even in his very late essay "Structuralism in Modern Linguistics" (1946) Cassirer prefers to contrast natural sciences to Geisteswissenschaften, and he offers a clear explication of his understanding of the term, an understanding he traces to Dilthey. Except when there is reason to distinguish between the terms *Kulturwissenschaften* and *Geisteswissenschaft*, I use the translation "human studies" to stand for both.

32. The "Erklären / Verstehen" (explanation / understanding) distinction is attributed to the German historian Johann Gustav Droysens (1808–84) who made use of it as early as 1843. Dilthey makes it the basis for the distinction between the natural sciences and human studies in his *Einleitung in die Geisteswissenschaften* (1883), first published in 1922 as volume 1 of the *Gesammelte Schriften*, ed. Bernard Groethuysen, 4th ed. (Stuttgart: B.G. Teuber and Göttingen: Vandenhoeck & Ruprecht, 1959).

33. *LH*, 165–66. Cf. "Structuralism in Modern Linguistics," 101.

34. In a discussion of changes in linguistic theory in relation to similar changes in theoretical physics and biology Cassirer says: "The former positivism was superseded by a new principle which we may call structuralism" (*EM*, 121).

35. Wilhelm Windelband, *Präludien: Aufsätze und Reden zur Philosophie und ihrer Geschichte*, 2 vols. (Tübingen: J.C.B. Mohr [Paul Siebeck], 1921), 2:145–49.

36. These two conceptions of culture are examined in Cassirer's systematic essay, "Naturalistische und humanistische Begründung der Kulturphilosophie, first published in *Göteborgs Kungl. Vetenskaps- och Vitterhets-Samhälles Handlingar*, 5e följden, ser. A, vol. 7, no. 3 (1939): 1–28. A translation of this essay was added as an introduction to the English translation of *Zur Logik der Kulturwissenschaften* (*LH*, 3–38).

37. In an article defending Heidegger's method of interpreting Kant in *Kant und das Problem der Metaphysik*, Edwin Alexander claims that Cassirer's ultimate criterion for interpreting a philosophical work is "author intention"; see "Hermeneutical Violence," *Philosophy Today* 25 (1981): 286–306. Alexander justifies his claim by citing the following translation of Cassirer's review of Heidegger's book: "Only the subject [*die Sache*] itself should speak. And one cannot do justice to an author in a better way than to seek to hear only the voice of the subject [*ihre Stimme*]. It would be a false and bad subjectivity that would not inspire us to such an objectivity and pledge us to it" (Alexander, 287). Alexander quotes this passage from the translation of Cassirer's article "Kant and the Problem of Metaphysics: Remarks on Martin Heidegger's Interpretation of Kant" in *Kant: Disputed Questions*, edited with translations by Molte S. Gram (Chicago: Quadrangle Books, 1967), 157. For the original passage, see "Kant und das Problem der Metaphysik: Bemerkungen zu Martin Heideggers Kant-interpretation," *Kant-Studien* 36 (1931): 25. By relying exclusively on the translation, Alexander misses completely the sense of Cassirer's comments. I have interpolated the original German above to show the source of confusion. By rendering "die Sache" (subject matter, topic of concern) as "the subject," the translator creates an ambiguity that can give the impression that Cassirer is speaking about the author of a text when this is not his meaning at all. In German, it is impossible to read *die Sache* as "the author," but the ambiguity of the English word *subject* makes this reading possible. This misleading translation recurs in the next sentence where "ihre Stimme" (its voice, that is, the voice of the *Sache* or subject matter) becomes "the voice of the subject." Cassirer here contrasts *Sachlichkeit* in interpretation with an orientation to the "bad subjectivity" of personal intention, the very opposite of what Alexander claims.

38. On Cassirer's agreement with the fruitfulness of new interpretations of Kant, see "Kant and the Problem of Metaphysics," 135. On his agreement with Heidegger's view of the productive imagination, see p. 139. He explains his rejection of Heidegger's reading on pp. 147–49.

39. On art, see *EM*, 137–70; *SMC*, 145–215. See also A. L. Boboc, "Ernst Cassirer und die semiotische Ästhetik," *Revue Roumaine des Sciences* 17 (1973): 157–61.

40. Cassirer, "The Problem of the Symbol," 423.

41. *PRE*, 184–86. On optimism, see below, chapter 5.

42. Cassirer, "Thomas Manns Goethe-bild" (1945), 190.

43. "The Problem of the Symbol," 427.

44. Paul Feyerabend, "Dialogue on Method," in Gerard Radnitsky and Gunnar Andersson, ed., *The Structure and Development of Science*, Boston Studies in the Philosophy of Science, vol. 59 (Dordrecht: D. Reidel, 1979), 72–79.

45. "Die Astrologie ist, reinformal gefaßt, einer der großartigsten Versuche systematisch-konstruktiver Weltbetrachtung, der je vom menschlichen Geiste gewagt wurde" (*WW*, 35).

46. Paul Feyerabend, *Against Method: Outline of an Anarchistic Theory of Knowledge* (London: New Left Books, 1975), 297.

47. Robin Horton, "African Traditional Thought and Western Science," *Africa* 3 (1967): part 1, 50–71; part 2, 155–87.

48. Horton, "African Traditional Thought and Western Science," 53.

49. Willard van Orman Quine, "Two Dogmas of Empiricism," in *From a Logical Point of View: 9 Logico-Philosophical Essays*, 2d ed. (New York: Harper & Row, Harper Torchbooks, 1961), 45.

50. See *SMC*, 188 on Hölderlin and Schiller.

51. Goodman, *Ways of Worldmaking*, (Indianapolis: Hackett Publishing Co., 1979), 6.

52. Cassirer, "Formen und Formwandlungen des philosophischen Wahrheitsbegriffs" (1929), 20.

53. "Formen und Formwandlungen des philosophischen," 22; cf. *EM*, 228.

54. "Erkenntnistheorie nebst den Grenzfragen der Logik und Denkpsychologie," 34.

CHAPTER IV. MORALITY AND LAW

1. Cassirer develops his theory of social morality and law in "Axel Hägerström." He indicates that he is merely working out an aspect of the philosophy of symbolic forms that he had conceived of many years before, and he refers the reader to his 1925 study *Language and Myth* (AH, 85n; cf. *LM*, 44). The earlier passage reads: "Theoretical, practical and aesthetic consciousness, the world of language [and of knowledge (*der Erkenntnis*), of art (*Kunst*), of law (*Recht*)] and of morality, the basic forms of the community and the state—they are all originally tied up with mythico-religious conceptions" (*LM*, 44; *WW*, 112). Langer's translation omits the portion in brackets.

2. W. D. Ross, *Foundation of Ethics* (Oxford: Oxford University Press, 1939), 1.

3. A. C. Ewing, *Ethics* (1953; reprint, New York: Free Press, 1965), 9.

4. Ewing says, "It is not the history of the development of ethical ideas that we are discussing but their validity which may be quite independent of the authority on which we accepted them" (*Ethics*, 154).

5. John Rawls, *A Theory of Justice* (Oxford: Oxford University Press, 1972), 11.

6. See Cassirer, "Logos, Dike, Kosmos in der Entwicklung der griechischen Philosophie," *Göteborgs Högskolas Arsskrift* 47, no. 6 (1941): 14–23.

7. "Indem der Mensch sich gegen die mythischen Mächte auflehnte, hat er damit nicht nur sich selbst gewonnen, sondern er hat auch das Bild des Göttlichen in seiner Seele gerettet. . . . In dem Augenblick, wo der Mensch ein anderer geworden ist, muss auch die Vorstellung des Göttlichen sich wandeln und zu einer reinen Gestalt geläutert werden." Ibid., 16–17.

8. Clytaemnestra says:

Can you claim I have done this?
Speak of me never
more as the wife of Agamemnon.
In the shadow of this corpse's queen
the old stark avenger
of Atreus for his revel of hate
struck down this man,
last blood for the slaughtered children.

Aeschylus, *Oresteia: Agamemnon*, trans. Richmond Lattimore (Chicago: University of Chicago Press, 1953), lines 1497–1504.

9. "Logos, Dike, Kosmos," 17–23.

10. "Logos, Dike, Kosmos," 18; cf. *MS*, 75.

11. Cassirer, "Wesen und Werden des Naturrechts" (1932), 8. See also *MS*, 172. Cf. Hugo Grotius, *The Law of War and Peace*, trans. Francis W. Kelsey (Indianapolis: Bobbs-Merrill, 1925), 13. Grotius argues that the validity of natural law holds "even if we should concede that which cannot be conceded without the utmost wickedness, that there is no God, or that the affairs of men are of no concern to him."

12. "Wesen und Werden des Naturrechts," 5; cf. *LS*, 450–51.

13. Cassirer refers to Plotinus, *Enneads* III, sec. 4. Cassirer makes the same claim about Heidegger's notions of *Geworfenheit* (thrownness) and *Geschick* (destiny). See *MS*, 293; and " 'Mind' and 'Life': Heidegger," *Philosophy and Rhetoric* 16 (1983): 162–63.

14. Leo Strauss, review of *The Myth of the State* by Ernst Cassirer, *Social Research* 14 (1947): 127–28.

15. Hägerström wrote an early work on Kant, *Kants Ethik im Verhältnis zu seinen erkenntnistheoretischen Grundgedanken* (Uppsala: Almqvist & Wiksells; Leipzig: O. Harrassowitz, 1902), in which he interpreted Kant's position as a subjective idealism. Cassirer discusses this work only briefly, since it antedates Hägerström's own systematic emotivist position. See *AH*, 32–35.

16. Cassirer points out that Hägerström is rationalistic, not a positivist, in the theory of knowledge, whereas in his ethics he can be regarded as a perfector and no mere precursor of the positivistic theory of values (*AH*, 13). Hägerström first presents his theory of value in his inaugural lecture *Om moraliska föreställningars sanning* (On the truth of moral ideas; Stockholm: A. Bonnier, 1911).

17. Jes Bjarup, *Skandinavischer Realismus: Hägerström–Lundstedt–Olivecrona–Ross* (Freiburg and Munich: Verlag Karl Alber, 1978), 10.

18. AH, 64, 74; cf. "Wesen und Werden des Naturrechts," 2–5.

19. "Wesen und Werden des Naturrechts," 3–5.

20. Cassirer followed Cohen in developing ethics as the philosophy of law—in direct opposition to Kant, who kept the moral and the legal spheres apart. Cohen says, "Die Ethik muss selbst als Rechtsphilosophie sich durchführen" (Ethics must develop itself as the philosophy of law). Hermann Cohen, *Ethik des reinen Willens*, 5th ed., vol. 7 of *Werke* (Hildesheim: Georg Olms, 1981), 225. The notion of the unity of will as the "infinite task" of striving for a universal ethics takes up another of Cohen's basic tenets. Cassirer diverges from Cohen less in point of content than in method. Cohen begins with the Faktum der Rechtswissenschaft (fact of legal science) whereas Cassirer begins with Rechtserfahrung (the experience of law). The latter encompasses a far greater historical field, going back to the mythic origins of social organization. Cassirer also pays close attention to the role of language in this development, a theme only touched upon by Cohen. Finally, Cassirer's ethics was developed in the direction of a theory of human rights, Cohen's as a theory of virtues.

21. See Immanuel Kant, *Groundwork of the Metaphysic of Morals*, trans. H. J. Paton (New York: Harper & Row, Harper Torchbooks, 1964), 88.

22. See "Die Sprache und der Aufbau der Gegenstandswelt," STS, 124 and *KW*, 127. The latter is translated as "act of speech" in *LH*, 216.

23. "Wesen und Werden des Naturrechts," 22–23.

24. The doctrine of the *Volksgeist* as the origin of law was first presented in Friedrich Carl von Savigny, *Vom Beruf unserer Zeit für Gesetzgebung und Rechtswissenschaft* (1814; 2d ed. 1828; reprint [from the Heidelberg 1840 edition], Hildesheim: Georg Olms, 1967), chap. 2. See *MS*, 182.

25. See G. W. F. Hegel, *Natural Law: The Scientific Ways of Treating Natural Law, Its Place in Moral Philosophy, and Its Relation to the Positive Sciences of Law*, trans. T. M. Knox (Philadelphia: University of Pennsylvania Press, 1975), 101–03; and Hegel, *Philosophy of Right*, trans. T. M. Knox (London: Oxford University Press, 1952), 155–60.

26. See esp. Karl Marx and Friedrich Engels, *Werke* (Berlin: Dietz, 1956), 1:363–66. Cassirer agrees with Hägerström's claim that there is a "social teleology" in Marxian philosophy that is more fundamental than the doctrine of economic determination on which it supposedly rests (AH, 73–75).

27. See *FF*, 357–68; *LH*, 30, 37–38; *SMC*, 108–20, 225–26, 227; *MS*, 248–76; "Albert Schweitzer as Critic of Nineteenth-Century Ethics," in A. A. Roback, ed., *The Albert Schweitzer Jubilee Book* (Cambridge, Mass.: Sci-Art Publishers, 1946), 241–57, esp. 248–57.

28. Hegel, *Natural Law*, 32.

29. "Wesen und Werden des Naturrechts," 27. Cassirer gives the example of the outcry against the handling of the Dreyfus case as an instance of how public conscience goes beyond written law. Dreyfus, a French officer, was accused of selling military secrets to the Germans. Questions were not admitted at Dreyfus's original trial for treason, but after his conviction and sentencing the protests against these irregularities led to a retrial and, eventually, to Dreyfus's acquittal. The Dreyfus affair gained much of its emotional burden from the fact that the accused was a Jew.

30. "Wesen und Werden des Naturrechts," 27.

31. See *The New Science of Giambattista Vico*, 3d ed., trans. Thomas Goddard Bergin and Max Harold Fisch (Ithaca: Cornell University Press, 1968), esp. paragraphs 394–98 and 922–24.

32. Axel Hägerström, *Inquiries into the Nature of Law and Morals*, ed. Karl Olivecrona and trans. C. D. Broad (Stockholm: Almquist & Wiksell, 1953), 55.

33. AH, 108; on Schopenhauer, see MS, 31–32.

34. For a discussion of this situation and its significance, see Kurt Sontheimer, *Anti-Demokratisches Denken in der Weimarer Republik: Die politischen Ideen des deutschen Nationalismus zwischen 1918 und 1933* (1968; reprint, Munich: Deutscher Taschenbuch Verlag, 1978), esp. chap. 4.

35. See the discussion in Cornelius F. Murphey, Jr., *Modern Legal Philosophy: The Tension between Experiential and Abstract Thought* (Pittsburgh: Duquesne University Press, 1978), chap. 2.

36. See Cassirer's discussion of Hägerström's exclusively psychological and sociological view of the unity of law (AH, 95–96).

37. Hans Kelsen, *The Pure Theory of Law*, 2d ed., trans. Max Knight (Berkeley and Los Angeles: University of California Press, 1967), 204. This claim is limited, since Kelsen did not follow the basic direction of Cohen's ethics—to show how ethics and law form a unity. Pure for Cohen means "transcendental"; Kelsen is not a transcendental thinker. For Cohen, the source of ethical norms is the "pure will"; Kelsen is an emotivist.

38. Kelsen, *Hauptprobleme der Staatsrechtslehre*, 2d ed. (1923; reprint, Aalen: Scientia Verlag, 1960), xvii.

39. Kelsen, *Der soziologische und der juristische Staatsbegriff*, 2d ed. (1928; reprint, Aalen: Scientia Verlag, 1962), 212–13. Cf. SF/ET, 210–11.

40. Siegfried Marck, *Substanzbegriff und Funktionsbegriff in der Rechtsphilosophie* (Tübingen: J. C. B. Mohr [Paul Siebeck], 1925), 3.

41. See Sontheimer, *Anti-Demokratisches Denken*, 75.

42. Cassirer argues against this view, claiming that the idea of "inalienable human rights" was first upheld by Leibniz and that this idea subsequently was developed in England and France; see *Die Idee der Republikanischen Verfassung*, Rede zur Verfassungsfeier am 11. August 1928 (Hamburg: Friederich, De Gruyter & Co., 1929), 13.

43. *Die Idee der Republikanischen Verfassung*, 19–24.

44. *Inter-Nationes: Zeitschrift für die kulturellen Beziehungen Deutschlands zum Ausland* 1 (1931): 57–59 and 83–85.

45. Peter Gay, *Weimar Culture: The Outsider as Insider* (New York: Harper & Row, Harper Torchbooks, 1970), 72.

46. According to David Lipton, Cassirer gave his support during the Weimar Republic to the liberal Deutsche Demokratische Partie; *Ernst Cassirer: The Dilemma of a Liberal Intellectual in Germany, 1914–1933* (Toronto: University of Toronto Press, 1978), 146.

47. "Wesen und Werden des Naturrechts," 21.

48. Ibid., 17. Kelsen was repeatedly criticized on the grounds that his doctrine permitted no other conception of the state's legitimacy but its power. See Sontheimer, *Anti-Demokratisches Denken*, 68. Cf. the discussion of this failure of Kelsen's theory in contrast to the Cohenian position in Steven Schwarzschild's introduction to Cohen's *Ethik des reinen Willens* in the new Olms edition of Cohen's *Werke*, 7:ix-xviii. Cassirer's concentration on the human rights doctrine of natural law distinguished his position radically from Kelsen's. Lipton's apparent association of Cassirer with Kelsen on the grounds of what Lipton calls Cassirer's "commitment to neo-Kantianism" (Lipton, *Ernst Cassirer*, 13–14) has an a priori rather than a historical justification. Lipton says: "Cassirer's neglect of ethics was not accidental. As a Kantian possessing an abstract and formalistic view of law and politics, he felt it was not within his competence to prescribe in concrete terms what was right and wrong for other people; he could only suggest the formal rules circumscribing all human activities" (ibid., 147). Here a position is attributed to Cassirer on the grounds that "as a Kantian" he naturally held such a view. In reality, Cassirer's position was not empty and formalistic like Kelsen's, but a theory of human rights.

49. "Wesen und Werden des Naturrechts," 10.

50. Heidegger, *Being and Time*, 410–11; cf. Cassirer, " 'Mind' and 'Life': Heidegger," 162–63.

51. William Stern, "Zur Wiederkehr seines Todestages," *Acta Psychologia* 5 (1940): 9. Cassirer agrees with Stern in opposing both a positivistic behaviorism and pure mentalism as a psychological method of research.

52. Cassirer employs this personalistic perspective in two of his historical works, *Kant's Life and Thought* and *Descartes: Lehre–Persönlichkeit–Wirkung*.

53. Kant, *Groundwork of the Metaphysic of Morals*, trans. H. J. Paton (New York: Harper & Row, Harper Torchbooks, 1964), 96.

54. For an example of this argument, see Adda B. Bozeman, "Human Rights in Western Thought," in Kenneth W. Thompson, ed., *The Moral Imperatives of Human Rights* (Washington, D.C.: University Press of America, 1980), 25–38. Bozeman bases the argument against universal human rights on differences between languages.

55. SMC, 266. From *Faust, Goethes Werke* sect. 1, 14:27, lines 372–73. The translation is from *Goethe's Faust*, trans. Walter Kaufmann (New York: Doubleday and Co., Anchor Books, 1963), 95.

56. SMC, 60, 232. Cf. "Albert Schweitzer as Critic of Nineteenth-Century Ethics" (1946), 250ff.

57. "Albert Schweitzer," 255.

58. Cassirer singles out Spengler and Heidegger; see SMC, 226–30, and cf. MS, 289–93.

59. "Albert Schweitzer," 255.

CHAPTER V. HISTORY

1. There is at present no literature on Cassirer's interpretation of history. Nathan Rotenstreich treats of historiography and even criticizes Cassirer for sometimes conceiving history materially rather than as a symbolic form. Rotenstreich appears to think that Cassirer's philosophy must be limited to epistemological concerns. See "Cassirer's Philosophy of Symbolic Forms and the Problem of History," *Theoria* 18 (1952): 155–63.

2. EM, 222–23. The passage from Heraclitus is fragment number 51 in Diels's *Die Fragmente der Vorsokratiker*; see also fragment 54. Cassirer cites an English translation by Charles M. Bakewell.

3. G. S. Kirk, ed., *Heraclitus: The Cosmic Fragments* (Cambridge: Cambridge University Press, 1954), 208; cf. 216.

4. Philip Wheelwright, *Heraclitus* (Princeton: Princeton University Press, 1959), 108.

5. Martin Heidegger and Eugen Fink, *Heraklit: Seminar Wintersemester 1966/67* (Frankfurt am Main: Vittorio Klostermann, 1970), 256.

6. Charles H. Kahn, *The Art and Thought of Heraclitus* (Cambridge: Cambridge University Press, 1979), 198.

7. Karl Kerényi, *Die Mythologie der Griechen*, vol. 1, *Die Götter- und Menschheitsgeschichten* (Munich: Deutscher Taschenbuch Verlag, 1979), 118.

8. Hesiod, *The Homeric Hymns and Homerica*, trans. Hugh G. Evelyn-White (Cambridge, Mass. and London: Harvard University Press and William Heinemann, 1936), 333.

9. Cassirer discussed this fragment early in his career in his contribution to Max Dessoir's *Lehrbuch der Philosophie*, vol. 1, *Die Geschichte der Philosophie* (Berlin: Ullstein, 1925), 23–25. Here the tension of opposites seems to be conceived mainly in terms of nature. He speaks of "Gesetz und Maß" (law and measure) as the way to conceive the *Lösung* (solution) of these tensions. In the *Essay on Man* Cassirer has culture, not nature, in mind. I do not think that Cassirer's solution to the tensions in culture is a rational "law or measure."

10. Cassirer's view is summarized in the chapters "From Animal Reactions to Human Responses" and "A Clue to the Nature of Man: The Symbol" in *An Essay on Man.*

11. For a concise discussion of this idea, see R. V. Sampson, *Progress in the Age of Reason* (London: William Heinemann, 1956), chapter 2.

12. *Kant's Werke*, Prussian Academy edition "Der Streit der Fakultäten," vol. 7 (Berlin: Georg Reimer, 1917), 85.

13. Cassirer felt an almost personal attachment to Goethe. See the comments in Toni Cassirer, *Mein Leben*, 86–88.

14. See Hans-Wilhelm Kelling, *The Idolatry of Poetic Genius in German Goethe Criticism*, European University Papers, series 1, vol. 27 (Berne: Herbert Lang, 1970).

15. Hegel called *Faust* "the absolute philosophical tragedy" because it dealt with the reconciliation of the finite subject and the quest for absolute knowledge. G. W. F. Hegel, *Sämtliche Werke, Jubiläumsausgabe*, vol. 14, *Vorlesungen über die Aesthetik* (Stuttgart: Fr. Frommanns Verlag, 1954), 564.

16. Ms 204, "Der junge Goethe," 8. This typescript, consisting of ninety-three numbered pages, is dated "Göteborg, 2. Oktober 1940."

17. The remarks by Goethe that Cassirer quotes can be found in Johann Peter Eckermann, *Gespräche mit Goethe* (Wiesbaden: F.A. Brockhaus, 1975), p. 555 (March 1830) and p. 386 (March 1832). On the idea of "world literature" and its significance for Goethe's theory of the development of culture, see Hans Joachim Schrimpf, *Goethes Begriff der Weltliteratur*, Dichtung und Erkenntnis 5 (Stuttgart: J.B. Metzlersche Verlagsbuchhandlung, 1968), esp. 9–14 where Schrimpf discusses the "Freihandel der Begriffe und Gefühle," the free exchange of concepts and feelings.

18. Bruno Bauch (1877–1942), a student of Rickert's, was a professor in Jena when his article "Vom Begriff der Nation" appeared in the *Kant-Studien* 21 (1917): 139–62. He defined a nation as a "natural community of birth"

(*Natürliche Abstammungsgemeinschaft*) that acquires a common culture through a common history (p. 157). The implications of Bauch's view are stated in his lengthy letter published in *Der Panther*, a nationalistic journal of politics. There, Bauch developed a "völkisch" view of German culture, according to which Jews were not Germans. Cassirer was especially repelled by Bauch's claim that on these grounds Cohen could not fully understand Kant. See Bauch's letter in *Der Panther: Deutsche Monatsschrift für Politik und Volkstum*, 4. Jahrgang, Heft 6 (June 1916): 742–46. Cassirer's lengthy rebuttal, "Zum Begriff der Nation: Eine Erwiderung auf den Aufsatz von Bruno Bauch," was never published; Ms 113, typescript, 31 pages. The liberation of the Rhineland occurred in January 1930. At the end of the summer semester 1930 Cassirer celebrated the liberation with an address entitled "Wandlungen der Staatsgesinnung und der Staatstheorie in der Deutschen Geistesgeschichte" (Transformations in attitudes toward the state and theories of the state in the German history of ideas); Ms 97.

19. "Goethes Idee der Bildung und Erziehung," *Pädagogisches Zentralblatt* 12 (1932): 351.

20. See *IG*, 28; cf. "Goethes Idee der Bildung und Erziehung," 350, 353. I am indebted to Hans Joachim Schrimpf for suggesting this translation of *Entsagung*.

21. *Goethes Werke* sect. 1 (Weimar: Herman Böhlau Nachfolger, 1903), 41/2:377, line 16.

22. *Goethes Werke* sect. 1, *Dichtung und Wahrheit* (Weimar: Herman Böhlau Nachfolger, 1891), 29:10.

23. Cassirer discussed self-liberation from Angst in his debate with Heidegger; "Davoser Disputation," in Heidegger, *Kant und das Problem der Metaphysik*, 4th ed. (Frankfurt am Main: Vittorio Klostermann, 1973), 259. Philosophy can liberate man only to the extent that he can be liberated; it cannot eliminate death, but it can free man from the fear of death. Cassirer had also discussed Heidegger's views on death in lectures prior to the debate. In his lecture notes he says that for Heidegger "dem Tode gegenuber gibt es keine *Gemeinschaft* und keine *Allgemeinheit*—hier ist das individuelle Selbst auf sich allein zurückgeworfen" (faced with death there is no community and no generality—here the individual self is thrown back upon itself *alone*), Beinecke Ms 94, p. 16. The philosophical reasons for Heidegger's view and the reasons why Cassirer disagrees with them are the subject of another discussion, written for the planned fourth volume of the *PSF*; see " 'Mind' and 'Life': Heidegger." There and in the debate Cassirer quotes from Schiller's poem "Das Ideal und das Leben" (see *Schiller's Werke, Nationalausgabe*, vol. 2, part 1, *Gedichte* [Weimar: Herman Böhlau Nachfolger, 1983], esp. 397). This poem's call to "throw off the fear of the earthly" expresses a sensibility like that discussed in Cassirer's *Descartes* (see below). Erwin Panofsky's contribution to the Cassirer festschrift, *Philosophy and History*, "Et in Arcadia Ego: On the Conception of Transcience in Poussin and Watteau," is about the misinterpretation of the iconography of death in these painters and other seventeenth- and eighteenth-century artists. Panofsky shows that for these artists "Et in Arcadia Ego" expressed the omnipresence of death—even in Arcadia there was death—and a serene resignation toward it. He also examines how the notion of the Arcadian gradually changed, finally becoming the idea of "having a good time"; *Philosophy and History*, ed. Raymond Klibansky and H. J. Paton (1936; rev. ed., New York: Harper & Row, Harper

Torchbooks, 1963), 223. There are no doubt connections between Panofsky's analysis and Cassirer's conception of the "heroic will of the seventeenth century" (see below). The differences between Cassirer's and Heidegger's views of death, themselves irreconcilable, could also be illuminated by a philosophical-historical study of changes in the conceptions of death.

24. *Faust, Zweiter Teil, Goethes Werke,* sect. 1 (Weimar: Herman Böhlau Nachfolger, 1888), 15/1:317, lines 11599–603.

25. "An Essay on Man," *The Poems of Alexander Pope,* ed. John Butt (New Haven: Yale University Press, 1963), 515.

26. W. H. Auden, "The Age of Anxiety," *Collected Longer Poems* (London: Faber and Faber, 1968), 255–56.

27. Edward Alexander Parsons, *The Alexandrian Library* (London: Cleaver-Hume Press, 1952), 386n.

28. Paul Natorp, *Philosophie: Ihr Problem und ihre Probleme,* 4th ed. Wege zur Philosophie, Ergänzungsreihe: Einführung in die Philosophie der Gegenwart, no. 1 (Göttingen: Vandenhoeck & Ruprecht, 1929), 14, 26. Cf. above, chap. 2, note 3.

29. "Thomas Manns Goethe-bild" (1945), 190–91. The bow and the lyre are also important symbols for Thomas Mann; he chose them as the emblem stamped in gold, along with his initials, for the cover of his works published by Fischer in the "Stockholmer Ausgabe." On Mann's use of this emblem, see Georg Potempa, *Bogen und Leier: Eine Symbolfigur bei Thomas Mann* (Oldenburg: Buchhandlung G. Holzberg, 1968).

30. H. and H. A. Frankfort, John A. Wilson, and Thorkild Jacobsen, *Before Philosophy: The Intellectual Adventure of Ancient Man* (1946; reprint, Baltimore: Penguin Books, 1972), 240–41.

31. See Alexander Heidel, *The Babylonian Genesis,* 2d ed. (1951; reprint, Chicago: University of Chicago Press, Phoenix Books, 1963), 42.

32. See E. A. Wallis Budge, *Babylonian Life and History,* 2d ed. (1925; reprint, New York: Cooper Square Publishers, 1975), preface.

33. See Raffaele Pettazzoni, "Der Babylonische Ritus des Akitu," *Eranos Jahrbuch* 19 (1950): 403–30, esp. 408.

34. H. Frankfort, et al., *Before Philosophy,* 240.

35. "The current amazement that the things we are experiencing are 'still' possible in the twentieth century is *not* philosophical. This amazement is not the beginning of knowledge—unless it is the knowledge that the view of history which gives rise to it is untenable." "Theses on the Philosophy of History," VIII. In Walter Benjamin, *Illuminations,* ed. Hannah Arendt, trans. Harry Zohn (New York: Schocken Books, 1969), 257.

36. Christoph Martin Wieland, as cited by Peter Gay, *The Enlightenment: An Interpretation,* vol. 2, *The Science of Freedom* (New York: W. W. Norton, 1977), 107–08.

37. Albert Speer, *Inside the Third Reich,* trans. Richard and Clara Winston (1970; reprint, New York: Avon Books, 1973), 85–86.

38. This important claim goes unmentioned in the following major reviews of *The Myth of the State:* Thomas I. Cook, *The American Political Science Review* 41 (1947): 331–33; Charles N. R. McCoy, *The Modern Schoolman* 25 (May 1948): 271–78; Hans J. Morgenthau, *Ethics* 57 (January 1947): 141–42; George H. Sabine, *The Philosophical Review* 56 (1947): 315–18; Leo Strauss, *Social Research* 14 (1947): 125–28.

39. A conference on *The Myth of the State* held at Abo in Sweden, Septem-

ber 6–8, 1971, took its name from Cassirer's book but was directed to historical aspects of ancient political myth. The papers were published as *The Myth of the State*, ed. Haralds Biezais (Stockholm: Almqvist & Wiksell, 1972). As far as I can determine, the only attempt to apply Cassirer's idea to present-day political life is a brief but insightful discussion by Michael J. Arlen, "The Air: The Governor's Brief Brush with Logic," *The New Yorker*, March 31, 1980, 112–14.

40. Despite the quite different style of argument, Cassirer's *Die Idee der Republikanischen Verfassung* has the same general intent as Mann's famous 1922 address "Von Deutscher Republik," *Reden und Aufsätze* 2 (Frankfurt: S. Fischer Verlag, 1965), 11–52.

41. " . . . bürgerliche Glucksansprüche wie Freiheit, Geistigkeit, Kultur" (p. 81). Mann, "Deutsche Ansprache: Ein Appell an die Vernunft," *Reden und Aufsätze* 2, 61–81. This address was given in 1930 in reaction to the enormous success of the National Socialist party in the September 14 election, which increased their seats in the Reichstag from 12 to 107. Mann, like Cassirer, was convinced that despite the economic conditions these election results "cannot be explained simply by economics" (p. 65).

42. Kurt Sontheimer shows the various sources and strands of thought that entered into the ideology of National Socialism in his *Anti-Demokratisches Denken in der Weimarer Republik* (1968; reprint, Munich: Deutscher Taschenbuch Verlag, 1978). See esp. chap. 6 and the summary on pp. 140–41.

43. On the differences between original and manufactured myth, see Karl Kerényi, "Wesen und Gegenwärtigkeit des Mythos 1964," *Die Eröffnung des Zugangs zum Mythos*, ed. Karl Kerényi, Wege der Forschung 20 (Darmstadt: Wissenschaftliche Buchgesellschaft, 1976), 235–39.

44. Cassirer once remarked that radio could be used to sell soap or the master race, cleaning powder or hatred of the Jews; Toni Cassirer, *Mein Leben*, 311–12.

45. A good pictorial report on the National Socialists' use of ritualization is Frank Grube and Gerhard Richter, *Alltag im Dritten Reich* (Hamburg: Hoffman und Campe, 1982).

46. An interesting documentation of this aspect of National Socialist ideology is found in Ernst Loewy, *Literatur unterm Hakenkreuz; Das Dritte Reich und seine Dichtung: Eine Dokumentation* (Frankfurt am Main: Fischer Bücherei, 1969), esp. "Die 'höhere Ordnung,' " 69–83. Hannah Arendt discusses this aspect of the technique of myth in *The Origins of Totalitarianism*, 2d ed. (1958; reprint, New York: Meridian Books, 1972), 348–51, 461–63. The idea of a "law of history" is, of course, the object of Karl Popper's critique of historicism.

47. George H. Sabine, review of *The Myth of the State* by Ernst Cassirer, *The Philosophical Review* 56 (1947): 317.

48. See Hermann Cohen's discussion of this problem in *Ethik des reinen Willens*, vol. 7 of Werke (Hildesheim: Georg Olms, 1981), 295 and 311.

49. "Auch die Technik stellt sich in ihrer Entfaltung nicht einfach neben die anderen Grundrichtungen des Geistes, noch ordnet sie sich ihnen friedlich und harmonisch ein. Indem sie sich von ihnen unterscheidet, scheidet sie sich zugleich von ihnen ab und stellt sich ihnen entgegen. Sie beharrt nicht nur auf ihrer eigenen Norm, sondern sie droht diese Norm absolut zu setzen und sie den anderen Gebieten aufzuzwingen" (*STS*, 78; cf. 39).

50. Siegfried Giedion, *Mechanization Takes Command: A Contribution to Anonymous History* (1948; reprint, New York: W.W. Norton, 1969), 41.

51. A detailed documentation of this genre is found in a history of the theater in the Weimar Republic: *Weimarer Republik*, herausgegeben vom Kunstamt Kreuzberg, Berlin, und dem Institut für Theaterwissenschaft der Universität Köln (Berlin and Hamburg: Elefanten Press, 1977), 763–822.

52. *Der Ozeanflug* (1929), in Bertolt Brecht, *Gesammelte Werke* (Frankfurt am Main: Suhrkamp, 1967), 2:565–85. *Der Ozeanflug* was first titled *Der Flug der Lindberghs*. See Brecht, *Versuche 1* (Berlin: Kiepenheuer Verlag, 1930), 1–18. This edition includes Brecht's comments on the importance of the use of radio as a pedagogical means.

53. The term *neue Sachlichkeit* has the senses of "new functionality," "new objectivity," and "new sobriety." See John Willett, *Art and Politics in the Weimar Period: The New Sobriety, 1917–1933* (New York: Pantheon Books, 1978), 111.

54. In the 1928 Schiffer-Spoliansky revue *Es Liegt in der Luft*, the title song begins:

There's something in the air called objectivity,
there's something in the air like electricity. . . .
What has come over the air these days?
Oh, the air has fallen for a brand-new craze.
Through the air are swiftly blown
Pictures, radio, telephone.
Through the air the whole lot flies,
till the air simply can't believe its eyes.
Planes and airships, think of that!
There's the air, just hear it humming!

Quoted from Willet, ibid. Fritz Lang's *Metropolis* is perhaps the most famous film based on the idea of a technological future. Siegfried Kracauer describes the theme of "inexorable fate" in German films during the 1920s in *From Calagari to Hitler: A Psychological History of the German Film* (Princeton: Princeton University Press, 1947), chap. 7.

55. Leo Kestenberg, ed., *Kunst und Technik*, Berlin: Wegweiser Verlag, 1930), 141–56. Leo Kestenberg was at the time the head of the Kroll Opera in Berlin and a member of the Prussian Cultural Ministry. His friendship with the Cassirer family is evident as early as 1916, when he was the editor of the journal *Der Bildermann*, published by the Paul Cassirer Verlag.

56. Toni Cassirer, *Mein Leben*, 177.

57. Numerous nonacademic books were also published on Technik in the 1920s. Titles like *Schönheit der Technik* (Beauty of technology), *Bildungswerte der Technik* (Educational value of technology), and *Friede mit der Technik* (Peace with technology)—all published in 1928—reflect the mixture of enthusiasm and concern elicited by the rapid development of technological society. See Jost Hermand and Frank Trommler, *Die Kultur der Weimarer Republik* (Munich: Nymphenburger Verlagshandlung, 1978), 58–69. An important personage deeply concerned with the significance of the rapid development of technology was the industrialist and statesman Walther Rathenau. Cassirer agreed with Rathenau's assessment and cites his work in "Form und Technik," STS, 87–88.

58. Georg Simmel, "On the Concept and the Tragedy of Culture," in *The Conflict in Modern Culture and Other Essays*, translated with an introduction by K. Peter Etzkorn (New York: Teacher's College Press, Columbia University, 1968), 44.

59. Simmel, ibid., 42. Cf. "The Fetishism of Commodities and the Secret Thereof" in Karl Marx, *Capital: A Critique of Political Economy* ed. Frederick Engels, trans. Samuel Moore and Edward Aveling (New York: Random House, The Modern Library, n.d.), 81–85.

60. Simmel, "The Tragedy of Culture," 42.

61. The first chapter in Cassirer's manuscript of the unfinished fourth volume of the *Philosophie der symbolischen Formen* is a criticism of this aspect of Lebensphilosophie, particularly in Simmel and Ludwig Klages. "Erstes Kapitel: 'Geist' und 'Leben,'" Ms 184a, pages numbered 1–79.

62. Simmel, "The Tragedy of Culture," 42–43; Cassirer, *STS*, 87–88.

63. "The number of tools that a machine can bring into play simultaneously, is from the very first emancipated from the organic limits that hedge in the tools of a handicraftsman," Marx, *Capital*, 408.

64. Marx's description of the introduction of machines into industry calls attention to the interchangeability of human effort and machine effort, while emphasizing the tremendous increase in productivity using the latter. See, e.g., *Capital*, 410.

65. The terms *Schicksalsgemeinschaft* and *Willensgemeinschaft* were taken from Friedrich Dessauer and Paul Natorp respectively. Dessauer uses "community of fate" to refer to the forced interdependence in society resulting from the spread of technology; see his *Philosophie der Technik* (Bonn: Friedrich Cohen Verlag, 1928), 132–33. The idea of a "community of will" is part of Natorp's ethics, the idea of an end point toward which society has a tendency; Natorp, *Philosophie: Ihr Problem und ihre Probleme*, 4th ed. (Göttingen: Vandenhoeck & Ruprecht, 1929), 81. Cassirer's use of these terms reflects their established meanings.

66. In Schweitzer's Olaus-Petri Lectures in Uppsala in 1922, he presented the ideas that were later published as *The Philosophy of Civilization*, trans. C. T. Campion (New York: Macmillan Co., 1950). Cf. *SMC*, 59–60.

67. In a work published not long before his death, *Der Mensch und die Technik: Beitrag zu einer Philosophie des Lebens* (Munich: C.H. Beck'sche Verlagsbuchhandlung, 1931), Spengler applies his mythic conception of necessity to the idea of Technik: "In fact, neither heads nor hands are capable of changing anything concerning the fate of the technology of machines, which has developed from its inner soul's necessity" (74).

68. Wolfgang Schivelbusch, *Geschichte der Eisenbahnreise: Zur Industrialisierung von Raum und Zeit im 19. Jahrhundert* (Munich: Carl Hanser, 1977), 15.

69. Walter Benjamin, "The Work of Art in the Age of Mechanical Reproduction," *Illuminations*, edited with an introduction by Hannah Arendt, translated by Harry Zohn (New York: Schocken Books, 1969), 217–51.

70. Ernst Krenek, "Bemerkungen zur Rundfunkmusik," *Zeitschrift für Sozialforschung* 7 (1938): 148–65, esp. 159–60.

71. Jacques Ellul, *The Political Illusion*, trans. Konrad Kellen (New York: Random House, Vintage Books, 1967), 53.

72. *Hegel's Philosophy of Right*, trans. T. M. Knox (London: Oxford University Press, 1952), 122–23.

73. Hegel emphasizes early in his career that *Willkür* and *Zufall*, whim and chance, are only "subordinate standpoints" and that they have no place in his conception of the science of the absolute. See G. W. F. Hegel, *The Difference between Fichte's and Schelling's System of Philosophy*, trans. H. S. Harris and Walter Cerf (Albany: State University of New York Press, 1977), 167.

74. On *tyche* in Peirce's sense, see *The Collected Papers of Charles Sanders Peirce*, 8 vols. (Cambridge, Mass.: Harvard University Press, 1931–58), 6: pars. 47–65.

75. For the ancient Greeks, *tyche* (chance) and *moira* (fate) were interconnected; pure chance was a foreign notion. See Ulrich von Wilamowitz-Moellendorf, *Der Glaube der Hellenen*, 3d ed., 2 vols. (Darmstadt: Wissenschaftliche Buchgesellschaft, 1959), 2:295–306.

76. Hannah Arendt, *The Origins of Totalitarianism*, 478.

77. Kant, *Critique of Pure Reason*, trans. Norman Kemp Smith (New York: St. Martin's Press, 1961), 34a (B xl).

78. See Brian Easlea, *Witch Hunting, Magic and the New Philosophy: An Introduction to Debates of the Scientific Revolution, 1450–1750* (Sussex and Atlantic Highlands: Harvester Press and Humanities Press, 1980), 206ff.

79. For an overall account of this phenomenon, see H. R. Trevor-Roper, *The European Witch-Craze of the Sixteenth and Seventeenth Centuries* (New York: Harper & Row, Harper Torchbooks, 1969). Cf. Barbara Rosen, ed., *Witchcraft*, The Stratford-upon-Avon Library 6 (London: Edward Arnold, 1969). Her book, which covers Britain, was conceived as a companion to Trevor-Roper's book, which concentrates on the witch trials on the Continent. See also Lynn White, Jr., "Death and the Devil," *The Darker Vision of the Renaissance*, ed. Robert S. Kinsman, UCLA Center for Medieval and Renaissance Studies Contributions, no. 6 (Berkeley and Los Angeles: University of California Press, 1974), 25–46, for a cross-cultural study of the belief in dark forces. The figure of 200,000 deaths is given by Wayne Shumaker, *The Occult Sciences in the Renaissance* (Berkeley and Los Angeles: University of California Press, 1972), 61. Shumaker says that it was above all Cassirer who interested him in the study of "extralogical patterns" (xviii).

80. Hegel notes in his lectures on the philosophy of history that the witch trials were based purely upon suspicion. No matter what the reactions of the accused were, they were seen as corroboration of guilt: "If the accused fainted under the torture it was averred that the Devil was giving them sleep; if convulsions supervened, it was said that the Devil was laughing in them; if they held out steadfastly, the Devil was supposed to give them power." G. W. F. Hegel, *The Philosophy of History*, trans. J. Sibree (1899; reprint, New York: Dover Publications, 1956), 426. This clearly illustrates the kind of analytic judgments typical of mythic thought. Whoever was suspected of witchcraft was considered guilty and all further information served only to verify the initial suspicion, for to be suspected meant ipso facto that one was guilty.

81. "Cassirers Arbeit über die 'Begriffsform im mythischen Denken' habe ich vor längerer Zeit mit viel Interesse gelesen. Fraglich blieb mir, ob der Versuch durchfuhrbar ist, das mythische Denken nicht nur in Begriffen—d.h. kritisch—darzustellen, sondern auch durch den Kontrast gegens Begriffliche hinreichend zu erleuchten." Letter to Hugo von Hofmannsthal, December 28, 1925. Walter Benjamin, *Briefe*, vol. 2, ed. Gerschom Scholem and Theodor W. Adorno (Frankfurt am Main: Suhrkamp, 1966), 407.

82. See *MS*, 269–73; *SMC*, 225–26; "Albert Schweitzer as Critic of Nine-teenth-Century Ethics," 256.

83. Charles N. R. McCoy, review of *The Myth of the State* by Ernst Cassirer, *The Modern Schoolman* (May 1948): 271–78, 277.

84. John Joseph Schrems, "The Political Philosophy of Ernst Cassirer: A Study in Modern Liberal Political Thought," Ph.D. dissertation, 1965, Cath-olic University of America, 131. In a later article Schrems agrees with Mc-Coy's review, stating that there are no "barriers" to action for Cassirer and suggesting that his theory of man conceives him purely as *homo faber*. See Schrems, "Ernst Cassirer and Political Thought," *Review of Politics* 29 (1967); 180–203, 200.

85. Schrems, "The Political Philosophy of Ernst Cassirer," 75.

86. Gustave Lanson, "Le héros cornélien et le'généreux' selon Descartes," *Revue d'histoire littéraire de la France* 1 (1894): 397–411. Cassirer was familiar with Lanson's article and subsequent treatments of this question; see *D*, 285n.

87. Descartes, "The Passions of the Soul" in *The Philosophical Works of Descartes*, vol. 1, trans. Elizabeth S. Haldane and G. R. T. Ross (Cambridge: Cambridge University Press, 1972), 401–02. "Cette libre disposition de ses volontez," Descartes, *Les passions de l'âme*, ed. Geneviève Rodis-Lewis (Paris: J. Vrin, 1955), article CLIII, 177.

88. This very un-Kantian position was also held by Hermann Cohen in his ethics. Whereas Kant considered virtue to require stoic apathy, the strength to be free of agitation, Cohen claims that "virtue is inconceivable without pathos." See Kant, *The Doctrine of Virtue*, part 2 of the *Metaphysics of Morals*, trans. Mary J. Gregor (Philadelphia: University of Pennsylvania Press, 1971), 70–71; cf. Hermann Cohen, *Ethik des reinen Willens*, 476. Cassirer sided with Cohen.

89. "Albert Schweitzer as Critic of Nineteenth-Century Ethics," 257.

90. In a recent article the claim is made that *Mythic Thought*, volume 2 of *The Philosophy of Symbolic Forms*, might be read as an attempt to make readers aware of the proximity of the "Völkishness" prevalent among certain circles in the Weimar Republic to mythic thought. This view goes against Cassirer's own statements in *The Myth of the State* (296). It seems systemati-cally appropriate, however, to apply the theory of myth to Völkisch sentiment even though Cassirer himself never examined this dimension. See Ivan Strenski, "Ernst Cassirer's *Mythical Thought* in Weimar Culture," *History of European Ideas* 5 (1984): 363–83.

91. Cassirer's point of view is perhaps best expressed in this passage from *The Myth of the State*: "It was 1933 that the political world began to worry about Germany's rearmament and its possible international repercussions. As a matter of fact this rearmament had begun many years before but had passed almost unnoticed. The real rearmament began with the origin and rise of the political myths. The later rearmament was only an accessory after the fact" (*MS*, 282).

BIBLIOGRAPHY

Rather than duplicate existing bibliographies, I have listed here (1) bibliographies of Cassirer's works and of secondary literature on Cassirer, (2) works by Cassirer cited but not included in the list of abbreviations of frequently cited works, and (3) works on Cassirer cited in the text. General works cited are documented in the notes.

1. BIBLIOGRAPHIES

Primary Literature

Hamburg, Carl H., and Walter M. Solmitz. "Bibliography of the Writings of Ernst Cassirer to 1946." In Paul Arthur Schilpp, ed., *The Philosophy of Ernst Cassirer*, 881–910. New York: Tudor, 1949. A chronological bibliography of Cassirer's publications.

Klibansky, Raymond, and Walter Solmitz. "Bibliography of Ernst Cassirer's Writings." In Raymond Klibansky and H. J. Paton, eds., *Philosophy and History: Essays Presented to Ernst Cassirer*, 338–53, Rev. ed. New York: Harper & Row, Harper Torchbooks, 1963. A systematic bibliography with subsections within the main divisions of "Systematic Philosophy," "History of Philosophy," and "Philosophy and German Literature." Adds later writings and translations to the original version of this bibliography published in the first edition (Oxford: Clarendon Press, 1936).

Klibansky, Raymond. "Bibliografia di Ernst Cassirer." In Ernst Cassirer, *Filosofia delle forme simboliche*, vol. 3, *Fenomenologia della conoscenza*, Tomo secondo, trans. Eraldo Arnaud, 335–78. Firenze: La nuova editrice, 1982. A revised version of the Klibansky and Solmitz bibliography in *Philosophy and History*, adding numerous new translations into various languages of Cassirer's writings, a separate section listing documents and material concerning the debate between Cassirer and Heidegger at the "Davoser Hochschulkurse" in 1929, and an eleven-page list of recent secondary literature. Some of the secondary works cited, including a body of writings in Russian from the 1970s, are not listed in other bibliographies.

Secondary Literature

Esthimer, Steven W. "Ernst Cassirer: Critical Work and Translations, 1969–1979. *Bulletin of Bibliography* 40, no. 1 (1982): 40–44. An extension of Donald Phillip Verene's bibliographies.

Nadeau, Robert. "Bibliographie des Textes sur Ernst Cassirer." *Revue Internationale de Philosophie* 28 (1974): 492–510. Lists 288 items; does not include M.A. theses listed in Verene's bibliography.

Verene, Donald Phillip. "Ernst Cassirer: A Bibliography." *Bulletin of Bibliography and Magazine Notes* 23–24, no. 5 (1964): 103, 104–06. A bibliography of work on Cassirer in all languages from the earliest studies until 1964; lists eighty-six items.

———. "Ernst Cassirer: Critical Work, 1964–1970." *Bulletin of Bibliography and Magazine Notes* 29, no. 1 (1972): 21–23, 24. Lists sixty-four items.

2.WORKS BY CASSIRER (excluding the frequently cited works given in the list of abbreviations)

Published Sources

Der Kritischer Idealism und die Philosophie des "gesunden Menschenverstandes." Philosophische Arbeiten vol. 1, no. 1. Gieszen: Alfred Töpelmann, 1906.

"Kant und die moderne Mathematik." *Kantstudien* 12 (1907): 1–49.

"Hermann Cohen und die Erneuerung der Kantischen Philosophie." *Kant-Studien* 17 (1912): 252–73.

Ed., *Immanuel Kants Werke*. 10 vols. Berlin: Bruno Cassirer, 1912.

"Erkenntnistheorie nebst den Grenzfragen der Logik." *Jahrbücher der Philosophie* 1 (1913): 1–59.

"Hermann Cohen." *Korrespondenzblatt des Vereins zur Gründung und Erhaltung einer Akademie des Judentums* 1 (1920): 1–10.

"Die Philosophie der Griechen von den Anfängen bis Platon." In *Lehrbuch der Philosophie*, vol. 1, *Geschichte der Philosophie*, ed. Max Dessoir. Berlin: Ullstein, 1925.

"Erkenntnistheorie nebst den Grenzfragen der Logik und Denkpsychologie." *Jahrbücher der Philosophie* 3 (1927): 31–92.

"The Problem of the Symbol and Its Place in the System of Philosophy" [1927]. Trans. John Michael Krois. *Man and World* 11 (1978): 411–28.

"Zur Theorie des Begriffs." *Kant-Studien* 33 (1928): 129–36.

Die Idee der Republikanischen Verfassung. Rede zur Verfassungsfeier am 11. August 1928. Hamburg: Friederich, De Gruyter & Co., 1929.

"Formen und Formwandlungen des philosophischen Wahrheitsbegriffs" [1929]. *Hamburger Universitätsreden* gehalten beim Rektoratswechsel, 17–36. Hamburg, 1931.

"Deutschland und Westeuropa im Spiegel der Geistesgeschichte." *Inter-Nationes: Zeitschrift für die kulturellen Beziehungen Deutschlands zum Ausland* 1 (1931): 57–59 and 83–85.

"Kant and the Problem of Metaphysics: Remarks on Martin Heidegger's

Interpretation of Kant" [1931]. In *Kant: Disputed Questions*, edited with translations by Molte S. Gram, 131–57. Chicago: Quadrangle Books, 1967. Originally published as "Kant und das Problem der Metaphysik: Bemerkungen zu Martin Heideggers Kant-interpretation." *Kant-Studien* 36: 1–26.

"Die Antike und die Entstehung der exakten Wissenschaften." *Die Antike* 13 (1932): 276–300.

'Goethes Idee der Bildung und Erziehung." *Pädagogisches Zentralblatt* 12 (1932): 340–58.

'Wesen und Werden des Naturrechts." *Zeitschrift für Rechtsphilosophie* 6 (1932): 1–27

"Henri Bergson's Ethik und Religionsphilosophie." *Der Morgen* 9, no. 1 (1933): 20–29.

"Schiller und Shaftesbury." *Publications of the English Goethe Society* 11 (1934): 37–59.

"Inhalt und Umfang des Begriffs: Bemerkungen zu Konrad Marc-Wogau: Inhalt und Umfang des Begriffs." *Theoria* 2 (1936): 207–32.

"The Concept of Group and the Theory of Perception" [1938]. Trans. Aron Gurwitch. *Philosophy and Phenomenological Research* 5 (1944): 1–35.

Review of *An Introduction to the Philosophy of Science* by A. Cornelius Benjamin. *Lychnos*, Annual of the Swedish History of Science Society (1938): 456–61.

"Naturalistische und humanistische Begründung der Kulturphilosophie." *Göteborgs Kungl. Vetenskaps- och Vitterhets-Samhälles Handlingar*, 5e följden, ser. A, vol. 7, no. 3 (1939): 1–28.

"Was ist 'Subjektivismus'?" *Theoria* 5 (1939): 111–40.

"Zur Logik des Symbolbegriffs." *Theoria* 4 (1939): 145–75.

"Mathematische Mystik und mathematische Naturwissenschaft." *Lychnos* (1940): 248–65.

"William Stern: Zur Wiederkehr seines Todestages." *Acta Psychologia* 5 (1940): 1–15.

"Logos, Dike, Kosmos in der Entwicklung der griechischen Philosophie." *Göteborgs Högskolas Arsskrift* 47, no. 6 (1941): 1–31.

"Galileo: A New Science and a New Spirit." *American Scholar* 12 (1942): 5–19.

"Giovanni Pico della Mirandola." *Journal of the History of Ideas* 3, no. 2 (1942): 123–44 and 319–46.

"The Influence of Language upon the Development of Scientific Thought." *Journal of Philosophy* 39 (1942): 309–27.

"The Place of Vesalius in the Culture of the Renaissance." *Yale Journal of Biology and Medicine*, 16, no. 2 (1942): 109–19.

"Hermann Cohen, 1842–1918." *Social Research* 10 (1943): 219–32.

"Remarks on the Originality of the Renaissance." *Journal of the History of Ideas* 4 (1943): 49–56.

"Thomas Manns Goethe-bild: Eine Studie über *Lotte in Weimar*." *Germanic Review* 20 (1945): 166–94. Reprinted in Helmut Koopman, ed., *Thomas Mann*. Wege der Forschung, vol. 335. Darmstadt: Wissenschaftliche Buchgesellschaft, 1975.

"Albert Schweitzer as Critic of Nineteenth-Century Ethics." In A. A. Roback, ed., *The Albert Schweitzer Jubilee Book*, 241–57. Cambridge, Mass.: Sci-Art Publishers, 1946.

"Structuralism in Modern Linguistics." Word, Journal of the Linguistic Circle of New York, 1 (August 1946): 95–120.

With Paul Oskar Kristeller and John Herman Randall, Jr. *The Renaissance Philosophy of Man.* 1948. Reprint. Chicago: University of Chicago Press, Phoenix Books, 1967.

"Science and Ethics: Equal Partnership." *Saturday Review*, March 2, 1957.

"A Discussion between Ernst Cassirer and Martin Heidegger. Trans. Franci. Slade. In Nino Langiulli, ed., *The Existentialist Tradition*, 192–203. New York: Doubleday & Co., Anchor Books, 1971.

Débat sur le Kantisme et la Philosophie et autres Textes de 1929–1931. Trans. Pierre Aubenque, J.-M. Fataud, and P. Quillet. Paris: Éditions Beauchesne, 1972.

"Davoser Disputation zwischen Ernst Cassirer und Martin Heidegger." Ir Martin Heidegger, *Kant und das Problem der Metaphysik.* 4th ed. Frankfur am Main: Vittorio Klostermann, 1973.

"'Geist' and 'Leben': Heidegger." *Philosophy and Rhetoric* 16 (1983): 164–66. Published with an English translation by John Michael Krois as "'Mind and 'Life': Heidegger,'' 160–63.

Unpublished Sources

New Haven. Beinecke Rare Book and Manuscript Library, Yale University Ernst Cassirer Papers on Deposit. (Cassirer's *Nachlaß* is contained in numbered envelopes that in some cases contain more than one manuscript. The manuscript numbers refer to the envelope. The titles in quotation marks are Cassirer's.)

Ms. 94. "Heidegger Vorlesung (Davos) 1929."

Ms. 97. "Wandlungen der Staatsgesinnung und der Staatstheorie in de: deutschen Geistesgeschichte."

Ms. 113. "Zum Begriff der Nation: Eine Erwiderung auf den Aufsatz vor Bruno Bauch."

Ms. 131. "Grundprobleme der Kulturphilosophie, Sommersemester 1929."

Ms. 132. "Leib und Seele als philosophisches Problem. Berlin 22.01.31."

Mss. 184a–c. Material for volume 4 of the *Philosophie der symbolischer Formen.*

Ms. 204. "Der junge Goethe. (Göteborg, 2. Oktober 1940)."

Carbondale. Southern Illinois University Library. Library of Living Philoso phers Archive.

Letter to Paul Arthur Schilpp, May 13, 1942.

Letter to Paul Arthur Schilpp, June 3, 1943.

3. WORKS ON CASSIRER

Adorno, Theodor W. Review of *Philosophy and History*, ed. Raymond Klibansky and H. J. Paton. *Zeitschrift für Sozialforschung* 6 (1937): 657–61

Alexander, Edwin. "Hermeneutical Violence." *Philosophy Today* 25 (1981) 286–306.

Blanshard, Brand. Review of *An Essay on Man* by Ernst Cassirer, *Philosophi cal Review* 54 (1945): 509–10.

Blumenberg, Hans. "Ernst Cassirers Gedenkend: Bei Entgegennahme de:

Kuno Fischer—Preises der Universität Heidelberg im Juli 1974." *Revue Internationale de Philosophie* 85 (1974): 456–63.

Boboc, A. L. "Ernst Cassirer und die Semiotische Ästhetik." *Revue Roumaine des Sciences*, Série de Philosophie et Logique, 17 (1973): 157–61.

Brameld, Theodore. "Philosophical Anthropology: The Educational Significance of Ernst Cassirer." *Harvard Educational Review* 26 (1956): 207–32.

Cassirer, Toni. *Mein Leben mit Ernst Cassirer.* Hildesheim: Gerstenberg Verlag, 1981.

Cook, Thomas I. Review of *The Myth of the State* by Ernst Cassirer. *The American Political Science Review* 41, no. 1 (1947): 331–33.

Doherty, Joseph E. *Sein, Mensch und Symbol: Heidegger und die Auseinandersetzung mit dem Neu-Kantischen Symbolbegriff.* Münchner Philosophische Forschungen, vol. 6. Bonn: Bouvier Verlag Herbert Grundmann, 1972.

Fetz, Reto Luzius. "Genetische Semiologie?: Symboltheorie im Ausgang von Ernst Cassirer und Jean Piaget." *Freiburger Zeitschrift für Philosophie und Theologie* 28 (1981): 434–70.

Fischer-Appelt, Peter. "Zum Gedenken an Ernst Cassirer." Ansprache zur Eröffnung der Wissenschaftlichen Tagung "Symbolische Formen" am 20. Oktober, 1974. Hamburg: Pressestelle der Universität, 1975.

Gawronsky, Dimitry. "Ernst Cassirer: His Life and His Work." In Paul Arthur Schilpp, ed., *The Philosophy of Ernst Cassirer.* New York: Tudor, 1958.

Gay, Peter. "The Social History of Ideas: Ernst Cassirer and After." In Kurt H. Wolff and Barrington Moore, Jr., eds. *The Critical Spirit: Essays in Honor of Herbert Marcuse.* Boston: Beacon Press, 1967.

Hamburg, Carl H. "A Cassirer-Heidegger Seminar. *Philosophy and Phenomenological Research* 25 (1964–65): 208–22.

———. *Symbol and Reality: Studies in the Philosophy of Ernst Cassirer.* The Hague: Martinus Nijhoff, 1956.

Heidegger, Martin. Review of *Das Mythische Denken* by Ernst Cassirer. *Deutsche Literaturzeitung* 21 (1928): 1000–1012.

———. "Review of *Mythic Thought.*" In *The Piety of Thinking: Essays by Martin Heidegger.* Trans. James G. Hart and John C. Maraldo (Bloomington: Indiana University Press, 1976).

Holly, Michael Ann. "Panofsky and Cassirer." In Holly, *Panofsky and the Foundations of Art History*, chap. 5. Ithaca: Cornell University Press, 1984.

Howe, Clarence S. "Translator's Foreword." In Ernst Cassirer, *The Logic of the Humanities*, x–xviii. New Haven: Yale University Press, 1961.

Itzkoff, Seymour. *Ernst Cassirer: Philosopher of Culture.* Twayne's World Leaders Series, 61. Boston: Twayne Publishers, 1977.

———. *Ernst Cassirer: Scientific Knowledge and the Concept of Man.* Notre Dame: University of Notre Dame Press, 1971.

Jenkins, Iredell. "Logical Positivism, Critical Idealism, and the Concept of Man." *Journal of Philosophy* 47 (1950): 677–95.

———. Review of *The Philosophy of Ernst Cassirer*, ed. Paul Arthur Schilpp. *Journal of Philosophy* 47 (1950): 43–55.

Kaufmann, Felix. "Cassirer's Theory of Scientific Knowledge." In Paul Arthur Schilpp, ed., *The Philosophy of Ernst Cassirer.* New York: Tudor, 1958.

————. Review of *An Essay on Man* by Ernst Cassirer. *Philosophy and Phenomenological Research* 8 (1948): 283–87.

Krois, John Michael. "Cassirer's Unpublished Critique of Heidegger." *Philosophy and Rhetoric* 16 (1983): 147–59.

————. "Ernst Cassirers Semiotik der symbolischen Formen." *Zeitschrift für Semiotik* 6 (1984): 433–44.

————. "Ernst Cassirer's Theory of Technology and Its Import for Social Philosophy." *Research in Philosophy & Technology* 5 (1982): 209–22.

————. "Peirce and Cassirer: The Philosophical Importance of a Theory of Signs." In Kenneth L. Ketner, Joseph M. Ransdell, Carolyn Eisele, Max H. Fisch, and Charles S. Hardwick, eds., *Proceedings of the C. S. Peirce Bicentennial International Congress.* Lubbock: Texas Tech University Press, 1981.

————. Review of *Ernst Cassirer: The Dilemma of a Liberal Intellectual in Germany, 1914–1933* by David R. Lipton. *Journal of the History of Philosophy* 20 (1982): 209–13.

Kuhn, Helmut. "Ernst Cassirer's Philosophy of Culture." In Paul Arthur Schilpp, ed., *The Philosophy of Ernst Cassirer.* New York: Tudor, 1958.

————. Review of *An Essay on Man* by Ernst Cassirer. *Journal of Philosophy* 42 (1945): 497–504.

Langer, Susanne. "De Profondis." *Revue Internationale de Philosophie* 28 (1974): 449–55.

————. "On Cassirer's Theory of Language and Myth." In Paul Arthur Schilpp, ed., *The Philosophy of Ernst Cassirer.* New York: Tudor, 1958.

Letkemann, Peter, Klaus P. Mader, and Günter Wollschlaeger. "Cassirer und Co.: Ein Beitrag zur Berliner Kunst- und Kulturgeschichte." *Mitteilungen des Vereins für die Geschichte Berlins* 69 (1973): 233–44.

Lipton, David R. *Ernst Cassirer: The Dilemma of a Liberal Intellectual in Germany, 1914–1933.* Toronto: University of Toronto Press, 1978.

Lübbe, Hermann. *Cassirer und die Mythen des 20. Jahrhunderts.* Veröffentlichung der Joachim Jungius Gesellschaft der Wissenschaften. Göttingen: Vendenhoeck & Ruprecht, 1975.

Makkreel, Rudolf A. "Wilhelm Dilthey and the Neo-Kantians: The Distinction between the *Geisteswissenschaften* and the *Kulturwissenschaften.*" *Journal of the History of Philosophy* 7 (1969): 423–40.

Marx, Wolfgang. "Cassirers Symboltheorie als Entwicklung und Kritik des Neukantischen Grundlagen einer Theorie des Denkens und Erkennens." *Archiv für die Geschichte der Philosophie* 57 (1975): 188–206, 304–39.

McCoy, Charles N. R. Review of *The Myth of the State* by Ernst Cassirer. *The Modern Schoolman* 25 (May 1948): 271–78.

Morgenthau, Hans J. Review of *The Myth of the State* by Ernst Cassirer. *Ethics* 57 (1947): 1–42.

Neue Deutsche Biographie, "Cassirer, Ernst Alfred."

Neumann, Karl. "Ernst Cassirer: Das Symbol." In Josef Speck, ed., *Grundprobleme der grossen Philosophen: Philosophie der Gegenwart*, vol. 2. Göttingen: Vandenhoeck & Ruprecht, 1973.

Oehler, Klaus. "Zur Logik einer Universalpragmatik." *Semiosis* 1 (1976): 14–23.

Paetzold, Heinz. "Ernst Cassirer und die Idee einer transformierten Transzendentalphilosophie." In Wolfgang Kuhlmann and Dietrich Böhler, eds.,

Kommunikation und Reflexion: Zur Diskussion der Transzendentalprag-matik. Antworten auf Karl-Offo Apel. Frankfurt am Main: Suhrkamp, 1982.
———. "Ernst Cassirers 'Philosophie der symbolischen Formen' und die neuere Entwicklung der Semiotik." In A. Lange-Seidl, ed., *Zeichenkonsti-tution. Akten des 2. Semiotischen Kolloquiums Regensburg, 1978.* Berlin: Walter de Gruyter, 1981.

Peters, Jens-Peter. *Cassirer, Kant und Sprache.* European University Studies, vol. 121. Frankfurt am Main: Peter Lang Verlag, 1983.

Randall, John Herman, Jr. "Cassirer's Theory of History as Illustrated in His Treatment of Renaissance Thought." In Paul Arthur Schilpp, ed., *The Philosophy of Ernst Cassirer.* New York: Tudor, 1958.

———. Review of *The Logic of the Humanities* by Ernst Cassirer. *History and Theory* 2 (1962): 66–74.

Roo, William A. Van, S. J. *Man the Symbolizer,* Analecta Gregoriana, vol. 222. Rome: Gregorian University Press, 1981.

Rosenstein, Leon. "Some Metaphysical Problems of Cassirer's Symbolic Forms." *Man and World* 6 (1972): 304–20.

Rosenzweig, Franz. "Vertauschte Fronten" (1929). In *Kleinere Schriften.* Berlin: Schocken Verlag, 1937.

Rotenstreich, Nathan. "Cassirer's Philosophy of Symbolic Forms and the Problem of History." *Theoria* 18 (1952): 155–63.

———. "Schematism and Freedom." *Revue Internationale de Philosophie* 28 (1974): 464–74.

Sabine, George H. Review of *The Myth of the State* by Ernst Cassirer. *The Philosophical Review* 56 (1947): 315–18.

Schilpp, Paul Arthur, ed. *The Philosophy of Ernst Cassirer.* The Library of Living Philosophers, no. 6. 1949. Reprint. New York: Tudor Publishing, 1958.

Schlick, Moritz. "Critical or Empiricist Interpretation of Modern Physics?" In Schlick, *Philosophical Papers,* vol. 1 (1909–1922), ed. Henk L. Mulder and Barbara F. B. Van de Velde-Schlick; trans. Peter Heath. Dordrecht: D. Reidel, 1979.

Schrems, John Joseph. "Ernst Cassirer and Political Thought." *The Review of Politics* 29 (1967): 180–203.

———. "The Political Philosophy of Ernst Cassirer: A Study in Modern Liberal Political Thought." Ph.D dissertation, Catholic University of Amer-ica, 1965.

Seltzer, Edward. "The Problem of Objectivity: A Study of Objectivity Re-flected in a Comparison of the Philosophies of E. Cassirer, J. Piaget and E. Husserl." Ph.D. dissertation, New School for Social Research, 1969.

Silverstone, Roger. "Ernst Cassirer and Claude Lévi-Strauss: Two Ap-proaches to the Study of Myth." *Archives de Sciences Sociales des Re-ligions* 21 (1976): 25–36.

Stearns, Isabel. Review of *The Problem of Knowledge* by Ernst Cassirer. *Review of Metaphysics* 5 (1951): 109–24.

Strauss, Leo. Review of *The Myth of the State* by Ernst Cassirer. *Social Research* 14 (1947): 125–28.

Strenski, Ivan. "Ernst Cassirer's *Mythical Thought* in Weimar Culture." *His-tory of European Ideas* 5 (1984): 363–84.

Troeltsch, Ernst. "Humanismus und Nationalismus in unserem Bildungswesen" [1916]. In Hans Baron, ed., *Deutscher Geist und Westeuropa*, 231–35. 1925. Reprint. Aalen: Scientia Verlag, 1966.

Weizsäcker, Carl Friedrich von. Review of *Determinismus und Indeterminismus in der modernen Physik* by Ernst Cassirer. *Physikalische Zeitschrift* 38 (1937): 860–61.

White, Leslie. Review of *An Essay on Man* by Ernst Cassirer. *American Anthropologist* 48 (1946): 461–63.

Wolandt, Gerd. "Cassirer's Symbolbegriff und die Grundlegungsproblematik der Geisteswissenschaften." *Zeitschrift für philosophische Forschung* 18 (1964): 614–26.

Wurmser, Leon. "Is Psychoanalysis a Separate Field of Symbolic Forms?" *Humanities in Society* 4 (1981): 263–94.

INDEX

Aeschylus, 145–46
Alienation, 199–200
Animal symbolicum, 31, 169
Apel, Karl-Otto, 8
A priori, 120–21
Architectonic, 79
Arendt, Hannah, 207
Aristotle, 75–76, 106–07
Art: in contrast to science, 132; distinguished from myth, 139; as realistic, 131; twofold character of, 132
Astrology, 93–96, 135
Axiomatization, 116, 118
Ayer, A. J., 153

Bauch, Bruno, 177, 243–44 n.18
Becker, Oskar, 69
Being, 46, 75–77, 100–01
Benjamin, Walter, 37, 185, 205, 210
Bergson, Henri, 67–68
Berlin, 15
Bjarup, Jes, 153
Blanshard, Brand, 11
Body (Leib), 56–57, 61, 87–88
Bonaventure, Saint, 95
Bondy, Toni, 15
Book burnings, 182
Brecht, Bertolt, 198
Breslau, 13
Brouwer, L. E. J., 68–69
Bruno, Giordano, 95
Büchner, Georg, 33
Büchner, Ludwig, 33, 125
Burkamp, Wilhelm, 48

Cassirer, Bruno, 15
Cassirer, Ernst; Anglo-American interpretation of, x, 4–5, 10–13; Continental interpretation of, x, 4, 6–10; life of, 1, 13–32 passim
Cassirer, Fritz, 15
Cassirer, Paul, 15–16
Cassirer, Richard, 15
Causality, 63, 113–15; in myth, 93, 137
Causal relations, 62
Certainty, 110–12
Christina, Queen of Sweden, 212
Cohen, Hermann, 6, 13–14, 38–42, 74, 163
Concept: extension of, 97; intension of, 97; of substance, 19; of symbolism, 3; theory of, 46–49
Corneille, Pierre, x, 212
Cosmopolitanism, 176, 177
Critique of meaning, 44
Croce, Benedetto, 10–11

D'Ascoli, Cecco, 94
Davos debate between Cassirer and Heidegger, 27, 42–43, 225–26 n.26, 244–45 n.23
Descartes, René, 211–12
Dewey, John, 19, 110
Dilthey, Wilhelm, 18, 74, 124–25, 126, 230 n.80

Einstein, Albert, 121
Ellul, Jacques, 206
Engels, Friedrich, 125
Enlightenment, 2, 26, 77, 188, 208–09
Erkenntnistheorie (theory of knowledge), origin of term, 34
Ethics: foundations of, 29; normative, 28; objective standards in, 144, 151–52, 157
Ewing, A. C., 142

Lorenzer, Alfred, 83–84
Luther, Martin, 94

McCoy, Charles N. R., 210–11
Magic, 103, 137–38
Mann, Thomas, 183, 191, 245 n.29
Marck, Siegfried, 163
Marduk, 148, 183–85
Marx, Karl, 125, 199–201; on human rights, 158
Mathematics, 68–70
Mayer, Robert, 111–12, 141
Merleau-Ponty, Maurice, 58, 90
Metaphor, radical, 97–98
Metaphysics, 63
Mimetic, analogical, and purely symbolic, 80–81, 233 n.24
Mirandola, Giovanni Pico della, 76–77
Moleschott, Jacob, 33
Morality and law: analogical phase of, 148–50; mimetic phase of, 144–48; purely symbolic phase of, 150–52; symbolic form of, 142, 238 n.1
More, Henry, 209
Morgenthau, Hans, 2
Morris, Charles, 45, 83
Music, 86–88
Myth, 21, 187; and action, 85; chief problem in interpreting, 91; impervious to argument, 189–90; nature of, 88; and psychoanalysis, 83–84; and science, 92, 96; and sense of time, 86–88; as starting point for philosophy, 60; technique of, 189, 191–96

Natorp, Paul, 6
Natural law, 150, 158, 162–65; contract theory of, 161–62, 211
Neo-Kantianism, 13, 224 n.7; Cassirer's relation to, 114–15, 121; Marburg school of, 6, 25, 41–42; origins of, 33–34
Nietzsche, Friedrich, 35, 67

Oehler, Klaus, 8–9
Ontology, 37, 63

Paetzold, Heinz, 9, 228 n.53
Panlogism, 36
Part-whole distinction, 97–98
Passmore, John, 10
Peirce, Charles Sanders, 7, 44, 206; and Cassirer, 52
Personality, 104; heroic ethical, 29; right to, 168–70, 188–89
Phenomenology: in Cassirer, 78–81, 104–05, 123–24, 229 n.66; of cultural forms, 172–73; in Hegel, 78–80; of moral consciousness, 142–43
Philosophy, 25–26, 81; of culture, 72; of science, 34, 35, 122; systematic, 5, 23,

37; transcendental, 37, 62, 121. See also Transcendental
Philosophy of Symbolic Forms, volume four, 31, 32, 35–36, 63, 66, 224 n.8
Physicalism, 122, 236 n.29
Plato, 75, 95, 101
Poincaré, Jules-Henri, 118
Pope, Alexander, 175, 181
Popper, Karl, 105, 128
Progress, historical, 175
Providence, 187

Quantum theory, 114, 115–16
Quine, Willard van Orman, 74, 75, 139

Randall, John Hermann, Jr., 10, 41
Rawls, John, 143–44
Reality, 19
Reason, 182
Recollection, 78, 130
Religion and morality, 148–50
Renaissance, 76–77, 94–95, 126
Representation (Repräsentation), 50
Rickert, Heinrich, 66
Ricoeur, Paul, 83–84
Riehl, Alois, 18
Ross, W. D., 142
Rotenstreich, Nathan, 9
Rousseau, Jean-Jacques, 169

Sabine, George, 196–97
Sartre, Jean-Paul, 105
Saussure, Ferdinand de, 52
Savigny, Friedrich Carl von, 158
Saxl, Fritz, 22
Scandinavian realism, 108, 153
Scheler, Max, 42
Schematization, 116
Schivelbusch, Wolfgang, 205
Schlick, Moritz, 117–18, 121
Scholasticism, 76
Schrems, John J., 211
Schweitzer, Albert, 165, 170–71, 186, 203–04, 208, 213
Science: aim of, 112; distinguished from myth, 135–39; origin of, 96; and reality, 110–11; as a symbolic form, 122
Scientific materialism, 33–34, 125
Self-liberation, 174–176, 179, 180, 181, 186, 213, 214
Semiotic, 7, 45, 52, 119
Signs, 51, 121, 122
Simmel, Georg, 14, 67, 198–99
Social forces, mythical and critical, 96, 185, 187, 197
Space: in myth, 120; in science, 117–20
Speech acts, 156–57
Speer, Albert, 189
Spengler, Oswald, 195, 203–04
Statistics, 127
Stern, William, 167
Stevenson, C. L., 153